AIR WE ARE

Balloon MUSEUM

BALLOON MUSEUM

FROM A TO Z

SilvanaEditoriale

Contents

Foreword

Roberto Fantauzzi

From the very beginning, the Balloon Museum has embraced the idea that the most authentic and pure elements of childhood can be transformed into powerful means of expression. This vision, as simple as it is revolutionary, was born during the uncertain months of 2020 as a creative response to the changing post-pandemic social and cultural scenarios.
At the center of this artistic conception, lies a key figure, revealed in its process of conceptual breakdown: the image of a balloon.
Pliable, light, almost ethereal in its purest and simplest form, it transcends physicality to become a symbol of freedom, a medium for expressing art that goes beyond physical and conceptual boundaries.
Iconographically, the balloon is seen as a bridge between two very forceful spheres of imagination: on the one hand, the world of childhood, a universe filled with purity and playful spontaneity; on the other, the realm of air, an ethereal metaphor of freedom and boundless horizons. In this dual symbolism, the balloon emerges as both an object and a powerful means of expression, capable of concentrating the lightness of being and containing air, through an exercise that provides the intangible with unexpected forms.
Thus, it was that in December 2021 the first Balloon Museum exhibition opened in Rome, marking the project's debut, followed by shows in Paris, Milan, Madrid, New York, and London during its first two years of existence.
On this journey, the Paris stop in the spring of 2022, with the *Pop Air* exhibition—a group show where works by artists using air to express themselves were shown — represented an important turning point. Distinguished by its immersive nature, *Pop Air,* with its inherently Pop character, introduced an unprecedented paradigm of interaction between art and the public, which participated together in an instantaneous and digital narrative of the experience.
With the Paris exhibition, and thanks to its success in terms of

quality and number of viewers, Balloon Museum has broadened its horizon and carved out a unique space in the panorama of immersive-experiential exhibitions. Its structured growth has extended to different project areas: from curation and production to communication.

Today, the Museum's three exhibitions, *Pop Air, Let's Fly* and *EmotionAir*, are seen as the result of a process as fast-paced as it is extraordinary, enabling the Balloon Museum to present shows with characteristics of unique, original, and recognizable intercontinental appeal. The exhibition design pivots on immersive pathways that invite the viewer to embark on a deep, singular, and collective exploration within a narrative fabric that evokes and celebrates each visitor's inner child.

In this process, interactivity is used to make each experience subjective and different from the others. The concept of museum visiting integrates discovery, not simply conceived in the form of artistic and creative expression but also as inner exploration. Each interaction becomes an act of co-creation, where the meaning of the work evolves with the active participation of the visitor.

This catalog came into being thanks to the involvement of 44 leading artists and the promotion of 64 installations. It is a collection designed to enhance the richness of the esthetic and conceptual expression of Inflatable Art and to celebrate the artists involved who now represent a new international community.

The publication also highlights the role of the Balloon Museum as a promoter and producer, an authentic case study and a shining example of Made in Italy: design capable of enhancing and developing new creative expressions with originality.

Today Balloon Museum is a place where art stirs emotions and invites the public to take on the role of director, actor, and spectator, in an open and ever-changing dialog.

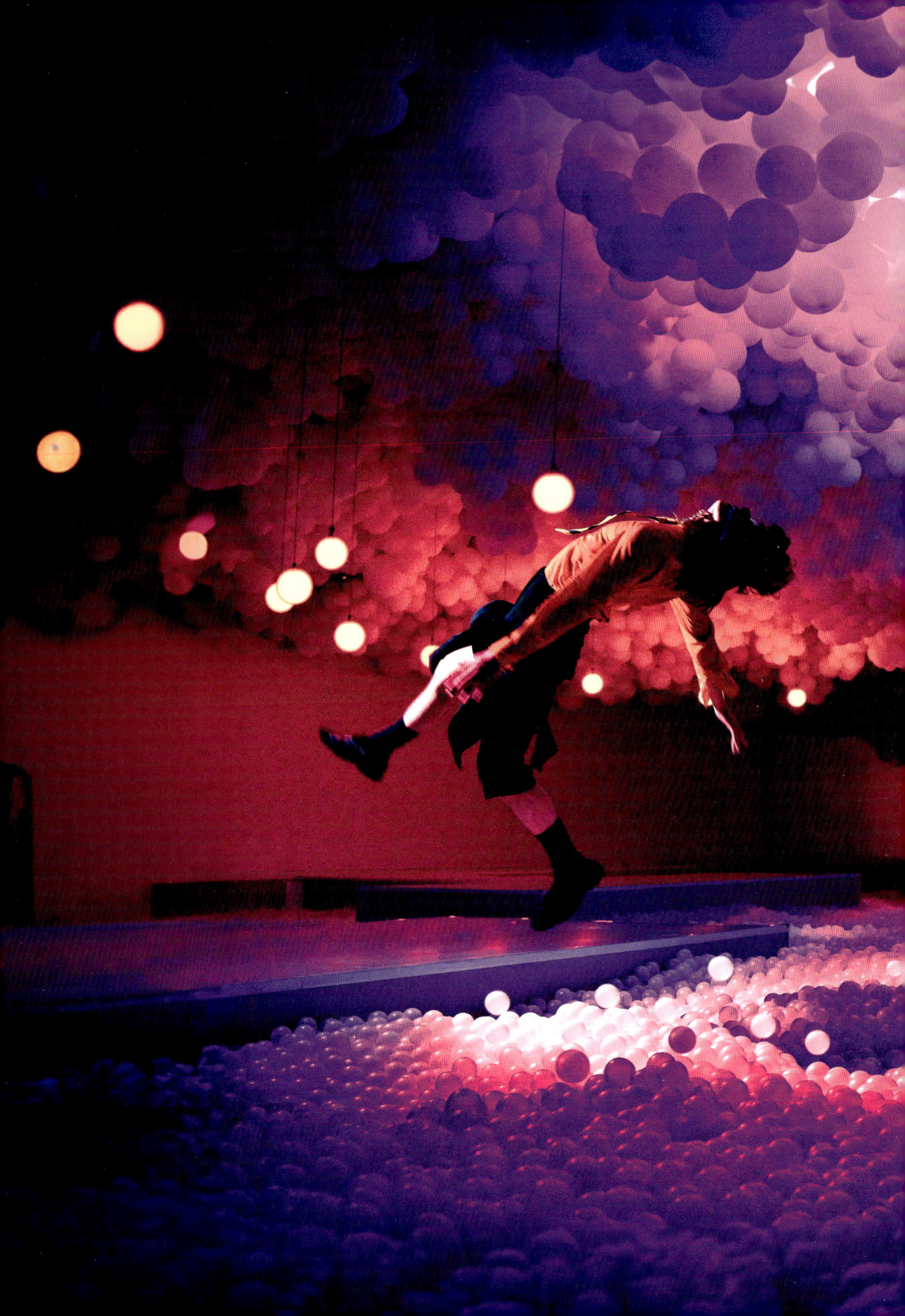

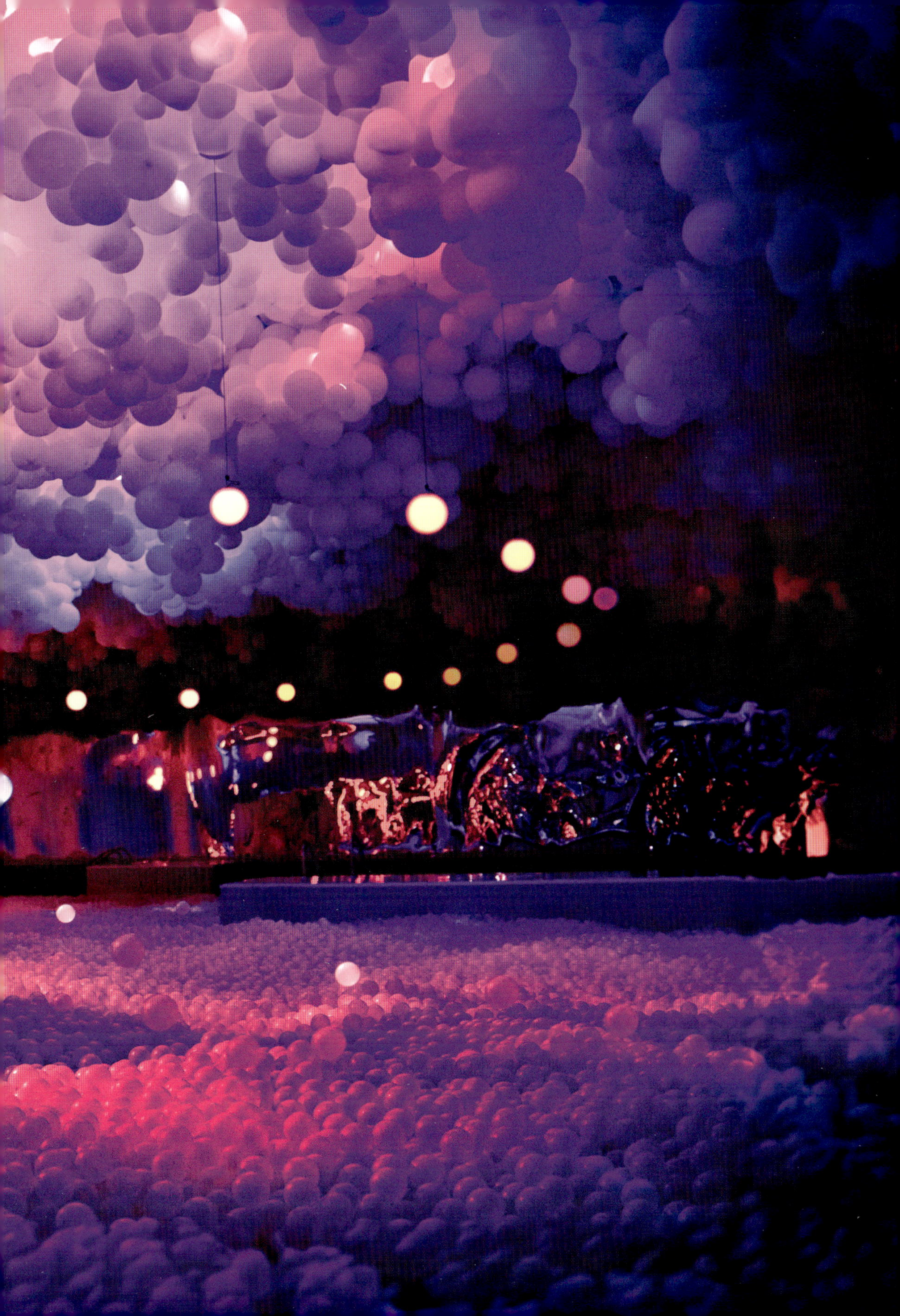

BALLOON MUSEUM

POP AIR – LET'S FLY – EMOTIONAIR

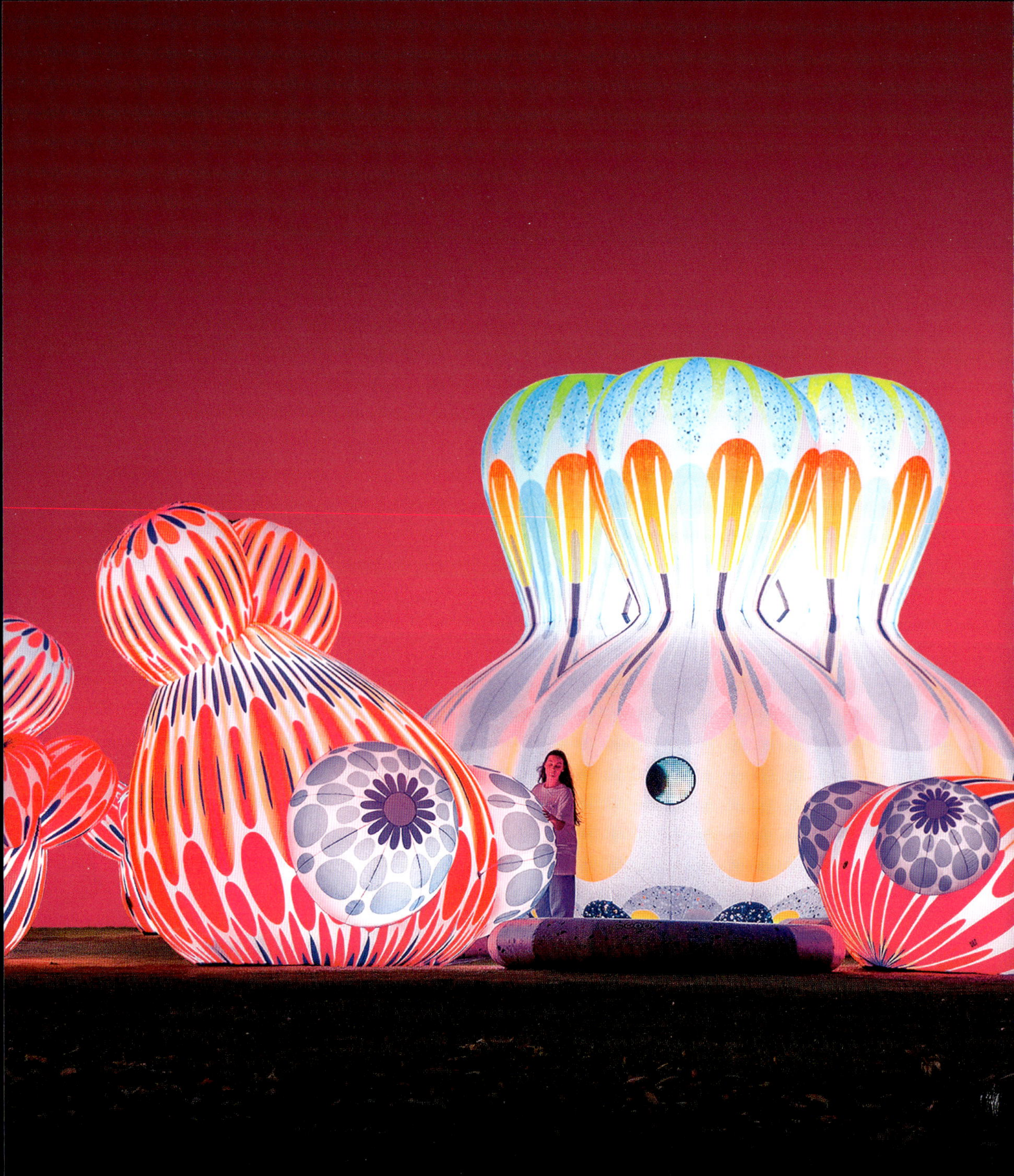

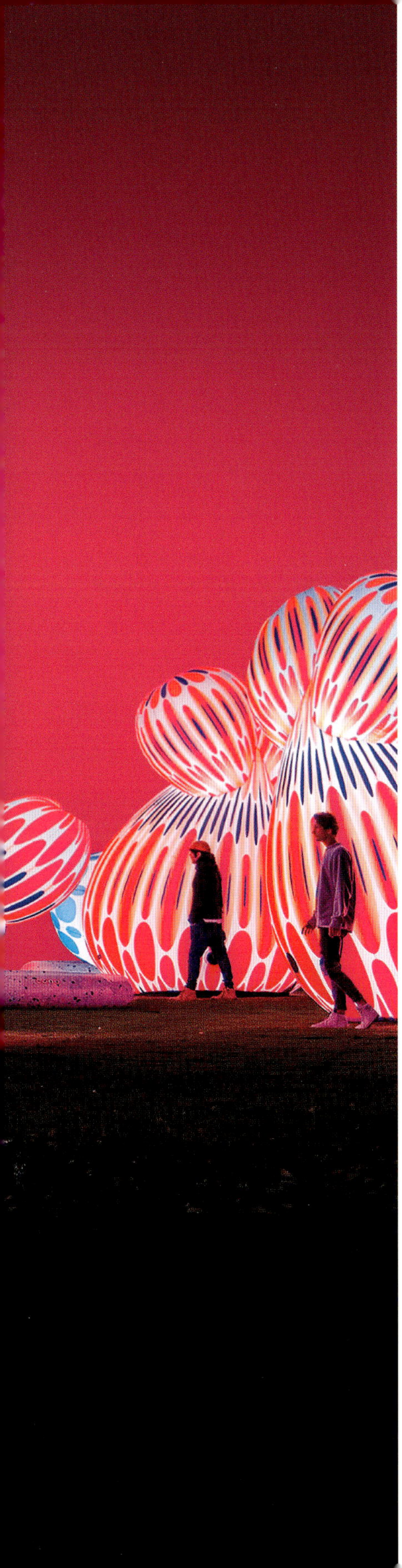

Pop Air

The first exhibition presented by the Balloon Museum dedicated to Inflatable Art is a group show where each work represents an interpretation of air through the ingenuity of international artists. *Pop Air* first opened to the public in Rome in December 2021.

Inspired by the Pop Art movement, when artists drew inspiration from mass and commercial culture, *Pop Air* adds a dimensional and architectural element, ensuring a unique experience that will characterize all the Balloon Museum's exhibitions.

The all-encompassing and immersive experience, designed after the prolonged period of isolation imposed by the pandemic, celebrates the power of human interaction, offering a new form of sociality through art. These traits are manifested through vibrant, fluorescent, and large-scale art installations.

Pop Air
Art is inflatable

Pop Air is an art project conceived with the unique aim of welcoming artists capable of creating an experience for all ages. Imagine interactive spaces where the visitor takes an active role at the center of the display, becoming the protagonist of new digital narratives. Through the creation of unique and precious memories captured in personal photos shared online, the capacity to produce a collective diary on a global scale arises.

Central to the curatorial selection of artworks for *Pop Air* is the idea of immersion and engagement. The exhibition is distinguished by its playful approach, encouraging the audience to physically interact with the installations. This distinctive feature manifests itself in the ability to stimulate visitors through continuous interaction and direct contact, subverting the traditional two-way relationship between audience and art. Viewers find a sense of youthful exuberance, freedom to interact with the art and be carried away in an engaging process that takes them back to carefree moments, creating a kind of collective childhood euphoria. It is an experience that reflects the universal appeal of Inflatable Art, reinforcing its status as an innovative and fascinating medium that transcends generations, capable of offering unique immersive experiences.

Today, *Pop Air* is a group show featuring some 20 artists, but its public debut involved only a few names whose works set the stage for the exhibition: Cyril Lancelin with his captivating red labyrinth, *Knot*; Pneuhaus and Bike Powered Events with the artwork *Canopy*, a forest in a state of continuous expansion and contraction; Kateřina Blahutová, who presented her enchanting *Living Forest*; MOTOREFISICO's *Never Ending Story*; Penique Productions, who transformed the space with *Deposito Vittoria*, named in honor of the old bus depot that hosted the experience, and enveloped the surroundings in a bright blue balloon; and Filthy Luker, who welcomed visitors at the entrance with one of his *Goofs*.

Over the years the exhibition has acted as a catalyst for artists from every corner of the globe. Each city has seen the inclusion of new masterpieces: studio ENESS presented their spouted chorus, *Cupid's Koi Garden,* in Paris; in Madrid, proverbial and literal Architects of Air brought their inflated, glowing city; and in Naples, Michael Shaw displayed his snaking, bulbous figure, *INF 22*. Also featured are the lively and mysterious *GINJOS* by Rub Kandy, and *Silenus* by sculptor Max Streicher—a sleeping giant of monumental dimensions. Investigating the concept of nature, the Hyperstudio collective recounts the story of balance between chaos and stillness in *Hypercosmo* in collaboration with the duo Quiet Ensemble, who form part of the multimedia performance and unveil another work that has become iconic of Balloon Museum: *A Quiet Storm*. Karina Smigla-Bobinski, inspired by neuro-scientific discoveries about the self-configuration of the brain, presented for the first time in Milan, *POLYHEADRA*, while the duo Plastique Fantastique pays homage to ancient temples reimagined in inflated fabric with their creation, *THOLOS*. Digital art makes its mark with Ultraviolетto's VR experience and *ARIA - The Breath Immersive Experience*, Pepper's Ghost's infinity room.

Pop Air remains a milestone for the Balloon Museum, an unprecedented success and a beacon of inspiration for subsequent and future exhibitions. A collection of visionary artists who have initiated this extraordinary journey into the fascinating world of Inflatable Art.

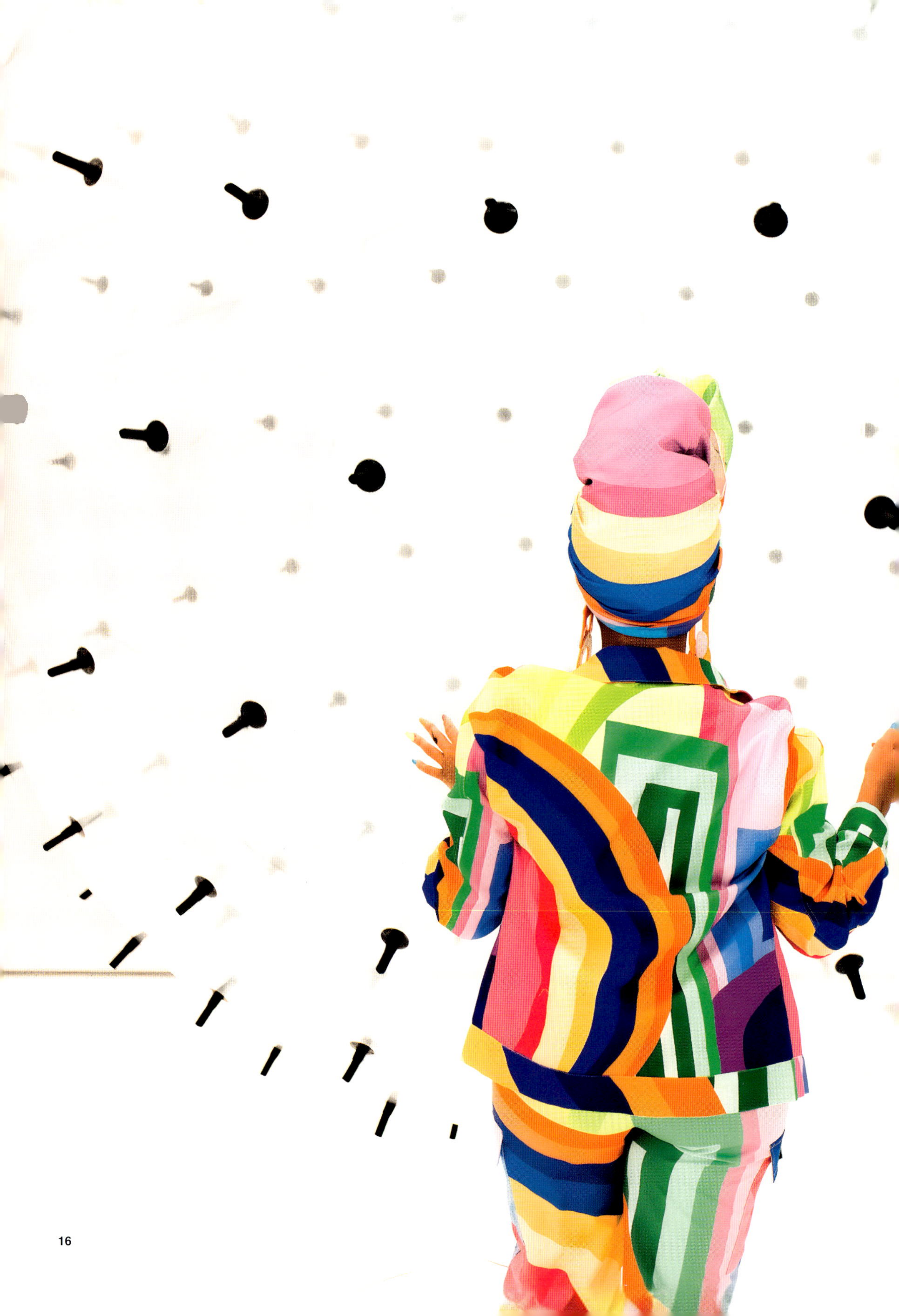

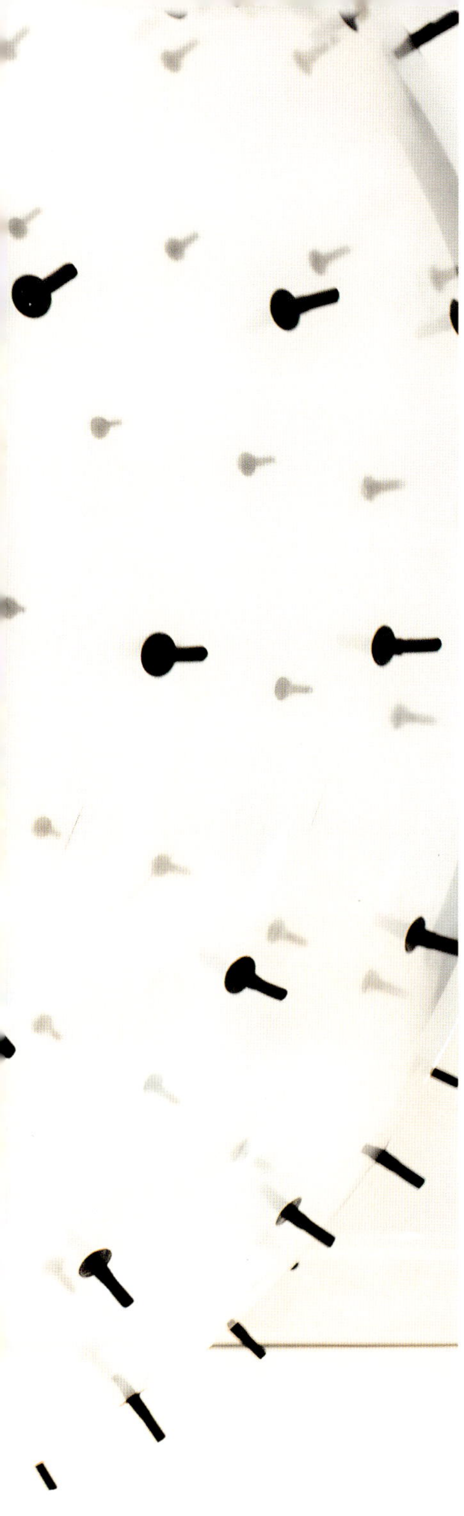

Let's Fly

Taking as its starting point the concept of flight, freedom, and lightness, Balloon Museum's second exhibition explores the medium of air as an idea of movement and limitless travel, both within ourselves and beyond. In the two years *Pop Air* has traveled throughout Europe, two million people have crossed its halls for romantic date nights, moments of laughter with family and friends, and to admire the latest celebrated installations from their favorite artists; the Balloon Museum has gathered an important collection of significant and well-known artworks as well as some newly designed for the experience, establishing an internationally recognized exhibition. Building on this solid foundation, the Balloon Museum opened the second art project, *Let's Fly*, in the United States. The task of taking the success of *Pop Air* overseas, inaugurating a new exhibition with its first location in New York City, involved significant logistical and cultural challenges. These obstacles were successfully overcome with the opening of *Let's Fly* at Pier 36 in Manhattan in October 2023. From there, the collection would embark on a journey through several U.S. cities, bringing with it the wonder of Inflatable Art and the inclusive character of the Balloon Museum.

Let's Fly
Art has no limits

For *Let's Fly*, the curatorial team dedicated significant efforts to the search for a new meaning, exploring sometimes opposing concepts such as stillness and energy, gravity and levity. This exhibition not only challenges our perspectives but also invites us to actively immerse ourselves in exploration, communicating to the audience the power of boundless imagination, dreams taking flight, and the courage required to face the unknown. Through the exhibited works, the experiential pathway offers an in-depth investigation into these contrasting concepts, highlighting how a solid grounding is essential to give meaning to our flight.

Visiting the *Let's Fly* exhibition, one encounters the impressive installations of the British artist Filthy Luker and his creatures from extraterrestrial planets, such as *Eye Scream* and *Octopus Attacks!* Entering the *AI Data Portal* of the Ouchhh collective, gathered air data of the cities visited by the museum are transformed into Digital Art. In the outside space, one can admire the vibrant inflatable sculptures of the Italian artist Camilla Falsini and their creation of mesmerizing visual effects.

The exhibition then hosts *ADA*, the large sphere by the German-Polish artist Karina Smigla-Bobinski, which with dozens of protruding tips of charcoal levitates in the room, leaving traces on the walls. *Lava Lamp*, the hypnotic and colorful installation by Michael Shaw, and *Spiritus Sonata*, by the Australian studio ENESS, envelop the viewer, evoking surprise and tenderness. The Hyperstudio collective, which

created the white universe of *Hypercosmo* for *Pop Air*, devised a new vision in *Hyperstellar* for *Let's Fly:* a sea of black spheres that reflect an infinite universe enveloping the audience. The work is executed with the creative contribution of Quiet Ensemble and the high-resolution images of Roman Hill. Still gazing skyward, one encounters the growing installation of Korean artist MyeongBeom Kim and the ethereal inflatable sculptures of the Canadian artist Max Streicher that hover above the heads of visitors, while reflective environments emerge along the path with minimalist sculptures like those of the *BB* series by Lithuanian artist Tadao Cern, and the silvery forms of *Fountain of Eternity* by Russian artist Sasha Frolova. Also present in this exhibition but in a fluorescent and spatial variant are the irreverent *GINJOS* by Italian artist Rub Kandy. The atmosphere is further enriched by the imposing work of the Spanish artist SpY, and his enigmatic, moving creature; by the graceful bubbles created by the Italian collective Quiet Ensemble, filling the space in a moment of contemplation; and, finally, by the monumental green labyrinth of Cyril Lancelin reminiscent of Renaissance gardens.
Absorbed in an almost ethereal realm, where art merges with the playful forces of air, the experience intensifies through group interactions and intergenerational synergies, promoting growth and change. Leading toward new heights, *Let's Fly* offers itself as a tool to soar into the infinite skies of Inflatable Art.

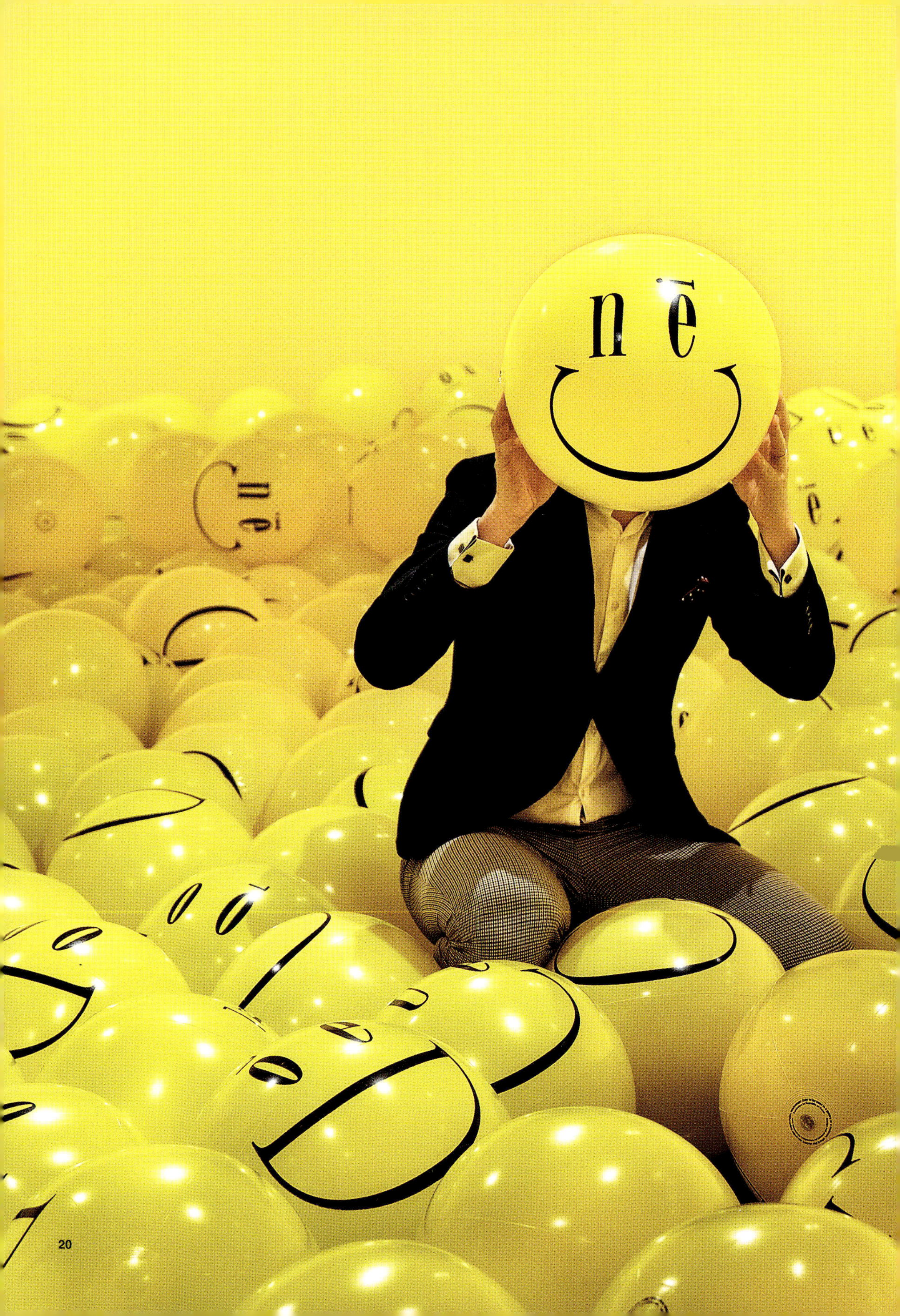
nē

EmotionAir

The *Pop Air* and *Let's Fly* exhibitions continue to thrill and engage a participative audience, but *EmotionAir* sets an even more ambitious goal. This latest exhibition, first presented in London in December 2023, is committed to the work of emotions, transforming artworks into mirrors to explore the profound relationship between art and emotions, action, and reaction. This is manifested tangibly through Inflatable Art, which offers itself as a medium to express the most intimate nuances of human feelings.

Through a mix of interactive installations, emotional projections, and performance art, *EmotionAir* aims to transport visitors on an unprecedented sensory journey. Artworks, rather than merely static objects, become vehicles for exploring and understanding the complex dynamics of human sentiments.

EmotionAir represents an audacious step in exploring the power of art to evoke and communicate emotions. Through the medium of Inflatable Art and a bold and innovative vision, the project aims to leave an indelible imprint on the hearts and minds of those privileged to participate.

EmotionAir
Art you can feel

Drawing on the six basic emotions—Happiness, Sadness, Anger, Fear, Disgust, and Surprise—the exhibition sought to transcend cultural, institutional, and geographical boundaries, offering a poignant exploration of the human condition. However, rather than confining the exploration to these six emotions, the exhibition expanded its scope.

EmotionAir offers a multisensory exhibition journey that balances the lightness of inflatable artworks with the complexity of human emotions. The installations are not mere works of art but portals through which to guide the visitor into a vibrant and intense world of feelings. Artists interpret and present works inspired by a wide range of emotions and behaviors, offering a varied and articulate narrative. Each artwork is designed to stimulate intimate dialog, providing a unique insight into the complexity of human experience.

A rich range of emotions is revealed through the presented works: Momoyo Torimitsu's large pink rabbits, constrained by a low and oppressive ceiling, tell a story of oppression and discomfort; Cyril Lancelin's imposing installation *Cube Abyss* confronts us with fear; while Jason Wilsher-Mills' reclining *Argonaut* figure and Lucas Zanotto's playful *SQUEEZED IN* celebrate joy in various forms. Kalman Pool's *Voyage* brings surprise, and its lively, translucent creatures lead viewers on a fantastic journey while Rub Kandy and his extravagant *GINJOS* celebrate

ecstasy. Michela Picchi's grand *Playground Love* inspires wonder in an audience of all ages, enchanting the youngest. The Hyperstudio collective returns with two significant works: *Too Many Thoughts* and *Hyperfeeling*. The latter, in collaboration with international studio Sila Sveta and the artist kissmiklos, is the centerpiece of the museum experience, inviting visitors to immerse themselves in a multitude of bright yellow spheres showcasing a whirlwind of conflicting emotions. From monumental installations that stand majestically to more intimate works that stimulate a dialog within oneself, *EmotionAir* offers a comprehensive overview of the diversity of artistic approaches. Visiting the exhibition stimulates all the senses, like listening to Thom Kubli's *Black Hole Horizon*, where resonant tones are trapped in floating bubbles; seeing and basking in the play of light in Alex Schweder's, *The Third Thing;* and the kinetic installation *ELECTRIC MOONS* by Christopher Bauder. Viewers are invited to immerse themselves in atmospheres with hypnotic visual effects, such as those created by Miranda Makaroff, and to meet the monstrous and fascinating, angry and playful creatures of the artist Motomichi Nakamura.
EmotionAir emerges as a celebration of the power of art to evoke, stimulate, and unite the complexity of human emotions through Inflatable Art.

WORKS

FROM A TO Z

ANOTHERVIEW

Anotherview is an art collective dedicated to researching and recording high definition views for 24 hours from different places around the world that are transmitted through portable digital windows. The collective is formed by Marco Tabasso, Tatiana Uzlova, and Robert Andriessen, who, as contemporary archivists, research, record, and save the unique locations captured in our present time in order to build an archive for future generations. From New York City, to the vast landscape of the Okaukuejo/ Etosha

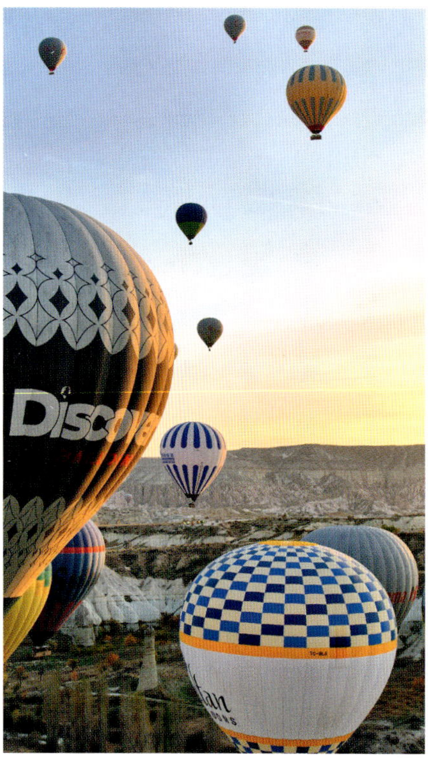

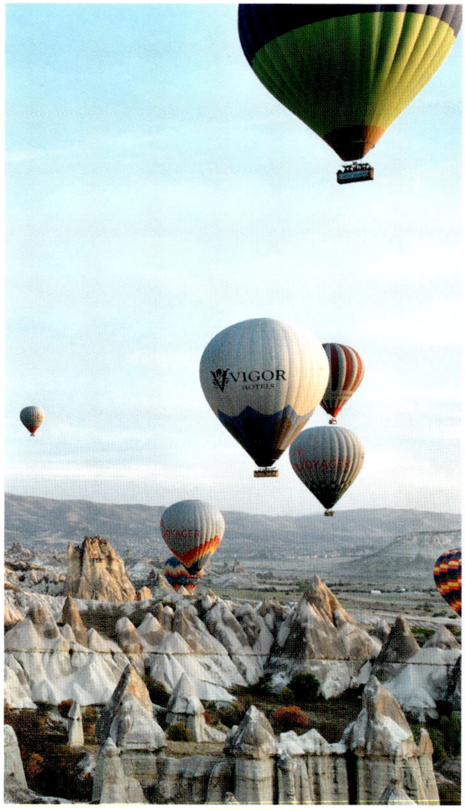

National Park in Namibia, the locations visited by the team are carefully selected for their storytelling. Each project connects to questions regarding the natural environment under threat and problems related to intensive urbanization. Anotherview "windows" have been presented at international fairs such as Jingart in Beijing, Art Basel/ Design Miami in Basel, Salone del Mobile in Milan, Salon NY, Art Miami and PAD in London.

Still frames from *Skyscape #1* by Anotherview Balloon Museum *EmotionAir* London, 2023

Skyscape #1 2023

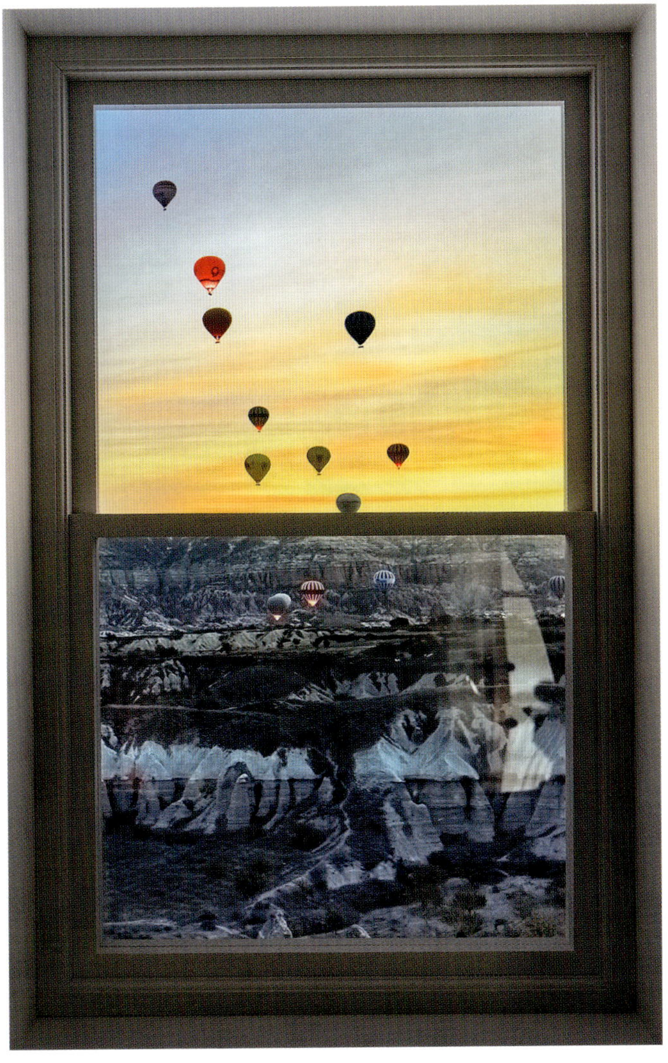

Anotherview
Skyscape #1
Balloon Museum
EmotionAir
London, 2023

Skyscape #1
This artwork of Anotherview has been specifically created for the Balloon Museum. The title originates from the fusion of two elements, the sky and escapes, beautifully encapsulating the experience of witnessing hot air balloons ascending and gracefully dancing through the magical panorama of Cappadocia.
Observers of *Skyscape #1* are confronted with an unexpected and surreal spectacle. Instead of gazing at the familiar landscape from the long row of windows, they are transported to the enchanting natural formations of Love Valley, witnessing the magical display of balloons rising at dawn. This engaging experience elicits a response akin to childlike wonder and irrational joy, accompanied by a fascinating sense of space-time detachment. It is an invitation to a deeper breath, a broader gaze, a way of being "differently present." The rugged rocky valleys of Cappadocia evoke a primordial, almost prehistoric time when humans were guests of Nature. The protagonists, in addition to the beauty of the landscape, are the air as a primordial element and the balloons, both in perfect symbiosis with the underlying concept of the exhibition.

ARCHITECTS OF AIR

Founder, designer and artistic director Alan Parkinson first started experimenting with pneumatic sculptures in the I980s and has since developed his own language of form in this plastic medium. The artist's intention is to stimulate visitors to a sense of wonder at the beauty of light and color, and create an environment where the visitor's experience is influenced by their own relation to space. From the Guggenheim in Spain to the Sydney Opera House in Australia, the monumental and interactive walk-in sculptures of Architects of Air have astounded audiences across the globe. Architects of Air has toured with their luminaria since 1992 and visited 43 countries.

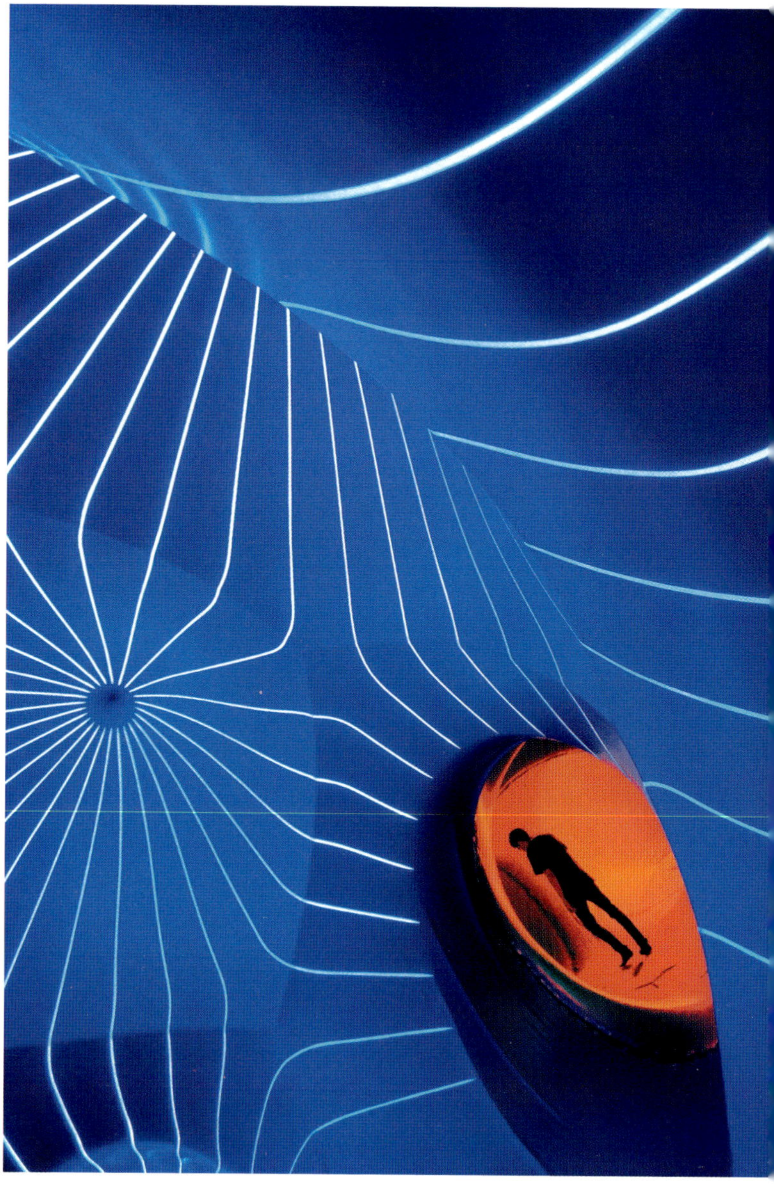

Architects of Air
Dodecalis Luminarium
(Blue Dome)
Malmö Festival, 2019

Dodecalis Luminarium 2019

Dodecalis Luminarium

A work designed by Alan and Meko Parkinson of Architects of Air, *Dodecalis Luminarium* was presented at the *Pop Air* exhibition in Madrid in 2023.
It is named after the dodecahedron—the 12-sided Platonic solid based on the pentagon. The work is a monumental immersive installation that invites the viewer to enter another dimension.
Dodecalis Luminarium offers a labyrinth in which to lose yourself, to be astounded by the beauty of this new world that is governed by the laws of physics. It is a place of contemplation, discovery, and wonder.
Dodecalis Luminarium presents the latest evolution of the dodecahedral dome in its most exciting manifestation, with a dazzling tracery of light lines animating the three Dodecadomes, entitled Green Dome, Blue Dome, and Red Dome. Advanced engineering design techniques enable a breakdown of the form into flowing neon-like contour lines of vibrant intensity. Above eye-level one can see more clearly the dome's pentagonal foundation and sense what it is like to be inside a Platonic solid.

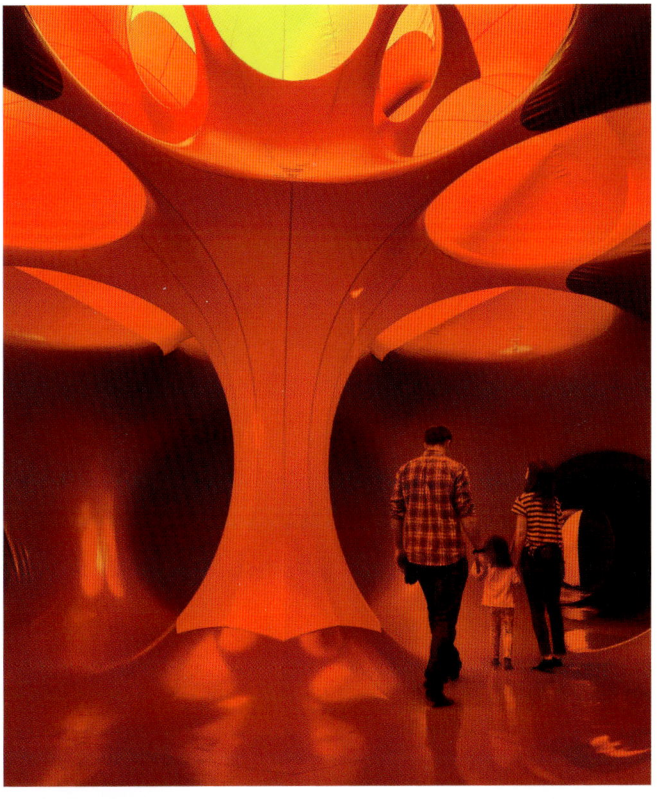

Architects of Air
Dodecalis Luminarium
(Red Tree)
Balloon Museum
Pop Air
Madrid, 2023

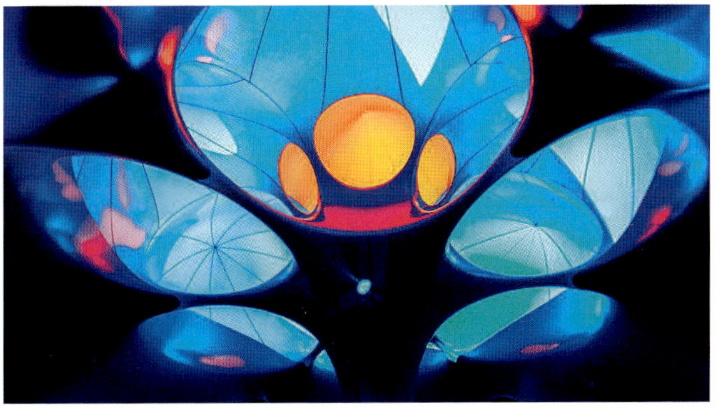

Architctects of Air
Dodecalis Luminarium
(Blue Tree)
Orlando, 2019

Architects of Air brings visual art to places where one would least expect it. *Dodecalis luminarium* offers a dazzling maze of winding paths and soaring domes where Islamic architecture, Archimedean solids, and Gothic cathedrals merge into an inspiring monument to the beauty of light and color, and where visitors can happily lose themselves. The installation awakens all the senses, creating a sense of wonder and enchantment for all ages. Visitors are transported to and immersed in an amazing world of light and subtle and saturated hues, providing a unique sensory experience.

The asymmetry of the pentagon serves to disorient the visitor in a way that makes exploration more exciting. *Dodecalis*' tranquil Main Dome continues the motif of neon-like tracery and its heptagonal foundation extends the principle of asymmetry. An imposing Blue Tree completes the ensemble of the large domes of *Dodecalis*.

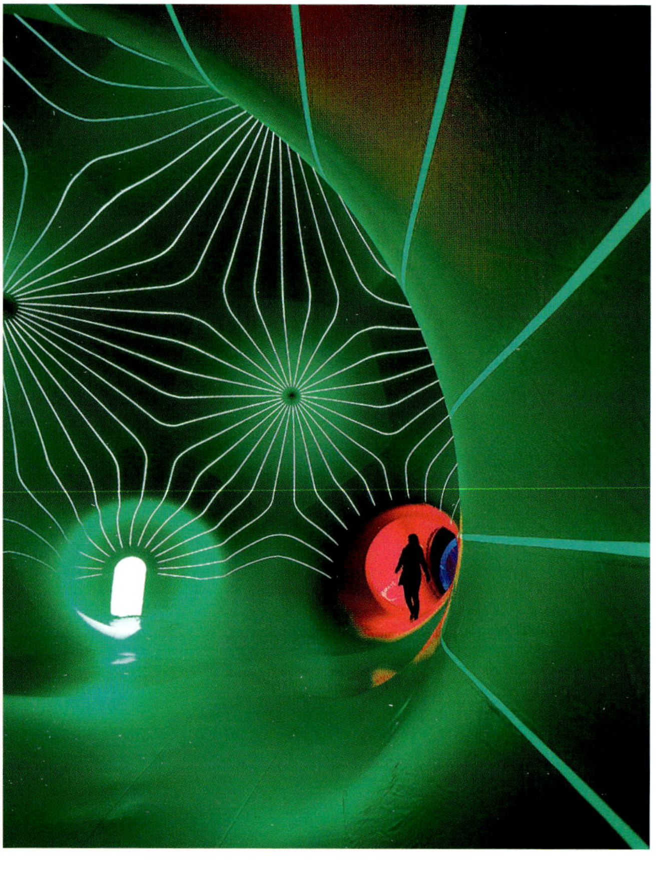

Architects of Air
Dodecalis Luminarium
(Green Dome)
Malmö Festival, 2019

Opposite

Architects of Air
Dodecalis Luminarium
Belgium, 2023

Sketch of
Dodecalis Luminarium
by Alan Parkinson

Dodecalis Luminarium 2019

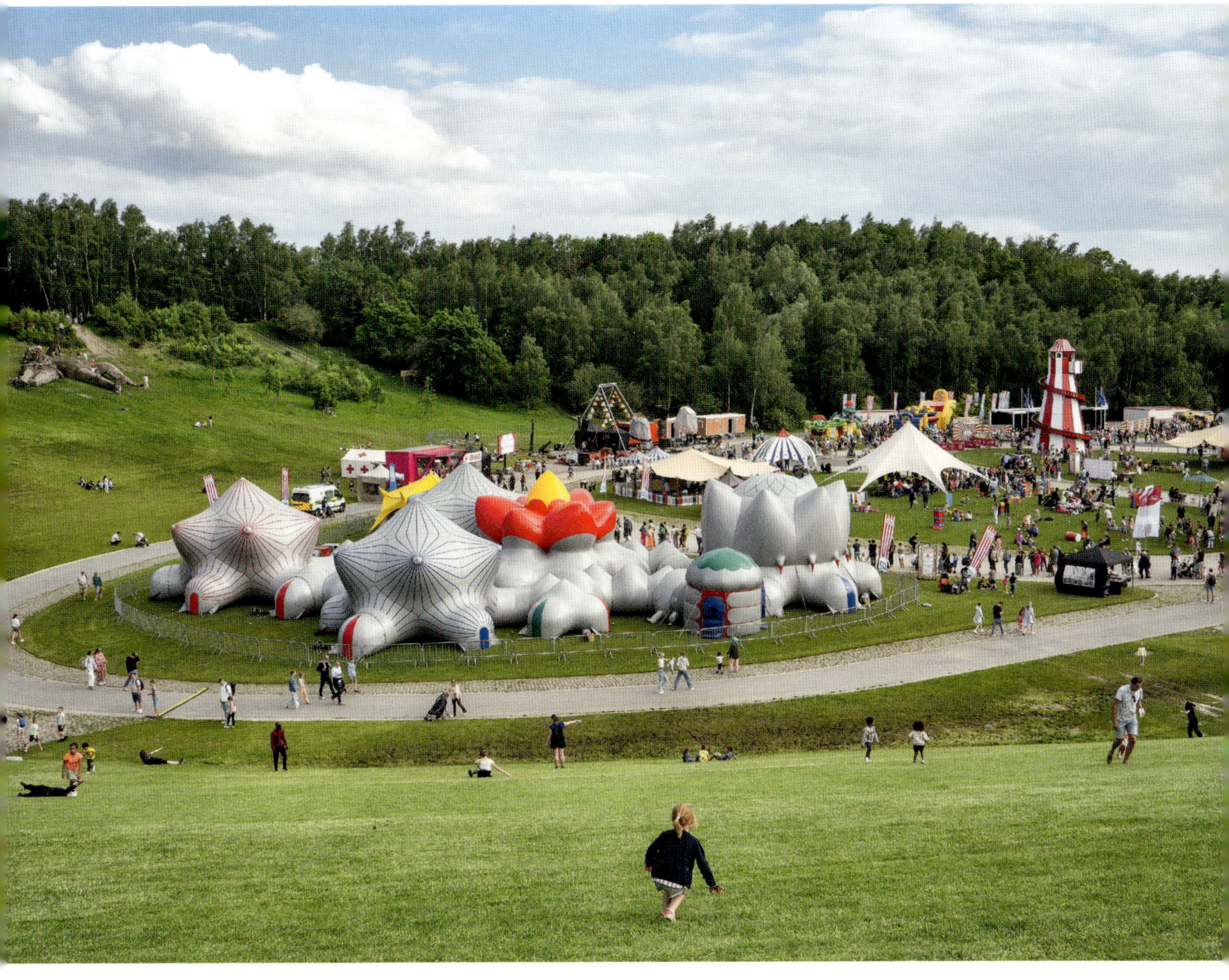

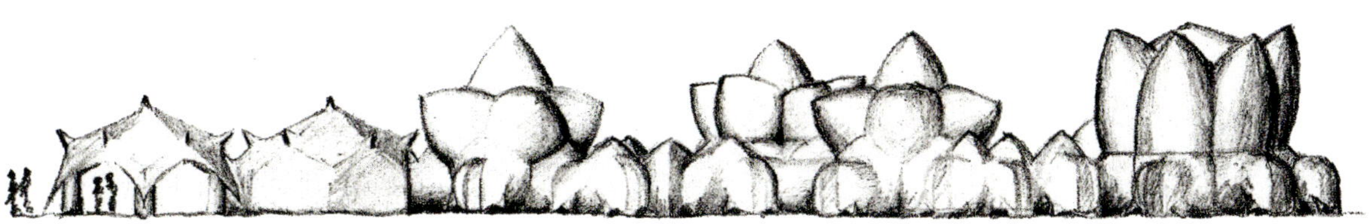

CLAIRE ASHLEY

Born in Scotland, Claire Ashley lives and works in Chicago, USA. She is famous for her very colorful inflatable sculptures, which she conceives as monumental creatures in bright tones. The artist designs burlesque artworks combining extravagant forms and attitudes. She teaches at the School of the Art Institute of Chicago in the United States.

"I encourage a sense of wonder and curiosity by welcoming people into a bizarre, extraterrestrial, totally kitsch world."

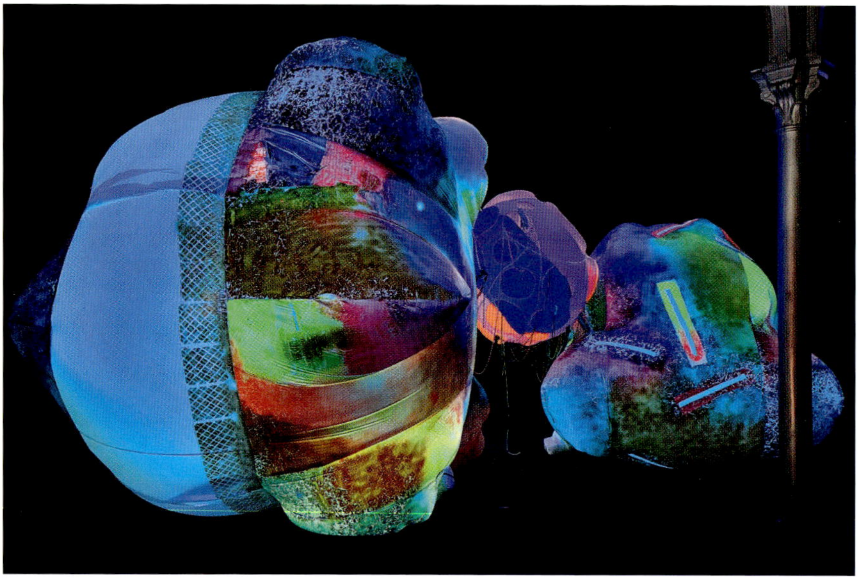

Claire Ashley
Clown (Star Patrick)
Balloon Museum
Pop Air
Paris, 2022

Clown (Star Patrick)
Claire Ashley's installation consists of three painted inflatable sculptures. *Clown (Star Patrick)* is a bulbous inflatable with six unequal protruding "legs" to signify the shape of a starfish. The form is spray painted in bright colors that take on an extraterrestrial hue in the black light overhead.

Inspired by the multiverse of popular culture, the artist immerses herself in imaginative alien landscapes, the universe of SpongeBob the cartoon character, and *Star Trek* the TV series.
Additional references from the natural world include: bioluminescent organisms, northern lights, and jellyfish.

Clown (Star Patrick) 2019

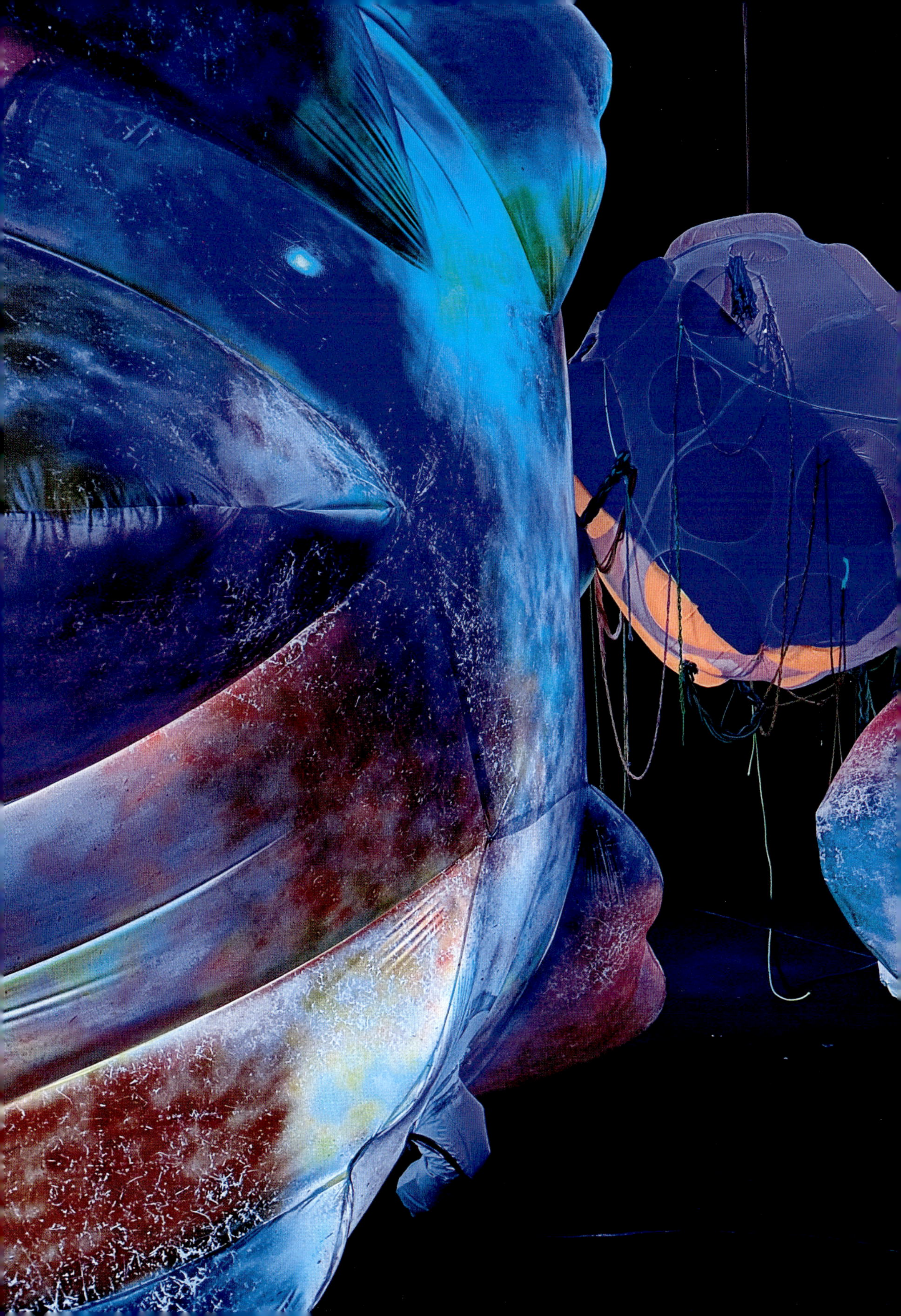

ATELIER SISU

This award winning Sydney-based art practice is led by Peruvian sculptor and industrial designer Renzo B. Larriviere and architectural designer and artist Zara Pasfield. The pair work with a multi-disciplinary team to create experiential environments, installations, and unique sculptural pieces. Their direction of work sits between the fields of art and architecture (art-chitecture), connecting audiences with their environment, with particular focus in the realm of public art. Each public artwork aims to provide a unique spatial experience for its visitor and is designed to be truly inclusive. The artists create large-scale site-specific works that enchant the viewer by reinventing spaces, while contributing to the visual identity of a place and promoting community interaction.

Atelier Sisu
Evanescent
Brisbane, 2021

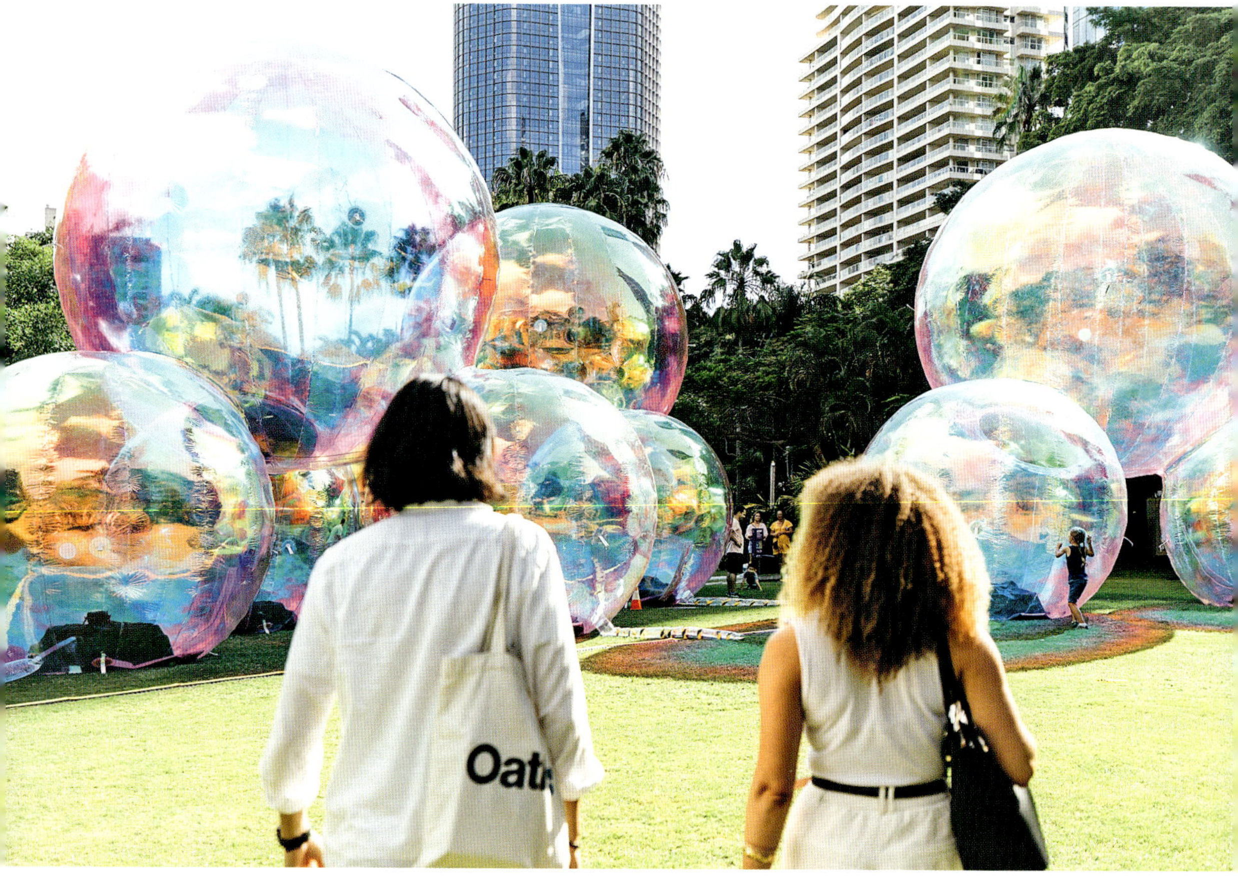

Evanescent 2020

Evanescent

For the title of their "art-chitecture" installation, the artists chose an adjective describing something fleeting or vanishing quickly and the quality of impermanence: *Evanescent*. The immersive light and sound experience aims to capture that ephemeral and transient feeling in visual form: the bubble.

The installation *Evanescent* is made from color-reflecting Dichroic film spheres that react to the changing sunlight as they move across the sky, causing a rainbow reflection on the ground that shifts and collides in brilliant formations.

The inspiration for the artwork came during the Covid-19 pandemic, when, noticing how the things that we would take for granted could disappear in an instant, the artists endeavored to communicate this feeling of transient beauty in physical form. By emulating the ethereal quality and the magic of bubbles, Atelier Sisu's *Evanescent* appeals to our universal playfulness and childlike wonder, encouraging us to consider the world around them as a space of transience and fragility, like that of a bubble.

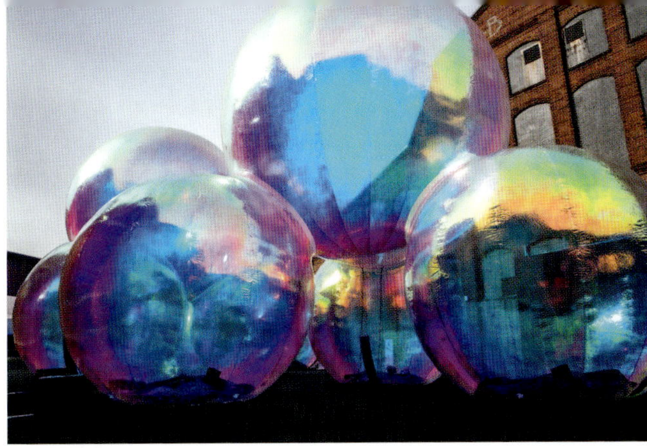

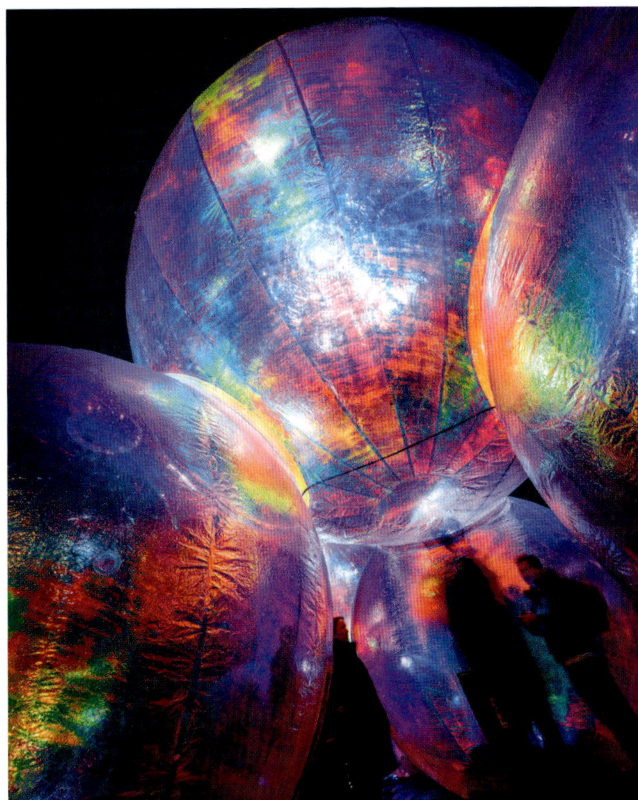

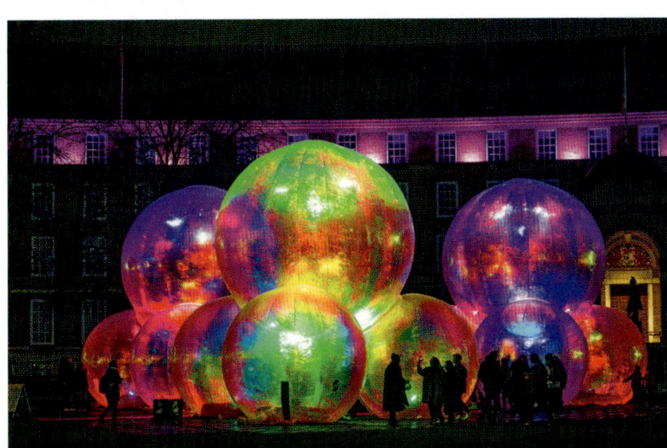

Atelier Sisu
Evanescent
Balloon Museum
Let's Fly
Atlanta, 2024

Atelier Sisu
Evanescent
Bristol, 2024

Atelier Sisu
Evanescent
Bristol, 2024

CHRISTOPHER BAUDER

A light and media artist, Bauder's large-scale spatial art installations focus on translating digital information into tangible objects and environments, with key elements including space, object, sound, light, and interaction. In 2004, Bauder founded the multidisciplinary art and design studio WHITEvoid in order to realize his large-scale and complex performance pieces. In 2021, *DARK MATTER*, the permanent exhibition for the interactive installations of Bauder, opened its doors to the public in Berlin.

Christopher Bauder has showcased his installations and performances globally, e.g. at the Centre Pompidou in Paris, The National Museum of Fine Arts in Taiwan, the Festival of Lights in Lyon, and at numerous other festivals. He has received multiple internationally renowned awards for his design and inventions. Bauder's notable works like *DEEP WEB* and *SKALAR* are lauded around the globe as is *Lichtgrenze*, a city-wide light art installation created for the 25th anniversary of the fall of the Berlin Wall.

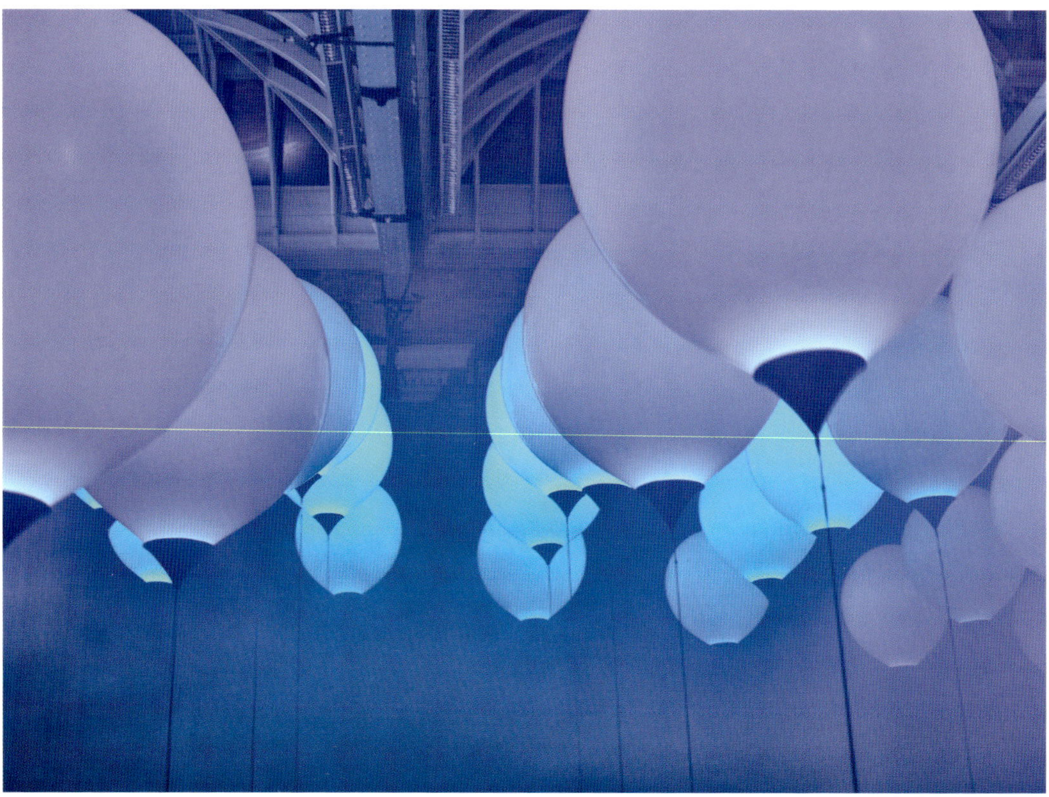

ELECTRIC MOONS 2018

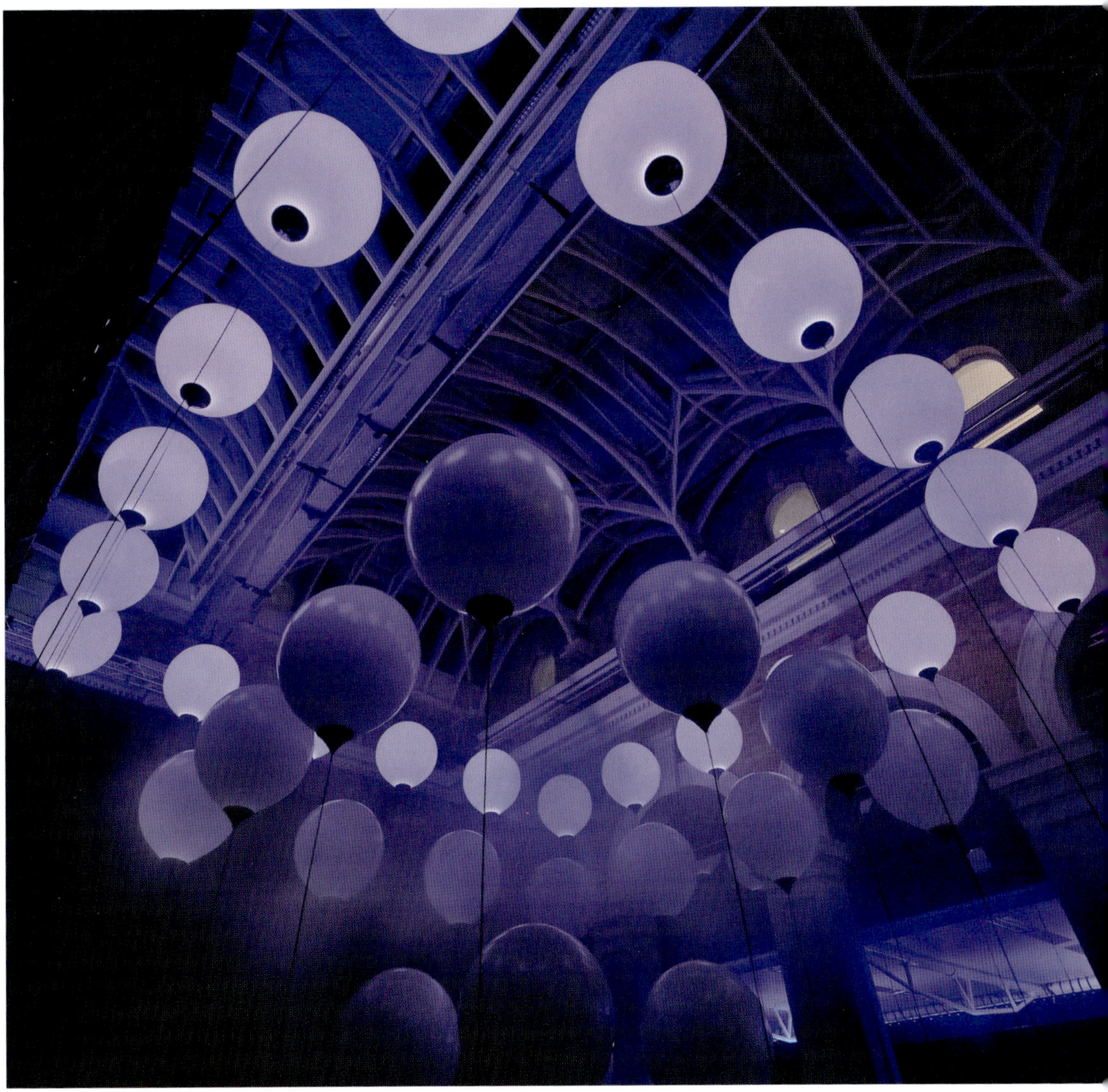

Here and overleaf
Christopher Bauder
ELECTRIC MOONS
Balloon Museum
EmotionAir
London, 2023

ELECTRIC MOONS

This kinetic installation celebrates the power of light and weightlessness. It consists of illuminated balloons arranged on a grid, evoking the image of celestial bodies dancing elegantly in the air. Through the deliberate interplay of movement, changing lighting, and atmospheric music, the viewer is immersed in a unique and ephemeral experience. The arrangement of the balloons is constantly evolving, creating new formations in space. *ELECTRIC MOONS* is a dynamic sculpture consisting of floating objects, light, and a synchronized rhythmic and textural sound composition. *ELECTRIC MOONS* invites the audience on a multi-sensory journey documenting the ephemeral nature of the creative act. An extraordinary experience that challenges the static nature of perception, opens the doors to new sensory perspectives, and encourages reflection on the fleeting and changing beauty of art.

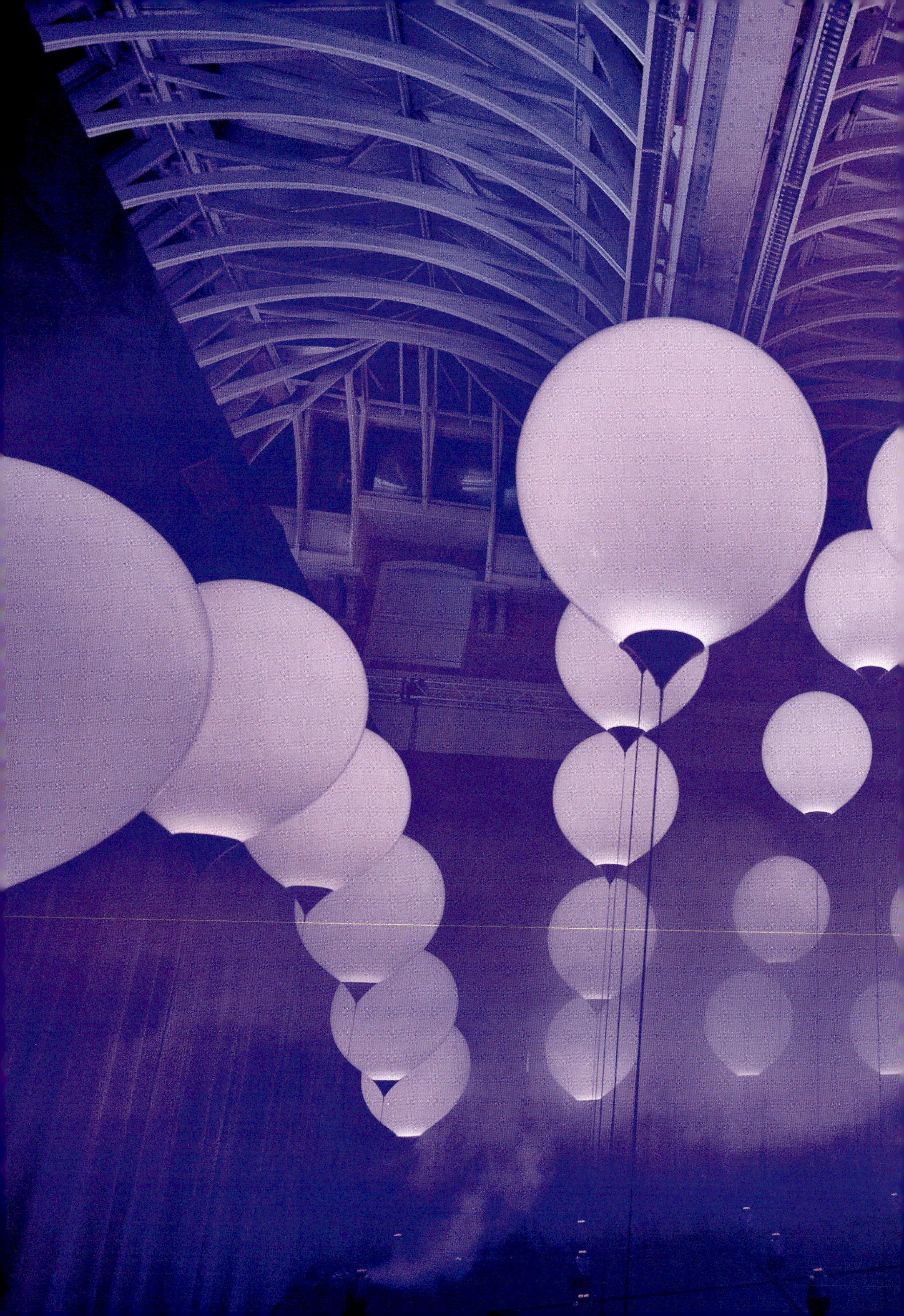

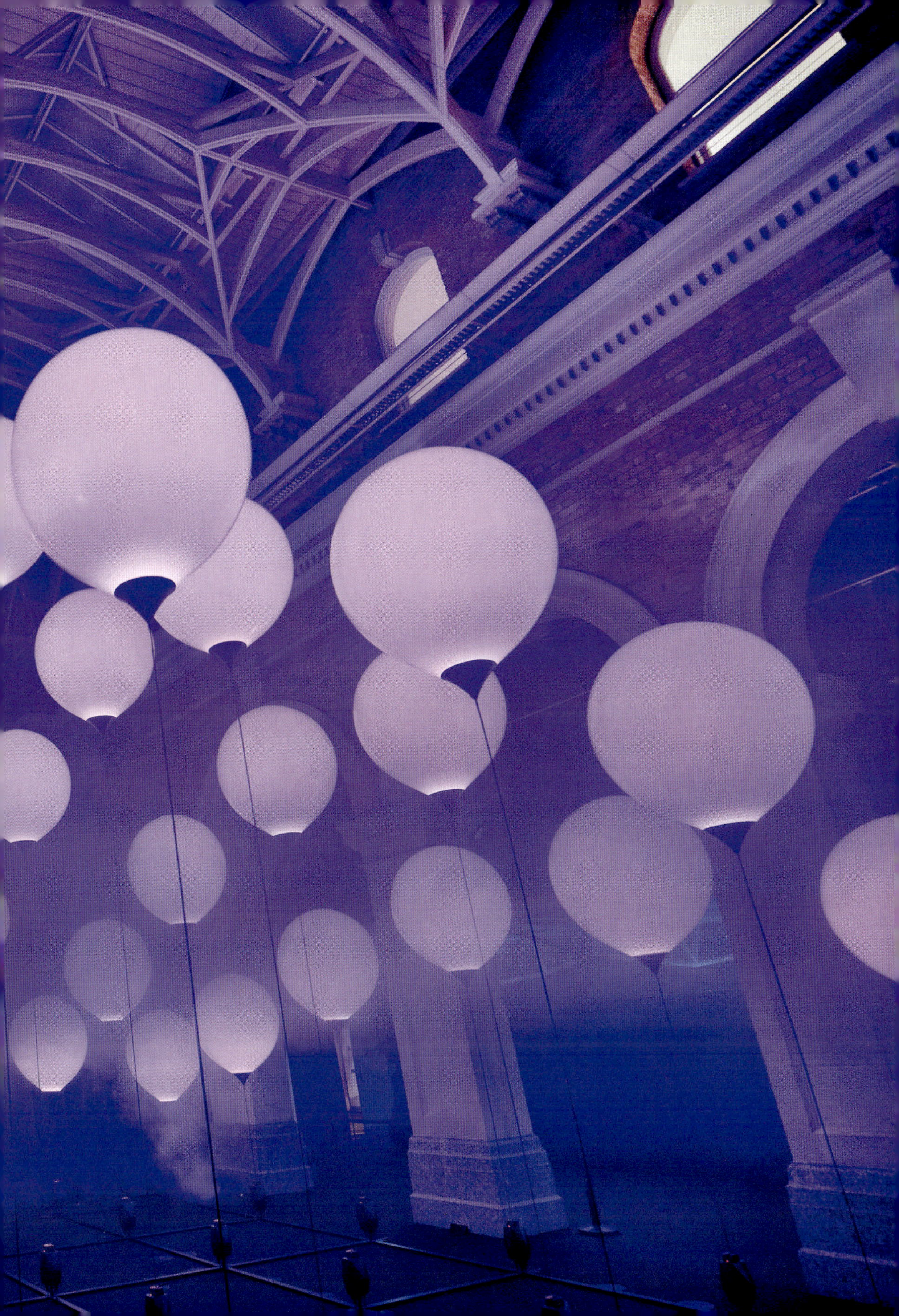

KATEŘINA BLAHUTOVÁ

A multifaceted creative professional, Kateřina Blahutová was born in the Czech Republic in 1987. She began her artistic journey by enrolling at the Czech Technical University in Prague, culminating in a Master's Degree in Architecture and Urban Planning from the esteemed Faculty of Architecture. From 2015 to 2018, Kateřina made her mark as both an artist and curator, contributing her talent and vision to the dynamic landscape of Lunchmeat Studio and Festival. *Living Forest* has been shown internationally including at Signal Festival in Prague and is emblematic of Kateřina Blahutová's common themes of sustainability in her artwork. In 2017 she relocated to Reykjavík, where she became part of the experimental collective RASK.

Kateřina Blahutová
Living Forest
Balloon Museum
Pop Air
Rome, 2021

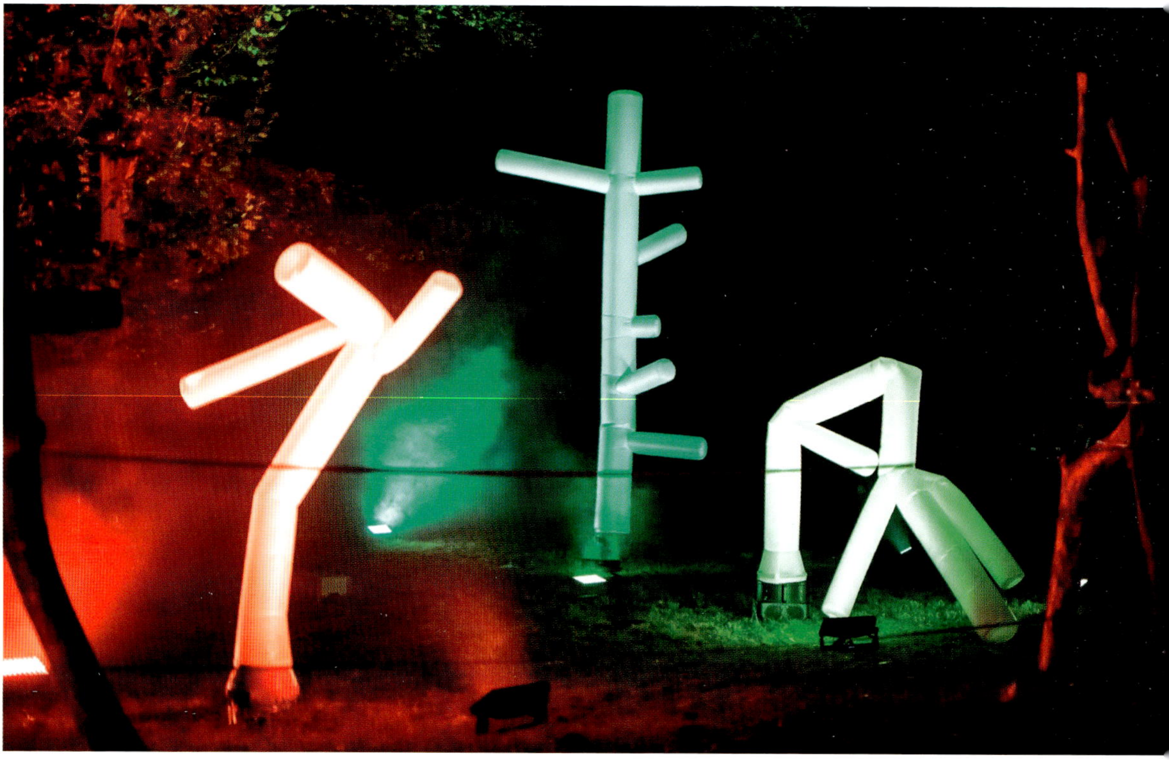

Living Forest 2021

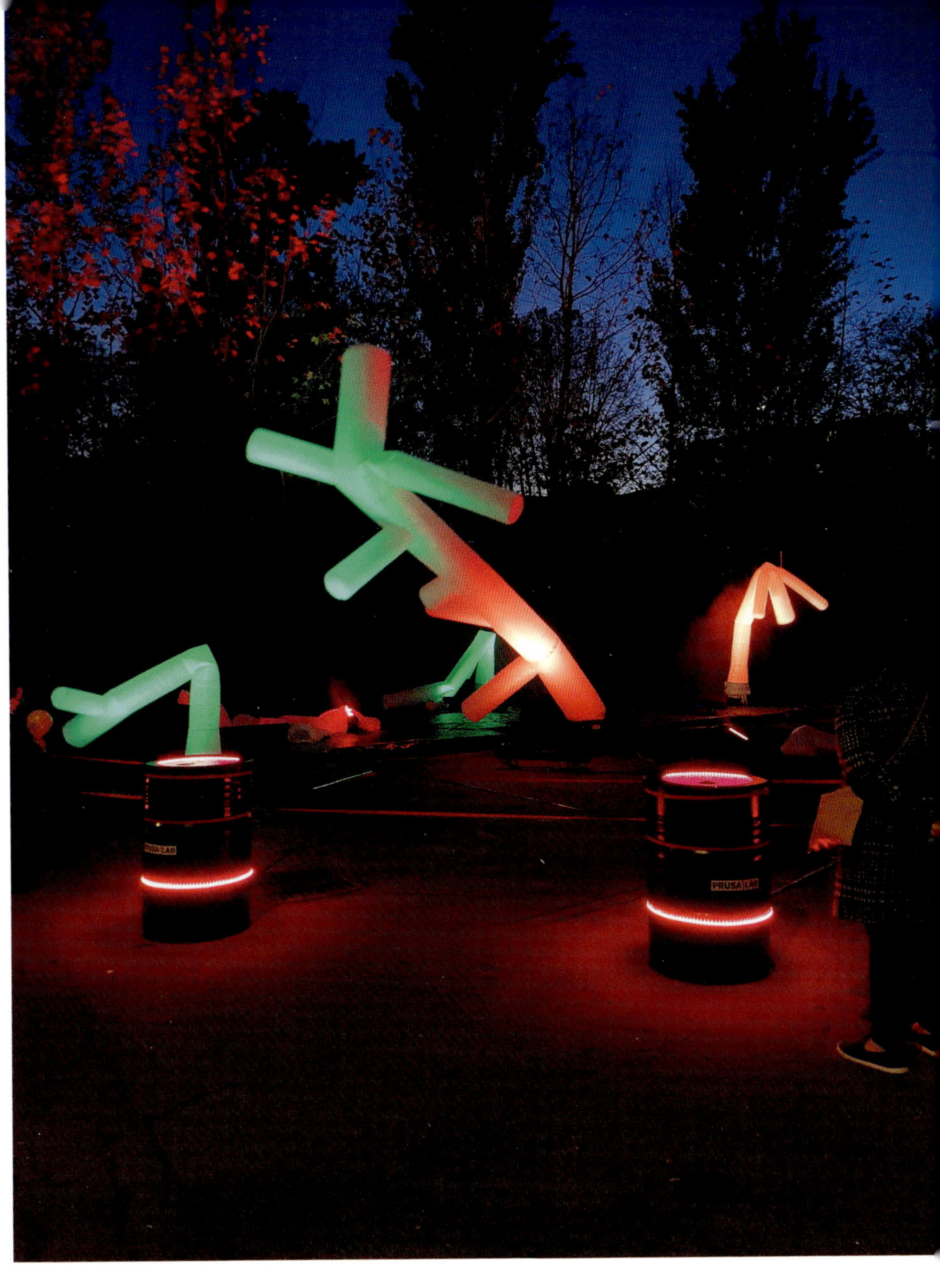

Kateřina Blahutová
Living Forest
Signal Festival
Prague, 2021

Living Forest

The temporary installation *Living Forest*, displayed at the *Pop Air* exhibition in Rome, confronts visitors with the pressing issue of the effects of the global climate situation. The vibrant, dancing figures are a whimsical embodiment of trees, capturing the attention of passersby with their playful and kinetic charm. But these seemingly jovial sentinels have a deeper meaning. *Living Forest* by Kateřina Blahutová is a call to action, expounding the belief that through the engagement of the community and through our determination and efforts, we can restore the natural landscape in which we live. Blahutová creates her *Living Forest* in direct response to The Dead Forest, a devastated landscape of the Czech Republic whose health has been disrupted by the interplay of the unfortunate management of recent centuries and the global climate situation.

TADAO CERN

Tadas Cerniauskas aka Tadao Cern was born in 1983, graduating in 2009 from Vilnius Gediminas Technical University with a Master's in Architecture. He currently lives and works in Vilnius, Lithuania. In 2011, he switched from architecture to photography and in 2016, he decided to move toward a more conceptual form of artistic expression with new plastic and sculptural projects such as his *BB* series, an artwork selected by the Balloon Museum for the *Let's Fly* exhibition. The artist now exhibits his creations worldwide, currently showcasing them on a global scale including at the Van Gogh Museum, Amsterdam and Saatchi Gallery, London. Cern has won numerous photo awards, which have brought him to opportunities to create campaigns for many high-end brands such as Samsung, New Yorker, BMW, and Chupa Chups.

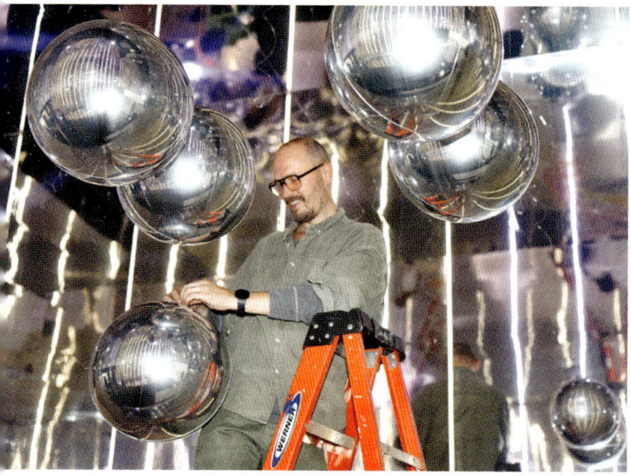

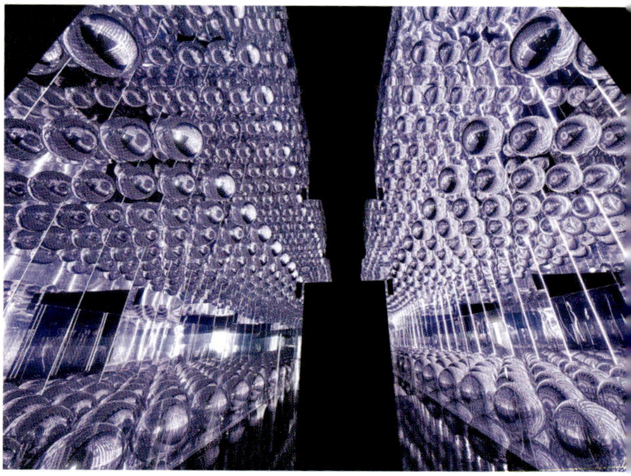

BB

Sometimes two, sometimes many more, the *BB* series comes in a variety of formats. Here, 180 silver balloons displayed in rows criss-cross the space with symmetrical, drawn lines. In this room of mirrors and stroboscopic lighting effects, the many reflections obscure our bearings. The boundaries between installation and space become blurred. Our compass goes astray. There's no more up, no more down. By dint of persistence, the viewer gradually discovers the illusion. Tadao Cern's work is reminiscent of the obsessions of the minimalist artists of the 1960s and '70s, such as repetition, the use of monochrome colors, and symmetry. Here, however, he makes a surprising shift by incorporating a soundtrack of nature sounds into his installation. The contrast between the visual and the aural reinforces our sense of disorientation.

Left
Artist Tadao Cern
setting up *BB*
Balloon Museum
Let's Fly
New York, 2023

Right and opposite
Tadao Cern
BB
Balloon Museum
Let's Fly
New York, 2023

BB 2023

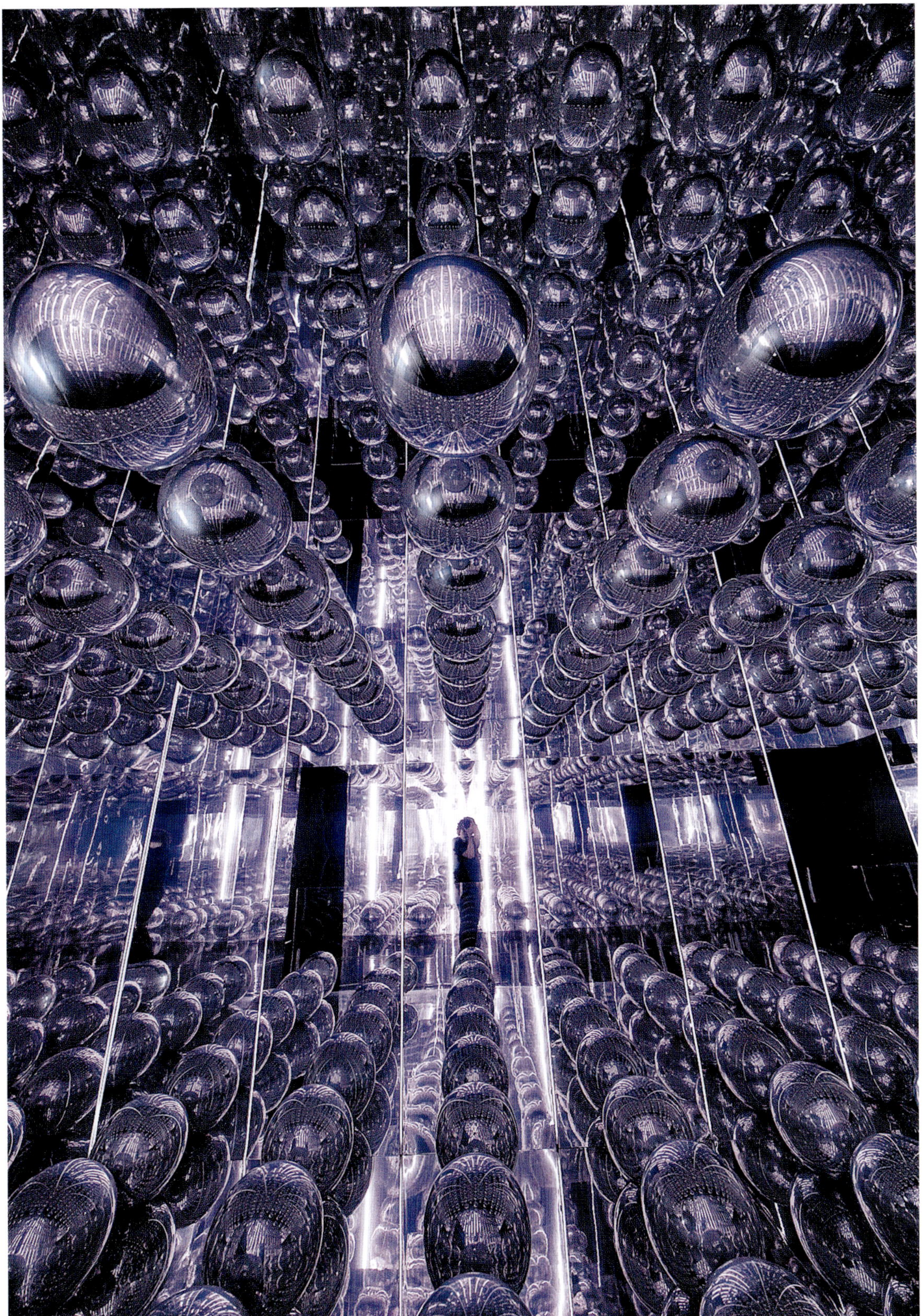

ENESS

Founded in 1997, ENESS is a multi-award-winning art and technology studio. The multidisciplinary team explores the intersection between the virtual and the physical world in the creation of both temporary and permanent interactive public art. Pioneers of new media art, ENESS artworks combine sculpture, textiles, design, furniture, software development, music and narrative. Led by artist and founder Nimrod Weis, the team delves into the deeper potential of interactivity to elicit emotive responses from audiences and discover how to make art appeal to people of all ages and backgrounds. The studio's style of work seduces viewers into getting closer and experiencing unexpected curiosities, taking digital art installations out of the gallery and into the realm of public space. The team's work questions how we view cities and their spaces and share ways in which technology and art bond us together. ENESS believes in the power of providing art in everyday life that fires the imagination; that provides joy, happiness and beauty in unexpected places—transformational experiences that change lives. In this way the team are 'happiness architects,' inspiring deeper moments between friends, family, and community. ENESS interactive installations are commissioned by urban and cultural precincts, festivals, galleries, and museums of modern art worldwide.

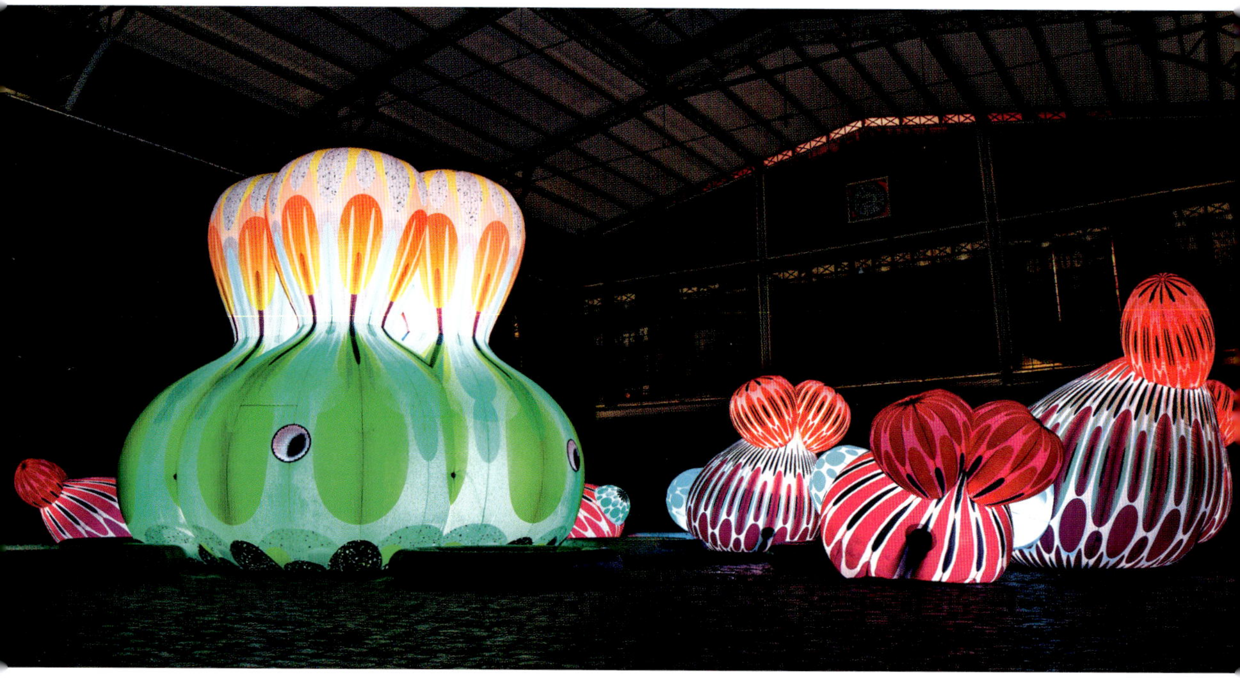

Cupid's Koi Garden 2022

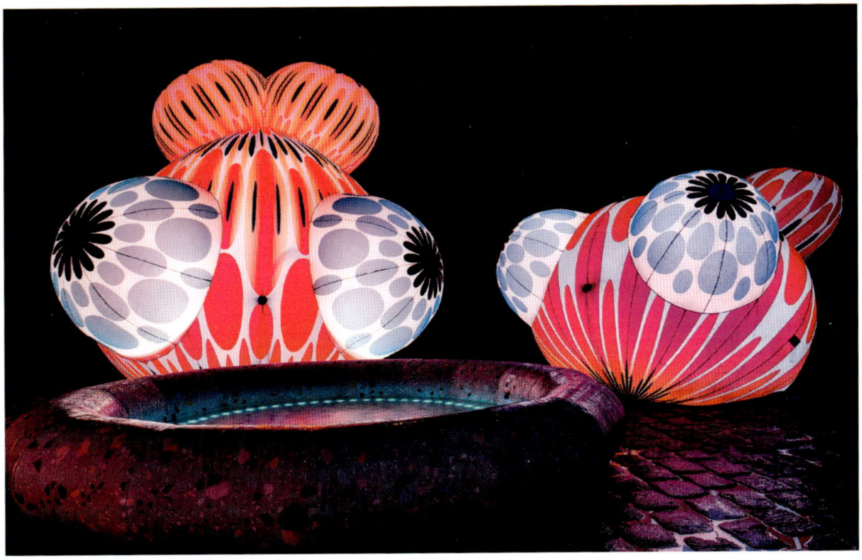

Cupid's Koi Garden

Cupid's Koi Garden, the first inflatable *kawaii* fountain displayed at the *Pop Air* exhibition at La Villette in Paris in 2022, is set up under the peristyle of the Grande Halle. Towering over 6 meters high, Eness's Cupid holds court among an adorable school of ten luminous and interactive Koi fish. Visitors stroll through the proverbial garden among the miniature tanks where cheeky koi fish spout water from phantasmagorical printed bodies into ponds set up throughout the installation. Giant roving eyes reveal themselves as one walks among the inflated sculptures. Cupid's Koi Garden combines technical innovations such as motion capture, interactive musical scores, and choreographed water streams. Symbols of love and friendship in Japan with which Nimrod Weis has a strong connection, the artwork aims to spread those same sentiments to its audience, as well as a little bit of watery mischief if you're not paying attention to where the next water stream might be directed.

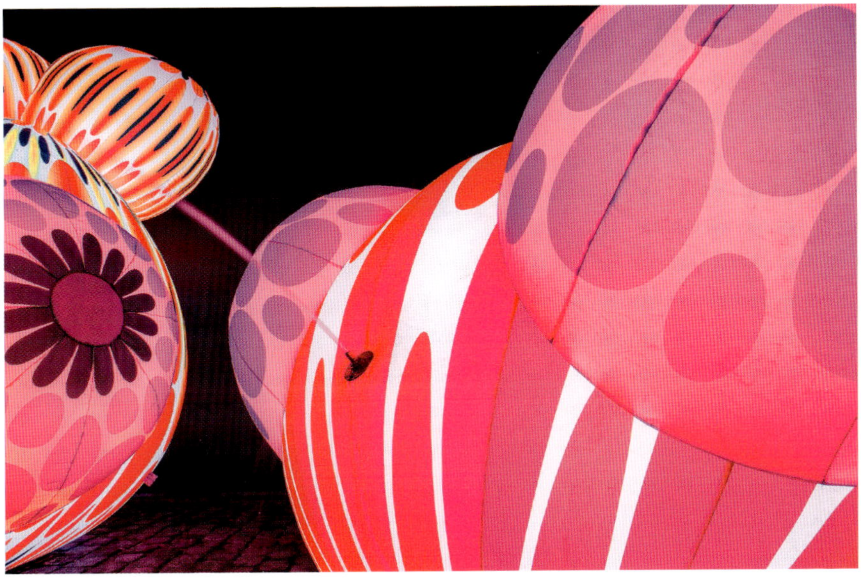

Here and overleaf
ENESS
Cupid's Koi Garden
Balloon Museum
Pop Air
Paris, 2022

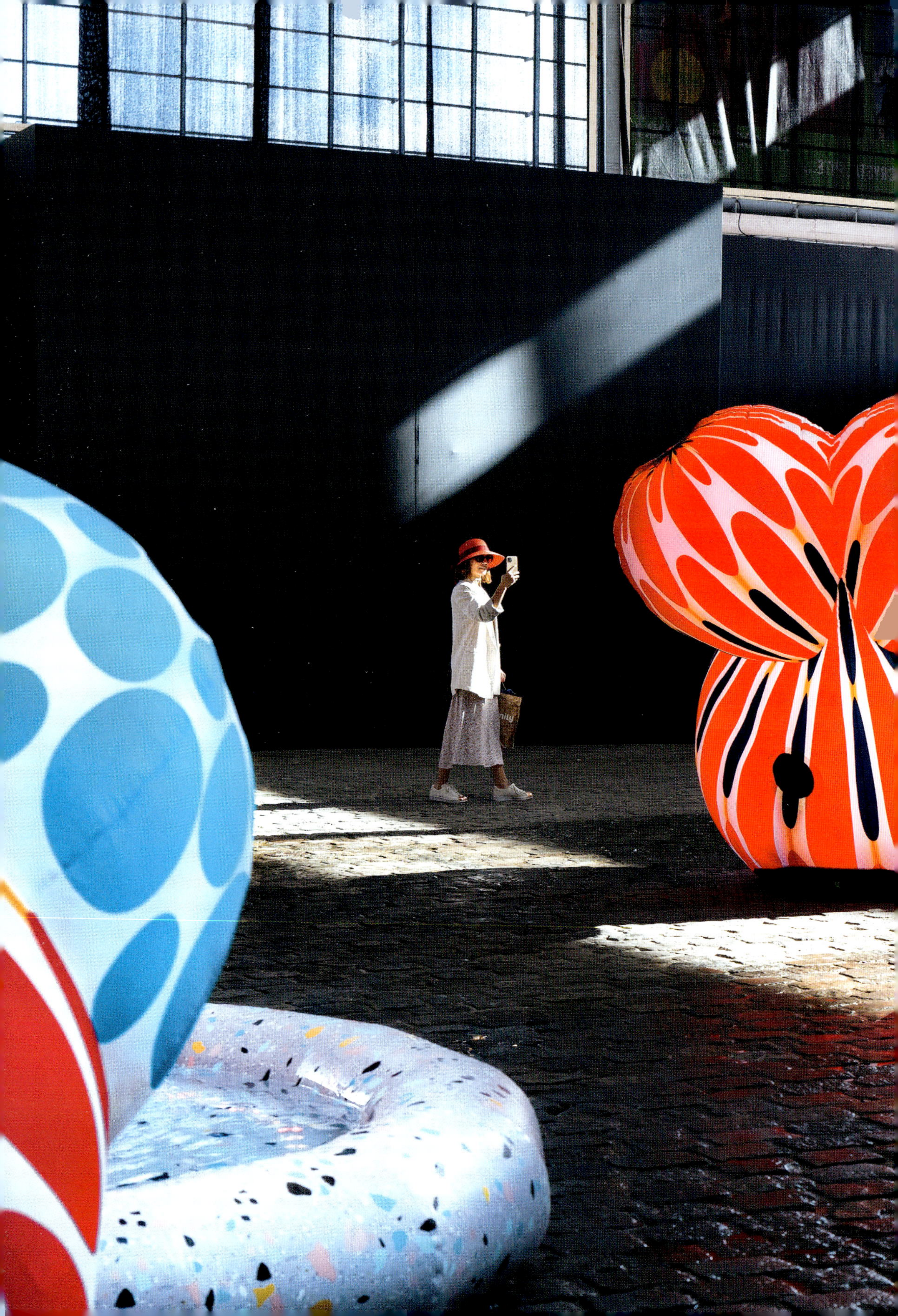

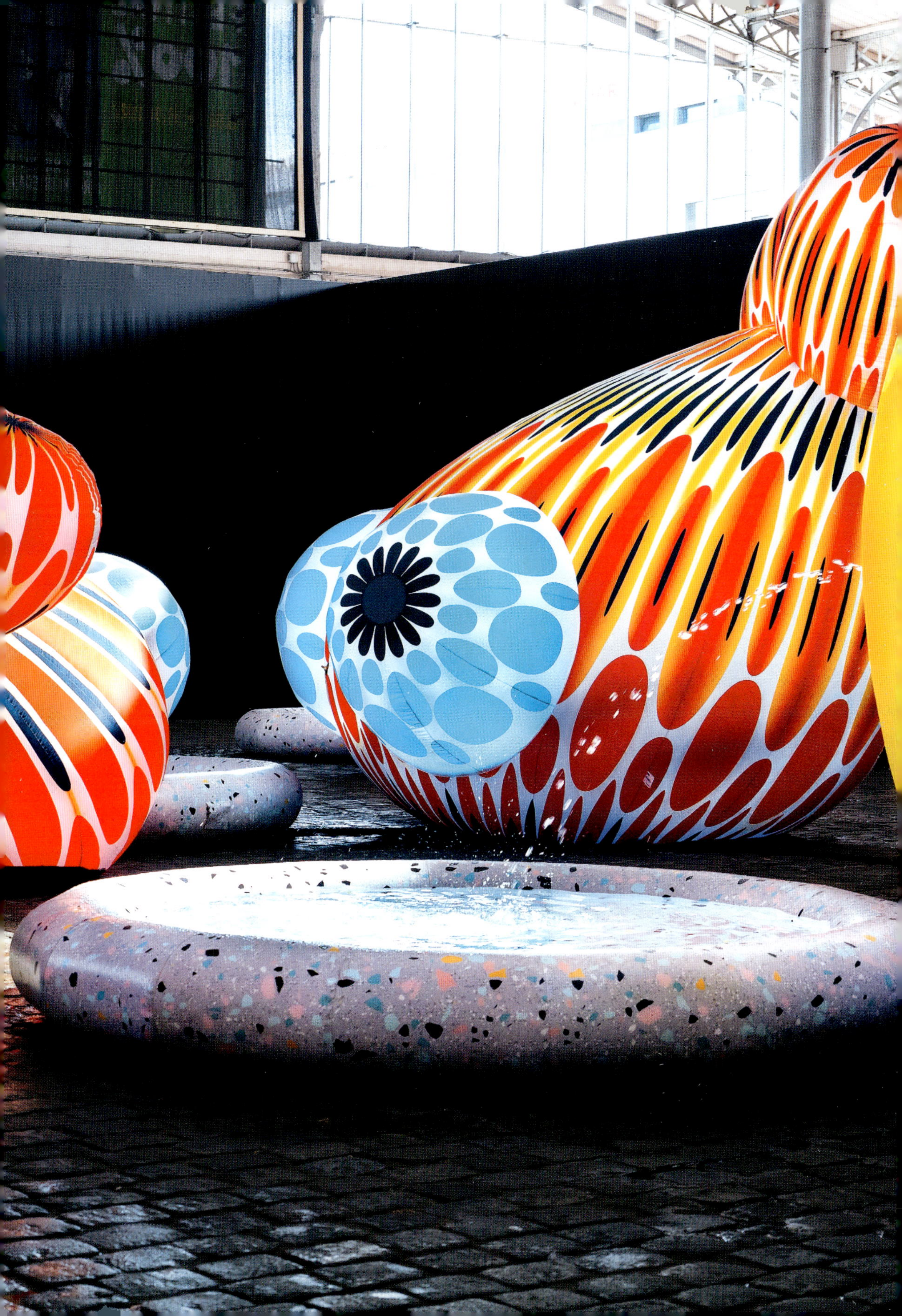

ENESS

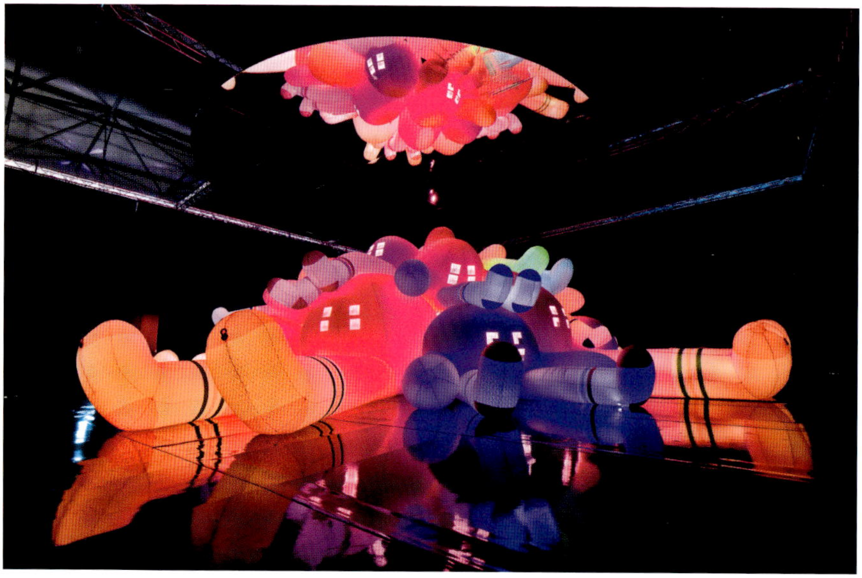

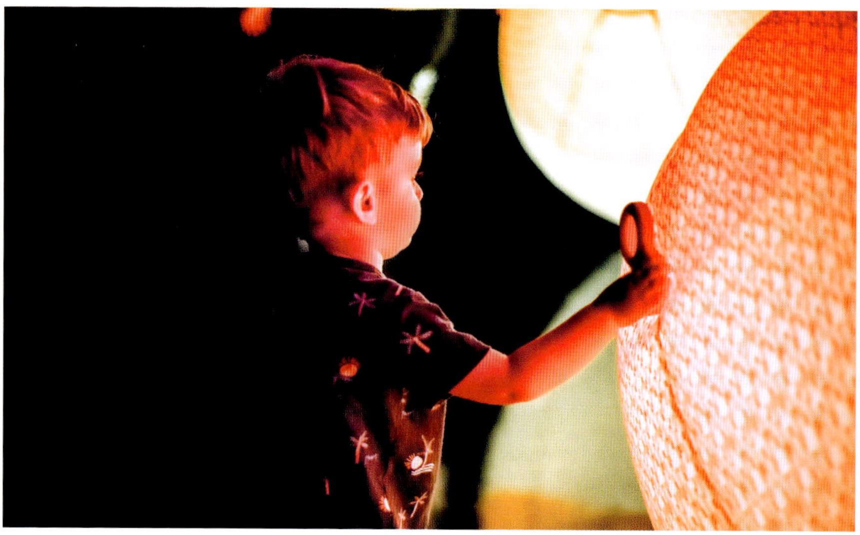

ENESS
Together Forever
Balloon Museum
Pop Air
Naples, 2023

Together Forever
This large inflatable installation is the artwork by ENESS specially conceived for the *Pop Air* exhibition at the Balloon Museum. *Together Forever* centers mainly around the concept of social bonding and the importance of people coming together. Its composition features 20 characters arranged one on top of the other—in close contact—in a messy, happy cluster that coexists in perfect harmony. This lively, joyous cluster is actually a carefully designed structure, a soft pyramid resembling a mold of jelly. Visitors are encouraged to interact with the work: tickling the feet of the different characters brings them to life, activating different sensory experiences. The installation's sound accompaniment recalls an organic soundscape, which evolves and intensifies in a fascinating succession of sounds such as human heartbeats, breaths, and liquid bubbles. In addition, scents are released that evoke memories of childhood and sharing, such as the smell of popcorn, chewing gum, freshly cut grass, and freshly baked bread.

Together Forever 2023

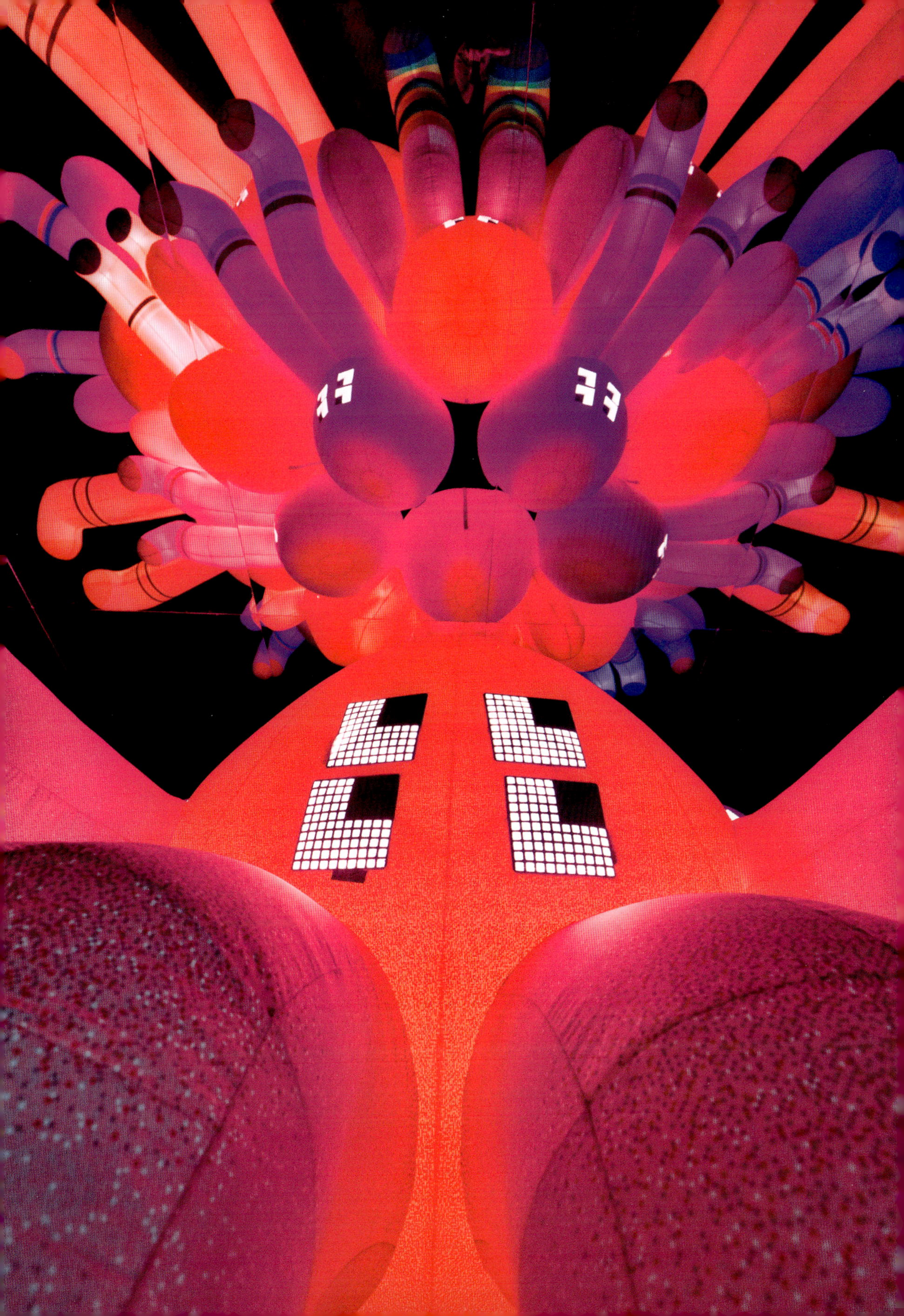

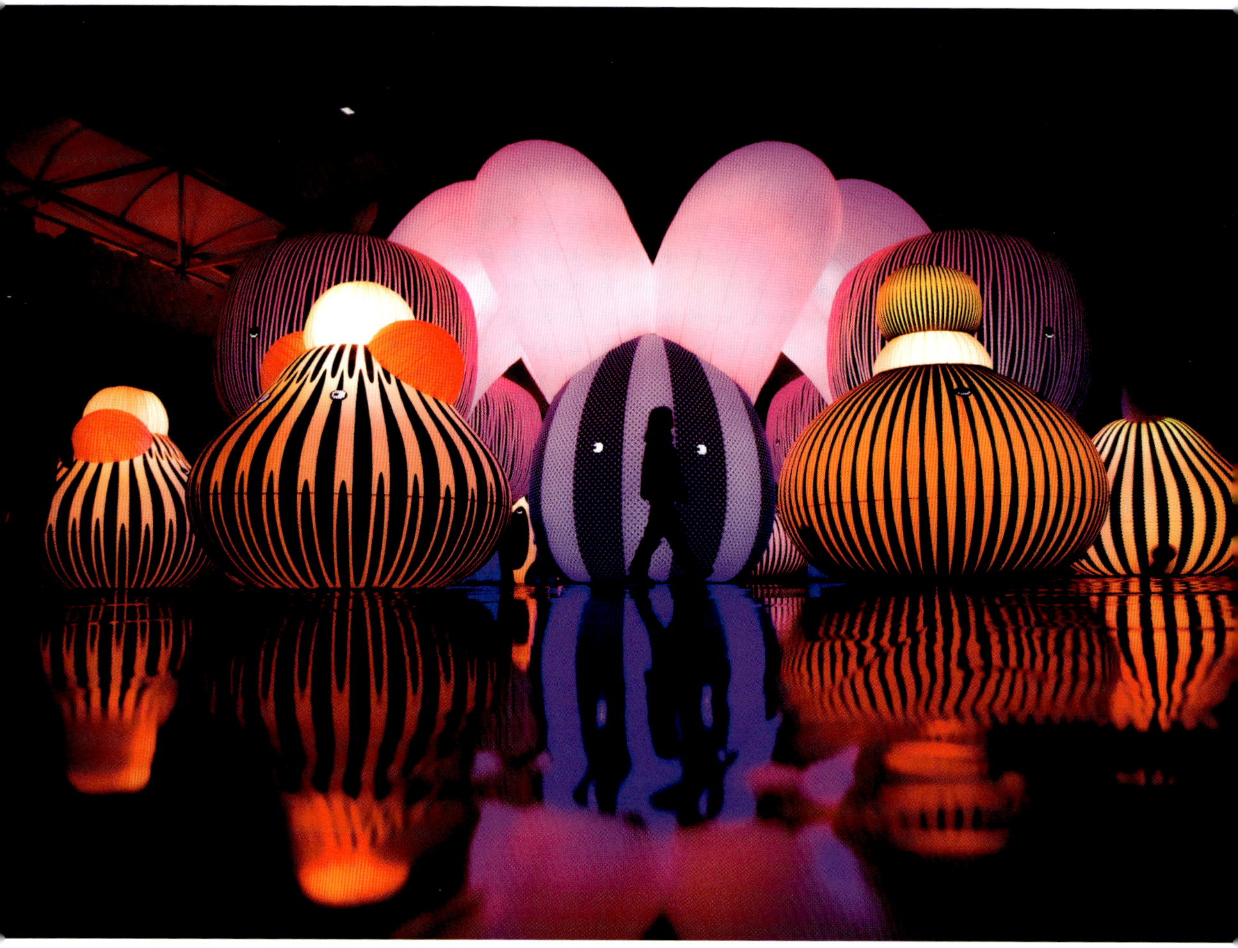

Airship Orchestra

Airship Orchestra gathers together a mystical tribe of otherworldly characters beamed from the night stars, skin streaked and voices like stardust. The sound experience is its own spatial environment, immersing visitors in an arresting score written character-by-character for a 20-person choir, with each shape emitting its own personal timbre. The generative soundscape synced with light, creates a mesmeric adventure that is esthetically dynamic both day and night. Visitors are beckoned inside the formation to bathe in volumetric sound and rhythmic light pulsations that change upon passer-by's interaction with the individual sound and lights emitted from the choir. The resulting music is minimal and reflective, enabling visitors to conjure their own interpretation of from where the Orchestra has materialized. As with all ENESS work, there are intriguing details to discover such as friendly LED eyes that blink and follow visitors from creature to creature. The diverse patterns on the characters, though primarily black, white, and pink during the day, come to life at night as a veritable aurora borealis of neon blues, greens, oranges, and fuchsia.

ENESS
Airship Orchestra
Balloon Museum
Pop Air
Madrid, 2023

Airship Orchestra 2020

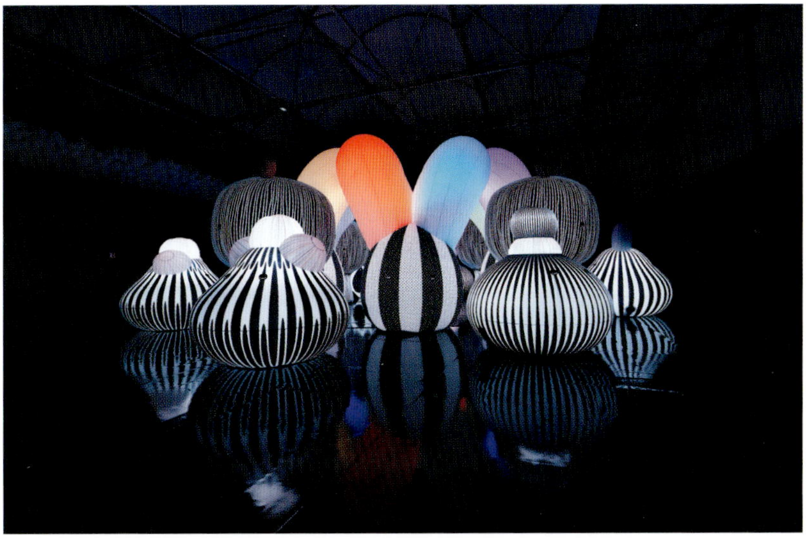

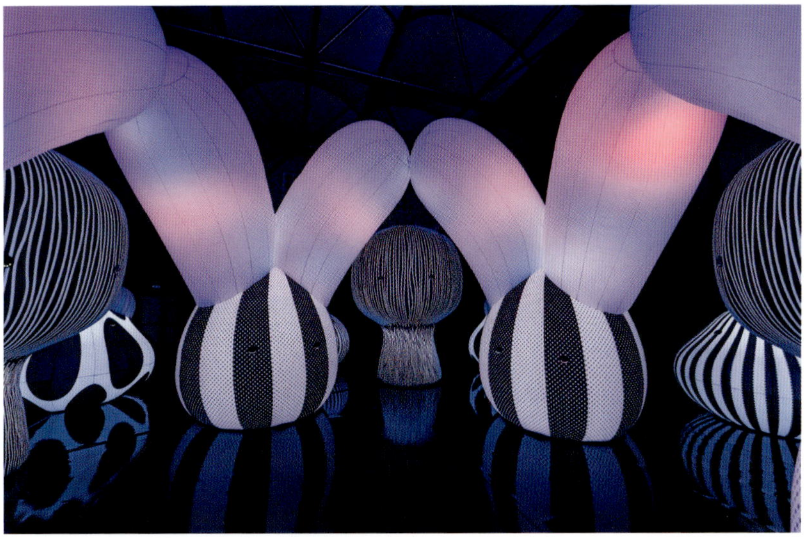

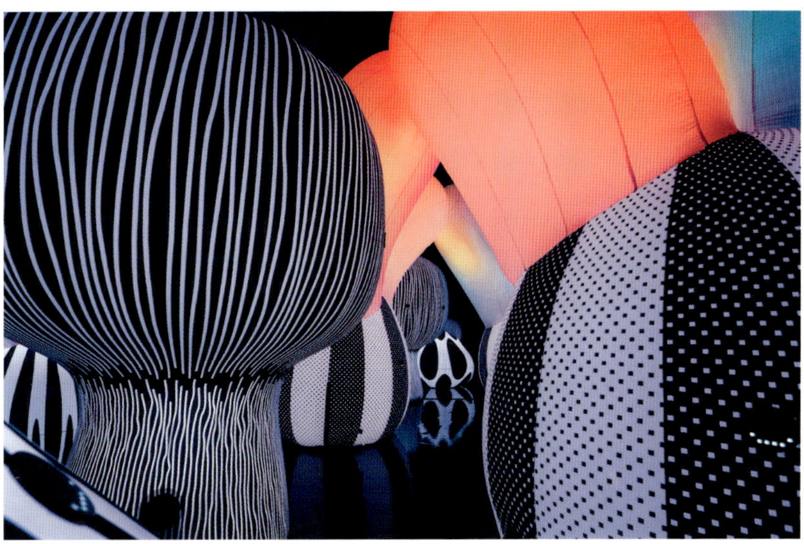

ENESS

Spiritus Sonata

Always committed to creating interactive artworks that engage the senses and strengthen ties with their public, ENESS created an original work entitled *Spiritus Sonata* for the *Let's Fly* exhibition. "Spiritus" can be translated as "breath" or "vital breath," and "Sonata" as "musical composition". This new inflatable and luminous creation invites the visitor to feel uplifted and connected. Evoking the magical, cottony ambience of early childhood discoveries, *Spiritus Sonata* envelops us, provoking surprise and tenderness. With its recognizable *kawaii* or "cute" esthetic, these veritable wind instruments use air to inflate the structures, enabling sounds to be created from the nasal extensions of each character. The layers of sound overlap, surrounding visitors in a celestial, vibratory continuum.

ENESS
Spiritus Sonata
Balloon Museum
Let's Fly
New York, 2023

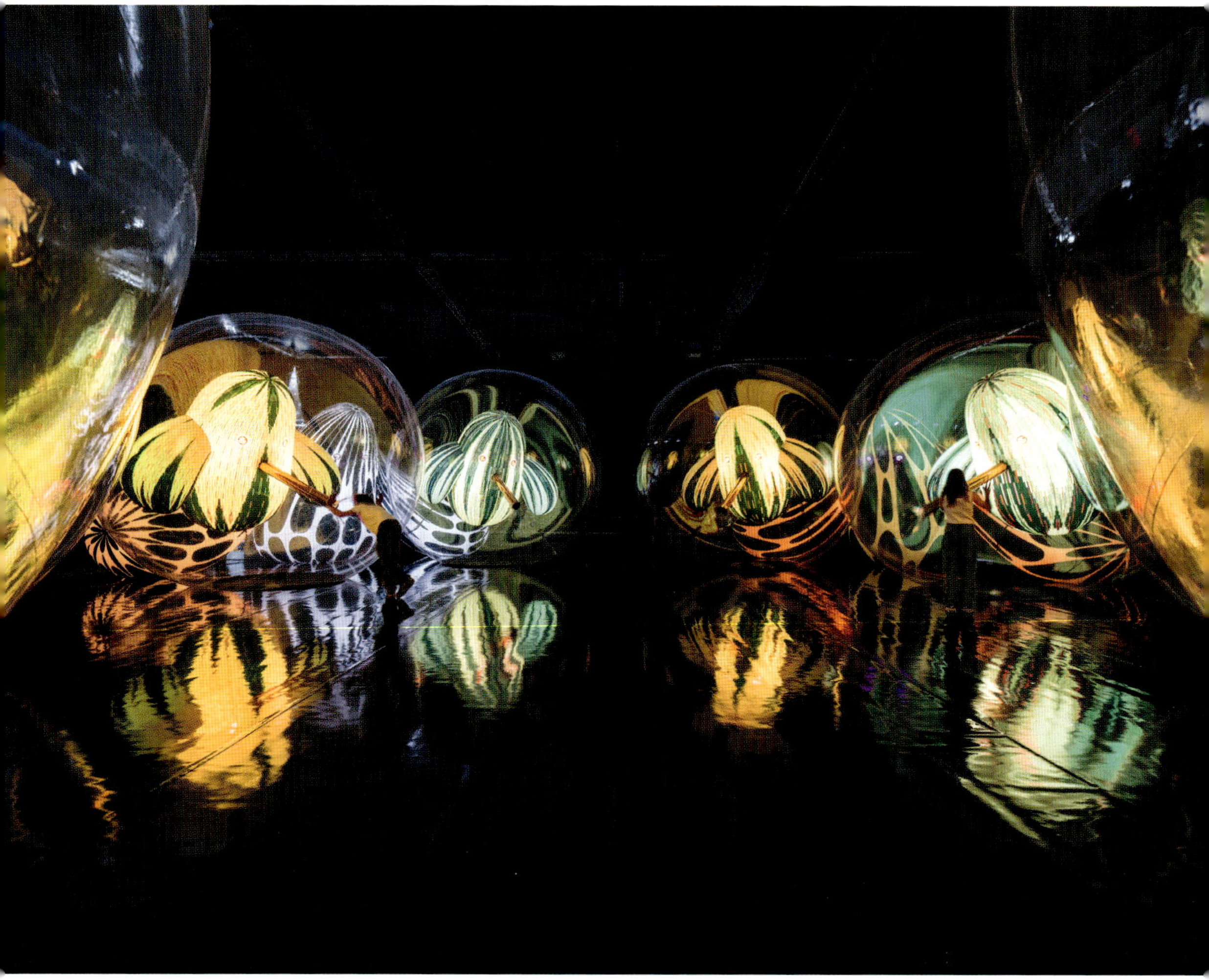

Spiritus Sonata 2023

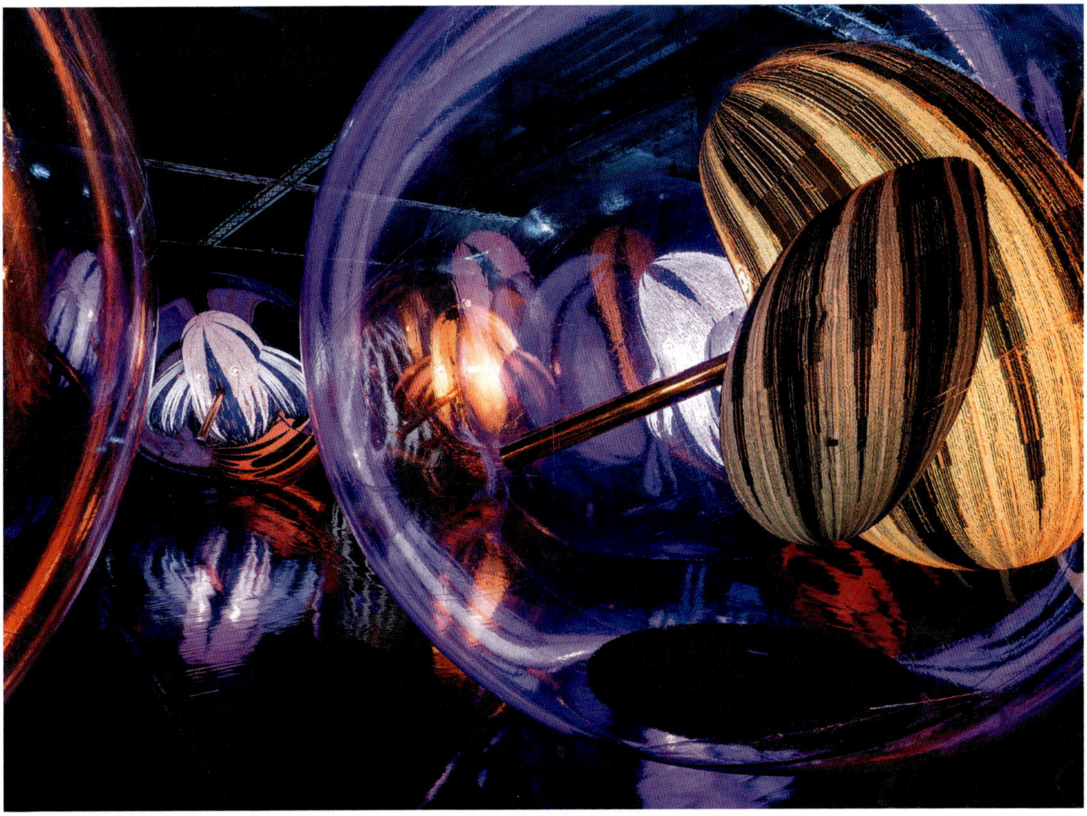

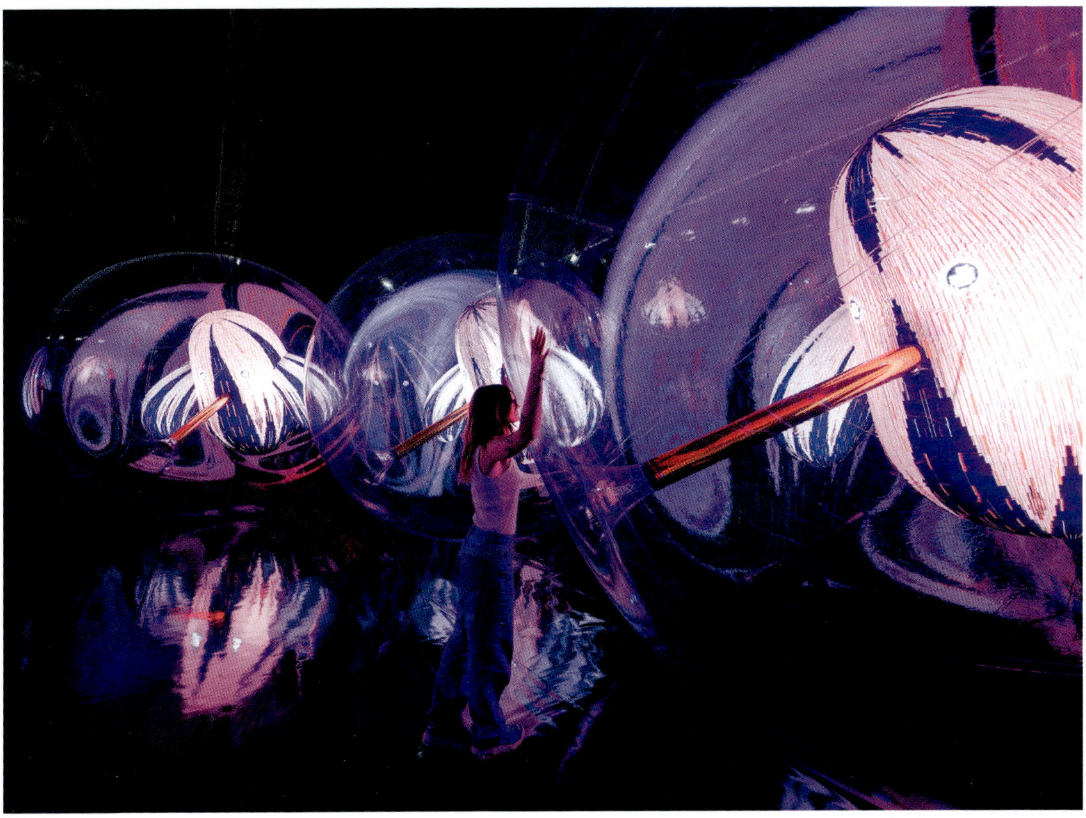

CAMILLA FALSINI

Camilla Falsini was born, lives, and works in Rome where she divides her work between illustrations and murals. She juxtaposes, composes, and decomposes simple shapes using them as modules, changing the meaning of an image in the same way that the letters of the alphabet can compose millions of words when juxtaposed differently. The artist is fascinated by themes such as language, writing, and the evolution of species. In 2020 she won, together with the WeAreJungle agency, the "Piazze Aperte" competition as part of the Redesign for the regeneration through urban planning intervention in Milan. She has published three illustrated books: *100 CHEVALIERS*, *ZOOM: The biggest circle ever*, and *5 WILD SHAPES* and her illustrations made the Official selection at the Bologna Children's Book Fair in 2017. She took part in group exhibitions organized at the Milan Triennale, the MACRO Museum in Rome, the MADRE Museum in Naples, among others, as well as in multiple solo shows in Ravenna, Florence, and Bologna, Italy.
Camilla Falsini started working as an illustrator collaborating with Italian and foreign publishing houses, agencies, newspapers and magazines, such as *Vanity Fair* and *The Washington Post,* the major Italian newspapers, and music and film festivals. She has created installations, large paintings and wall paintings for Samsung, Zalando, Napapijri, ILIAD, Lavazza and many others. Her murals can be found in Rome, Milan, Turin, Palermo, Naples, Padua, Brescia, Monza, Ravenna, Bologna, and in small towns of Tuscany, Emilia Romagna, Molise, Marche, Basilicata, Veneto, Lombardy, and Sardinia.

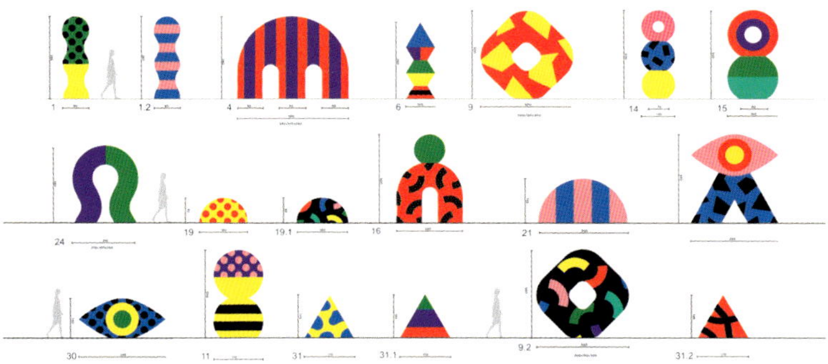

Renders of the sculptures for *D.R.E.A.M.S. Dove Raggiungere E Ammirare Mondi Straordinari* Balloon Museum *Let's Fly* New York, 2023

Opposite
Camilla Falsini *D.R.E.A.M.S. Dove Raggiungere E Ammirare Mondi Straordinari* Balloon Museum *Let's Fly* New York, 2023

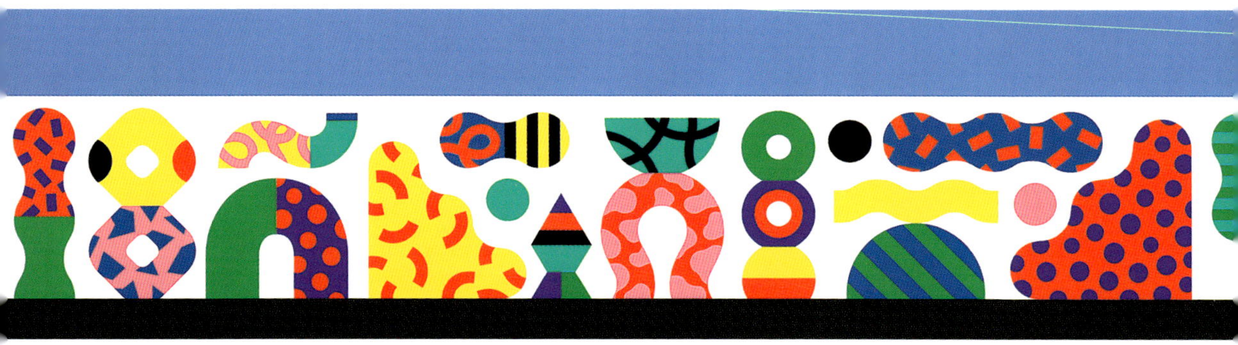

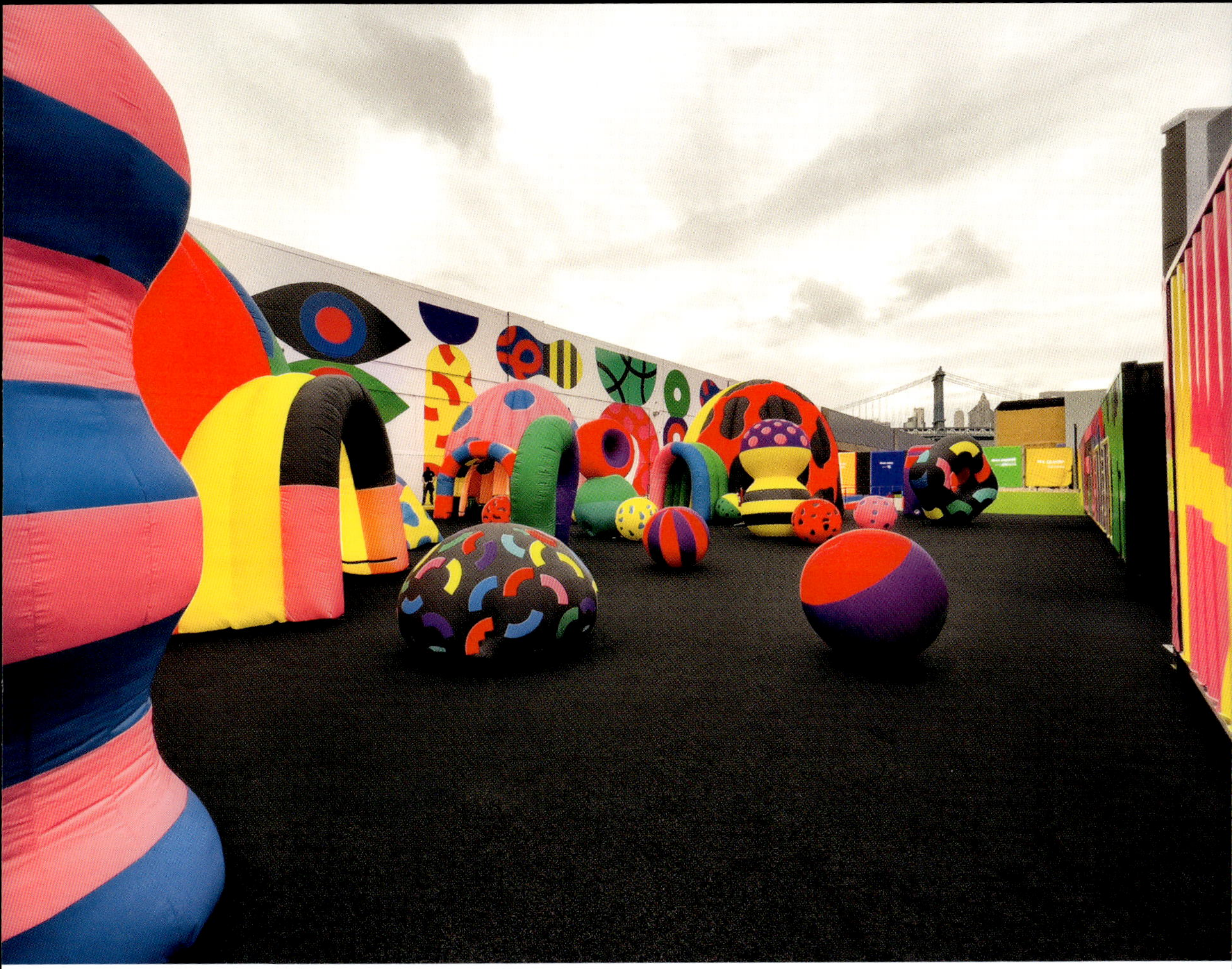

D.R.E.A.M.S.
Dove Raggiungere E Ammirare Mondi Straordinari

For the Balloon Museum *Let's Fly* exhibition, Camilla Falsini has worked on the adjacent walls and three-dimensional structures. We are surrounded by gigantic printed graphic compositions made of a multitude of colorful shapes, symbols, and igloos accessible to the public, outlining a dreamlike city in which we wander among mysterious figures: are these plant forms in an imaginary village or strange inhabitants of a surreal world? The effect is like being inside a utopian space where the public can play and interact with the artworks. Moving from 2D to 3D, Camilla Falsini takes us into a playful world where vivid colors and Pop motifs coexist. With her attraction to asymmetrical shapes and primary colors, Camilla Falsini's artistic practice is inspired by the Memphis group, a design and architecture movement created in Italy in the 1980s whose ambition was to end ambient "good taste." The Memphis style countered in favor of colorful interiors, where chic materials were combined with kitsch.

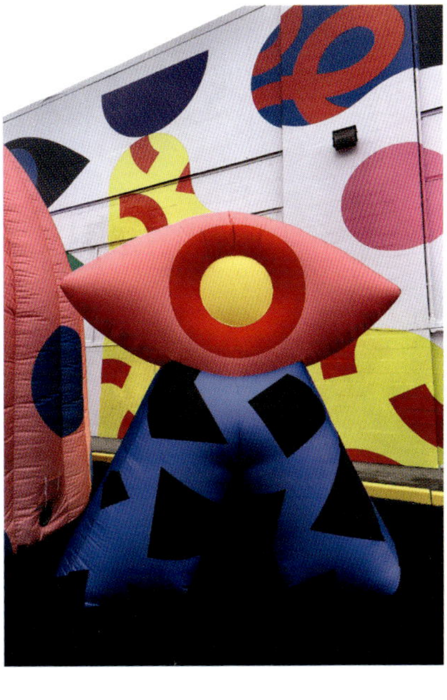

FILTHY LUKER

Formed in 1994 by artists Filthy Luker and Pedro Estrellas, Designs in Air is a pioneering inflatable design company from the UK renowned for their artistic flair and innovative installation concepts. Their work has featured at hundreds of major events and exhibitions worldwide as well as publicity stunts and art endeavors. Designs in Air is supported by specialist technicians and logistics team who have helped propel the artists onto the international arena. The team's originality and fantastical style have undeniably influenced the inflatable medium as well as carving out a unique niche in the international Street Art movement with their pop-up and often site specific sculptures. Whether they are 12m-long tentacles bursting from the windows of a sky scraper, traffic-stopping banana skins, or giant eyeballs staring out from otherwise overlooked city-center trees, Designs in Air's urban interventions never fail to delight.

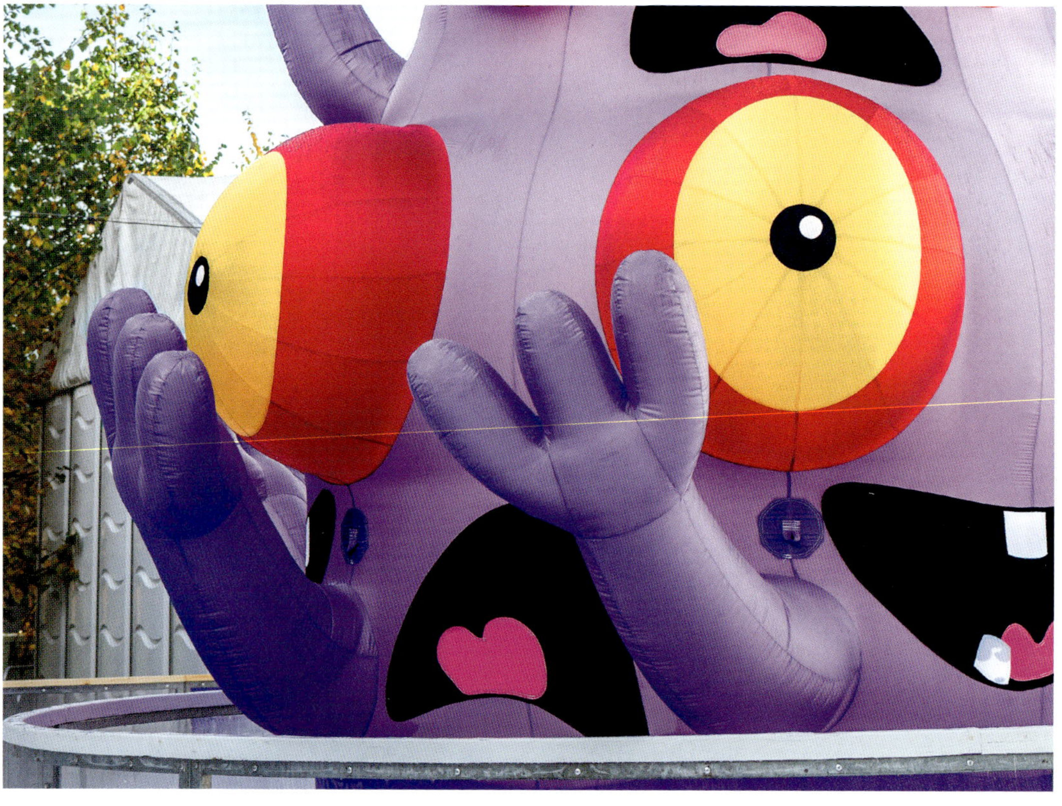

Eye Scream 2022

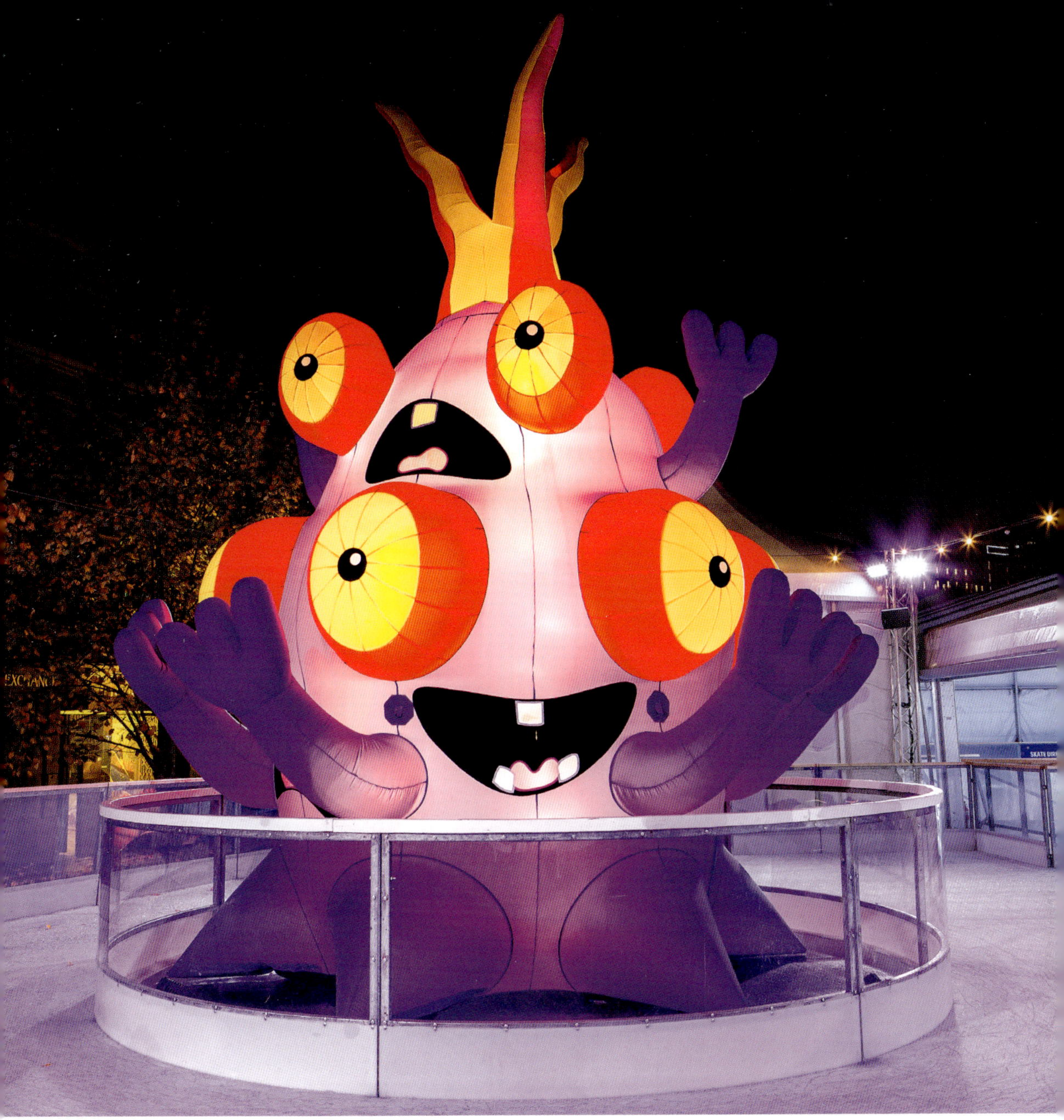

Designs in Air
(Filthy Luker
and Pedro Estrellas)
Eye Scream
Balloon Museum
Let's Fly
New York, 2023

Eye Scream

The main motive of Filthy Luker is to make the world a more soft and surreal place, as a kind of vendetta against the hard, concrete world we live in. The artist creates site-specific work and aims to transform everyday cityscapes into strange new ones in the hope of lifting people's eyes from their phones and raising a chuckle, or at least an eyebrow. In recent years, Filthy Luker has created pop-art monsters to sit on top of big buildings, breaking the skyline and pulling faces at the world below—it might not be high art, but it is high UP art! Each of the monsters has its own funny character and expression. For Balloon Museum, the artwork is titled *Eye Scream* and seems to be hysterically laughing and crying simultaneously, much like anyone in their right mind should be.

FILTHY LUKER

The Goofs
The Goofs are part of an entourage of inflatable monsters that are taking over the world, but how they got here and what their motives are is unknown. These peculiar gentle giants are often found in public places, silently observing our ways. Some suggests that they are talking to us via telepathy and are trying to make friends, some that they feed on our emotions—especially surprise and happiness, some say that they are conspiring to cause mischief...

Maybe one day someone will be able to let us know what they are thinking?
The Goofs made contact with the Balloon Museum audience as an ensemble for the first time in 2023, when all four of them arrived at the exhibition at Casa de Campo in Madrid, Spain.
The four inflatable creatures, one green, one blue, one red, and one yellow, with their colorfully protruding appendages look curiously down upon the visitors as they approach the entrance.

Filthy Luker
The Goofs
Balloon Museum
Pop Air
Rome, 2021
Madrid, 2023

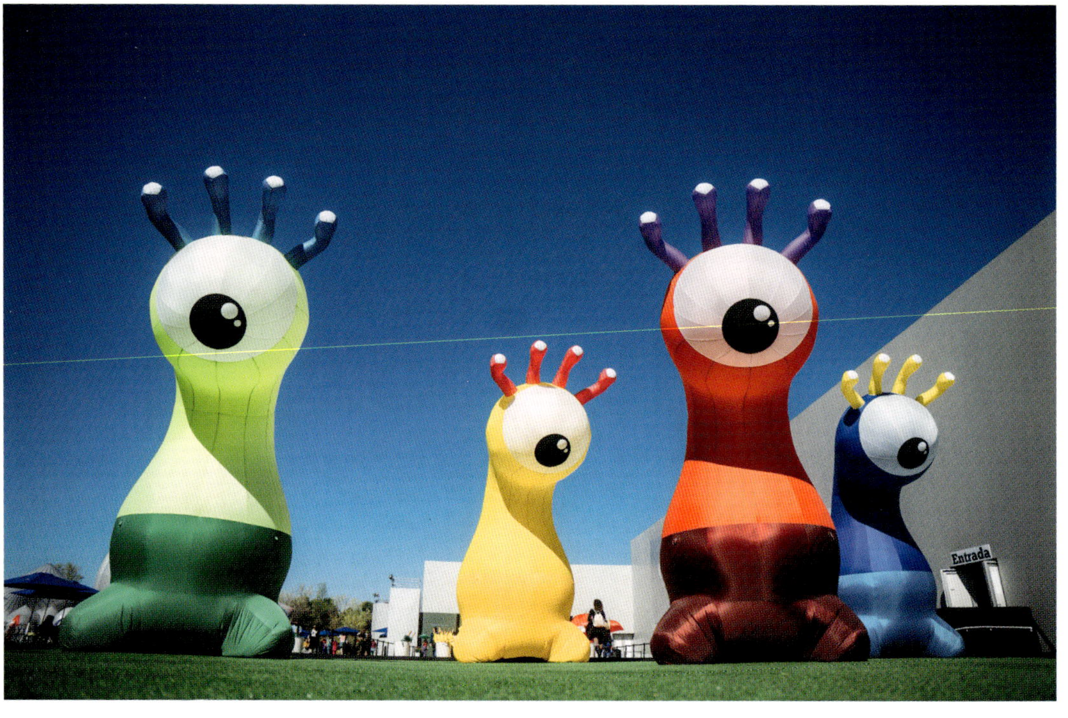

The Goofs 2021

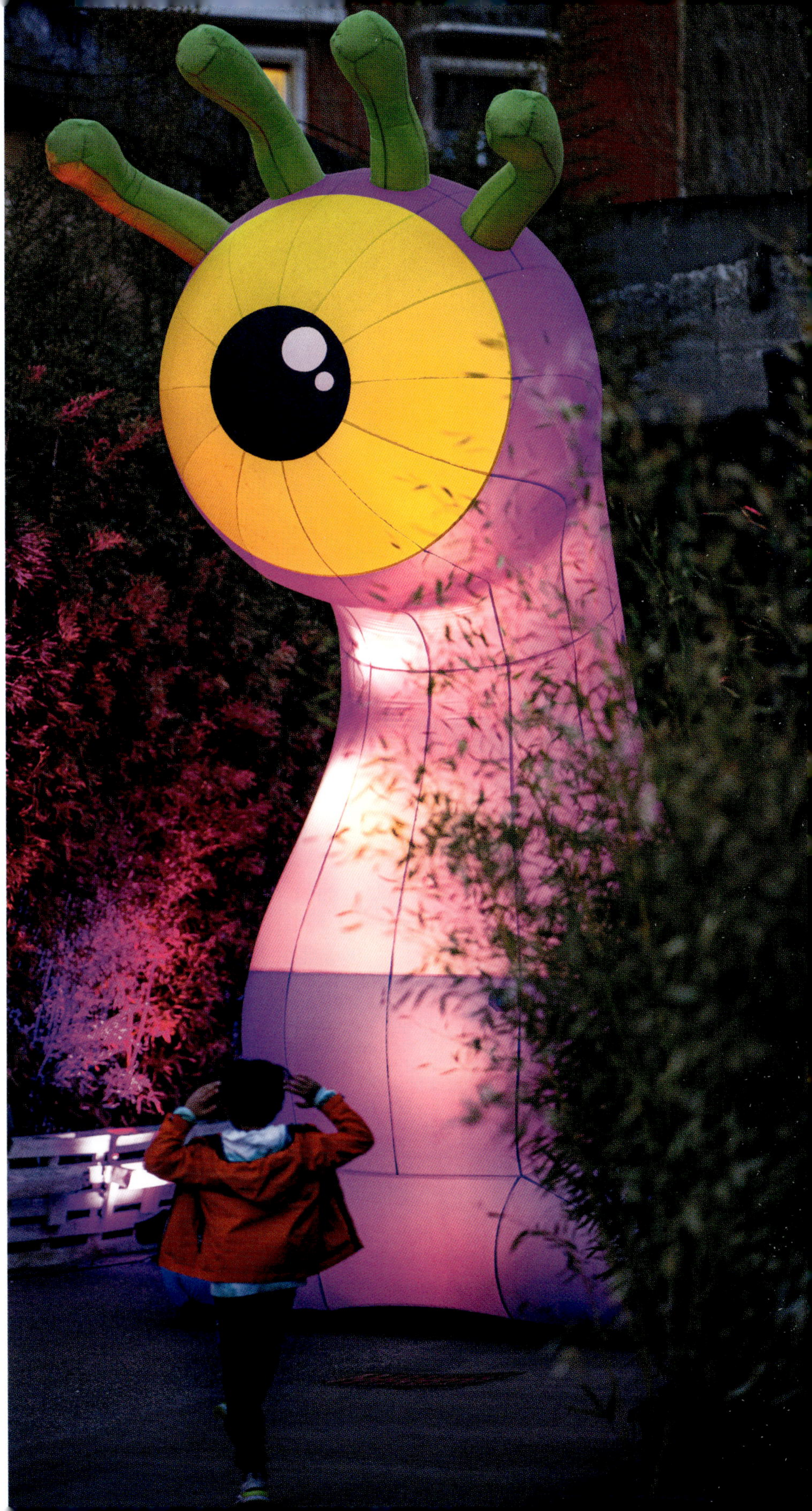

FILTHY LUKER AND PEDRO ESTRELLAS

Octopus Attacks!

Filthy Luker and Pedro Estrellas' world famous giant tentacles are attacking the Balloon Museum! The irrepressible Kraken has taken over the Pullman Yard (location of the exhibition *Let's Fly* in Atlanta) and is breaking through the brickwork, "waving its arms in the air like it just doesn't care!"[1]
This ground-breaking design is one of the most recognizable inflatable artworks on the planet. Bursting onto the international Street Art scene in 2004, the Kraken and its many colored offspring have disrupted the art world and city skylines around the globe ever since. The 40ft-long tentacles, eerily buoyant, become wildly animated in the wind. But fear not—for this often misunderstood creature really just wants to give you a massive hug!

[1] Lyrics from the song *The Roof Is on Fire* by Rock Master Scott & the Dynamic Three, 1984

Below
Designs in Air
(Filthy Luker
and Pedro Estrellas)
Octopus Attacks!
Le Grand Theatre
Angers, 2017

Opposite and overleaf
Designs in Air
(Filthy Luker
and Pedro Estrellas)
Octopus Attacks!
Balloon Museum
Let's Fly
Atlanta, 2024

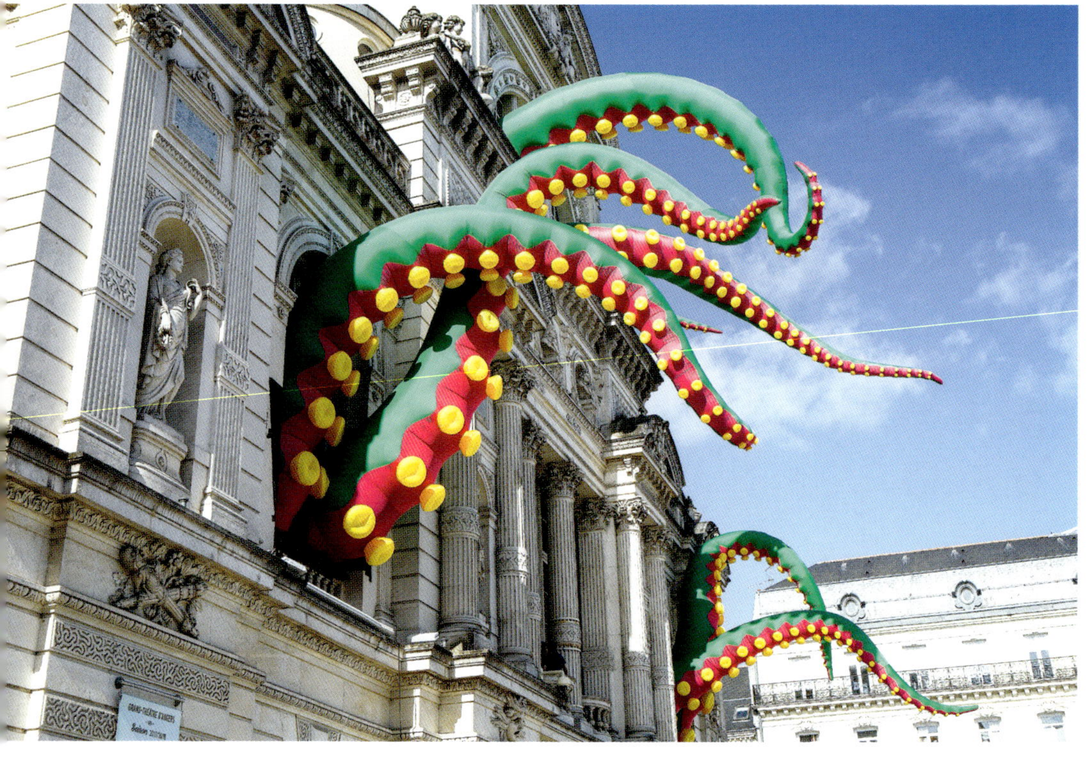

Octopus Attacks! 2004

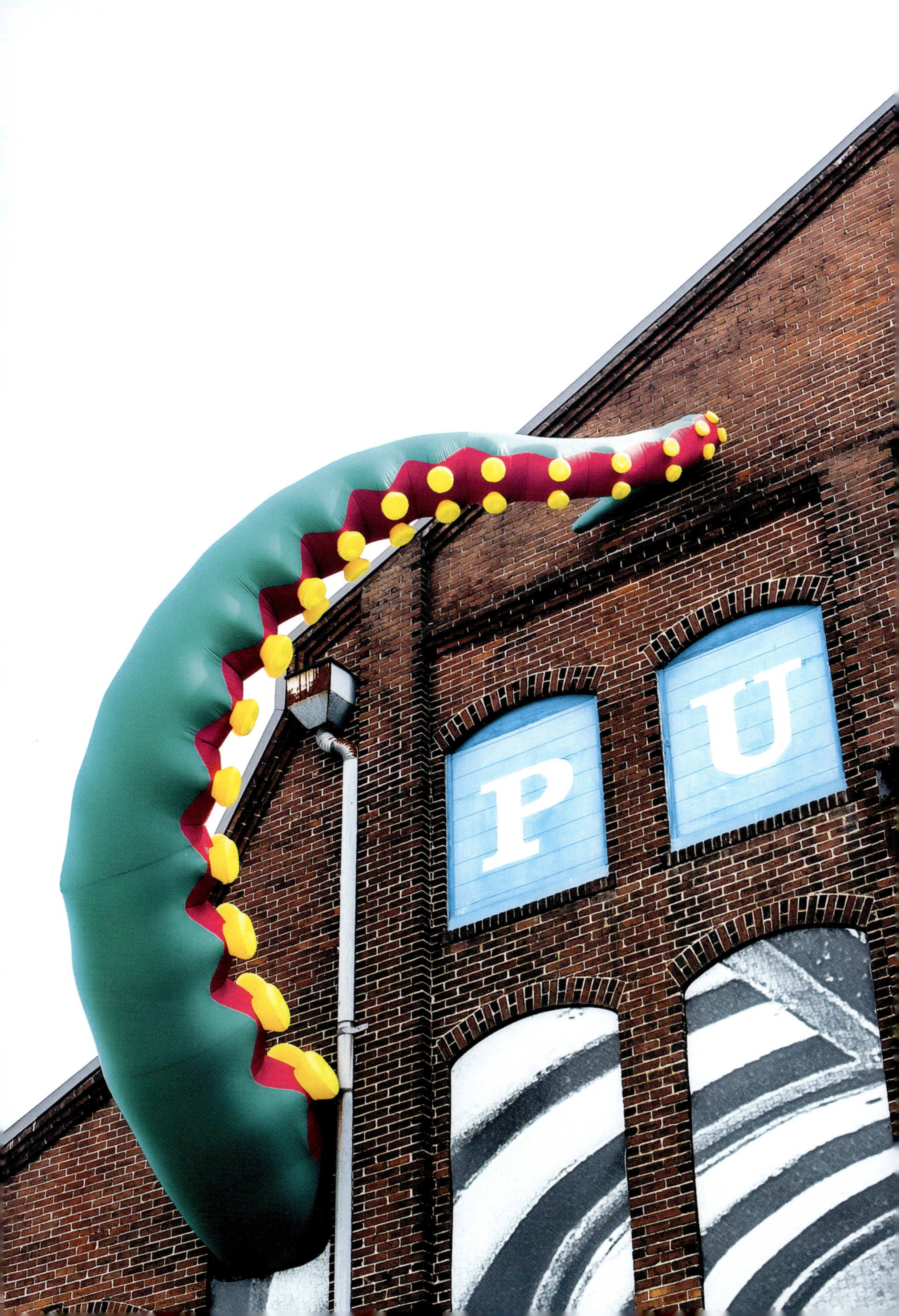
P
U

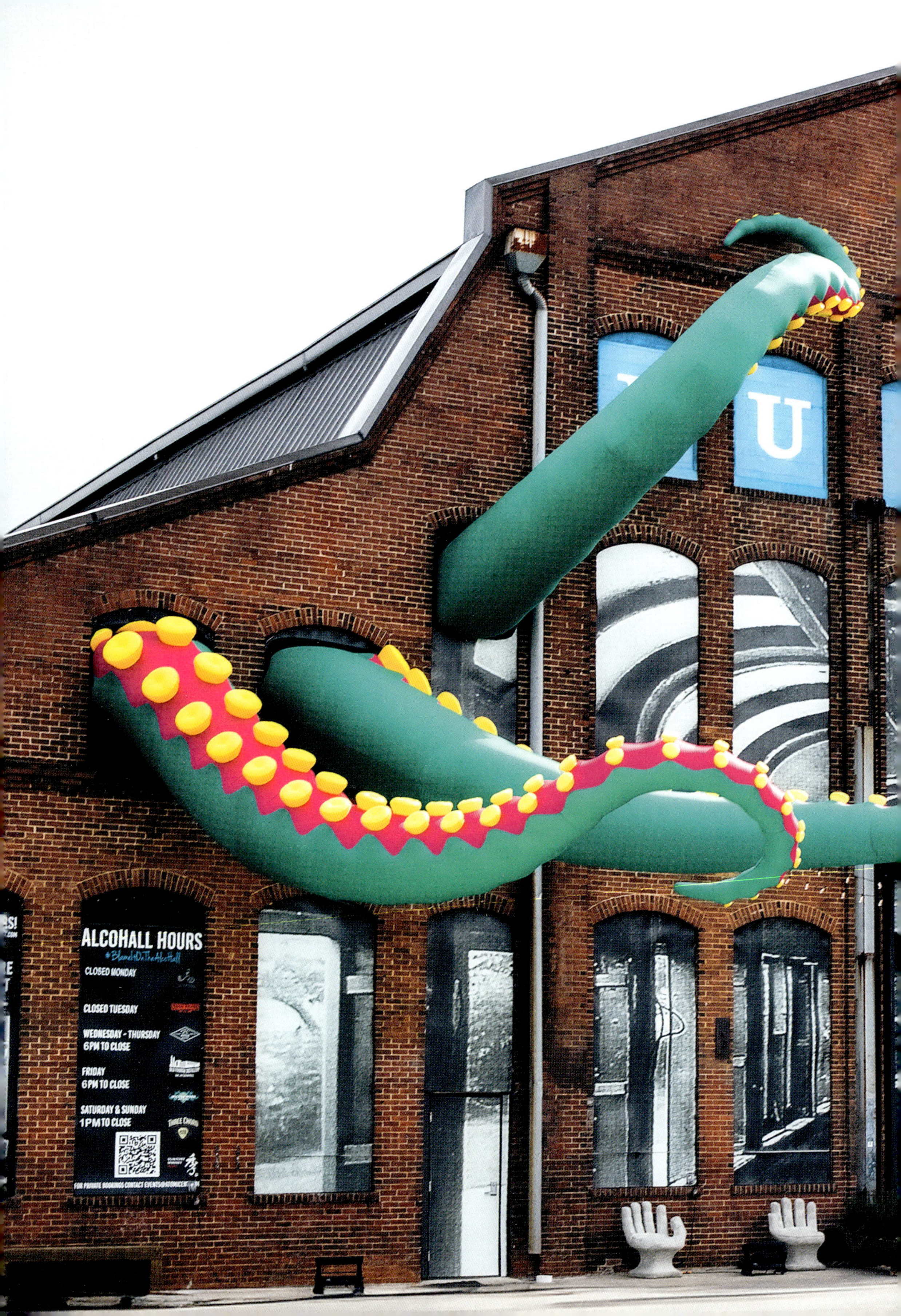
ALCOHALL HOURS
CLOSED MONDAY
CLOSED TUESDAY
WEDNESDAY - THURSDAY
6PM TO CLOSE
FRIDAY
6PM TO CLOSE
SATURDAY & SUNDAY
1PM TO CLOSE

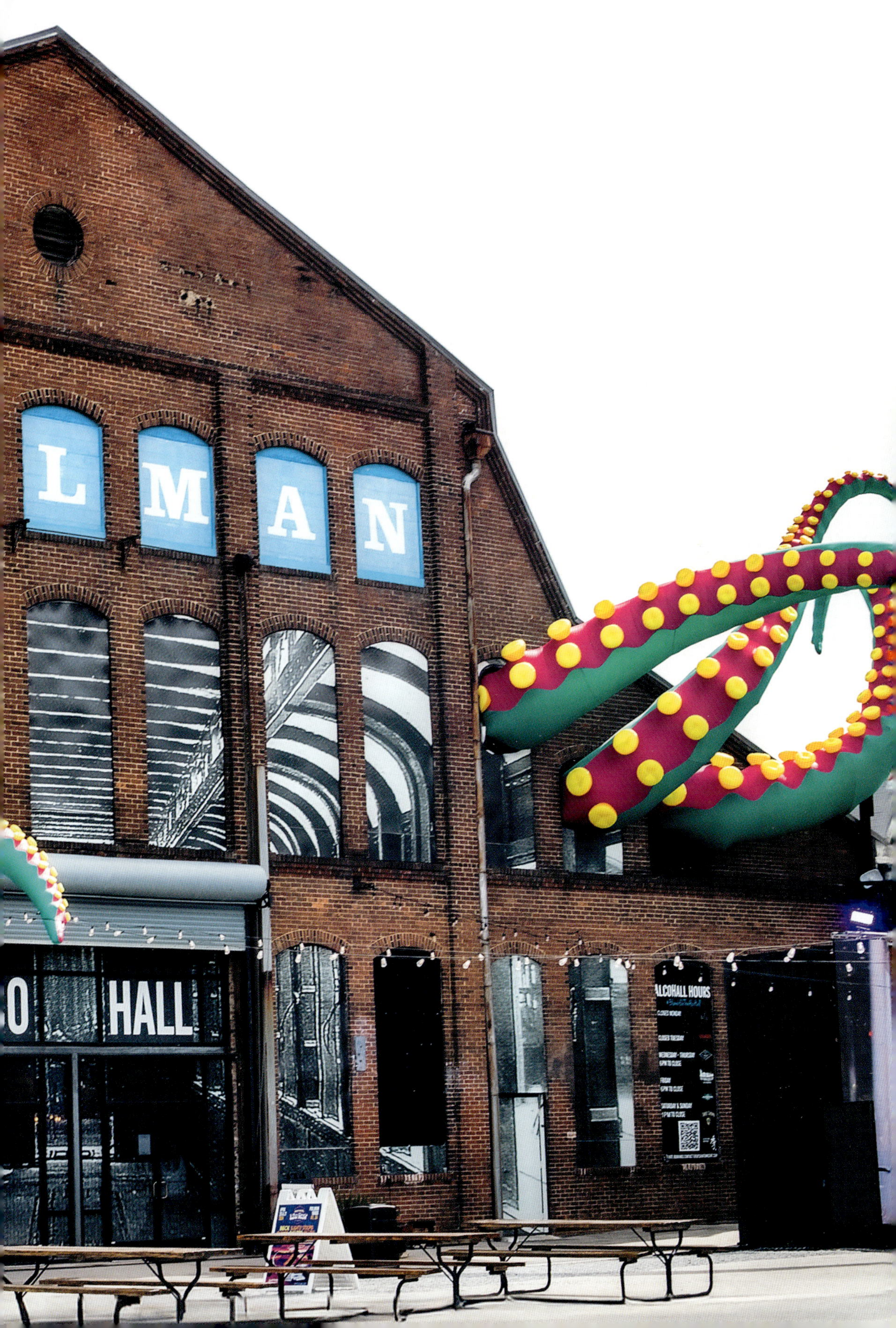
LMAN
HALL
ALCOHALL HOURS

SASHA FROLOVA

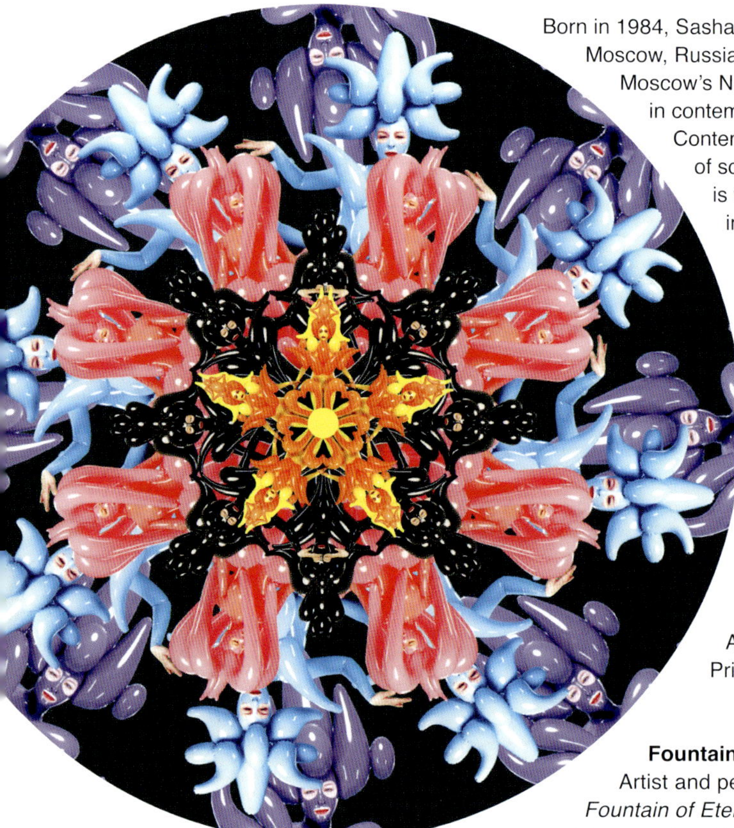

Born in 1984, Sasha Frolova currently lives and works in Moscow, Russia. A graduate in graphic design from Moscow's National Design Institute, she specialized in contemporary art at Moscow's Institute of Contemporary Art. She is active in the fields of sculpture and performance art and she is widely known for her extravagant, inflatable sculpture creations and elaborate costumes made out of latex. Sasha Frolova defines herself as a visionary artist. In her work she tries to foresee the future by creating its innovative esthetics today. Frolova has showcased her projects on the international stage, presenting at prestigious venues such as the 291 Gallery, Whitechapel Gallery, and Riflemaker Gallery in London, United Kingdom. Notably, Frolova was a finalist in the "Young Artist" category of the Kandinsky Prize 2009 and the ARTE LAGUNA PRIZE 12.13 at Arsenale, Venice and secured the Special Prize in the category "Personal Exhibition".

Fountain of Eternity & Kaleidoscope

Artist and performer Sasha Frolova presents *Fountain of Eternity*, an inflatable transparent and silver sculpture, and a video work entitled *Kaleidoscope*. In this video, projected onto a ceiling-mounted circular screen, the artist appears dressed in colorful, inflatable latex costumes. We see smooth, plastic silhouettes with the allure of burlesque, dancing rhythmically to the sound of soothing music. The artist creates a kaleidoscopic, hypnotizing self-portrait with a taste for pop and baroque esthetics. Adorned with a silver coating, *Fountain of Eternity* is a veritable alchemical symbol that resonates with our subconscious, inspiring dreams and fantasies. Sculpture on a human scale, the pistil-like fountain confirms the essence of a drink sipped in the form of a sweet, bewitching nectar.

Sasha Frolova
Fountain of Eternity
& Kaleidoscope
Balloon Museum
Let's Fly
New York, 2023

Fountain of Eternity & Kaleidoscope 2022

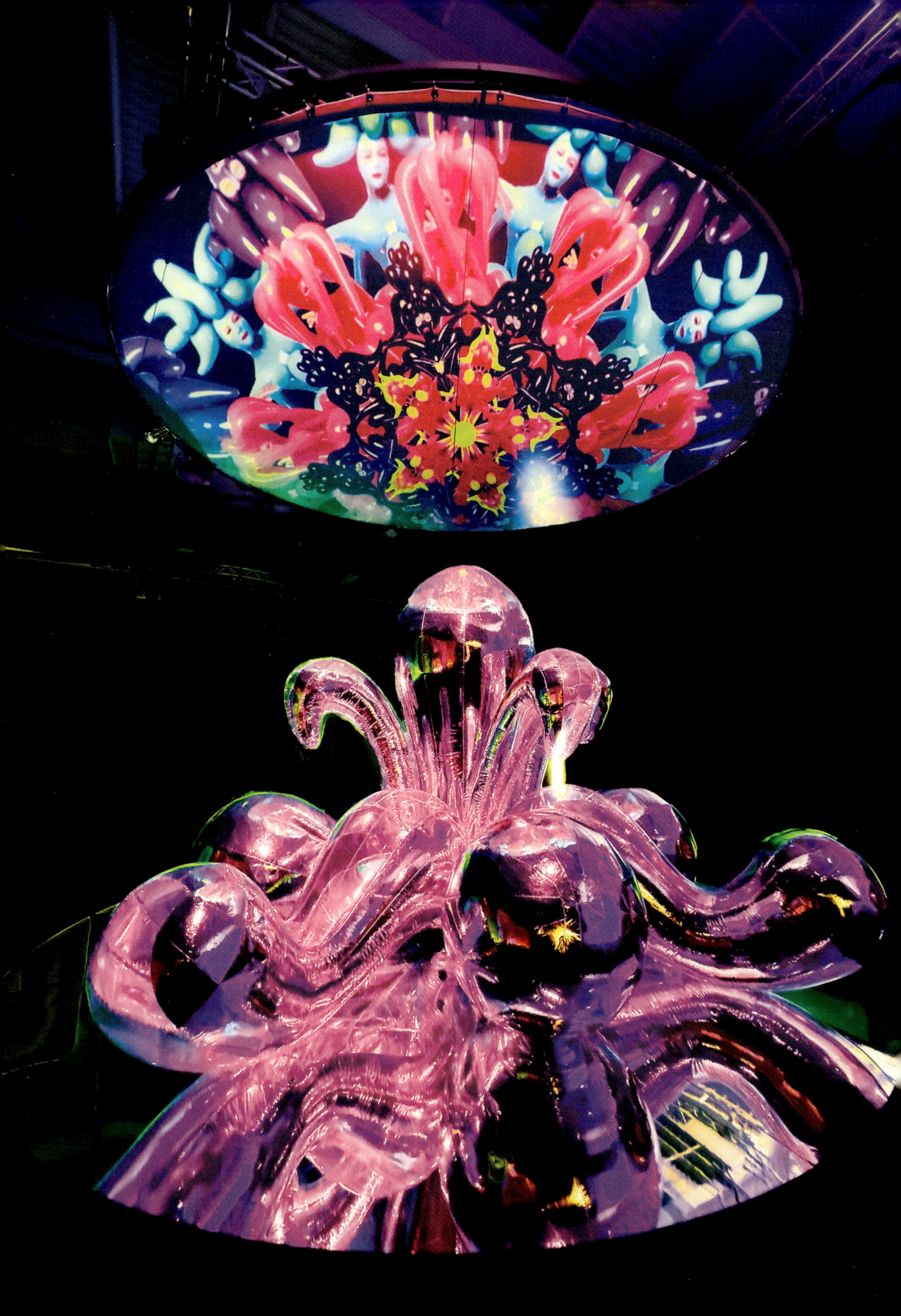

LINDSAY GLATZ AND CURIOUS FORM

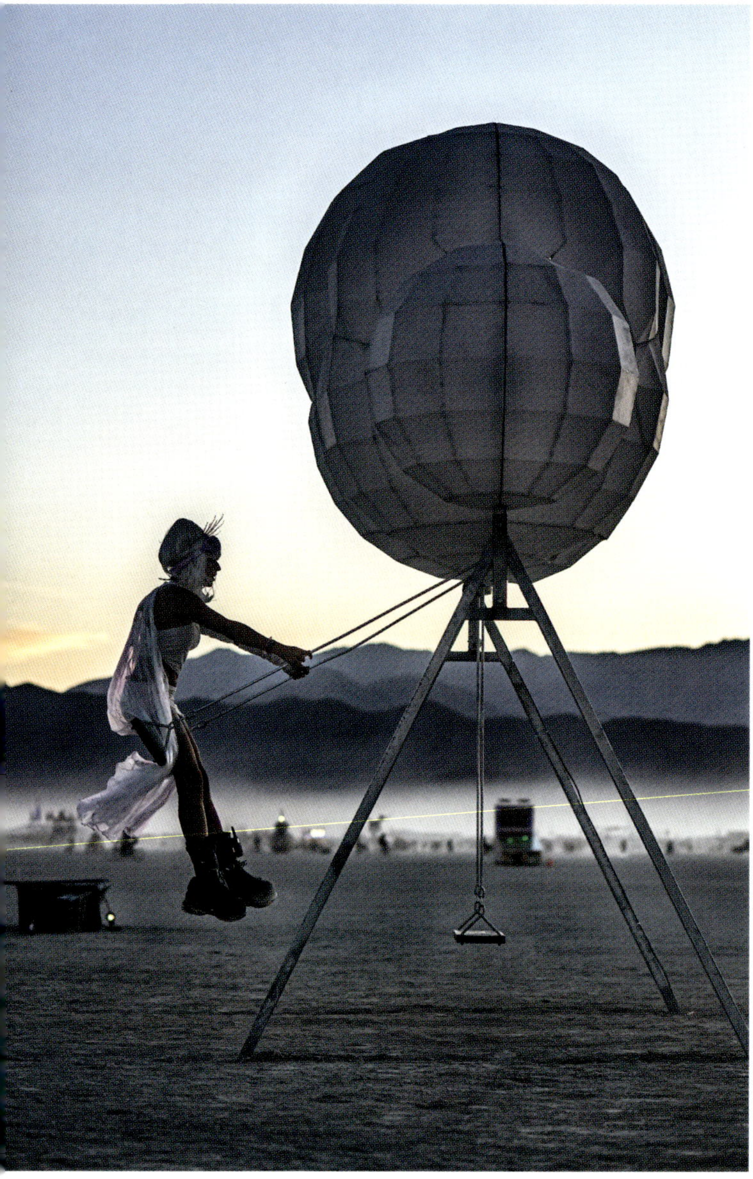

Lindsay Glatz is a visual storyteller with a mission to infuse the world with wonder. Glatz began her career abroad in the tech industry, sparking her interest in working at the intersection of technology, art, and tourism. In both her artistic and curatorial practices, she seeks to add vibrancy to public space as a means of inserting magic into everyday life and captivating the civic imagination. Glatz often encapsulates elements of childhood and nostalgia within her work as a basis for exploring human connection.

William Nemitoff is the founder of Curious Form, a creative fabrication studio, where he leverages his knowledge of diverse materials and building methods to craft innovative concepts, custom furniture, collaborative art, and impactful public installations. 3D modeling and cutting-edge machinery enable Nemitoff to create precise organic shapes with bold clean lines. Always curious, Nemitoff seeks inspiration from his interests in science, technology, and the natural world.

Lindsay Glatz
and Curious Form
Cloud Swing
Burning Man
Black Rock City, 2019

Cloud Swing 2019

Cloud Swing

This playful and interactive experience is intended to invoke a sense of wonder, nostalgia, and delight for participants. The artist uses a ubiquitous symbol of youth and childhood, swings suspended from glowing clouds, which create color and light as people engage with the artwork. Dormant, a soft light from the hovering cloud glows on the empty seat, waiting and inviting the audience passing by to push off into the rhythmic weightlessness. Once someone begins to swing, the transformation begins, and the white glow is replaced by vibrant color and lighting effects. Demonstrating that, despite the obstacles that hold you back, joy and delight will always find a path to propel you forward. *Cloud Swing* made its debut at Burning Man in 2019 to international acclaim, and made its way to the Balloon Museum *Pop Air* exhibition in 2022.

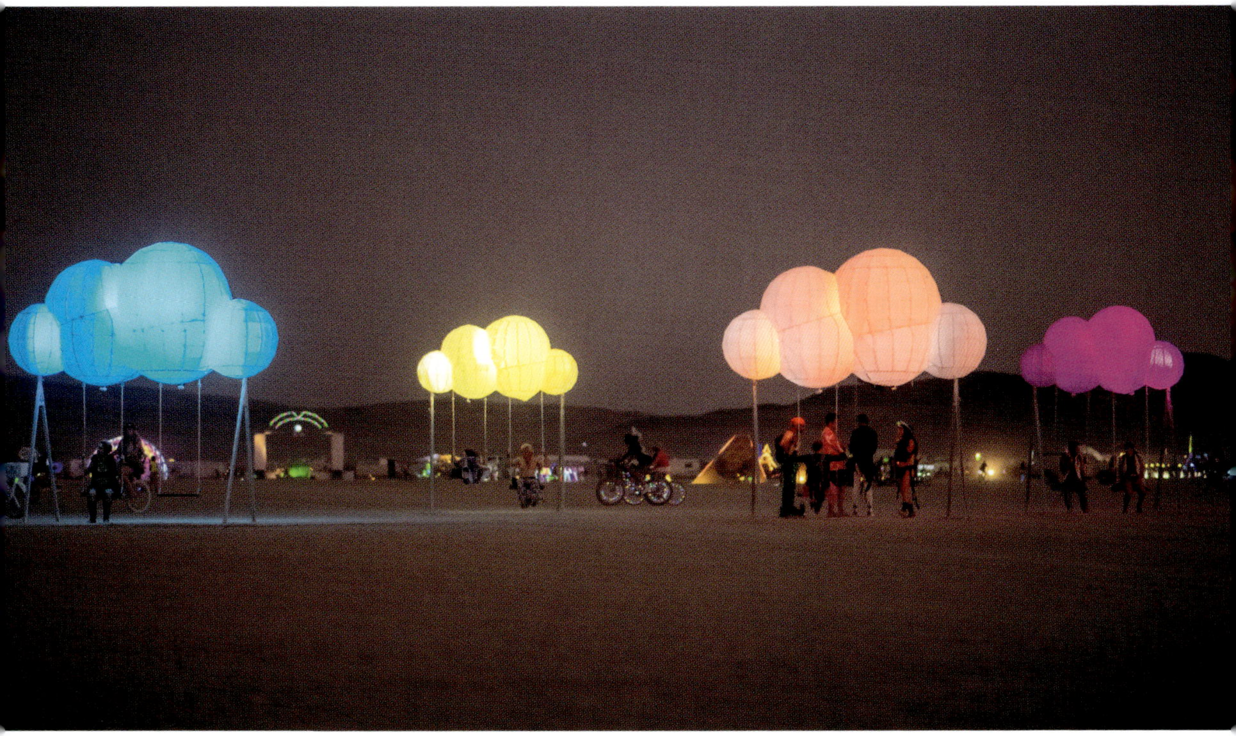

HYPERSTUDIO

At the border between reality and imagination there is a place where space and time become equal. The work by Hyperstudio is neither a beginning nor an end, just a narrative in which the distance between artwork and the viewer vanishes. Founded in 2020, Hyperstudio is a multidisciplinary collective of Italian artists and designers who conceive immersive installations in which art, artist, and visitor are placed in a universe where imagination is free. It is a dynamic meeting point for art, culture, and entertainment, creating amazing ecosystems and immersive experiences. Hyperstudio's installations allow the audience to be led and catapulted onto true sensory journeys unbounded by real time and space: effects of light and color, absence of perspective, and environments that are made to disorient. This is how, between the unfolding of imagination and a landscape that moves beyond the fourth wall, entering art becomes possible. The three installations—*Hypercosmo*, *Hyperstellar*, and *Hyperfeeling*—form the heart of the Balloon Museum, offering a complete immersion for visitors. Each installation aligns with the exhibition's theme, providing visitors with the central experience as they progress through the exhibition pathway.

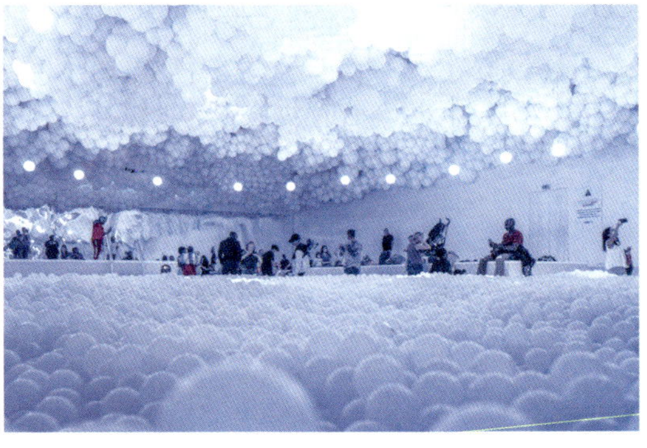

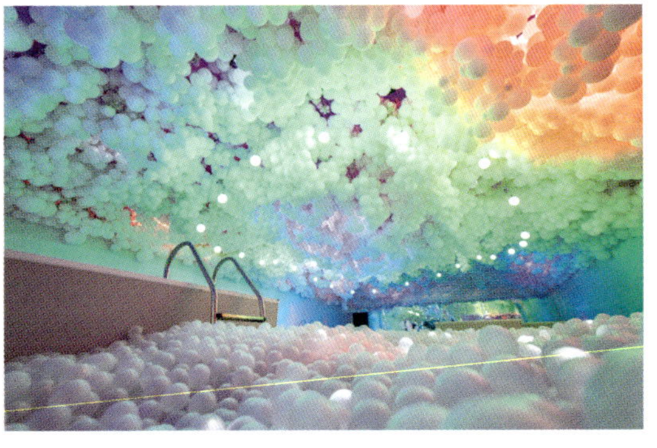

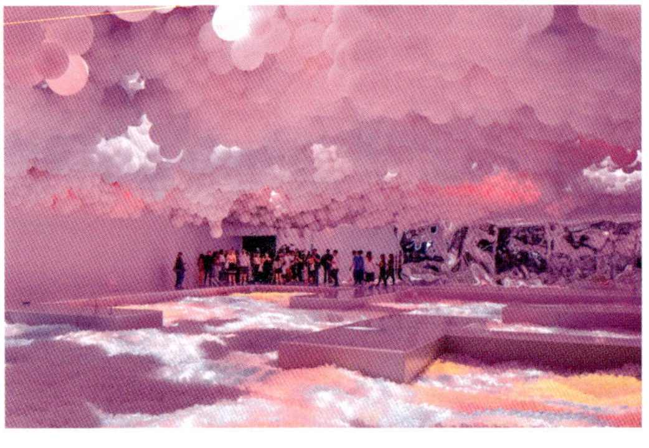

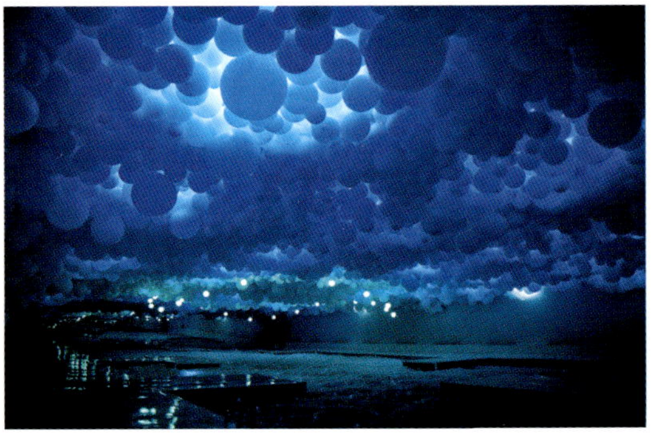

Hypercosmo 2021

Hypercosmo

Created in collaboration with Quiet Ensemble, *Hypercosmo* represents the essence of the entire *Pop Air* exhibition. The Hyperstudio collective takes us to a new macrocosm, a re-imagining of a natural environment in which the upper and lower parts are in direct communication and involve what is at the center: man. Projections, sounds, and movements of different elements accompany the experience: the sky, the sea, and the earth merge until they mingle for the spectacle of the cycle of life. The viewer is invited to immerse themselves, play, and be lulled by a candid environment, becoming an integral part of the work. An unexpected development draws the attention until it leads to a unique spectacle. A totalizing installation that offers a harmonious and imaginative view of the contradictory links between nature and new technologies. This installation is in collaboration with Quiet Ensemble.

Hyperstudio with
Quiet Ensemble
Hypercosmo
Balloon Museum
Pop Air
Rome, 2022
Paris, 2022
Milan, 2022
Madrid, 2023
Naples, 2023

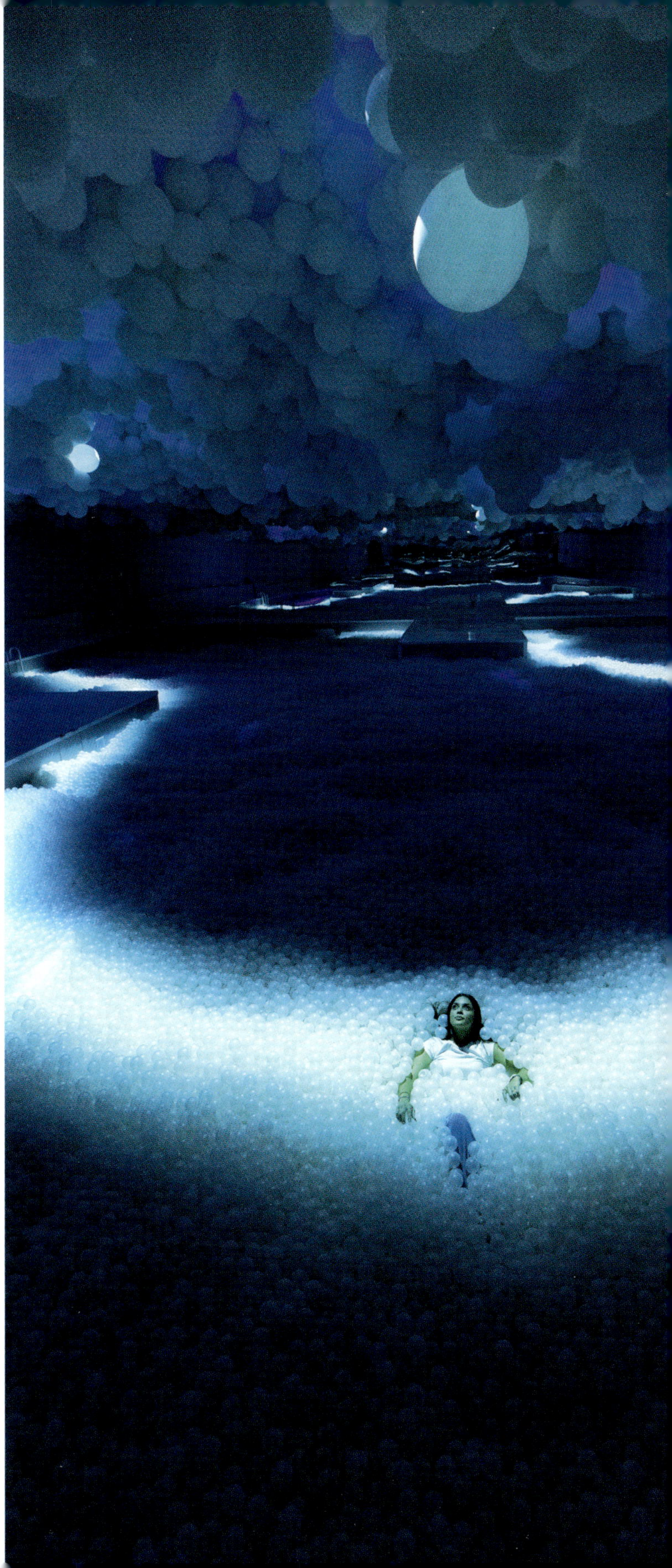

Hyperstellar

Hyperstellar is a sensory journey that challenges the perception of our place in the universe, leading the audience to experience the infinite size and complexity of the cosmos in the *Let's Fly* exhibition. The installation, in collaboration with Quiet Ensemble, is conceived as a total immersion in a mysterious universe, represented by a pool of black balls and a ceiling composed of a sky of balloons of the same color. This environment creates a perfect contrast for the cosmic wonders that will be revealed on the circular LED screen placed at 360 degrees, which dominates the room. Here, the magic begins to unfold. The hypnotic abstract shapes before our eyes, made by Roman Hill, are actually high-resolution shots of exploding water droplets and air bubbles. The inversion of perspective is astonishing: the grandeur of the cosmos is not only out there in space, but is also present near us all, inside a drop of water and within a bubble of air. The audience finds itself an integral part of a totalizing system, in which microscopic elements become carriers of magnified mysteries. Each element, rendered unrecognizable by its exaggerated size, emphasizes that the beauty of the universe is present even in the smallest and often overlooked details. The kinetic lights synchronize with the sounds that accompany the images, creating a synesthetic and immersive experience. The audience, enveloped in this multimedia and multisensory spectacle, finds itself catapulted onto a journey on which the dimensions of reality expand and contract in a hypnotic dance of light, sounds and forms. *Hyperstellar* invites viewers to reflect on their own place in the universe, suggesting that in order to perceive cosmic immensity, it is not necessary to travel through space, but only to look closely at our surroundings. In this collective experience, we are brought to the realization that, although microscopic, we are all part of a vast and extraordinary universe.

Bottom left
Riccardo Lionello, Creative Director of Balloon Museum and part of the Hyperstudio collective
Let's Fly
New York, 2023

Below and opposite top and bottom left
Hyperstudio,
Hyperstellar
Balloon Museum
Pop Air
New York, 2023

Opposite bottom right and overleaf
Hyperstudio
Hyperstellar
Palazzo Pitti
Florence, 2023

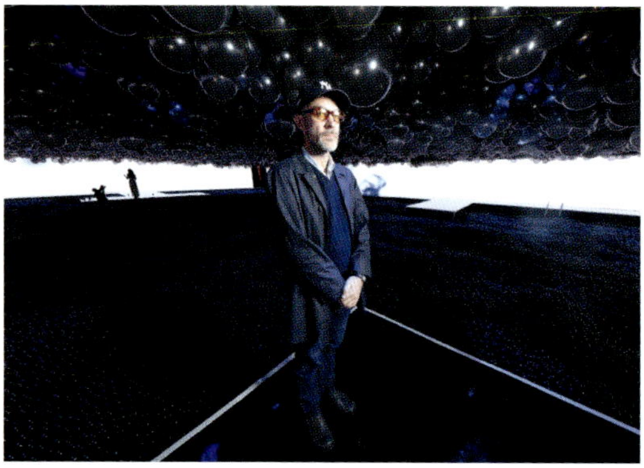

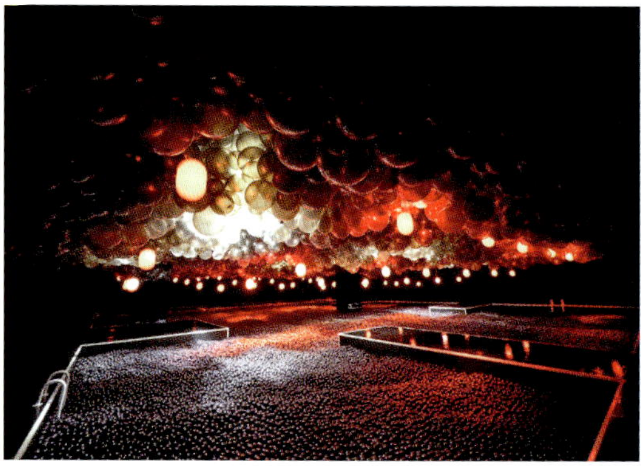

Hyperstellar 2023

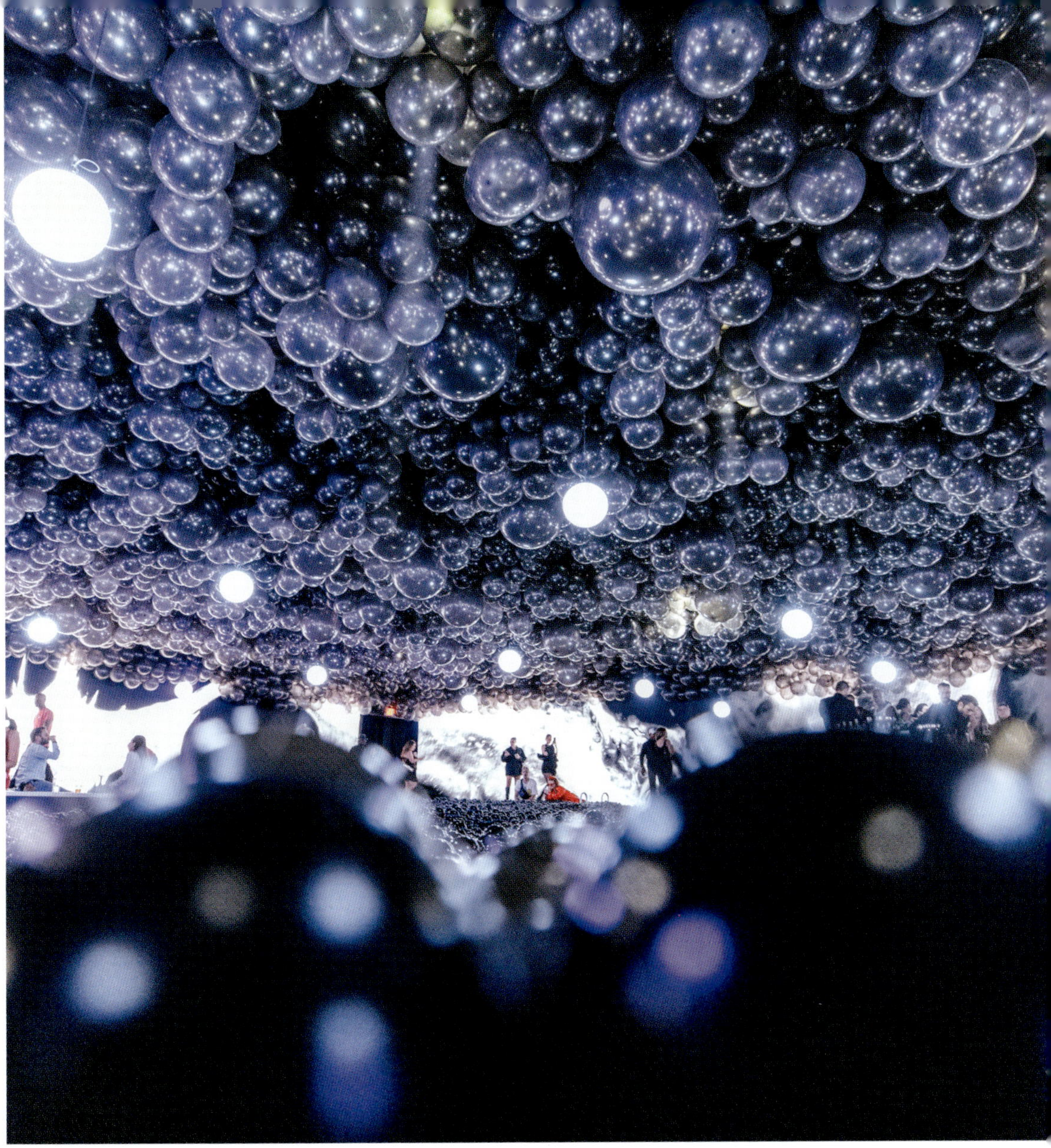

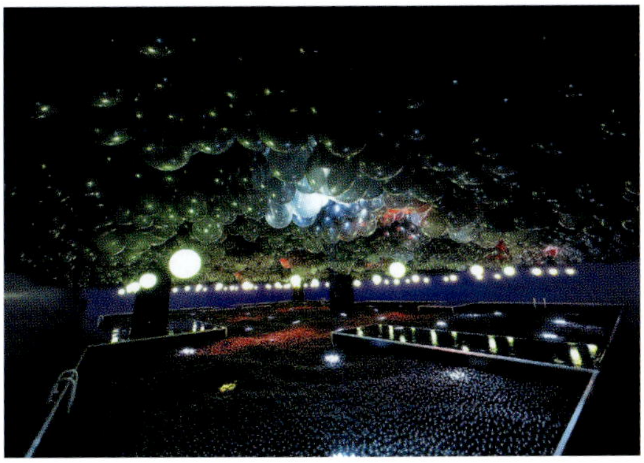

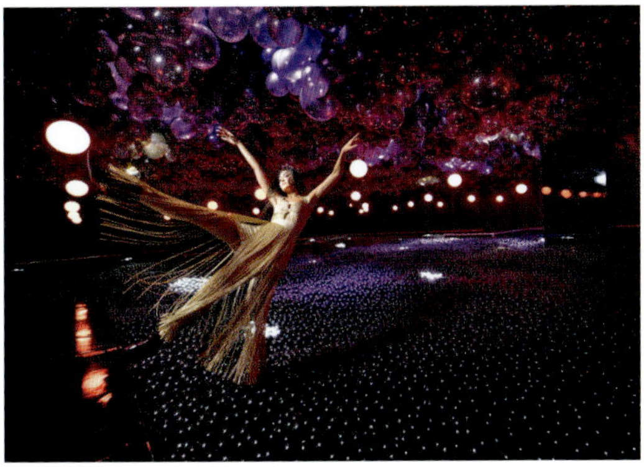

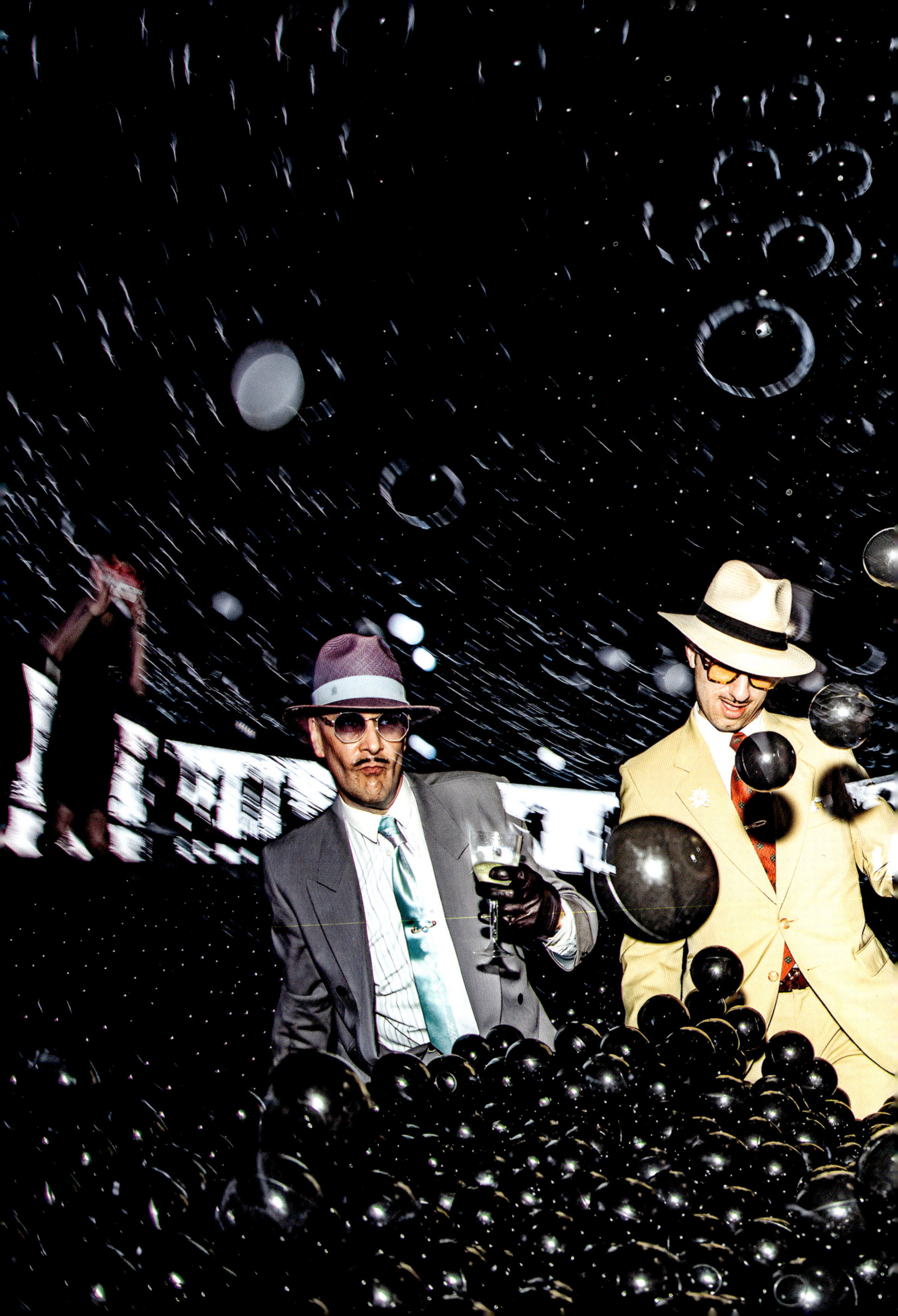

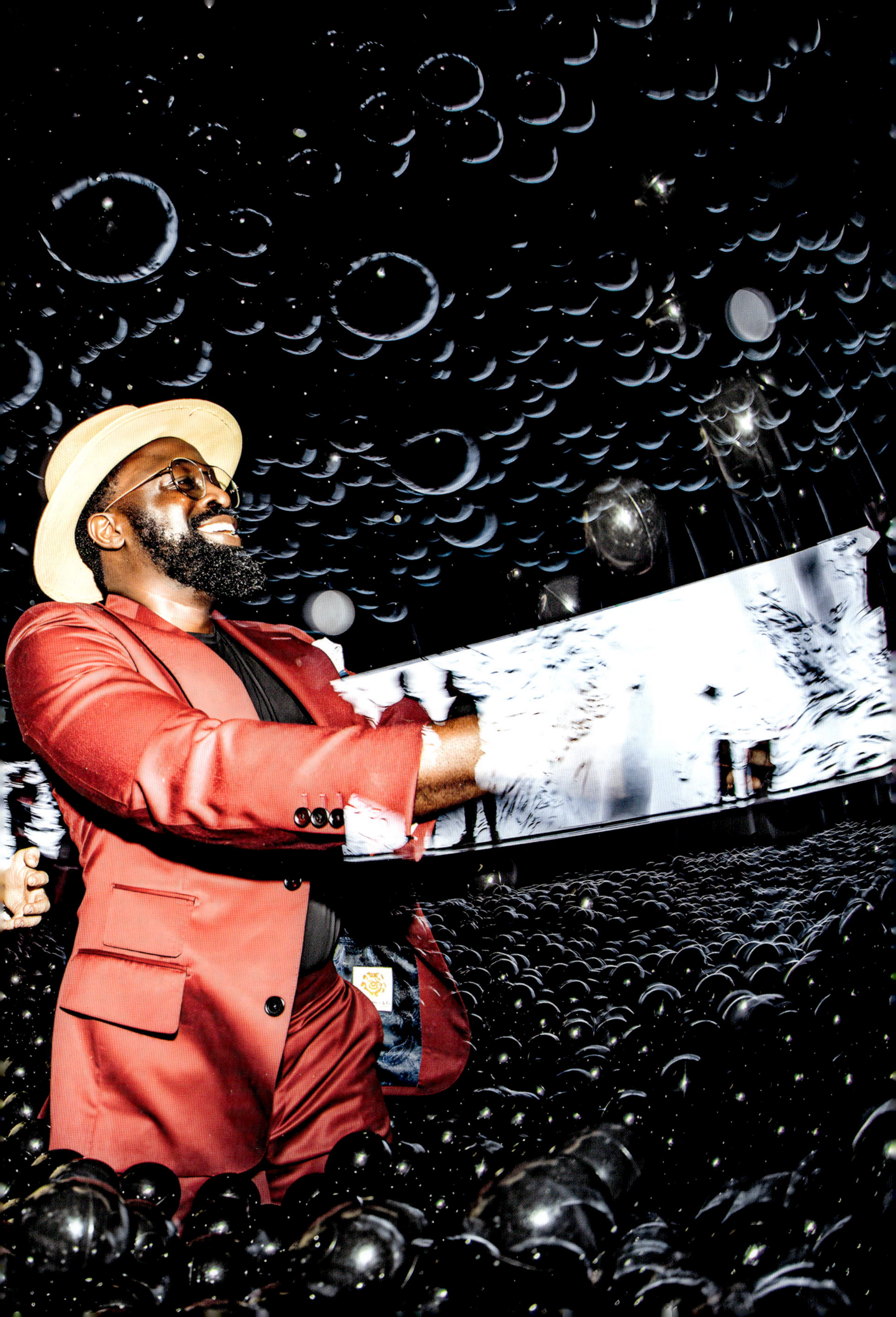

HYPERSTUDIO WITH ROMAN HILL

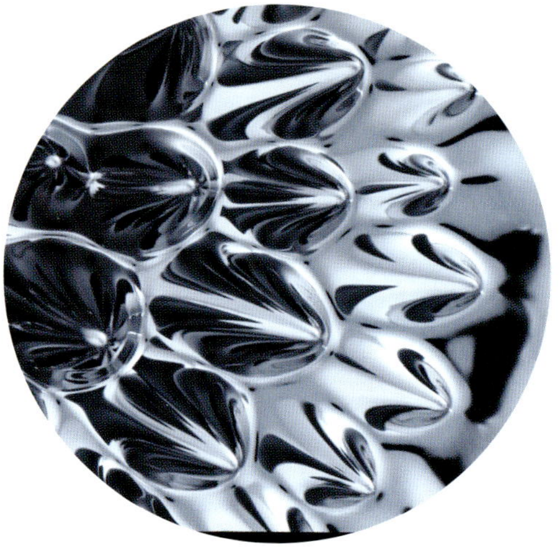

Roman Hill
Roman Hill, a gifted artist with dual French and American heritage, is celebrated for his Paris-based works that transcend conventional art forms. His unique approach involves an intricate exploration of the microscopic realm, bridging the gap between the minuscule intricacies of the microcosm and the vast expanse of the cosmos. This philosophical journey is more than an artistic pursuit; it's a quest to unravel the profound connections that underpin the universe. Roman's artistry is rooted in the utilization of organic-looking chemical reactions, a technique that blurs the lines between the animate and inanimate. His work is testament to his relentless exploration of life's origins and its very essence, transcending traditional boundaries of perception and understanding. Through the creation of immersive macro worlds, Roman Hill crafts hypnotic, abstract imagery that stems from a myriad of physical phenomena and intricate chemical interactions. In this unexplored universe of textures, movements, and colors, he masterfully redefines scale. The transformation of minute, inert elements into dynamic, evolving universes is a signature of his work. His art not only captivates the eye but also invites deep reflection on the nature of existence and our place in the universe.

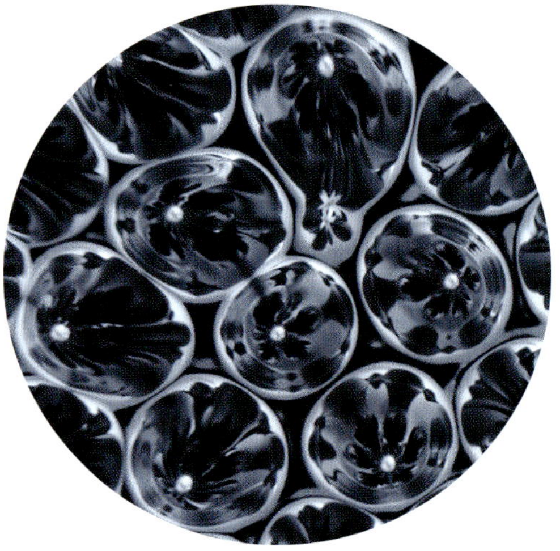

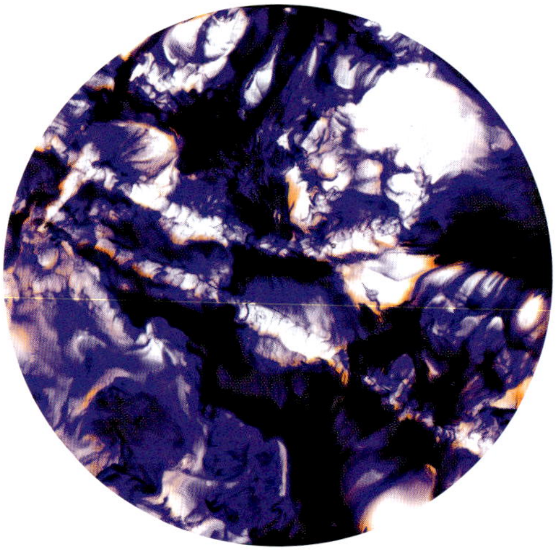

Still frames from *Hyperstellar* performance by Roman Hill Balloon Museum *Let's Fly* New York, 2023

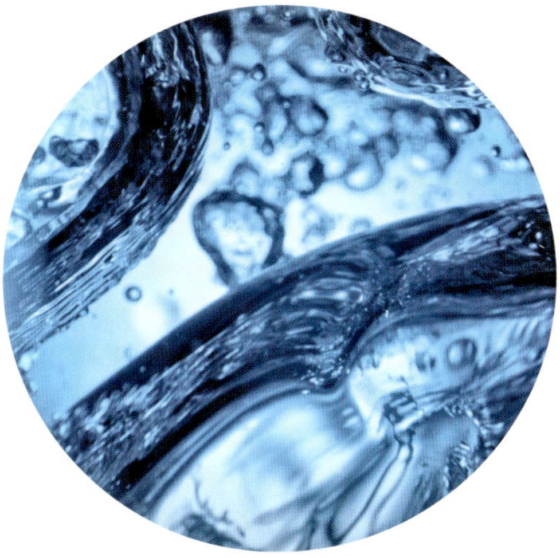
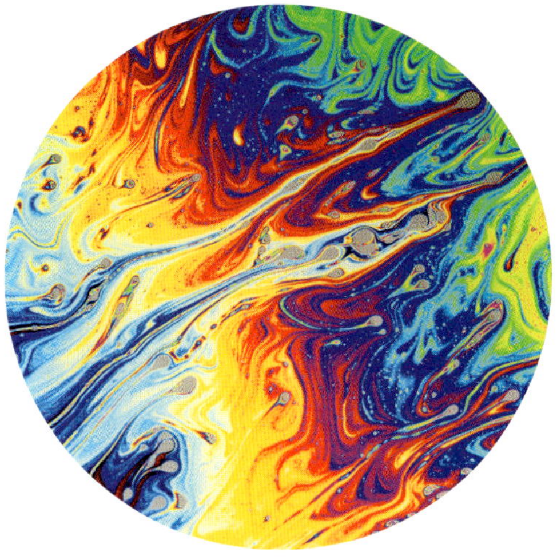
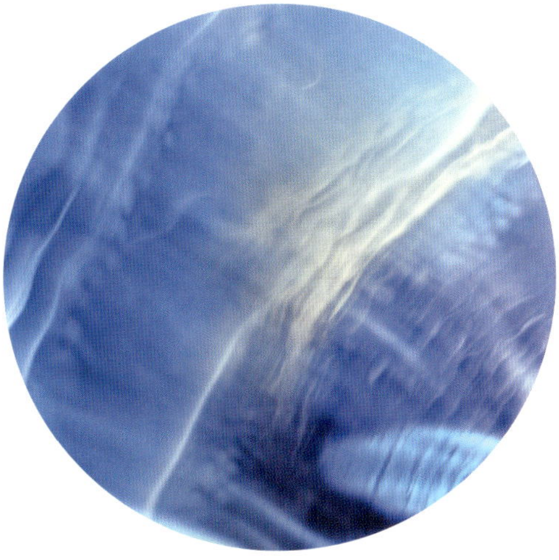
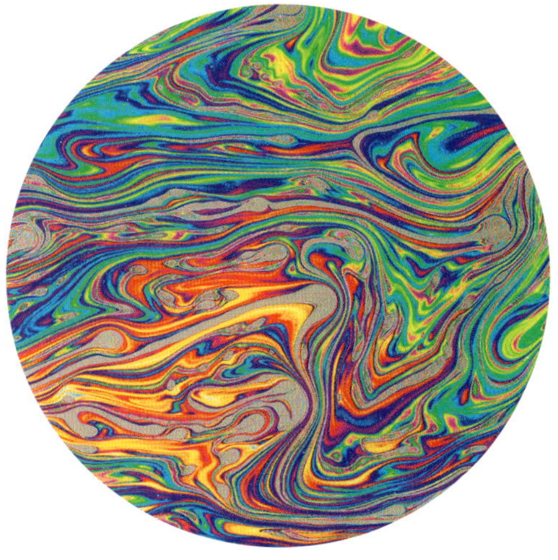
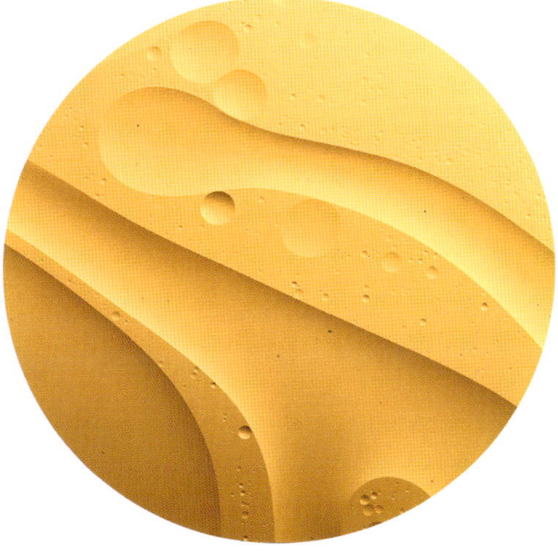
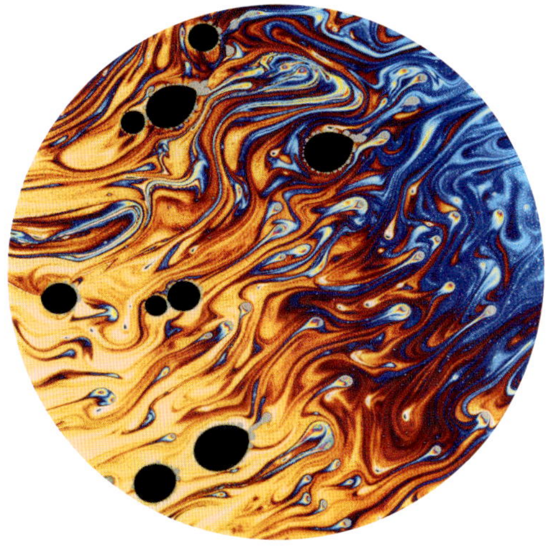

HYPERSTUDIO WITH SILA SVETA (PP 146-147) AND KISSMIKLOS

Hyperfeeling

This artwork aims to be the representation of all emotions, a large installation expressing the entirety of human feelings where one can touch, perceive, and see the complexity of emotions in Balloon Museum's *EmotionAir* exhibition. The artwork is conceived as a total immersion in a luminous and radiant universe, represented by a pool of small yellow balls and a ceiling composed of a sky of balloons of the same color. Additionally, there is a multimedia and multisensory show curated by Sila Sveta.

The audience is catapulted onto a journey where emotions flow rapidly on the large sphere, accompanied by sounds and lights to amplify the sensation. Joy, sadness, anger, fear, disgust, and surprise take shape, becoming images, lights, and sounds to engage the audience in a unique spectacle. In the large pool, some balls feature kissmiklos's *Emogram*, a work that aims to convey, through the typographic use of letters, the words that have contracted into emojis with contemporary communication. *Hyperfeeling* invites spectators to reflect on their own emotions in relation to themselves and the world, a personal experience that becomes collective at the same time, suggesting that to feel, one simply needs to carefully observe what surrounds us.

Bottom right, opposite and overleaf
Hyperstudio with Sila Sveta and kissmiklos
Hyperfeeling
Balloon Museum
EmotionAir
London, 2023

Bottom left
A model in
Hyperfeeling
Balloon Museum
EmotionAir
London, 2023

Below
Emograms by kissmiklos

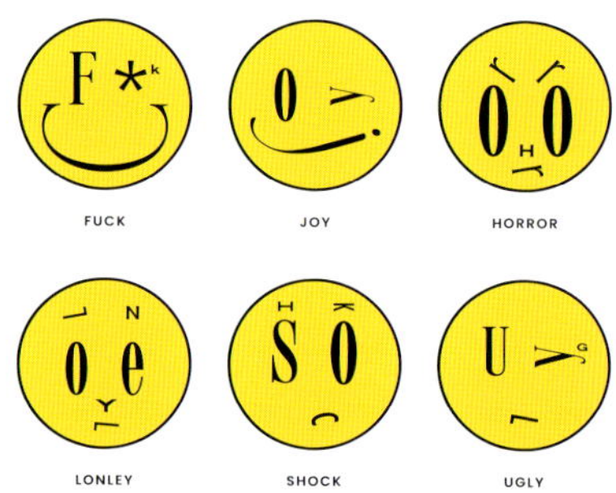

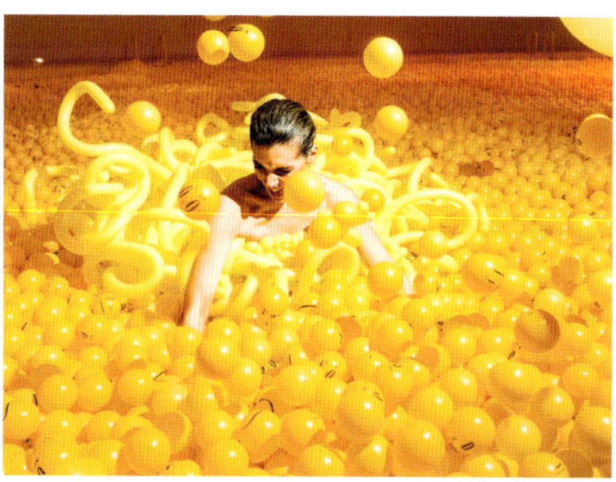

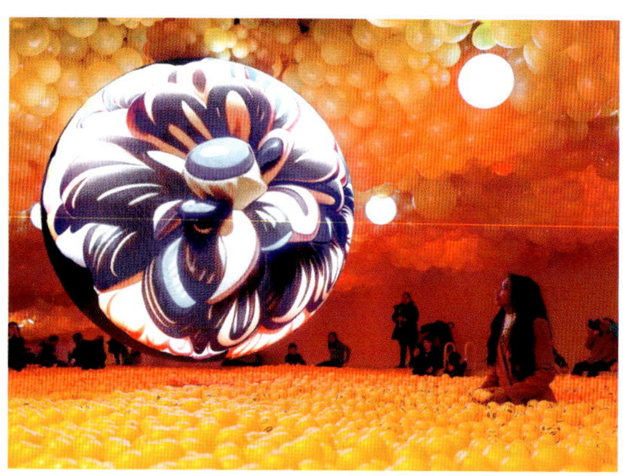

Hyperfeeling 2023

kissmiklos

A visual artist and designer, kissmiklos is known for incorporating elements of fine art, typography, illustration, graphic and interior design into his work. His art is characterized by a strong conceptual approach and an outstandingly colorful playfulness. The artist's most iconic works are his emograms. These figures' faces are made up from letters of a word, mostly expressing an emotion or thought. Kissmiklos's works have already been exhibited in many European and Asian museums and galleries. His practice challenges the boundaries between high and low art and reflects on the entangled relationship between art, social media, capitalism, and the individual. Such playful dichotomies and an acute awareness of art history are central to kissmiklos's oeuvre, which lends a new esthetic and conceptual dimension to the contemporary canon. His artworks oscillate between different systems of meaning and perception, while always maintaining a humorous, ironic, and tongue-in-cheek edge.

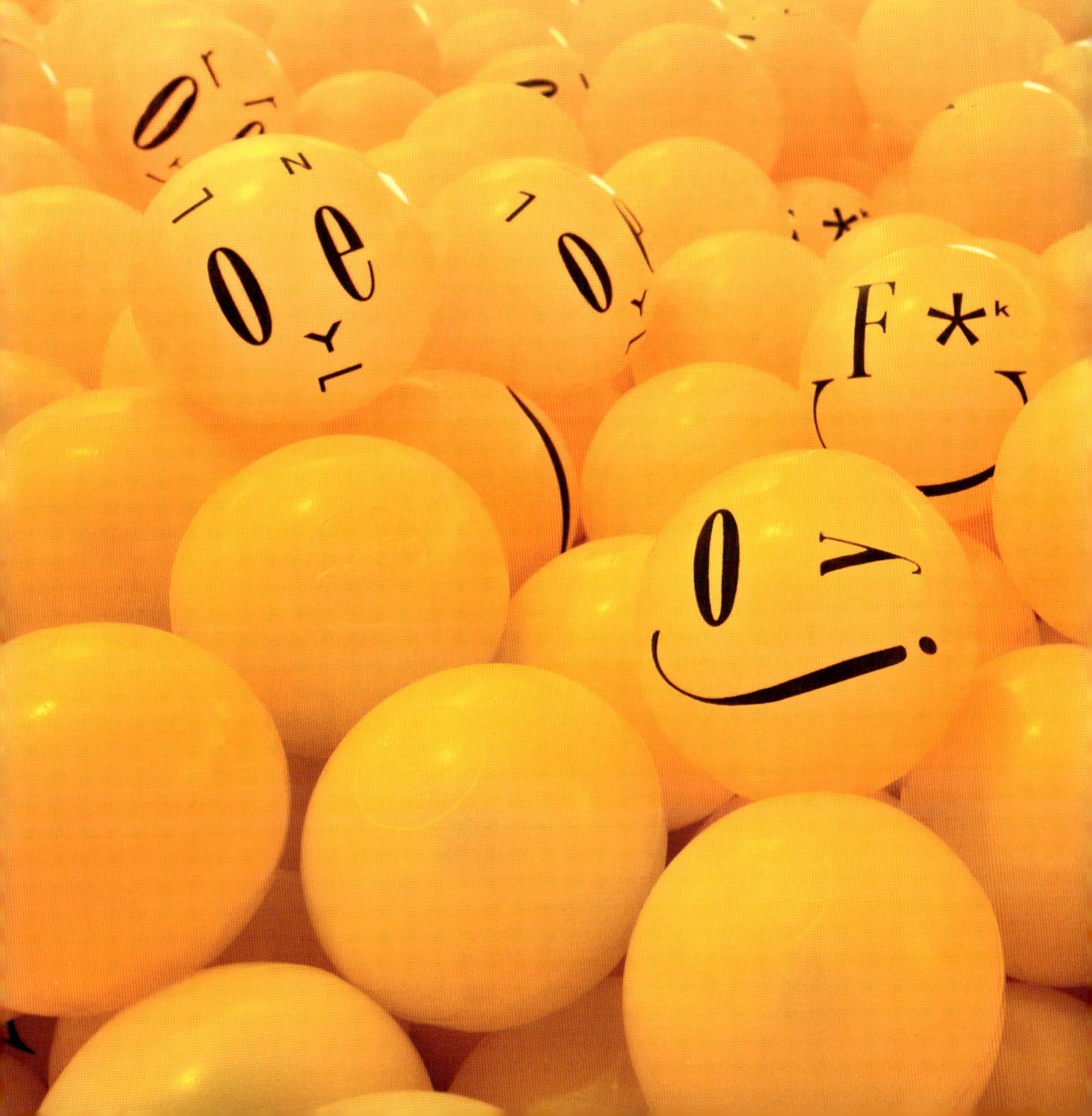

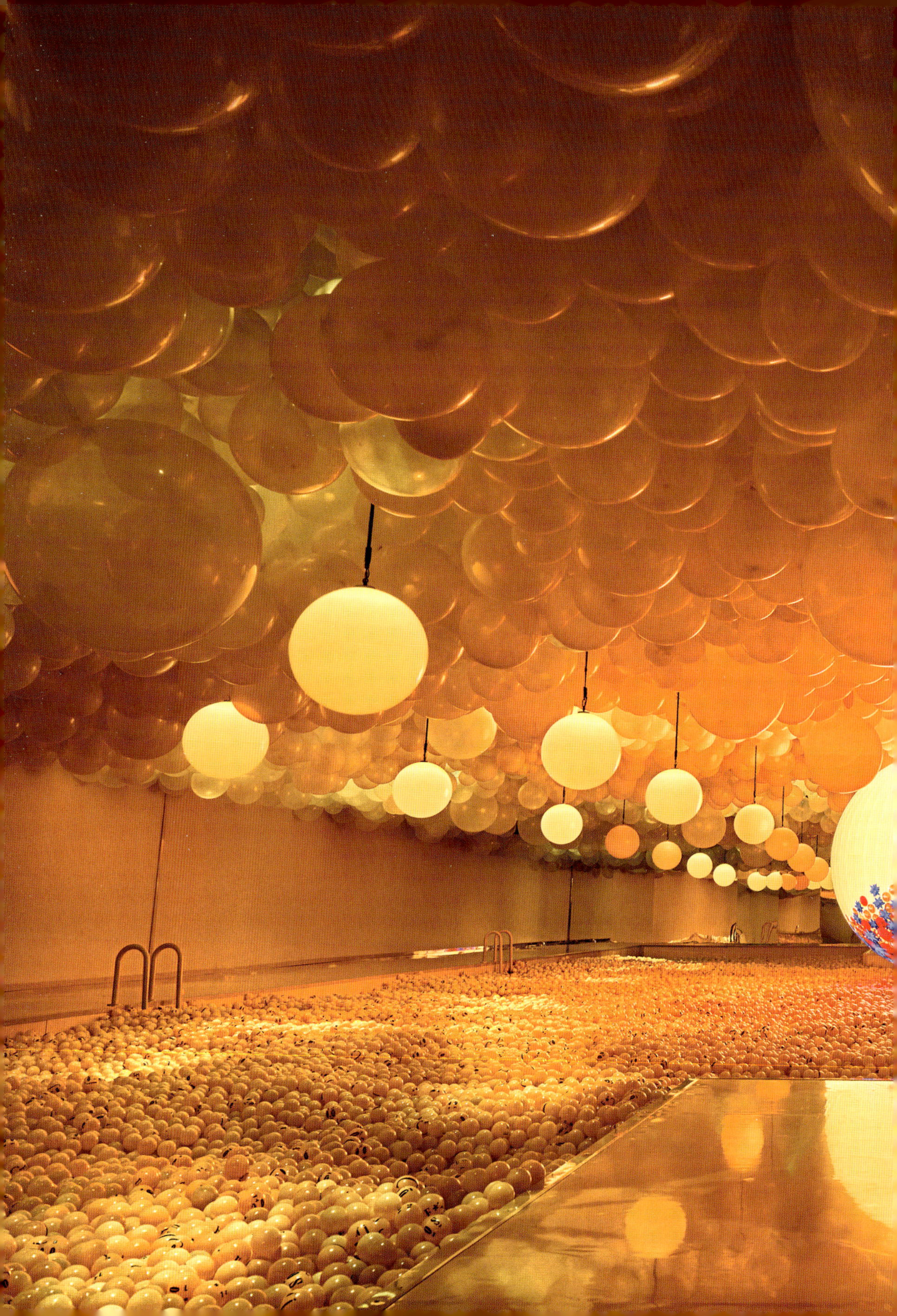

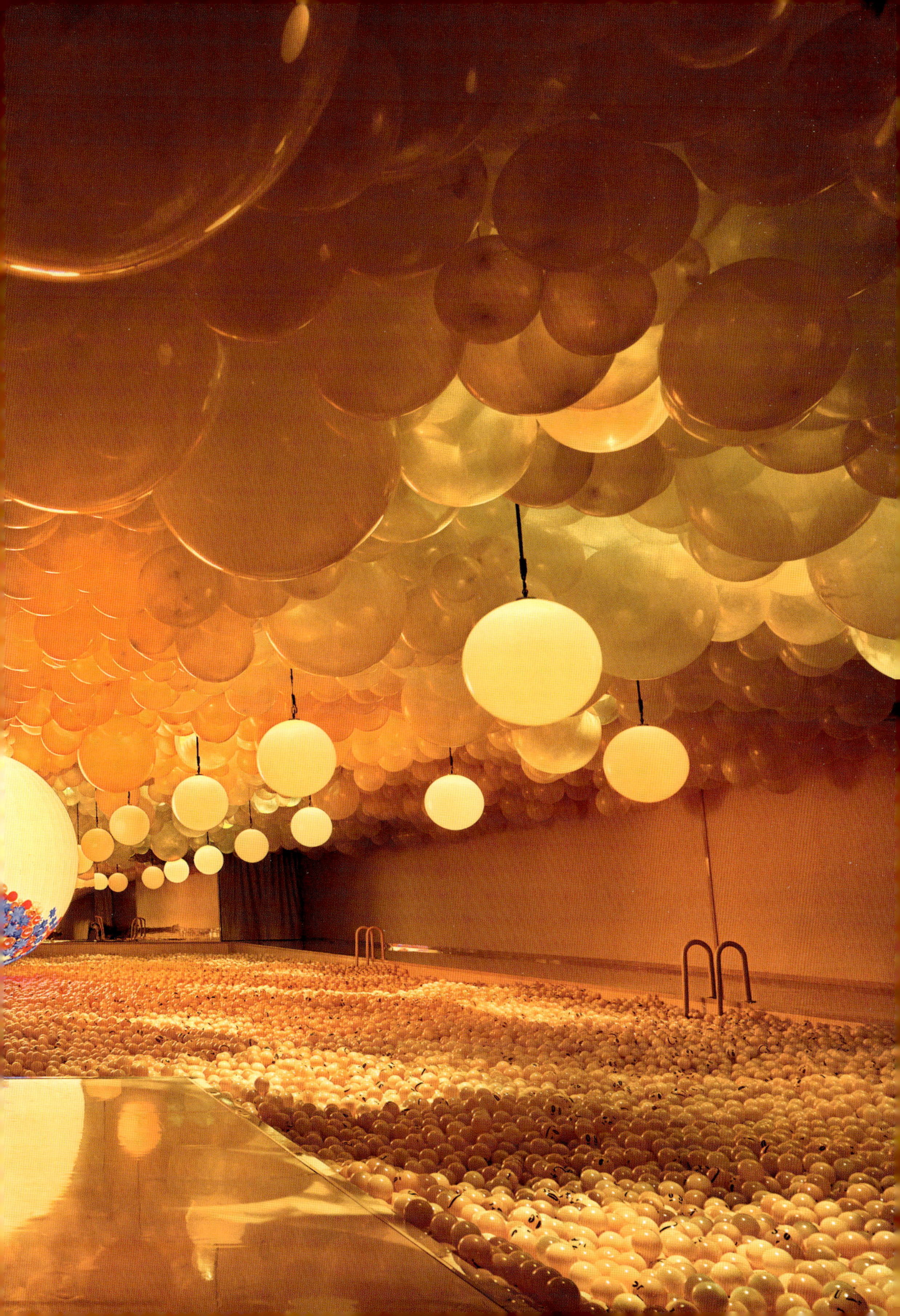

HYPERSTUDIO

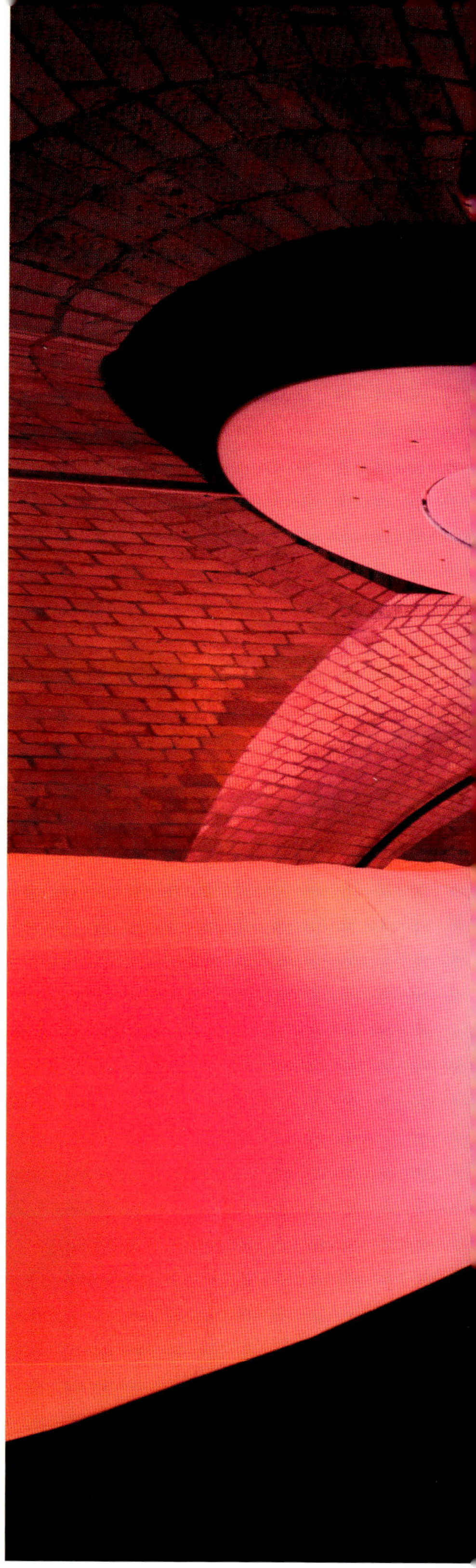

Too Many Thoughts
Engaged for a long time in the conception and creation of multisensory installations, the Hyperstudio collective presents *Too Many Thoughts*: imposing, cumbersome spheres that invade the space, filling every corner. The visitor finds themselves immersed in a constantly transforming room; the large spheres, akin to living organisms, move in harmony with the breath, expanding and contracting, creating a path that gives the sensation of being inside something larger than ourselves. A play of dynamic lights amplifies this effect, further emphasizing the perception of a space that contracts and expands in a brief span of time. The installation offers an engaging and stimulating experience, inviting the audience to explore the emotional nuances of space in constant transformation, prompting reflections on the individual's dimension in the face of external and ever-changing forces.

Hyperstudio
Too Many Thoughts
Balloon Museum
EmotionAir
London, 2023

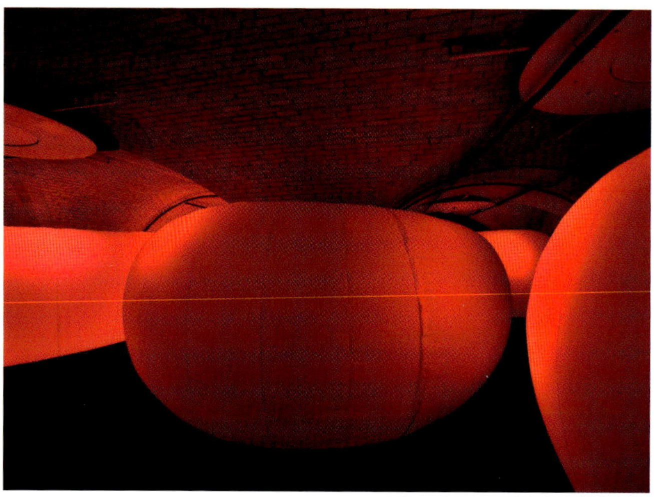

Too Many Thoughts 2023

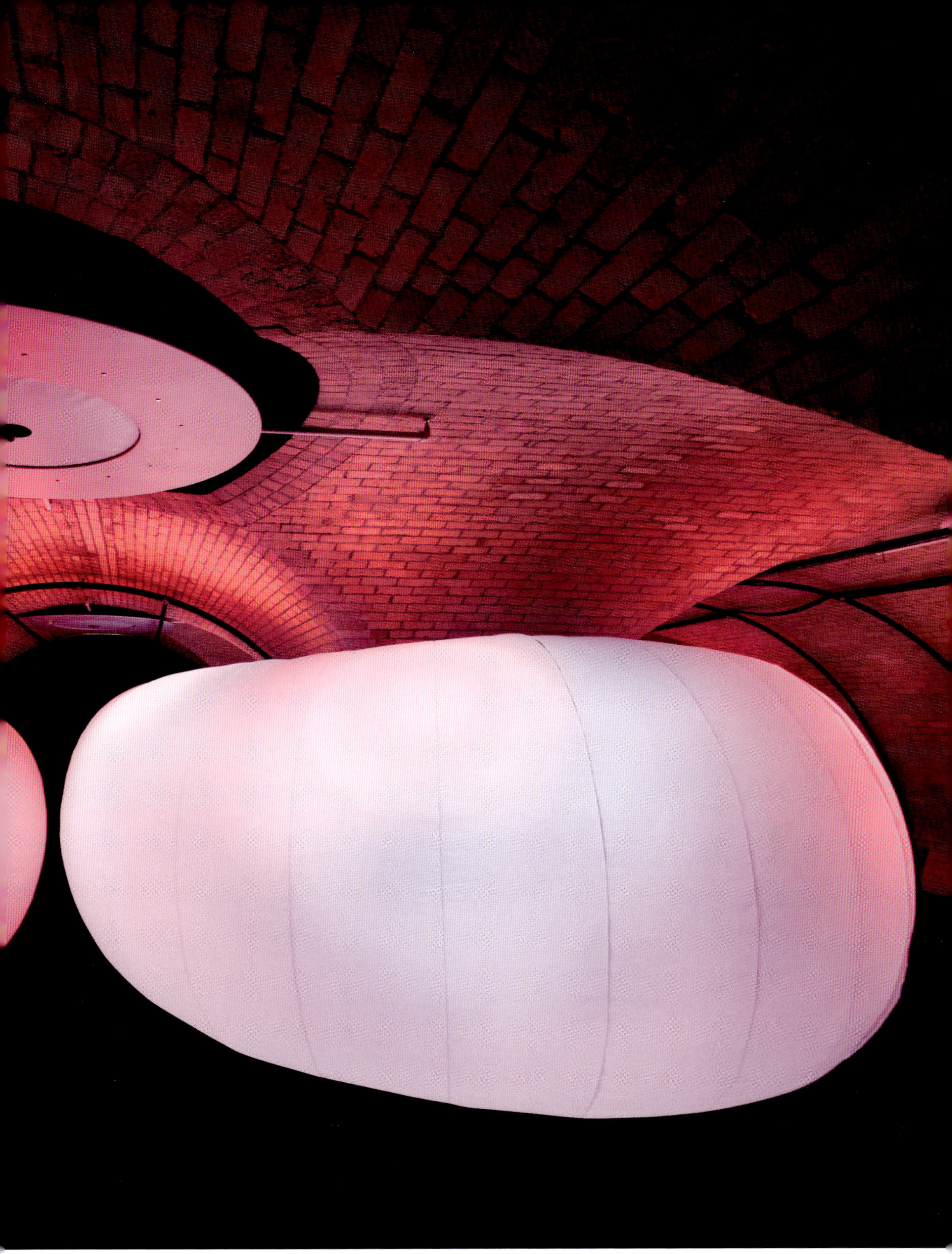

MYEONGBEOM KIM

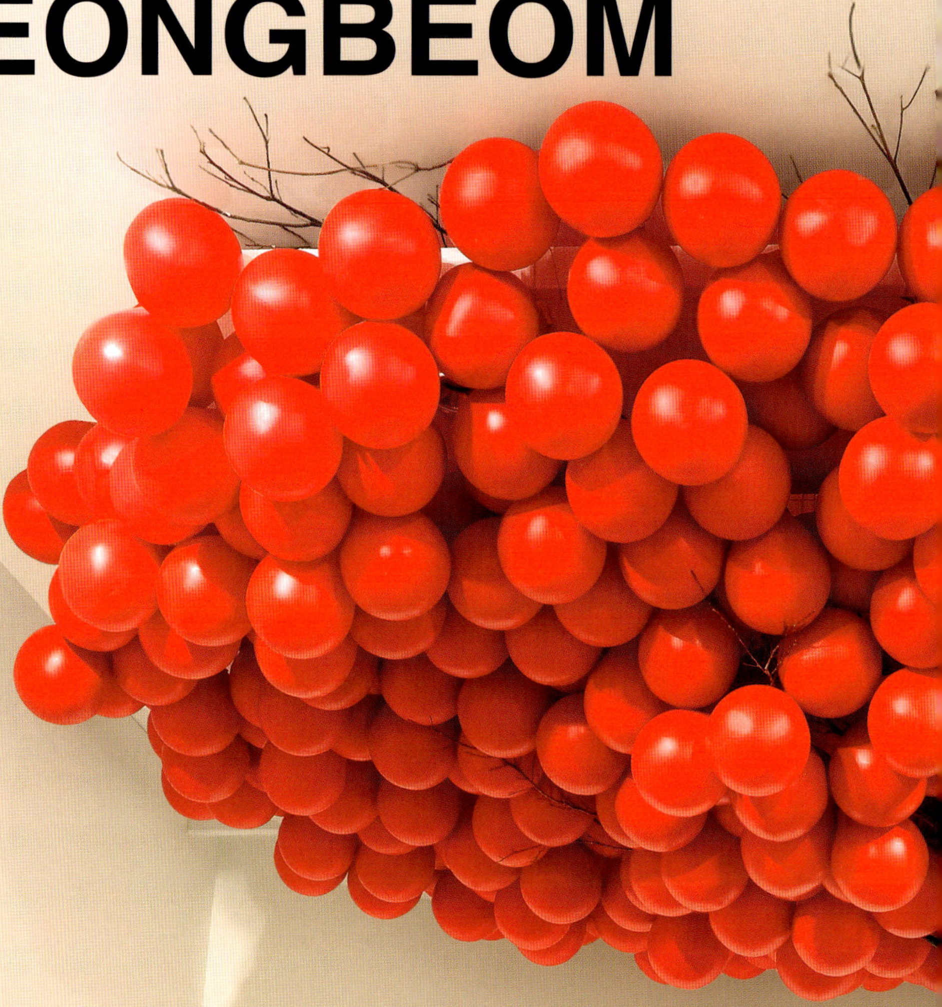

MyeongBeom Kim was born in Busan, South Korea, graduating with a bachelor's degree in fine arts from the University of Seoul where he studied environmental sculpture, and then received an M.F.A. in sculpture from the School of the Art Institute of Chicago. He featured in many solo exhibitions including *Breath* at Thomas Masters Gallery in Chicago, his relay exhibition, *One*, at Doosan Gallery in New York City and others in Seoul, and many group shows in Paris, UK, Switzerland, Rome, Hong Kong, Taiwan, Brussels, Montpellier, Puerto Rico, Daegu, and Busan, to name but a few.

MyeongBeom Kim
Balloon Tree
Jeju Museum of Art
Jeju-do, 2016

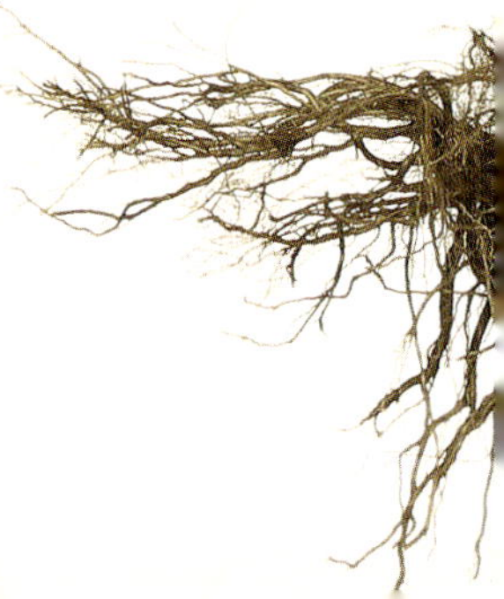

Balloon Tree 2009

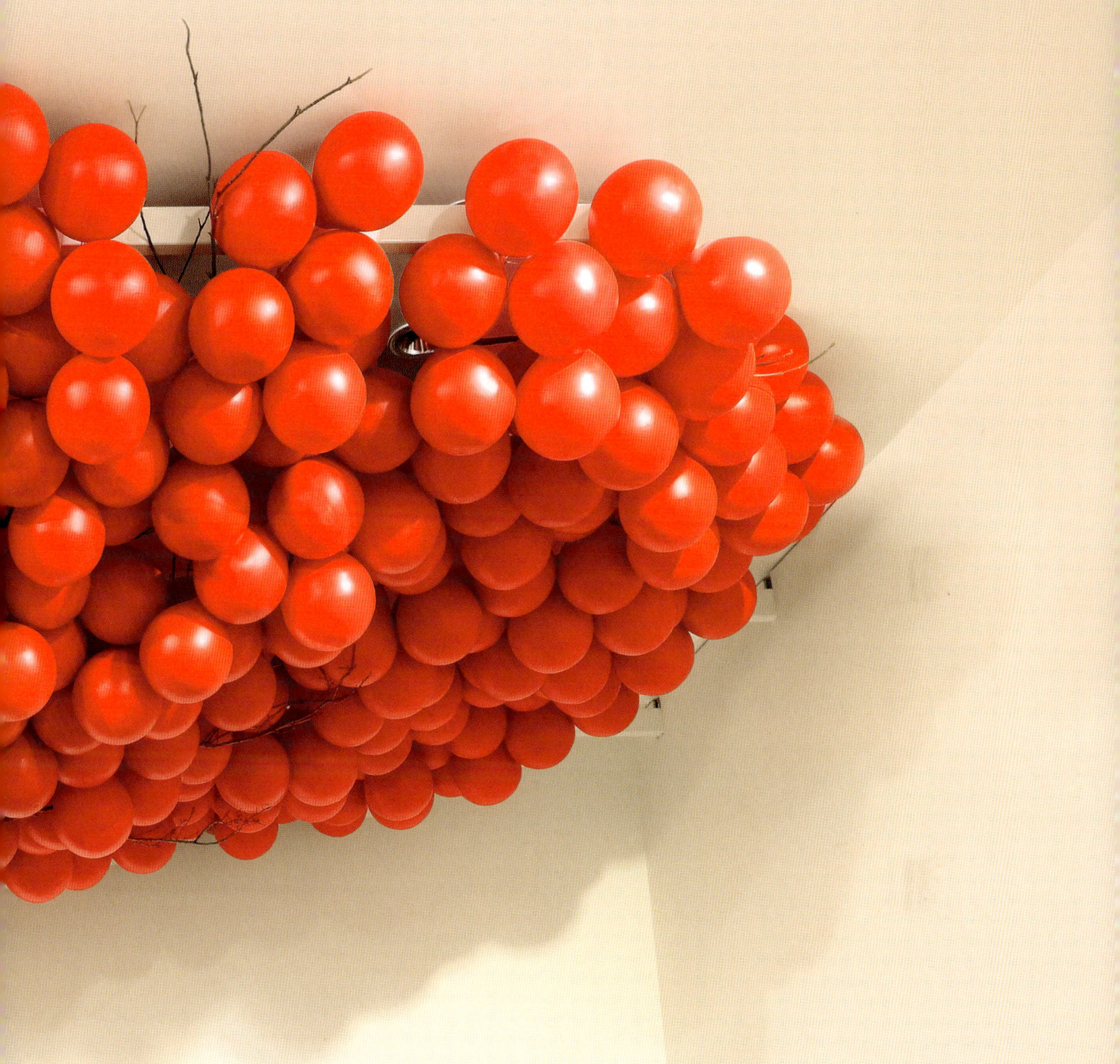

Balloon Tree

This artwork floats above the audience with a crown of red balloons clustered around the branches of a young tree with visible roots. The seemingly bizarre and illogical association of objects is a way of melding practical juxtaposition and combination of natural and man-made elements in time and space, erasing stereotypes connected to the objects and drawing out the expansion of subjective cognition. This approach draws out subjective appreciation and perception, and becomes the source of new stories and energy for new diverse possibilities that open up while looking at an object or event. To understand the essence of authenticity, the artist believes that a process of acquiring experience is necessary and should not be random or blind to the a priori ideas of others. Rather than superficial issues and trendy methods of expression, the artist strives to maintain the authenticity of the work by recognizing, reflecting, and expressing objects through deeply rooted experiences and perspectives.

THOM KUBLI

Swiss-German composer and artist Thom Kubli is known for his installation art and sculptures, with a distinctive emphasis on deploying sound as a pivotal element. Based in Berlin, Kubli's multidisciplinary approach blends composition, sculpture, and conceptual approaches. Kubli's body of work frequently delves into digital innovations, probing sensitive facets of social dynamics. Kubli often collaborates with scientific institutions like the MIT Media Lab or the Rensselaer Polytechnic Institute to devise new technologies and materials. Kubli's performances and installations have been shown in many art galleries internationally, among others, at the New Museum of Contemporary Art, NYC, Ars Electronica, Linz, Transmediale, Berlin, Laboratorio Arte Alameda, Mexico City, FILE, São Paulo, and LABoral, Spain. His composition pieces and experimental radio plays have been widely broadcasted on public radio stations.

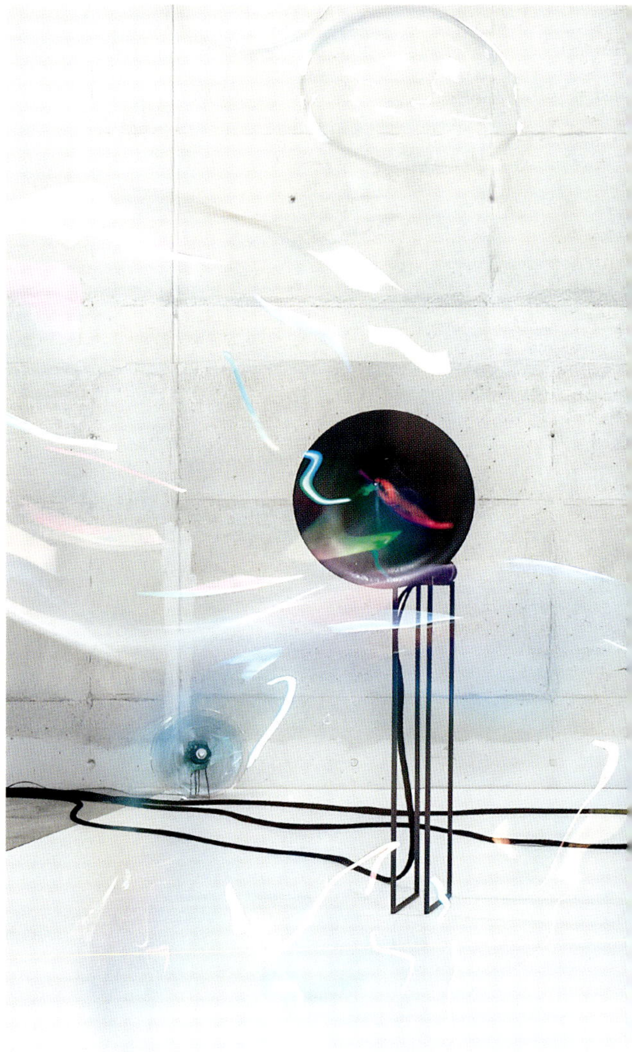

Thom Kubli
Black Hole Horizon
Ars Electronica Festival
Linz, 2016

Overleaf
Thom Kubli
Black Hole Horizon
Balloon Museum
EmotionAir
London, 2023

Black Hole Horizon 2012–2015

Black Hole Horizon

Black Hole Horizon is a kinetic installation composed of three sculptures of varying sizes, reminiscent of ships' horns, emerging in exponential funnels. These sculptures are able to generate sounds using compressed air; with each tone, large soap bubbles are emitted from the funnels. Growing in size with the duration of the sound, they eventually detach from the horn and float through the room until they burst at an unpredictable moment and place in space. The title, *Black Hole Horizon*, refers to the astrophysical phenomenon of the event horizon, a boundary in spacetime beyond which events are no longer perceptible to the observer. Enchanted by the sound, visitors follow the choreography and flight of these bubbles with their eyes. Each bubble is never identical to any other; their unpredictable movements and spatial situation create a different experience each time. *Black Hole Horizon* becomes a captivating fusion of sound, movement, and chance, transforming the spectator into a participant in an ever-evolving artistic narrative.

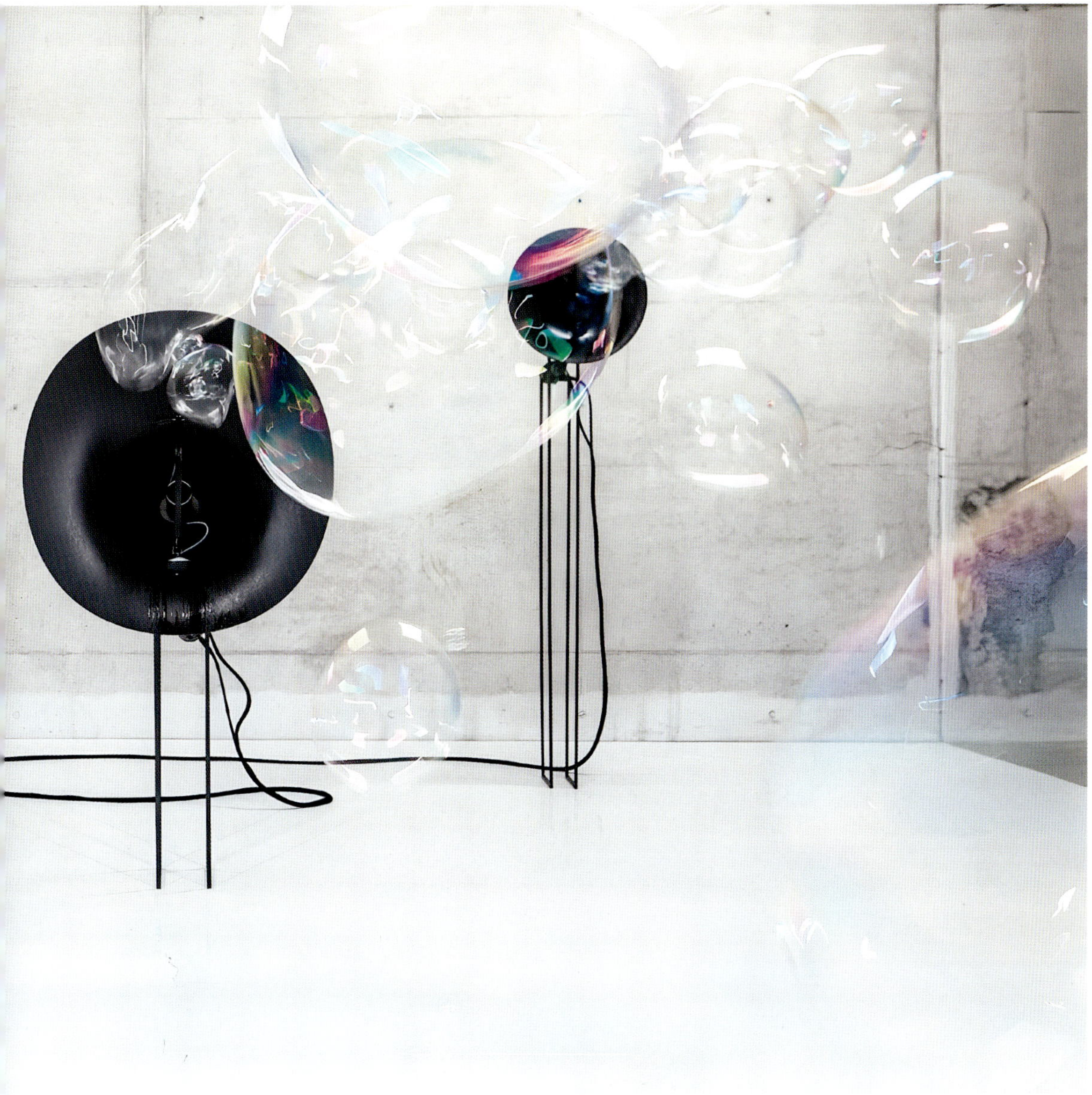

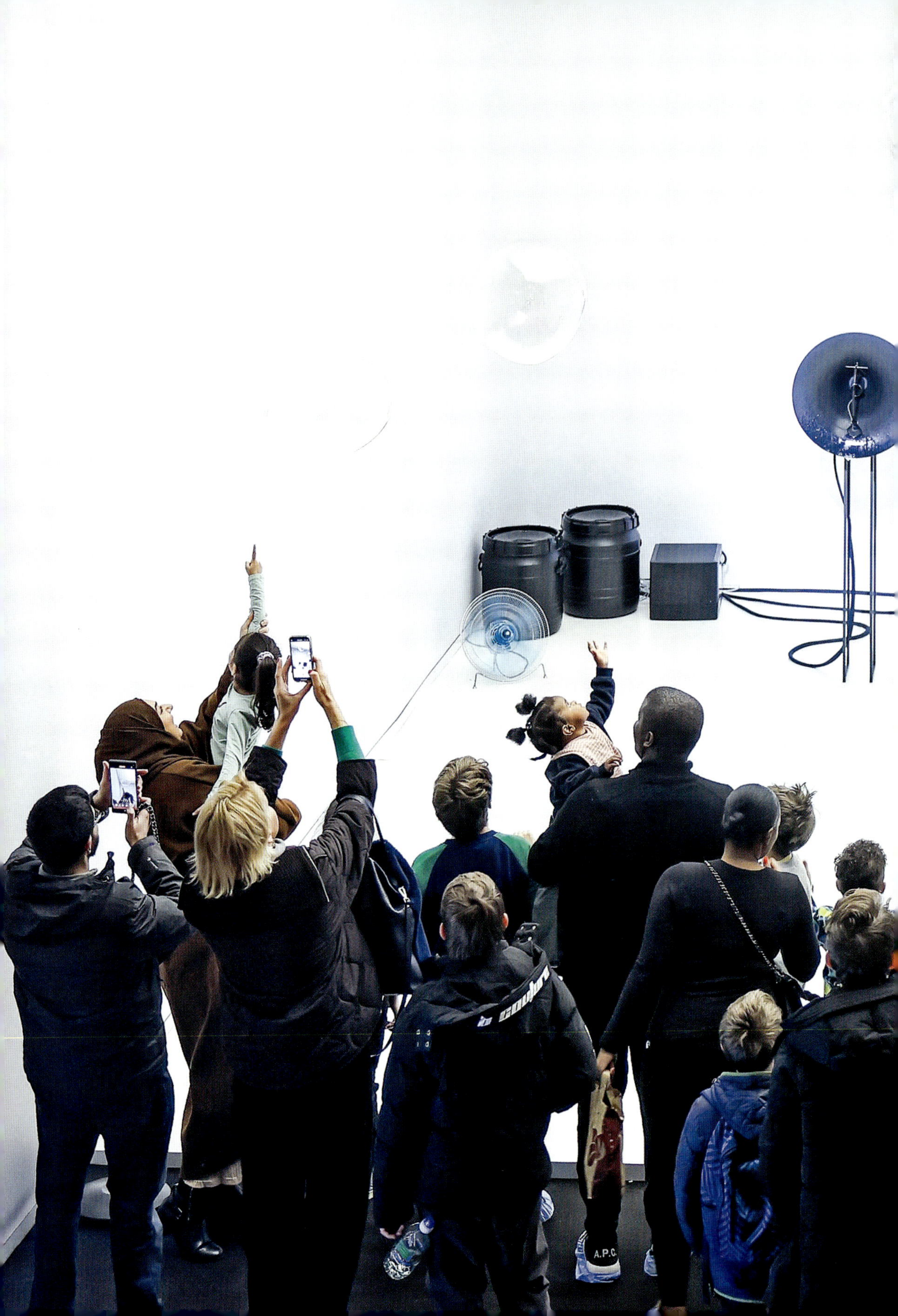
A.P.C.

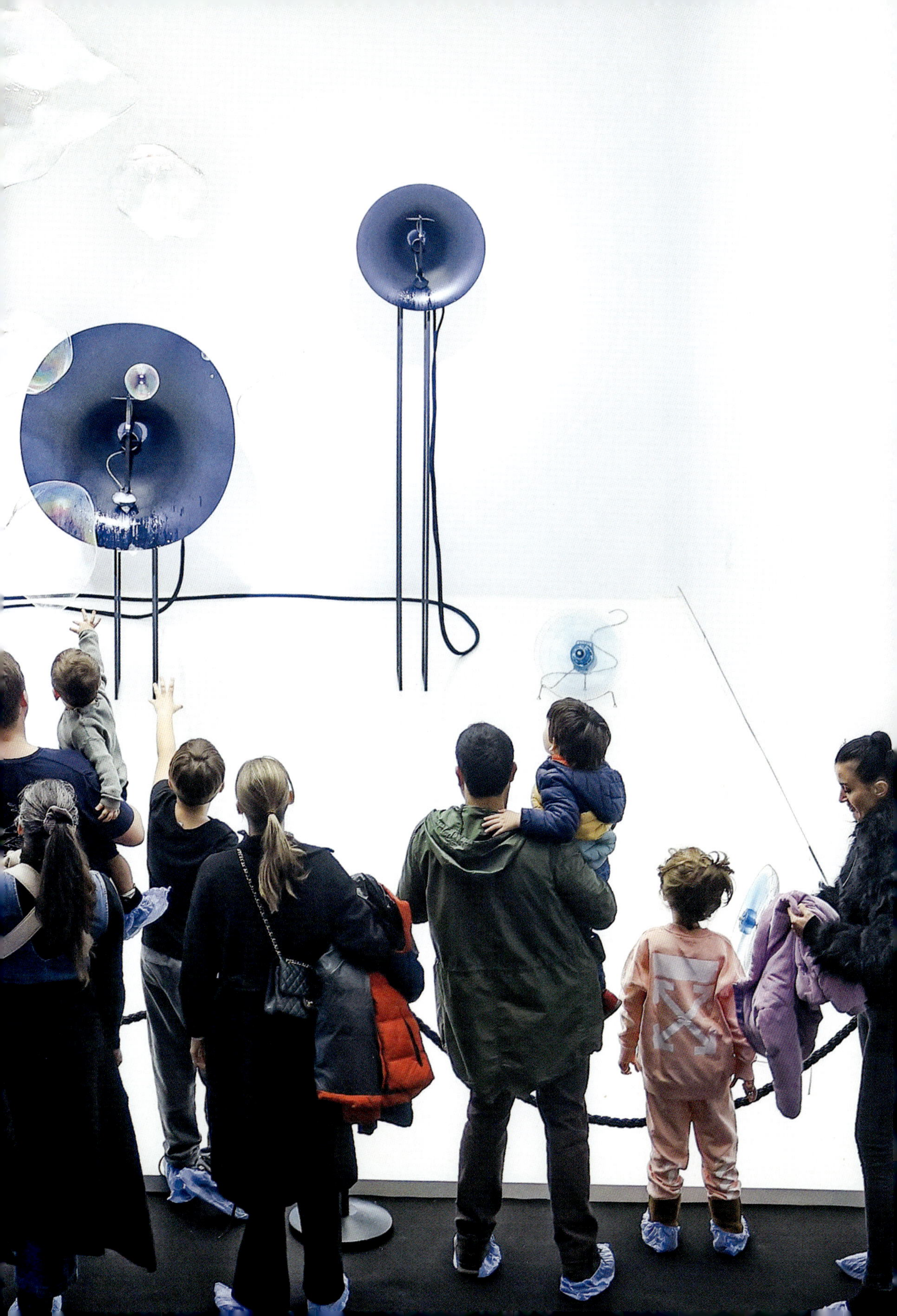

JIMMY KUEHNLE

Jimmy Kuehnle has exhibited in the United States and internationally. In 2014, he was selected for the national survey exhibition *State of the Art: Discovering American Art Now* at the Crystal Bridges Museum of American Art of Bentonville, Arizona. In 2015 he installed a large kinetic inflatable in the atrium of MOCA Cleveland as part of the group exhibition, *How to Remain Human*. His 2016 solo exhibition at the Hudson River Museum in Yonkers, New York was favorably reviewed in *The New York Times* and featured in *New York Magazine's* "Approval Matrix", among many other accolades. His 2016 monumentally scaled, site-specific inflatables at the Akron Art Museum, *Wiggle, Giggle, Jiggle,* were widely reviewed and in 2019 he opened *Wow, Pop, Bliss,* an exhibition of four new interactive inflatables at the Columbia Museum of Art in Columbia, South Carolina. Kuehnle is Professor/Chair of Sculpture + Expanded Media at the Cleveland Institute of Art and received his MFA from the University of Texas at San Antonio. Kuehnle was awarded a Fulbright Graduate Research Fellowship to study and research public art in Japan.

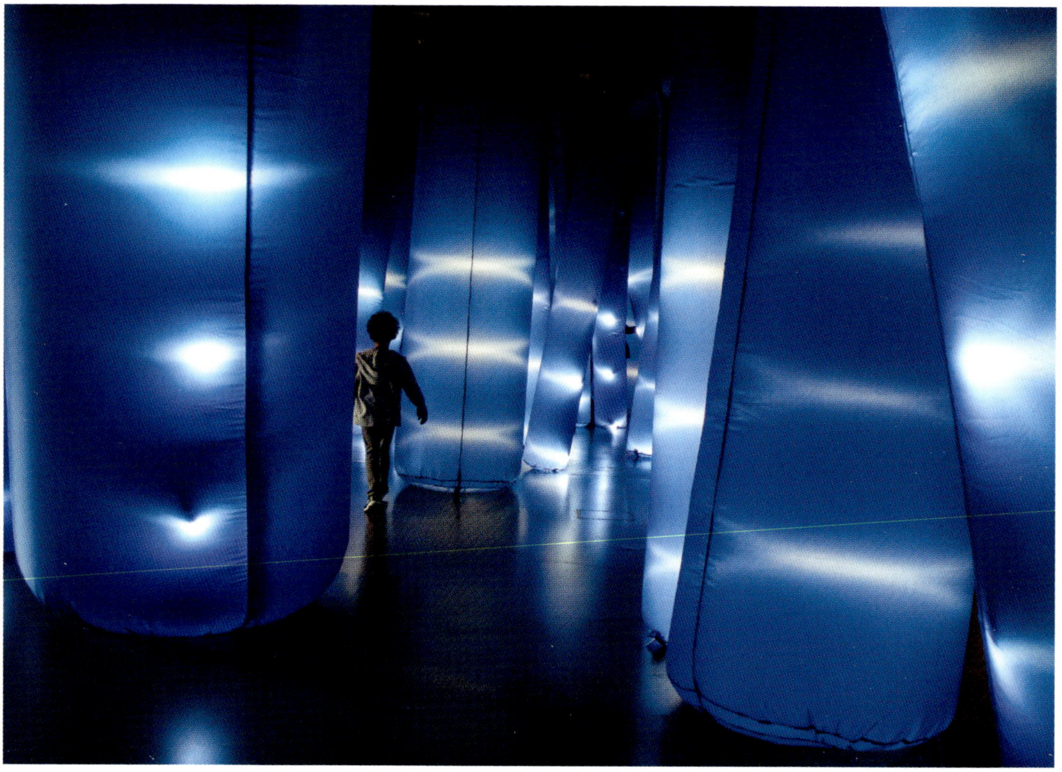

Bau(ncy) Haus 2018

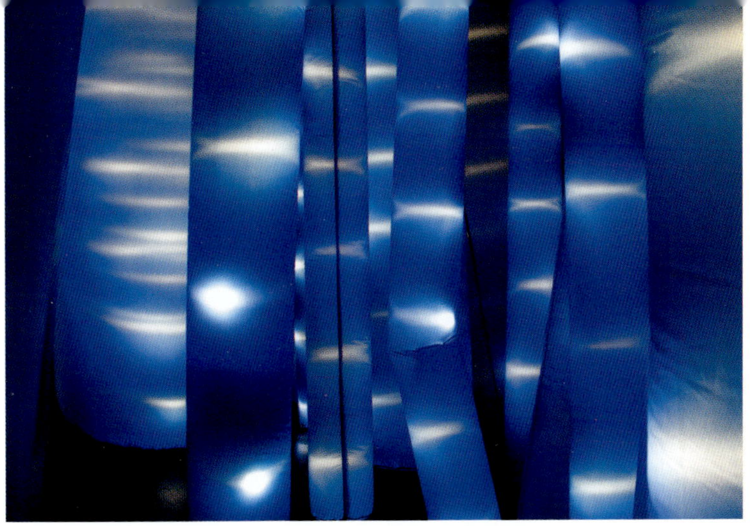

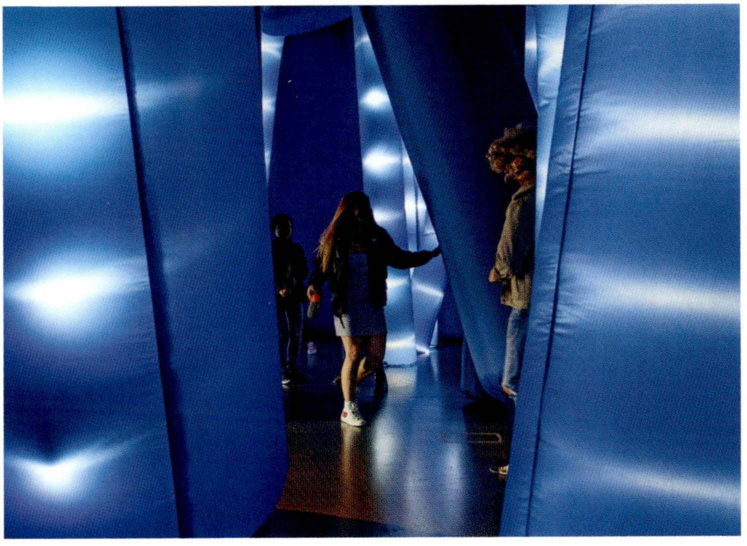

Jimmy Kuehnle
Bau(ncy) Haus
Exploratorium:
The Museum
of Science,
Art & Human
Perception
San Francisco, 2018

Bau(ncy) Haus

Step into a whimsical realm where the mundane rules of physics are playfully defied. A freestanding inflatable labyrinth, where each curve and corner is a mystery of its own, beckons you into a maze of variously-sized tubes that promise an adventure at every twist and turn, giving the feeling of immersion without being trapped. The inflatable comes alive with a symphony of LED lights, performing orchestrated sequences that dazzle the senses, at times blinking out completely only to come roaring back from the darkness. Depending on where the viewer stands, patterns and animations come alive in the lights. This installation doesn't just exist for its own sake—it exists for the viewers. Without their curious gaze and eager hearts, it's merely potential, coiled within inanimate fabric. The audience's engagement breathes life into it, crafting memories that cling to social media posts long after guests have departed.

"I want visitors to experience real delight and joy. I want them to forget where they are and what they were doing just a moment ago and experience light, sensation, space, and interaction. I want them to bump into strangers as they navigate the labyrinth and have their own trial and error experience. I want them to enjoy the moment and enjoy the human community of others that surrounds them in something that is not necessary for survival—art, but hopefully makes survival more enjoyable."

CYRIL LANCELIN

Cyril Lancelin was born in Lyon, France, in 1975 and is today a major figure in the world of Inflatable Art. Cyril Lancelin develops a hybrid work made up of sculptures, immersive installations, drawings, virtual experiences in the Metaverse, and videos that forge links between the physical and the fictional. It is from a plastic vocabulary based on primitive geometry that he links architecture and the human body, the everyday and the functional, the perennial and the ephemeral, science, and nature. He uses Virtual Reality and Augmented Reality in his exploration of tridimensional matter research. His practice is shaped by immersion and movement, by the porosity of limits, by innovation, by a search for a world that is half data, half real. The notions of repetition and parametric generation are recurring themes in his work. Digital or real, they offer an essentially optimistic vision, drawing an artificial and experiential landscape. Lancelin has exhibited and collaborated internationally at Design Miami/Art Basel, Festival de Cannes, and Glow Shenzhen among many other venues.

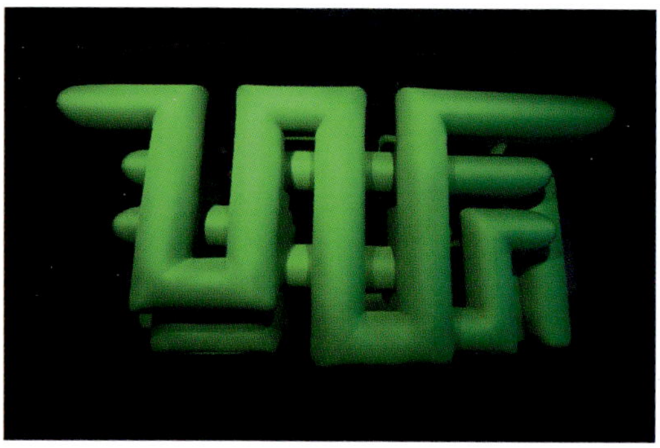

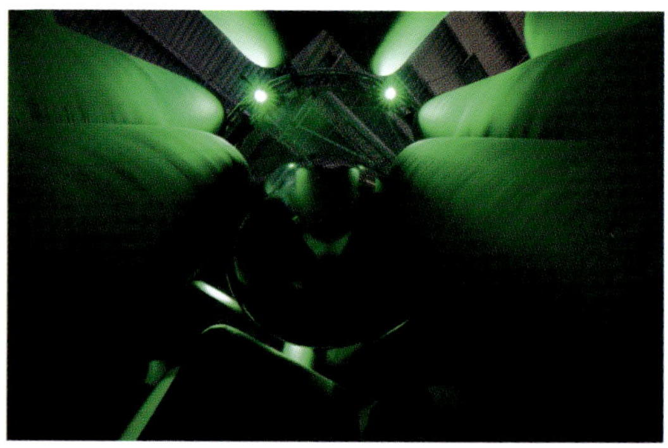

Here and overleaf
Cyril Lancelin
Flying Maze
Balloon Museum
Let's Fly
New York, 2023

Flying Maze
This new work has been specially crafted for the *Let's Fly* exhibition. This 10-meter by 10-meter sculpture takes the form of an immense inflatable maze. Green in color, the sculpture is reminiscent of vegetal labyrinths, a very fashionable construction during the Renaissance. Symbolizing the quest for self and the elevation of the spirit toward knowledge, the labyrinth is a very old motif. In fact, it already appeared on coins, pottery, and mosaics in the 15th century AD.
Cyril Lancelin invites visitors to venture into the labyrinthine world of this work-architecture. The impressive dimensions and enveloping curves of the work hypnotize the eye, which loses itself between the lines. At the heart of the labyrinth, there's no Minotaur, but an inflatable, reflective sphere suspended like a well-guarded treasure.

Flying Maze 2023

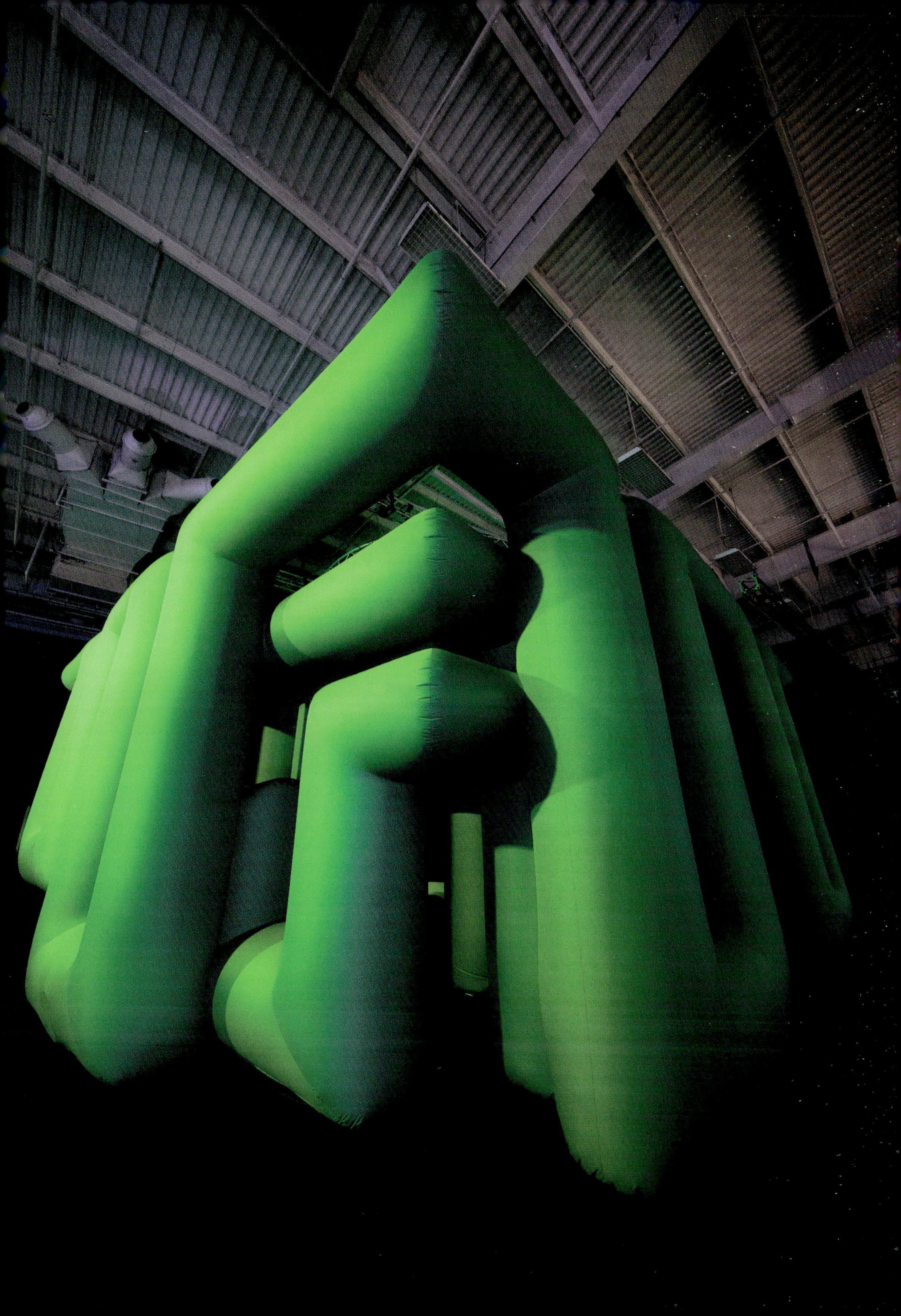

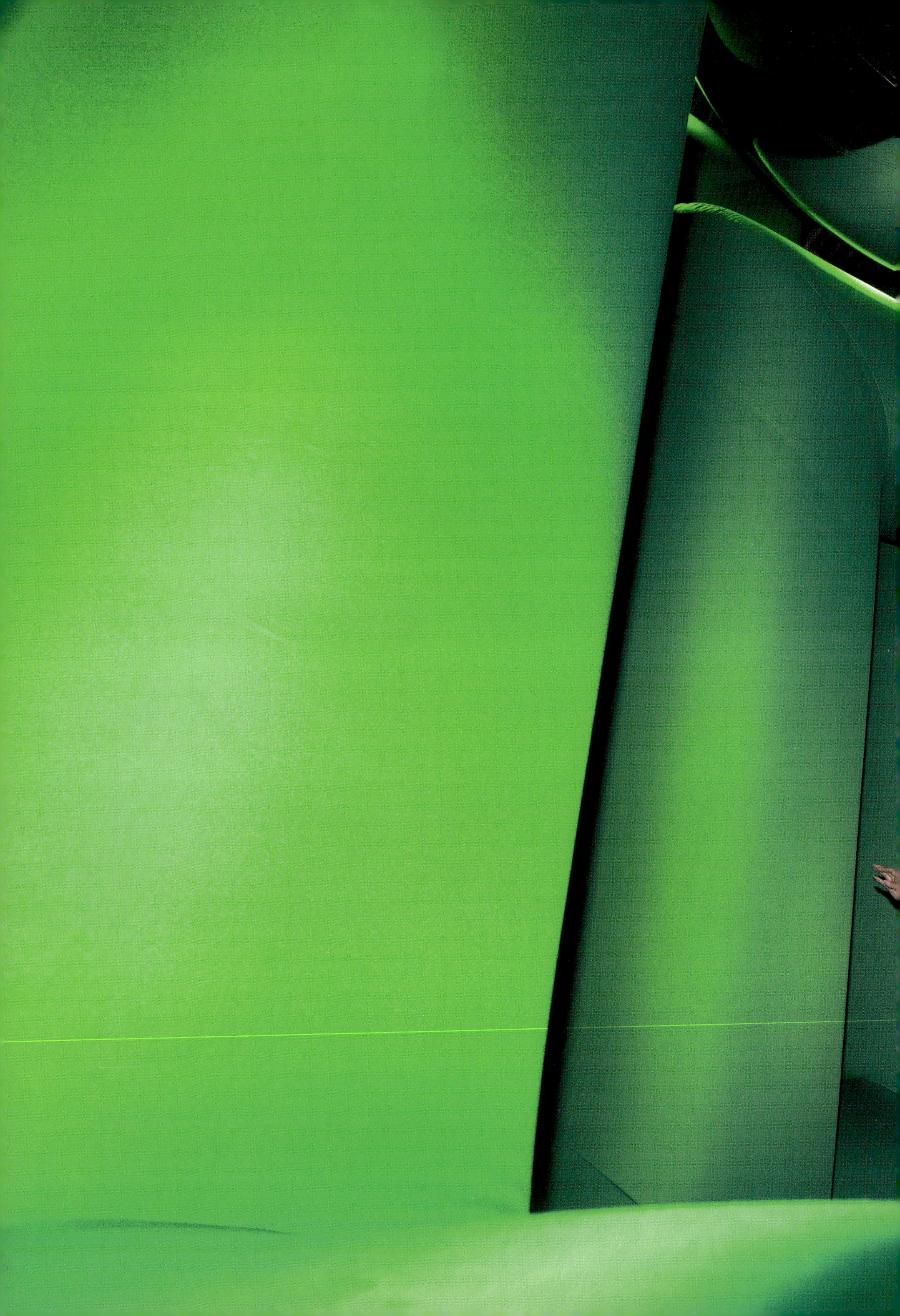

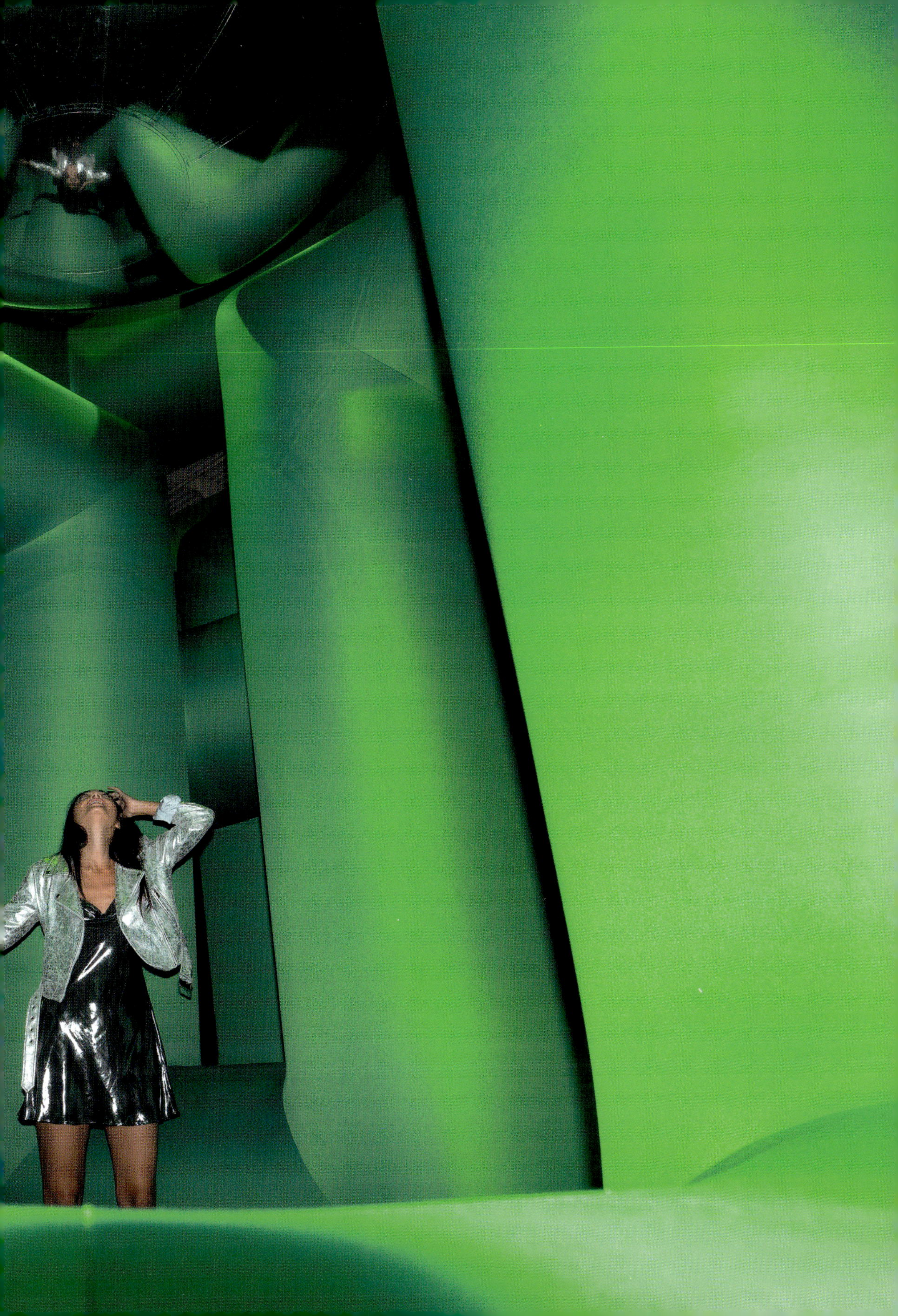

CYRIL LANCELIN

Knot

Huge installations with bright colors and impressive interactive geometric sculptures are the stylistic signature of Cyril Lancelin. *Knot*, as its title indicates, is an installation inspired by a clover knot, a primitive shape on which the three-dimensional structure is modeled; a line of which there is no perception of the beginning and the end but only of its development. The boundaries of separation created by his work lead the viewer to interact and immerse themselves, while the volume does not allow an overview of the surrounding space. What is experienced by the public is an essential component of the artist's approach: the labyrinth form stimulates him to take unknown directions, overcome possible obstacles, get lost and be surprised until he stumbles, almost by chance, on the right path. The red color, in full contrast with the environment that houses it, allows the viewers to distance themselves from their usual perceptions.

Cyril Lancelin
Knot
Balloon Museum
Pop Air
Paris, 2022
Milan, 2022
Madrid, 2023

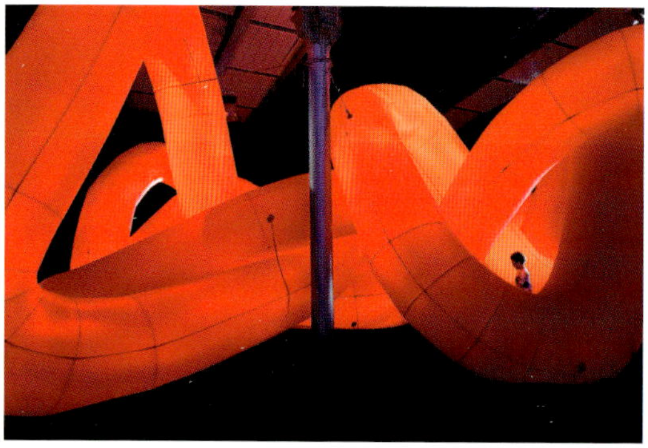

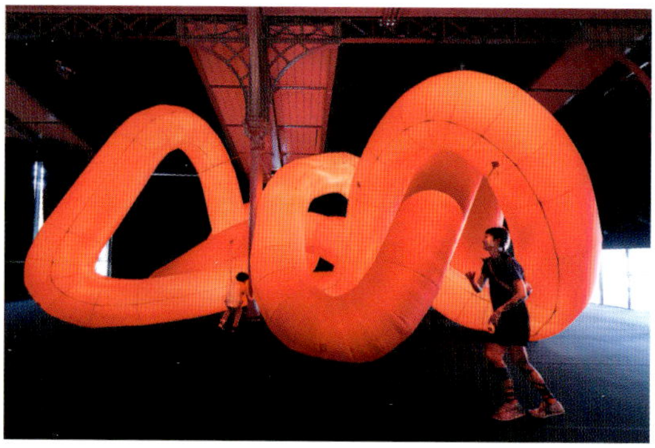

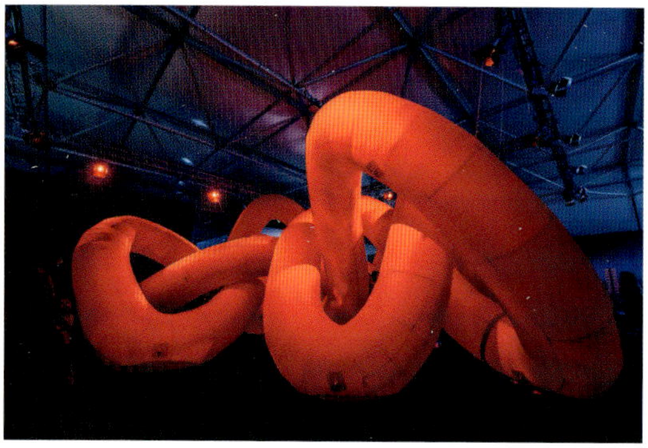

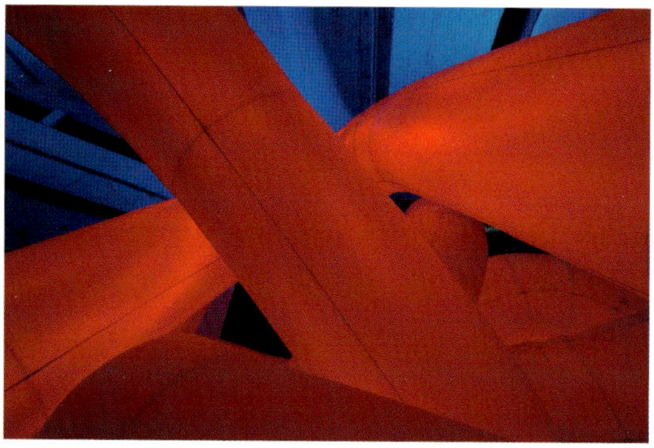

Knot 2021

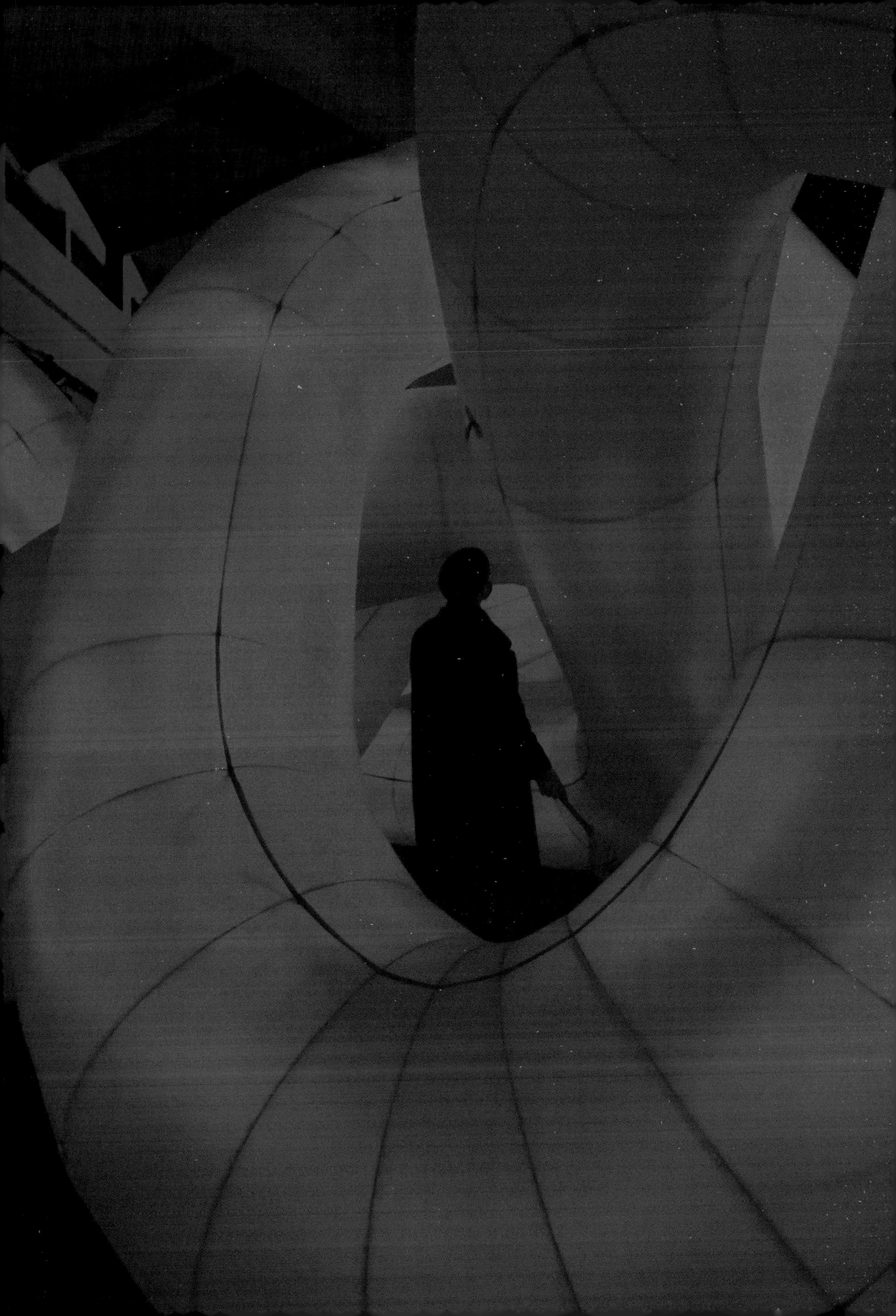

CYRIL LANCELIN

Cube Abyss
Cube Abyss is a structure designed for exploration that evokes the imagery of the ocean depths—a progression between shadows and light, encapsulating themes of discovery, close observation, and an openness to the unknown. Cyril Lancelin delves into the concept of fear, not in the traditional sense, but as an exploration of the anxiety linked to the unknown. Viewed from above, the installation takes on the form of a grid, where each space becomes a microcosm, a three-dimensional labyrinth. The inflatable element, soft to the touch, reveals itself only upon close contact, while, seen from a distance, it transforms into a grand and imposing sculpture that occupies the entire available surface. The skillful interplay of light and sound accentuates the labyrinthine atmosphere and the geometric structure. Cyril Lancelin's artwork transforms the environment into an immersive experience in which the spectator is invited to take the necessary time to explore, to sit within, navigating the voids and curves of the volume while observing the ever-evolving play of lights.

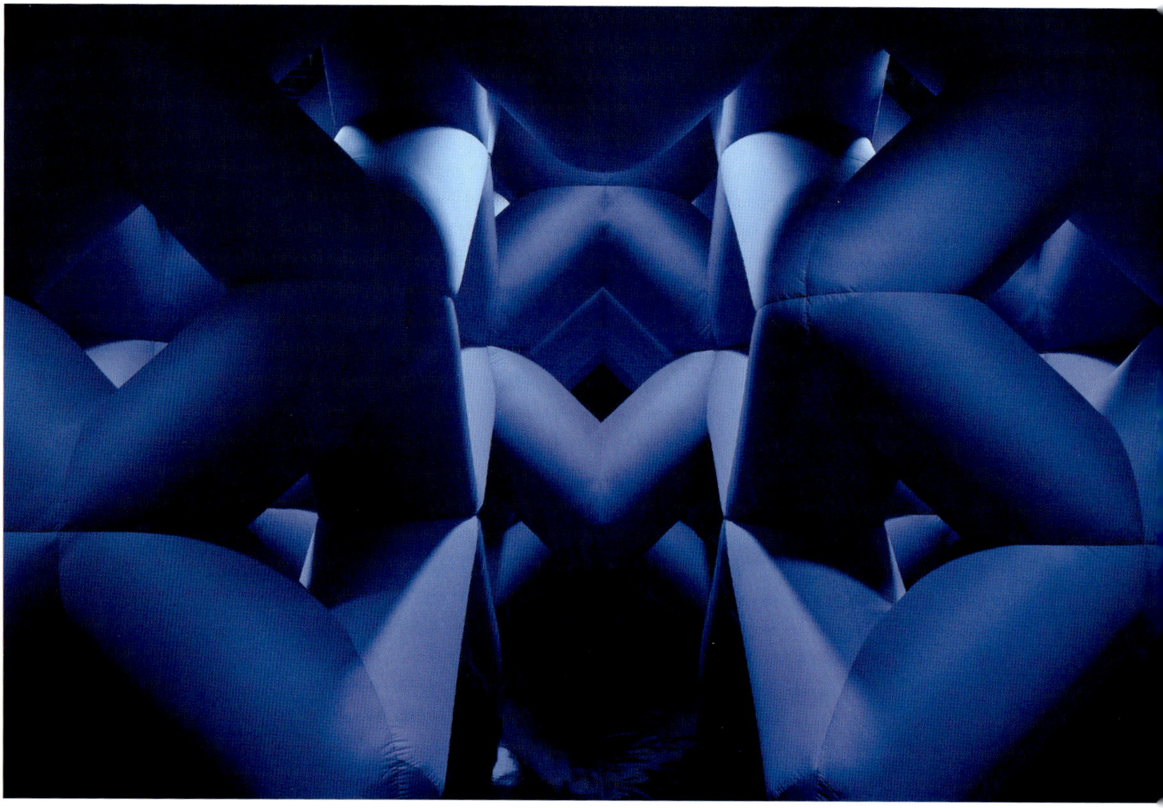

Cube Abyss 2023

Duck One Arch

Once an architect by profession, now an artist with vision, Cyril Lancelin creates colorful inflatable structures inserted in contrast to the surrounding architecture to give a new experience to the viewer. *Duck One Arch* represents all of this: a yellow inflatable winding through space with a duck head at each end. This duck, derived from the imagery of children's toys and the pop universe, is a stylized representation of the animal. For the artist, the work also becomes a representation of endangered animal species and the limits of our planet's resources, a symbol of the transformation our planet is undergoing now.

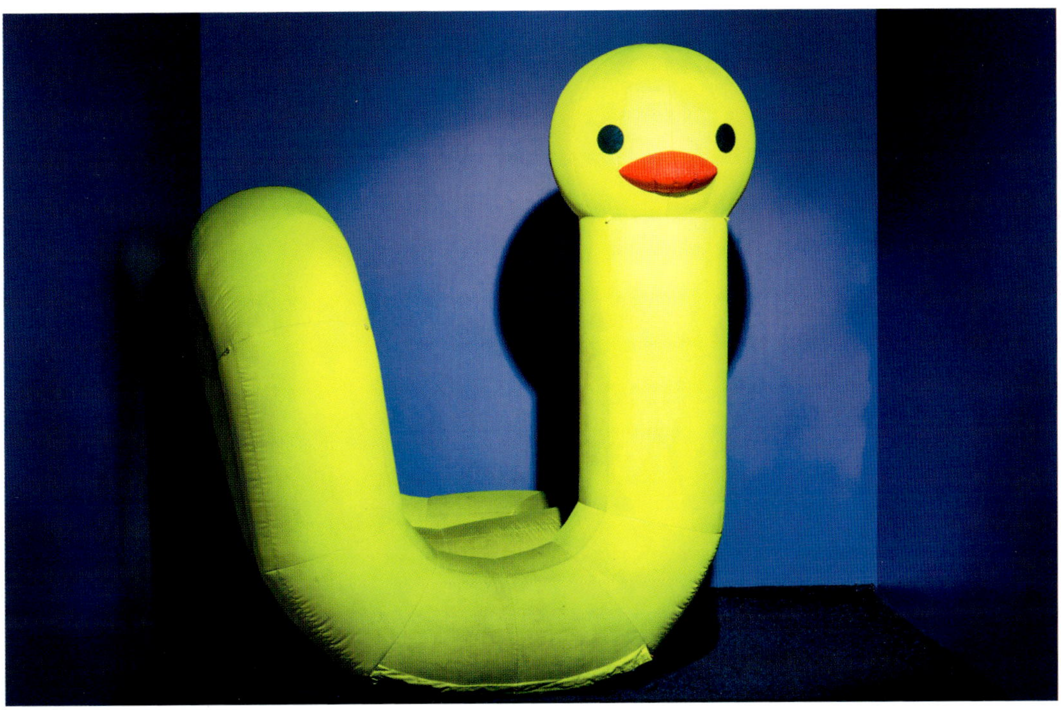

Cyril Lancelin, *Cube Abyss*
Balloon Museum, *EmotionAir*,
London, 2023

Cyril Lancelin, *Duck One Arch*
Balloon Museum, *Pop Air*
Paris, 2023

Duck One Arch 2021

MIRANDA MAKAROFF

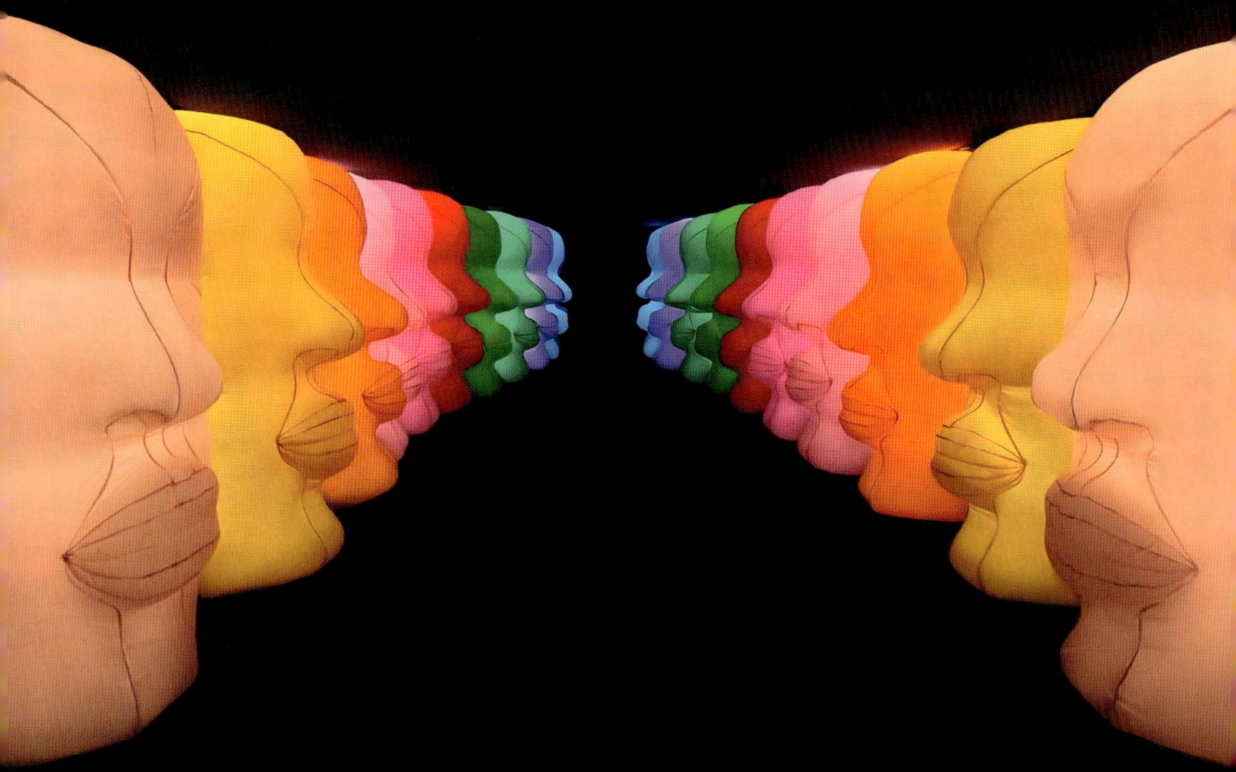

Synchronized Chaos 2023

Miranda Makaroff was born in Spain in 1984, of an Argentine father and Spanish mother, both of whom were artists, musicians, and fashion designers. This artistic milieu allowed Miranda the freedom to play and investigate various media, leading her to discover her own language, in which all the arts could coexist. A lexicon built on her multi-disciplinary interests as painter, sculptor, designer, and actress. Her work is showcased at Moco Museum Barcelona in 2023 and London in 2024, Art Basel's 2019 Miami Beach, Mirat Projects in Madrid (a solo show under the name of *Pamplemousse*), Mirat Gallery also in Madrid and in 2021 in Estudi Tur Costa, Ibiza, Spain. Makaroff's work moves between the theatrical and playfulness of the outer world and the solemnity of the inner. She unabashedly celebrates women—all the while, exploring a visual universe without restrictions or preconceived principles, giving way to a vastly diverse palette, all sharing the common denominator, of vivid color and tongue-in-cheek humor.

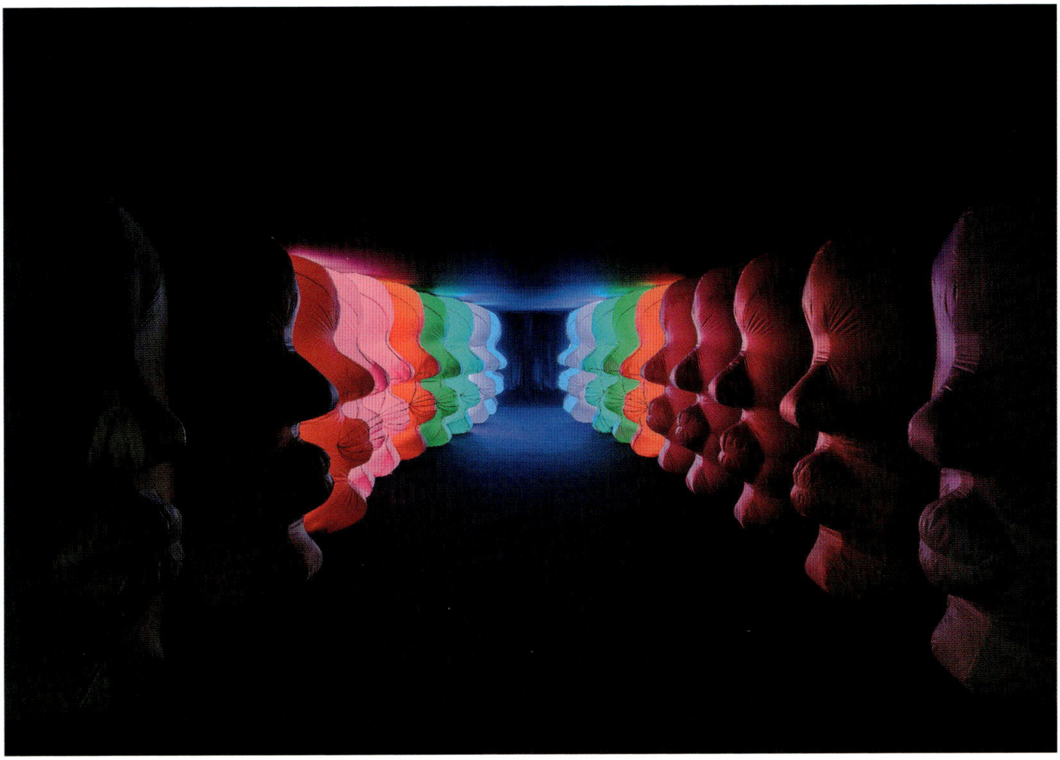

Miranda Makaroff
Synchronized Chaos
Balloon Museum
EmotionAir
London, 2023

Overleaf
Miranda Makaroff
with her artwork
Synchronized Chaos
Balloon Museum
EmotionAir
London, 2023

Synchronized Chaos

A vivid universe, inhabited by a diverse array of characters with myriad personalities, *Synchronized Chaos* is the creation of Spanish artist Miranda Makaroff for *EmotionAir*. Along an infinite corridor, the repetition of brightly colored faces unfolds, becoming, for the artist, eloquent symbols of human existence and the intrinsic complexity of our minds. At the heart of this captivating scenario lies the central theme of the artwork: self-awareness and the journey of individual growth. Venturing along the darkness of the corridor, the visitor finds themselves enveloped solely by the luminous expressions of the characters. This face-to-face encounter creates a direct confrontation, almost like engaging in a continuous dialogue with the voices that inhabit our minds. The emotion selected by the artist is self-confidence and the ability to evolve, transforming every obstacle into a positive opportunity for growth. The sensory experience thus becomes an emotional journey, inviting the audience to immerse themselves in the intricate narrative of *Synchronized Chaos*.

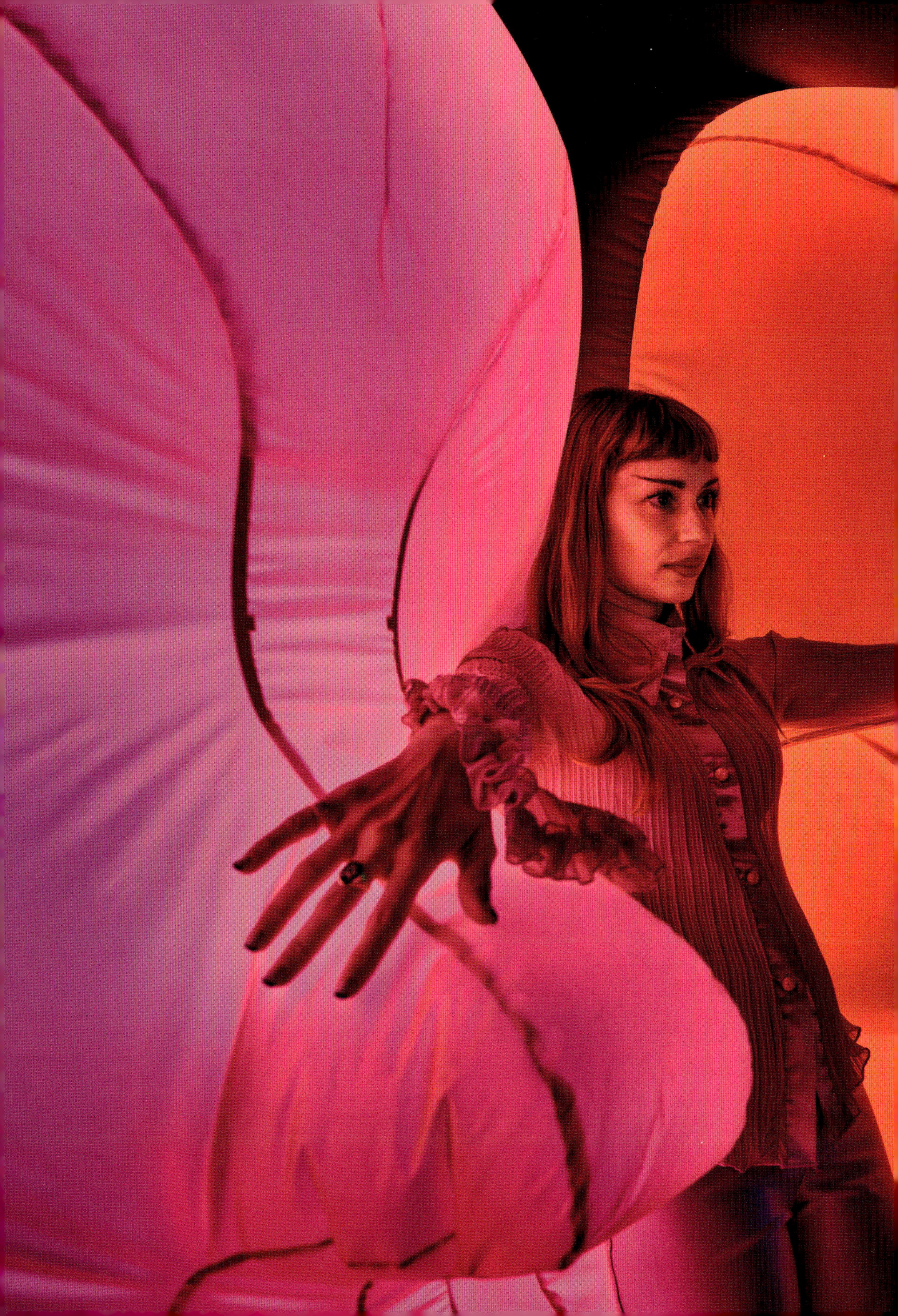

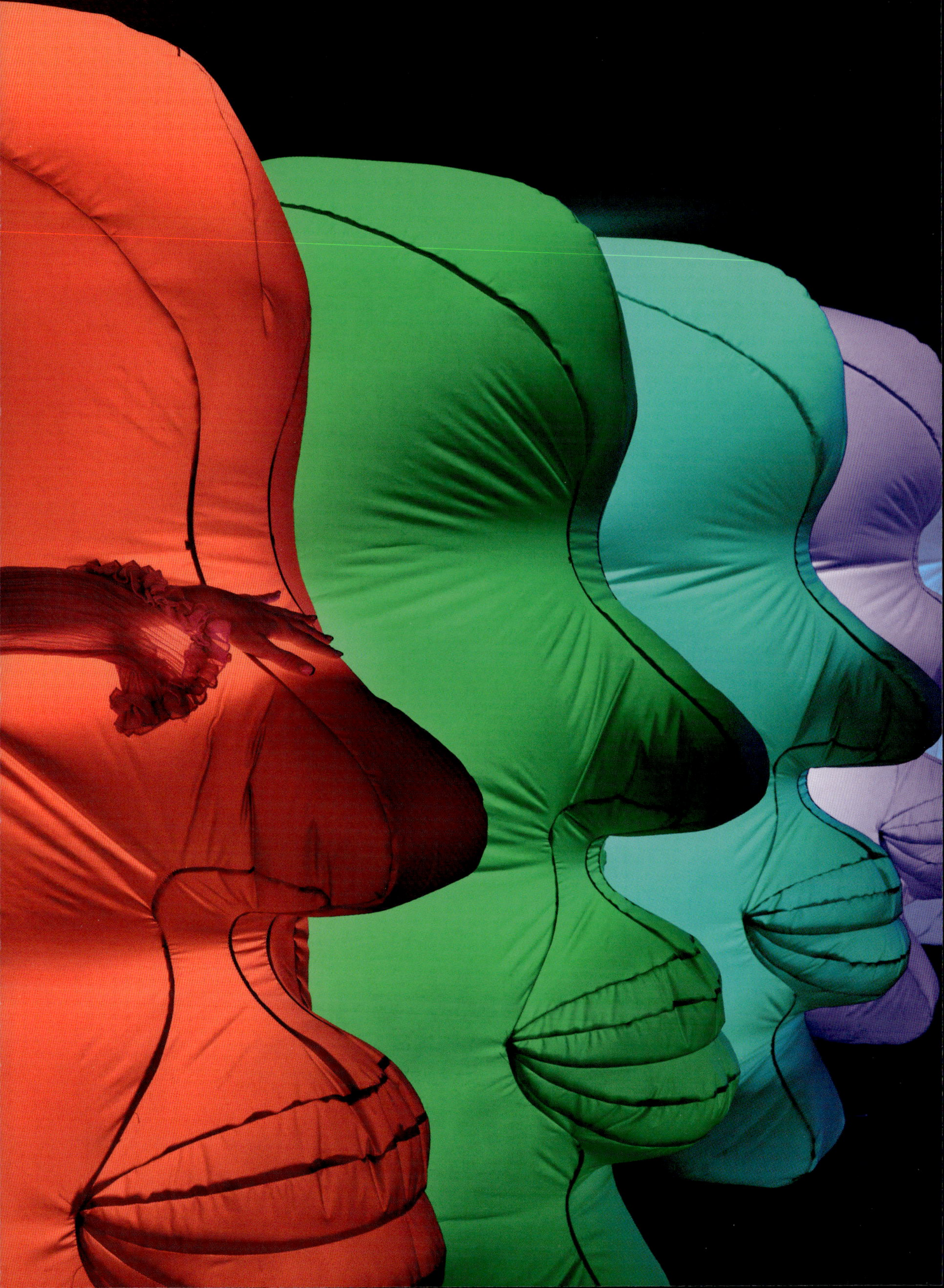

STEVE MESSAM

Steve Messam is an environmental artist based in County Durham, UK. His ephemeral site-specific installations re-imagine the every day, interrupting historical landscapes and vacant architecture to help us perceive the familiar environment in a new way. Messam's works seek to explore and uncover the layers of narrative within the rural environment, frequently drawing on existing uses of the land and reflecting an understanding of the geological, cultural, and agricultural practices already being used to shape the landscape. Working on a scale that is typically "bigger than a house," his works explore the color and scale of place. Messam created the first off-site installation at the 2006 Shanghai Biennial followed by a number of site-specific installations across the Venetian Lagoon during the 2009 Venice Biennale. In 2021 he was recognized as Visual Artist of the Year at the Newcastle Journal Culture Awards.

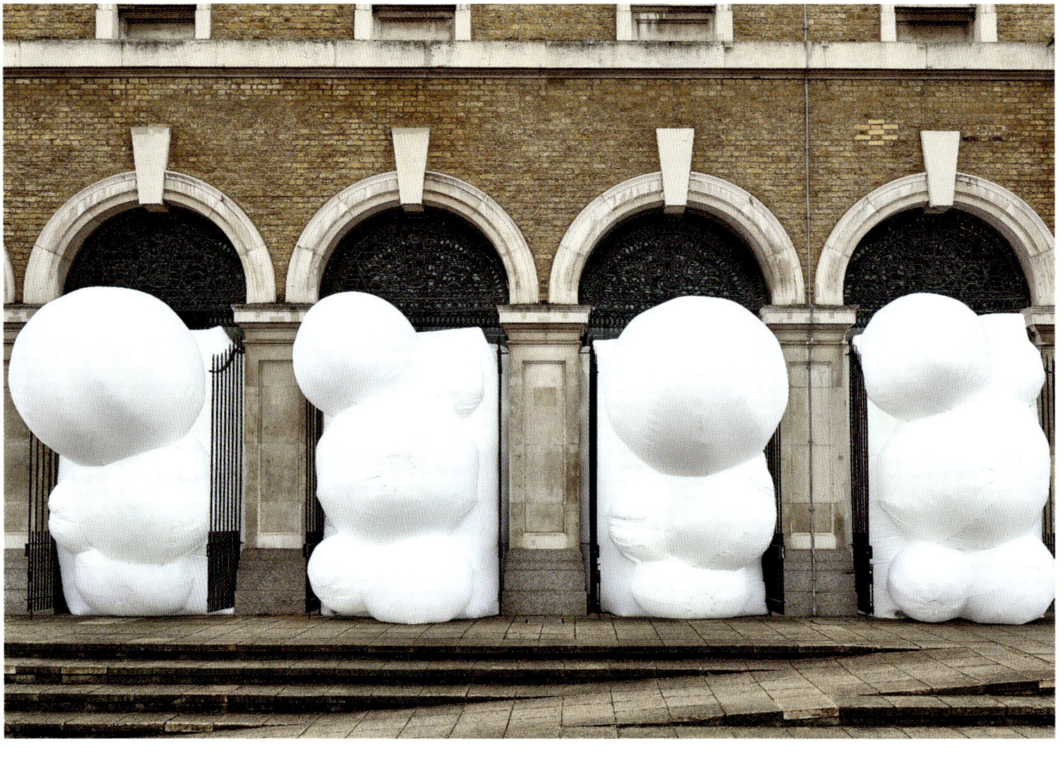

Façade

With *Façade*, the artist presents a site-specific work designed for the entrance of Old Billingsgate. This installation fully embodies Messam's artistic exploration, uniquely interacting with the surrounding environment and architecture, delving into themes of transitoriness and the relationship between art and landscape. The white and the irregularity of the piece contrast sharply with the colors of the façade and its strong architectural symmetry. The rounded and inflatable forms seem to emerge assertively from the arches with the public invited to contemplate this transformation. Messam appears to transform the entrance with an installation that goes beyond mere esthetics, challenging convention and prompting a deeper reflection on the relationship between artistic creation and architectural surroundings. *Façade* becomes an emanation of Messam's artistic vision, inviting observers to explore new perspectives and contemplate the meaning and purpose of art in the urban context.

Here and overleaf
Steve Messam
Façade
Balloon Museum
EmotionAir
London, 2023

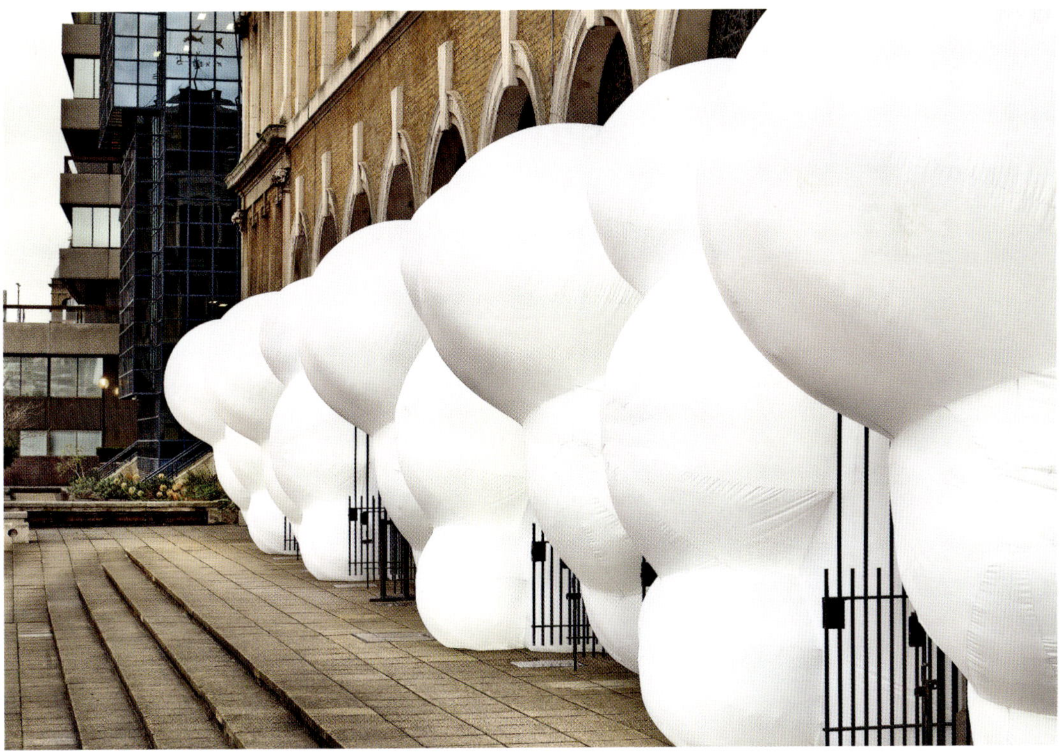

STEVE MESSAM

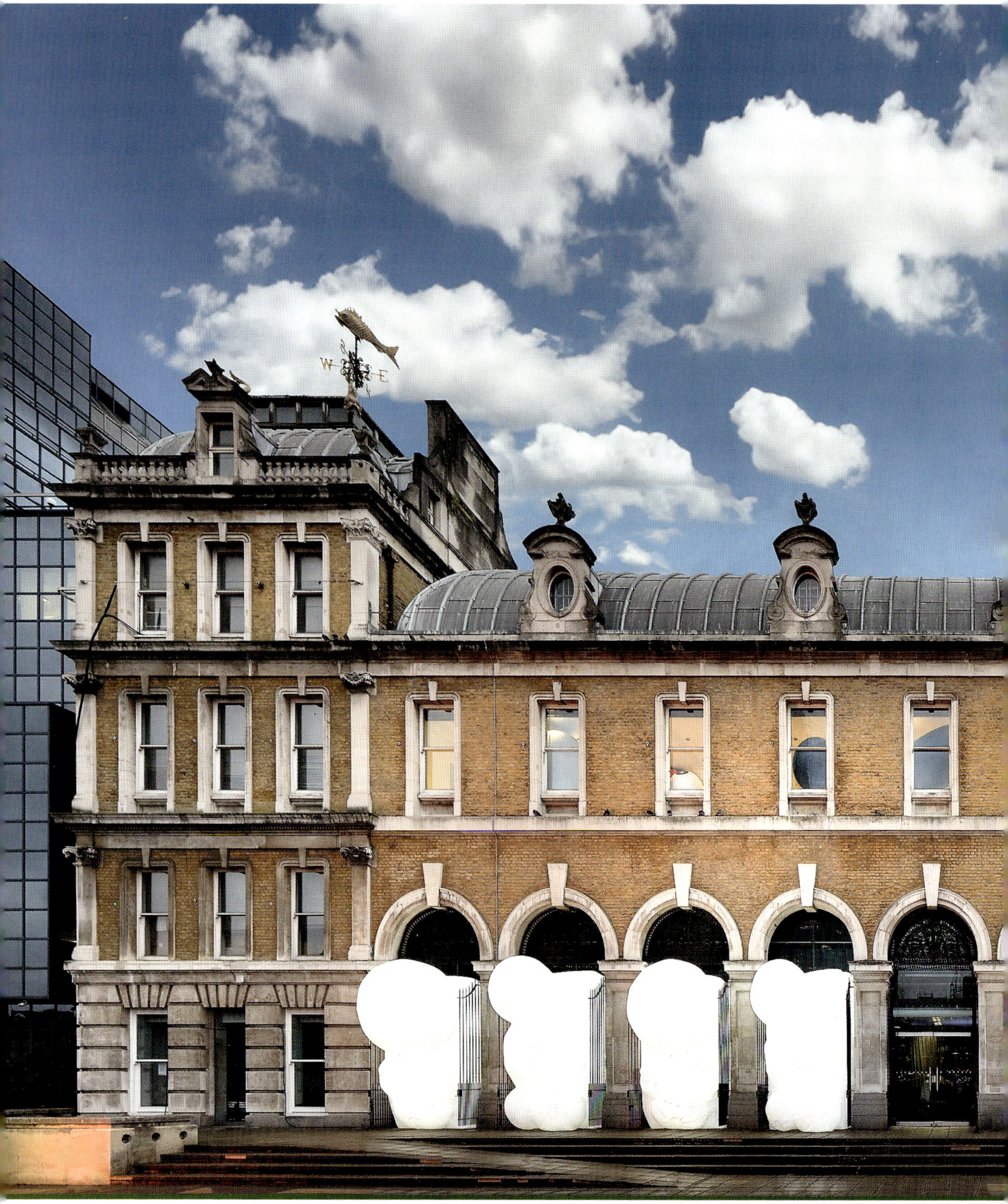

Façade 2023

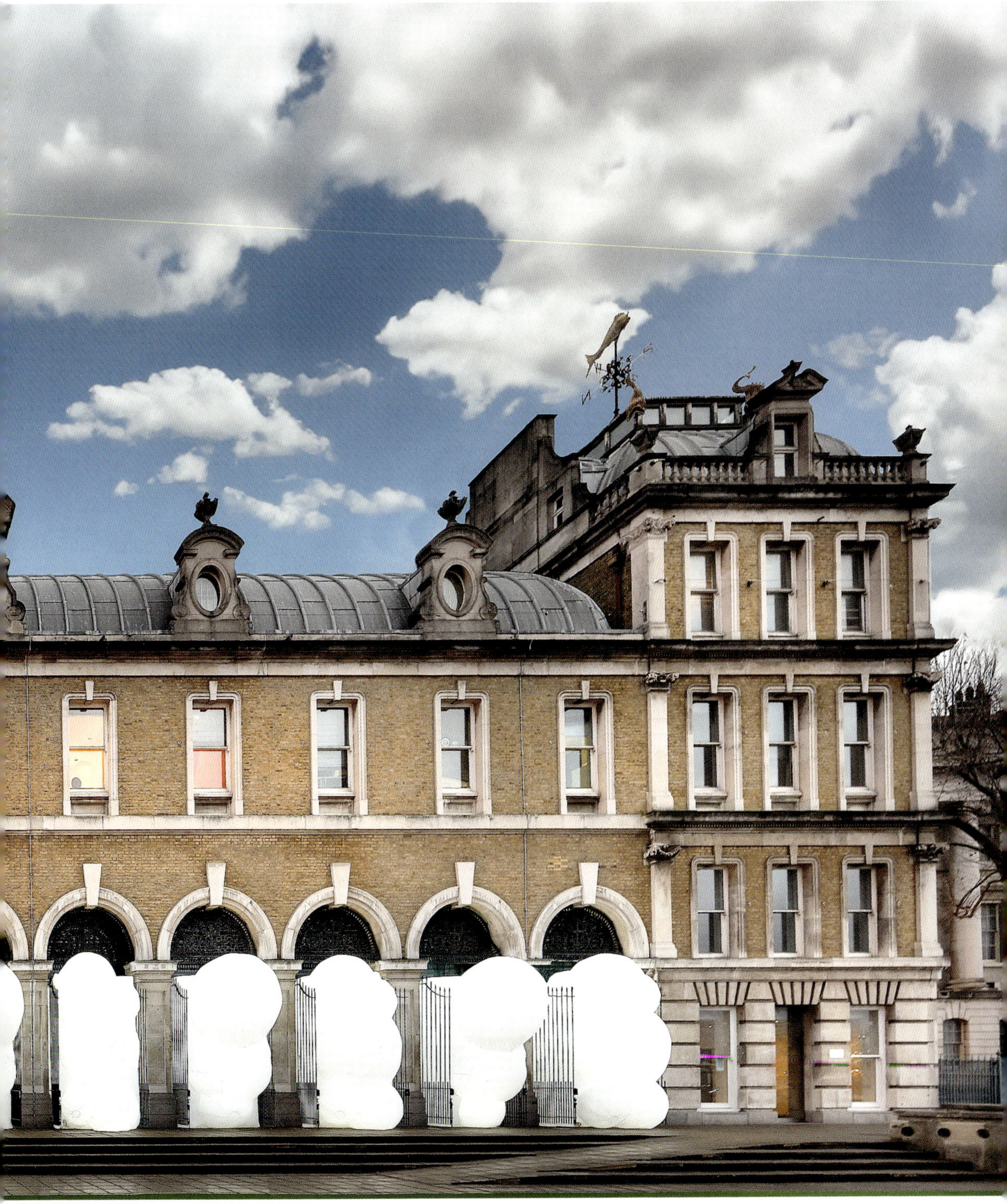

MOTOREFISICO

MOTOREFISICO is a project born in 2015 from the collaboration between designer and architect duo Lorenzo Pagliara and Gianmaria Zonfrillo. The project encompasses three distinct facets: Street Art, interior design, and audiovisual installations. The artistic activity of MOTOREFISICO is characterized at every level by abstract composition, geometric lines, often monochromatic tones, the organized arrangement of elements, and strong optical and kinetic influences. Over the years, the work of the Roman duo has expanded worldwide, from the USA to South Korea, from Russia to across the European continent. The contexts vary widely, ranging from exhibitions such as the Balloon Museum or the Blooming Festival to commissions for brands like Zalando, British American Tobacco, and Under Armour. MOTOREFISICO's expertise is frequently applied in the setup of large events such as the Formula E or the Commonwealth Games in the United Kingdom.

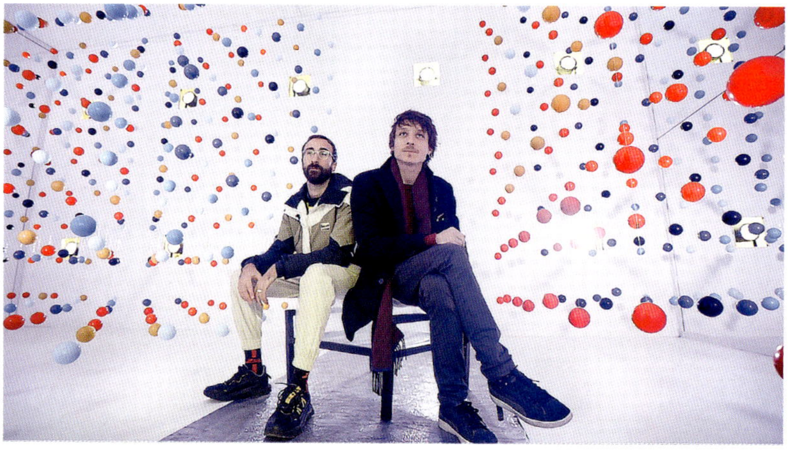

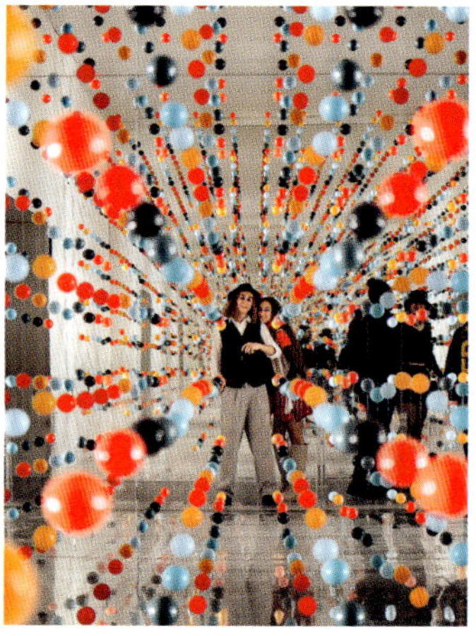

Above
Gianmaria Zonfrillo and Lorenzo Pagliara of MOTOREFISICO
Balloon Museum
Pop Air
Rome, 2021

Right and opposite
MOTOREFISICO
Never Ending Story
Balloon Museum
Pop Air
Rome, 2021
Madrid, 2023

Never Ending Story 2021

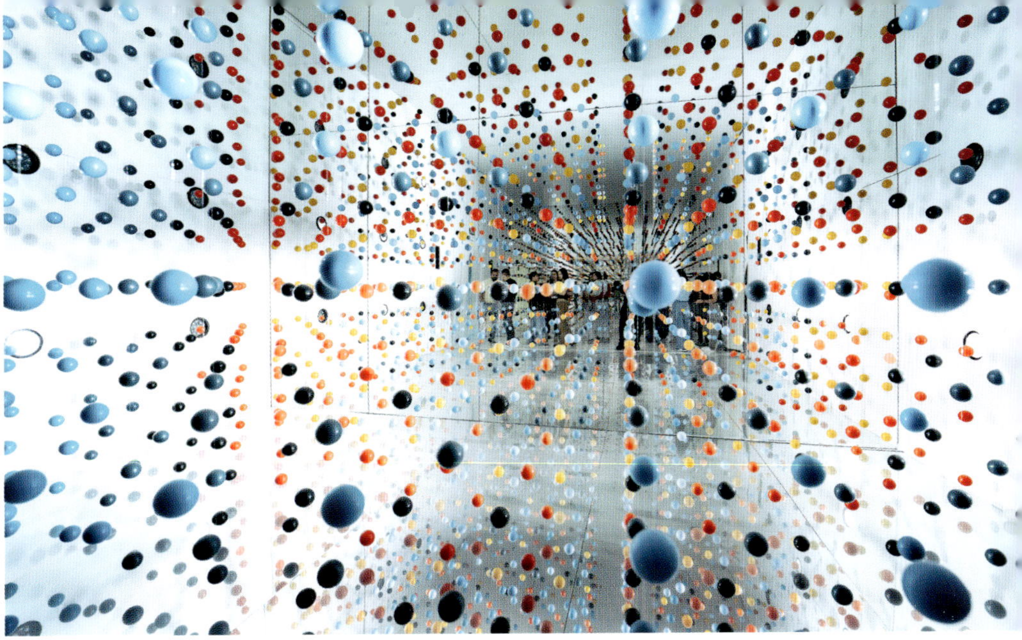

Never Ending Story
MOTOREFISICO transports us to a realm where traditional spatial cues are lost, and the observer becomes fully immersed in a multifaceted universe. Here, everything appears suspended and motionless, with human presence as the sole source of movement.
Never Ending Story is a captivatingly optical, immersive installation that capitalizes on the reflection between two mirrored surfaces, conjuring an infinite tunnel. Within this room, some 2700 colorfully suspended balls give the illusion of floating in mid-air, effectively enrolling spectators as integral components of the artwork as they step into the space. Appearances can be deceiving, as a comprehensive light and sound performance transforms the environment, ushering in an unexpected energy to the space and altering its perception.

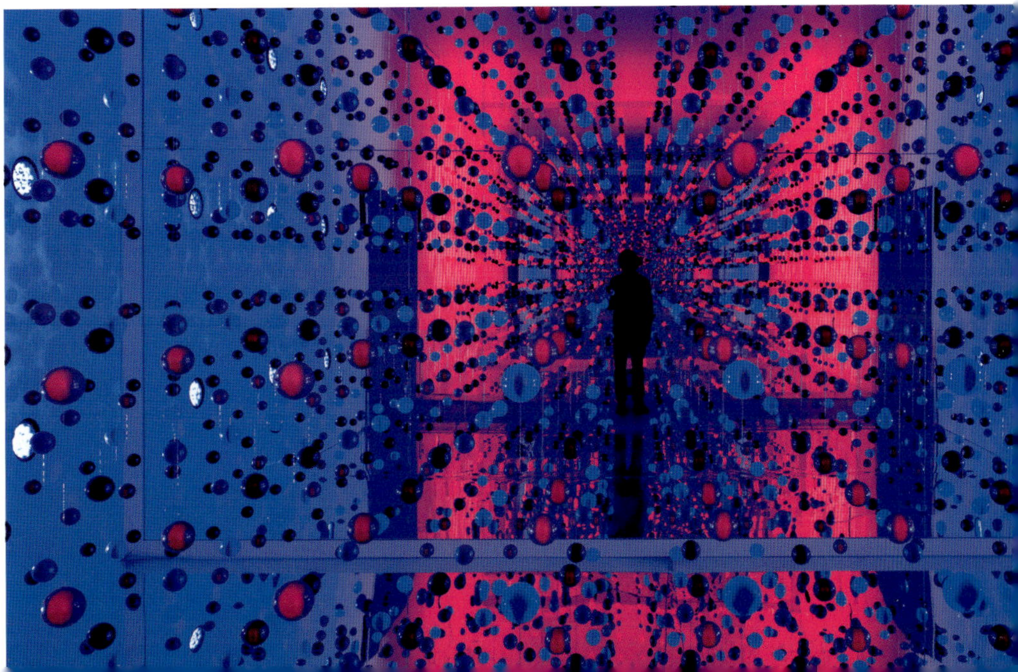

MOTOREFISICO

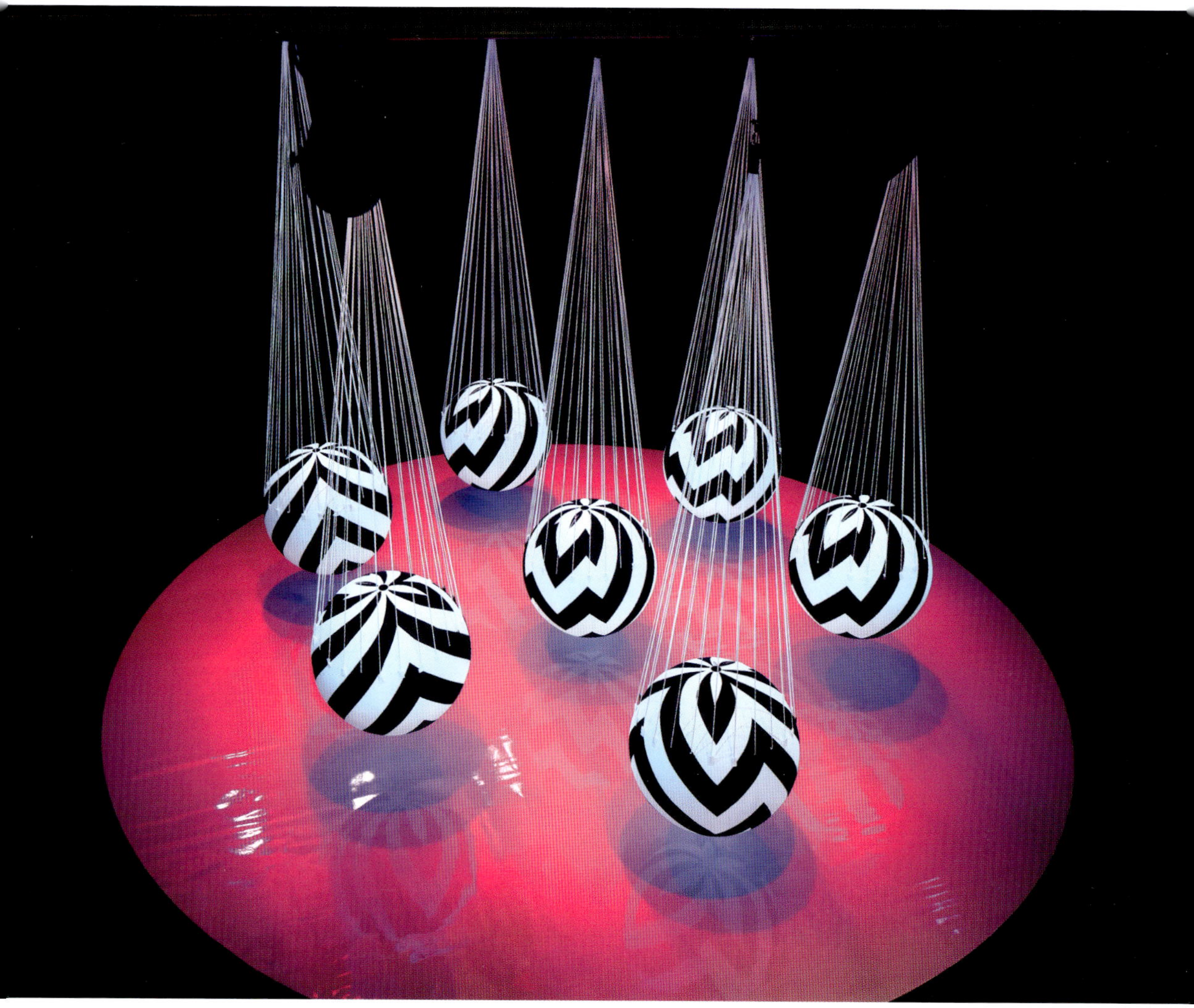

MOTOREFISICO
Swing
Balloon Museum
EmotionAir
London, 2023

Swing 2023

Swing

From the conceptualization of the physical system of the conical pendulum, MOTOREFISICO presents their new work *Swing* for the *EmotionAir* exhibition. This installation, composed of a series of spheres suspended from the ceiling, comes to life through engaging interaction with the audience. The spheres move in space, bouncing and spinning vortex-like, creating a dynamic and captivating play environment. The spectator is an integral part of the artwork, encouraged to move freely in the surrounding space, causing the spheres to oscillate, potentially colliding with others in motion. The connection between the visitor and the artwork becomes a moment of mutual trust, where active participation translates into a collective dance of spheres capturing the essence of the human experience. In this context, *Swing* is not just an installation but an interactive platform that explores the delicate balance between trust, movement, and the joyful unpredictability of human interaction.

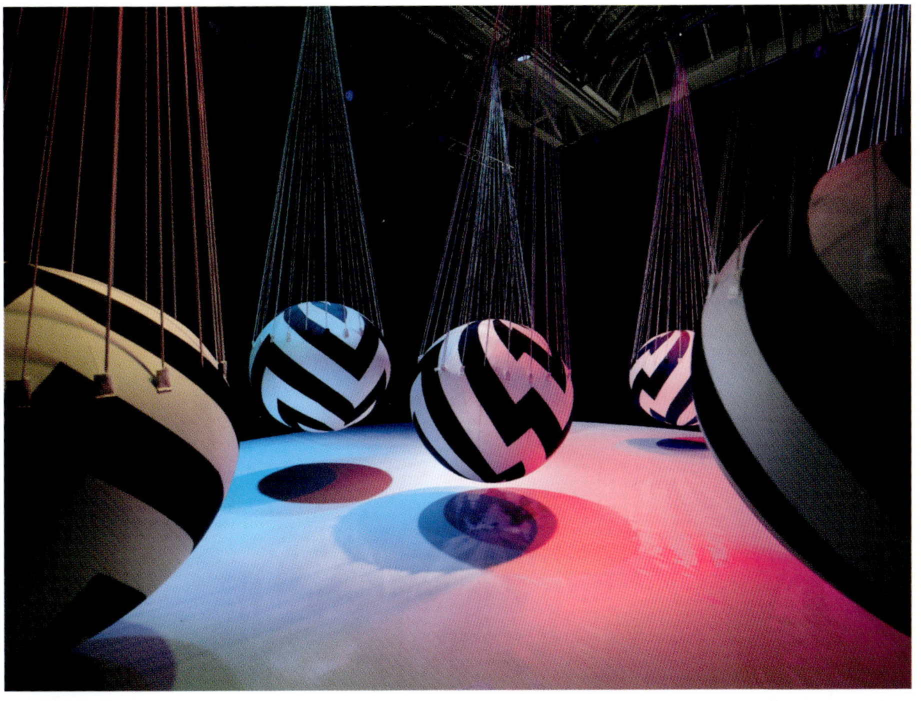

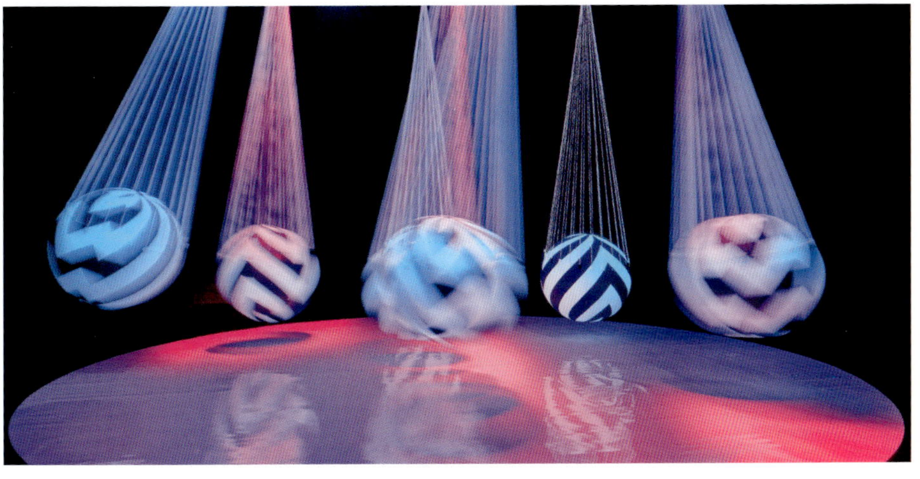

MOTOMICHI NAKAMURA

Japanese-born, award-winning digital artist and animator based in Croton On Hudson, NY, Motomichi Nakamura graduated from Parsons School of Design in New York. He is a versatile multimedia artist and designer, renowned for his extensive work ranging from Video Art to installations. Nakamura is known for the use of black, white, and red, as well as monsters created with minimalist graphic elements inspired by cryptozoology and mythology. He has exhibited worldwide in numerous museums and galleries including the New Museum in New York, Moscow Contemporary Art Center Winzavod, MARCO in Monterrey Mexico, Olympia Park Munich, Maison de la culture du Japon à Paris, and La Gaîté Lyrique. His animated films have been screened at the Sundance Film Festival, Onedotzero Festival, and Edinburgh International Film Festival and his recent film *Okami* won in The Leeds International Film Festival. Commercially, he has worked on projects for clients such as EA, MTV, USA Networks, and Sony, and produced music videos for artists including Nicola Cruz and the Swedish band The Knife which earned him international recognition.

Motomichi Nakamura
Cannonballs
Balloon Museum
EmotionAir
London, 2023

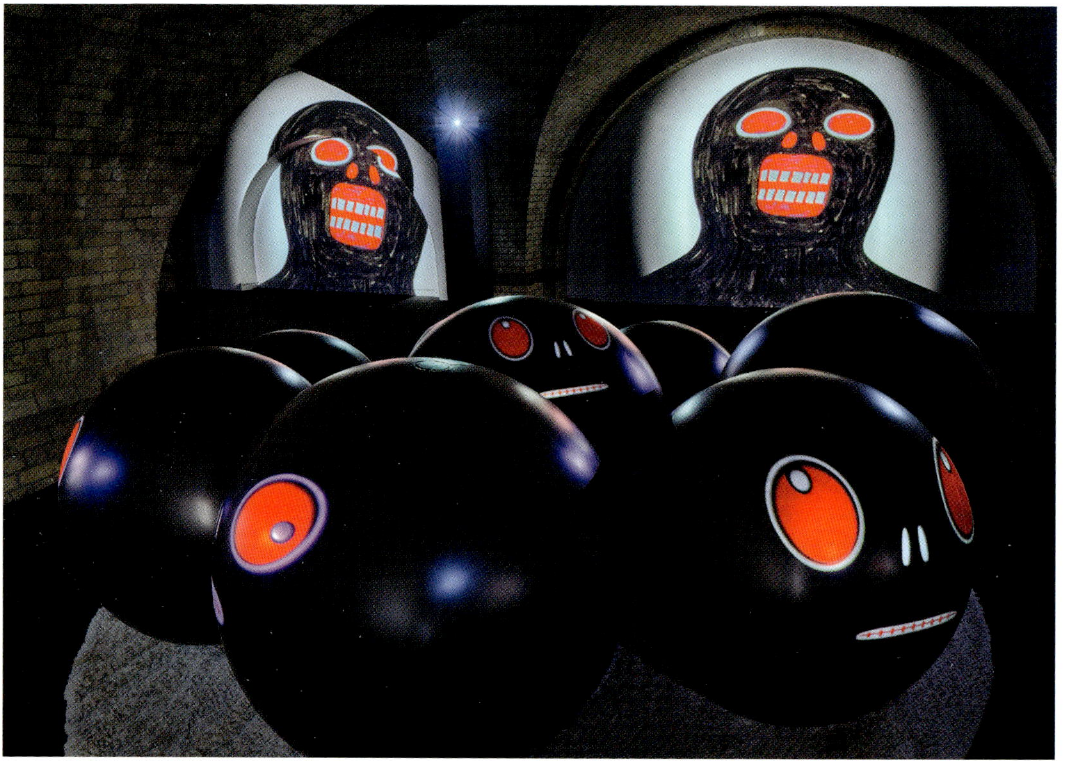

Cannonballs 2021

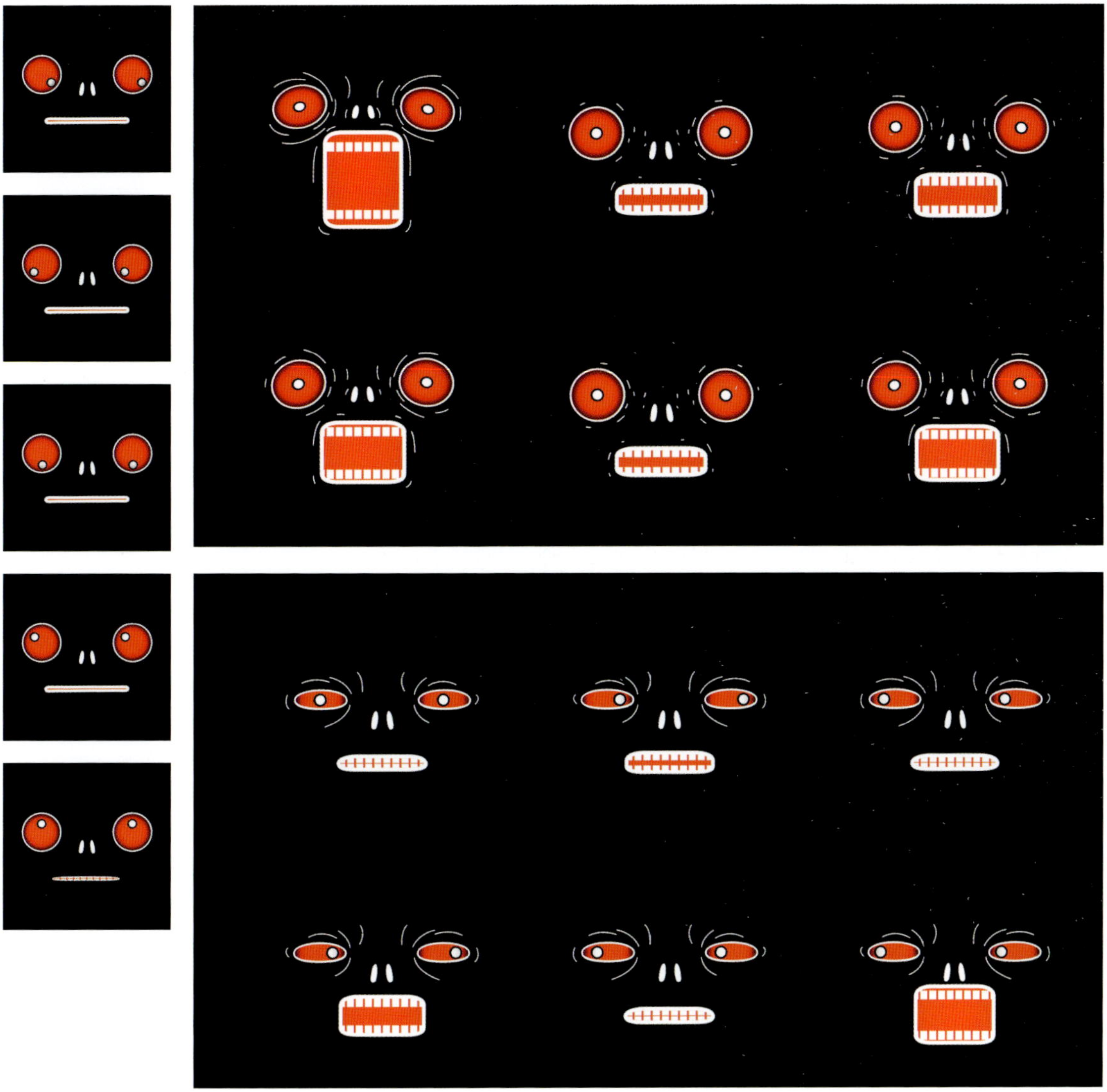

Still frames from video projection of *Cannonballs* Balloon Museum *EmotionAir* London, 2023

Cannonballs

Motomichi Nakamura's artistic versatility is epitomized in his piece titled *Cannonballs*; the paradoxical nature of inflatables as an artistic medium, filled with weightless air, yet capable of creating a substantial sense of presence and weight. The centerpiece of this installation consists of eight large balloons portraying the faces of imaginary monsters, varying in degrees of menace. These faces are accompanied by the projection of other ominous characters onto the surrounding walls.

Nakamura aims for the characters he creates to be nuanced entities and multifaceted creatures that can be simultaneously monstrous and enchanting, conflictual and playful. We can perceive Motomichi's work as if it were a mirror, reflecting upon ourselves as we examine how we perceive his characters that gaze back at us. It is up to the audience to ponder the reason for their presence and the intentions of these creatures. The answers to these questions unveil the myriad meanings encapsulated in Motomichi's characters, offering a fascinating perspective on the complexity of our interactions with the world created by the artist.

OUCHHH

Based in Istanbul, Turkey, Ouchhh is an international digital design studio specializing in data sculpture and immersive experiences. They collaborate with institutions and festivals from around the world. Ouchhh's interdisciplinary expertise covers graphic design, motion design and monumental digital projections. The collective has created approximately 60 public art projects for every continent. Their studio works have received multiple accolades and awards in the international arena such as Red Dot Design Best of the Best Award, German Design Award, Iconic Best of the Best Award, MUSE Awards in the USA, the 10th Annual IDA Awards The International Design Awards in LA, Asia Design Award in Seoul, Korea, and ADC Awards The Art Directors Club in NY, CODAwards, and the AVIXA Awards in Las Vegas to name a few. Today, the collective works with partners based in Los Angeles, Vienna, Barcelona, Paris, London, and Berlin.

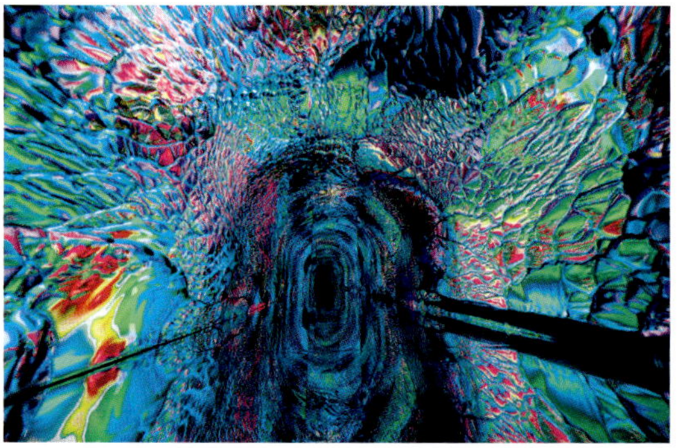

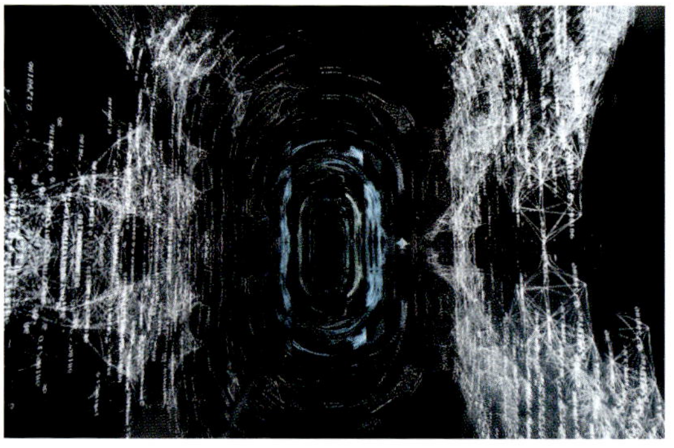

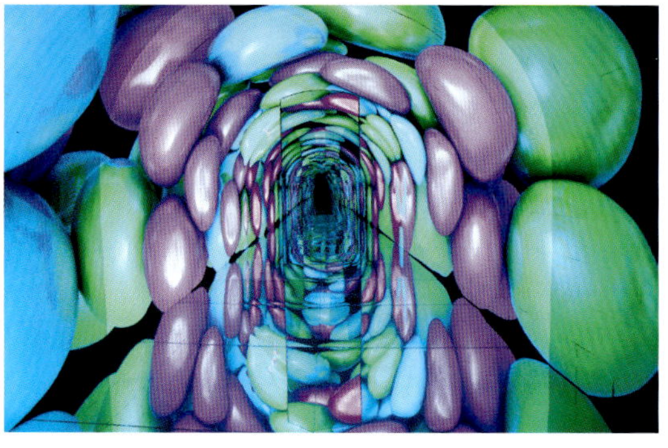

Ouchhh
AI DATA PORTAL
Balloon Museum
Let's Fly
New York, 2023

AI DATA PORTAL 2023

AI DATA PORTAL

This artwork is an immersive tunnel of LED screens. With this installation, the Ouchhh collective makes use of millions of pieces of data from the cities visited by the exhibition. Excel spreadsheets, documents and graphs disappear in favor of abstract, hypnotizing digital forms. The collective engages in Data Art: the creation of works generated from data such as statistics, flows and inventories. Information in all its dimensions, which is typically hidden or incomprehensible, is transformed into projected images.

This is an artistic trend developed with the aim of producing and offering sensations to visitors. Entering *AI DATA PORTAL* is like plunging into Plato's allegory of the cave, where sunlight doesn't exist and truth is solely projected onto walls. Despite the artifice, it's hard to look away from this impressive spectacle.

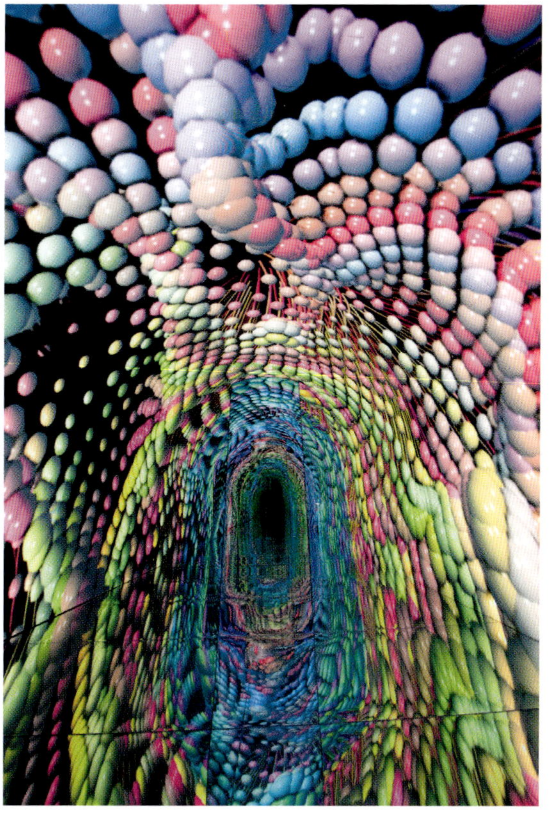

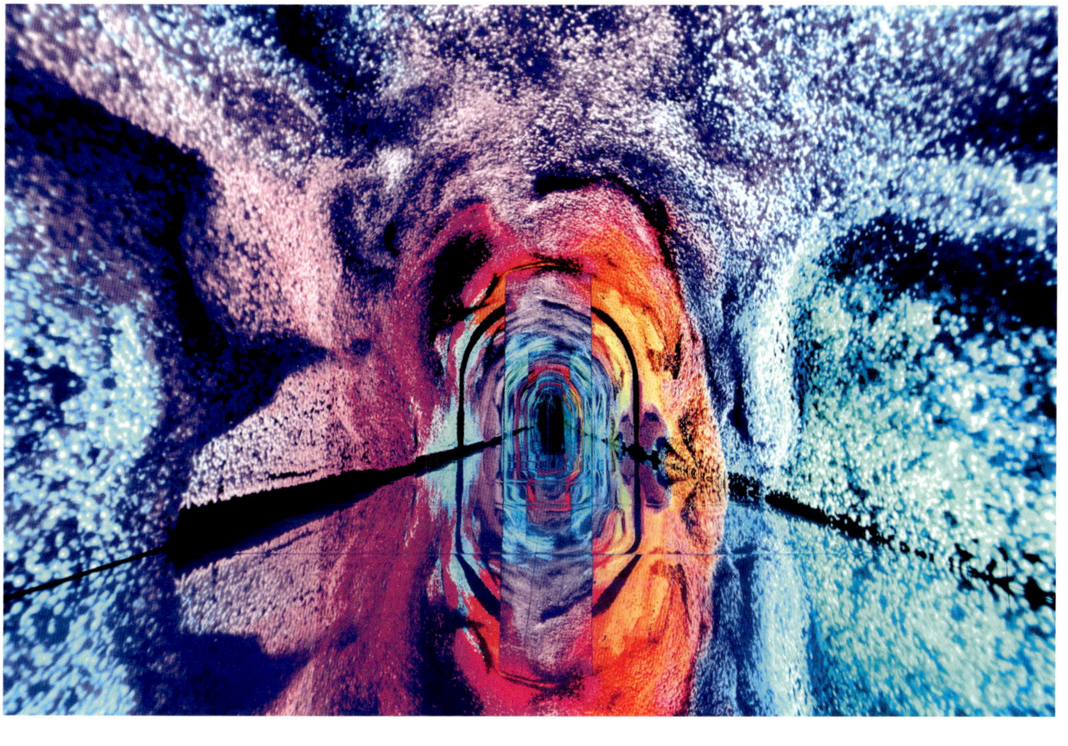

PENIQUE PRODUCTIONS

Penique Productions is an art project founded in Barcelona in 2007 that focuses its research on site-specific, inflatable, and ephemeral installations. Since 2008, Penique Productions has also operated from Rio de Janeiro, Brazil, and in 2009, the group won first prize at the Cerka'l Festival in Piera, Barcelona with *La Capella* installation. From there the group's diverse installations range from sites like the Market State Project with *18 Clocktower Place*, an initiative in response to the proposed demolition of the Market State Residential complex in London; a patio in an old monastery in Mexico; an arts school palace, with a pool, in Rio de Janeiro; or transforming a tattoo shop, *Box 33*. In 2023, Penique Productions took over the space at 103 Avenue Champs-Élysées for the Louis Vuitton Spring-Summer show during Paris Fashion Week, using a two-tone orange inflatable, the largest the artists had attempted to date.

Far left
Artist
Sergi Arbusà of Penique Productions with Francesco Dobrovich, Head of Art and Curation of Balloon Museum
Balloon Museum
Pop Air
Rome, 2021

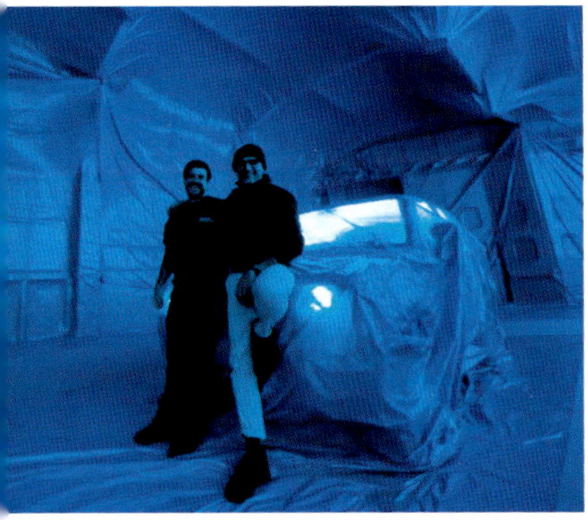

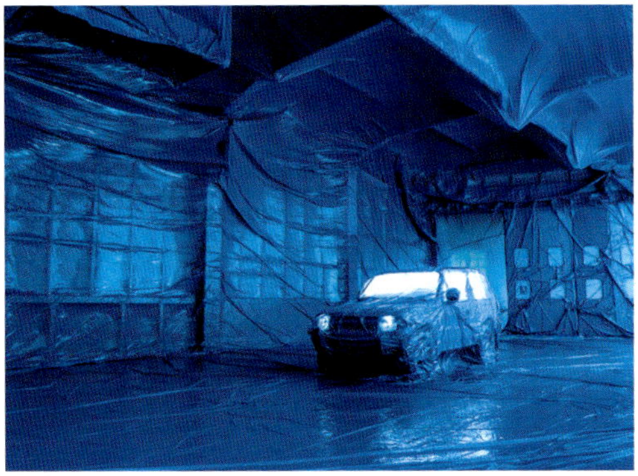

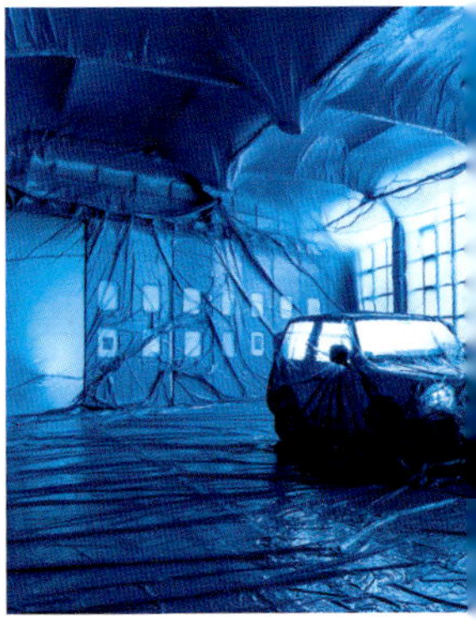

Deposito Vittoria
The first installation created for Balloon Museum, *Deposito Vittoria,* debuted in Rome in 2021. The space, conquered by the inflatable, is transformed by a new light, a new texture, and a new monochromatic color. Blue plastic envelops every visible surface in the room, casting a blue hue over everything, including the ground, walls, ceiling, and even a parked car. As visitors explore this altered environment, the car's lights illuminate, bathing the space in a deep glow. The title chosen is meant to recall the previous life of the work's location—in the past the exhibition space was a bus depot for the city of Rome's public transport company.

Penique Productions
Deposito Vittoria
Balloon Museum
Pop Air
Rome, 2021

Deposito Vittoria 2021

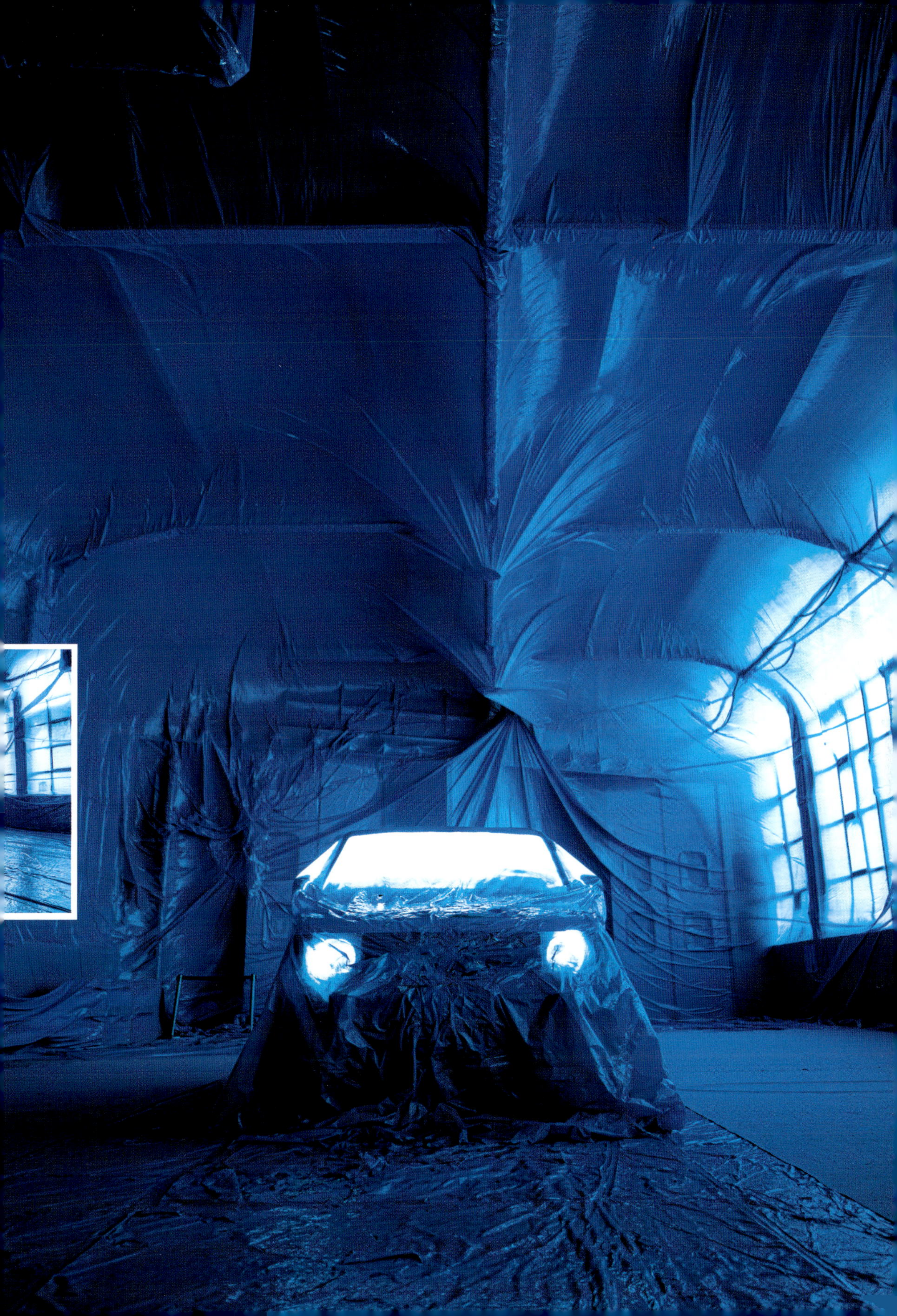

PENIQUE PRODUCTIONS

For Penique Productions, the room is a pretext for reflecting the way we interact with space. Always site-specific, the monochromatic plastic shell covers the interiors with the help of fans, appropriating the space and modifying its perception. Covering the room and making it “unusable” reveals the essence of spatiality and being present in space, disorienting those who cross it. Made of a light plastic, the “balloon” grows and expands as the air becomes the supporting structure and forces the inflatable to enlarge, consuming everything in its path. The viewer is transported through sensory experience to an environment that is both familiar and new at the same time. Having lost its original function, the site is given a new identity. The balloon acts as a barrier from multiple realities—framing and creating a new space—like a container, it confuses the concept of an object of art. Each work is temporary and aims to enhance the architecture that hosts it and at the same time tell its story.

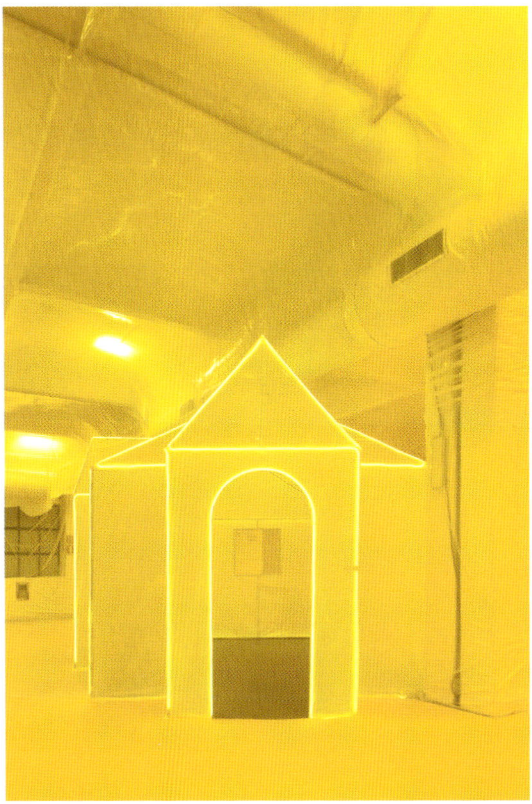

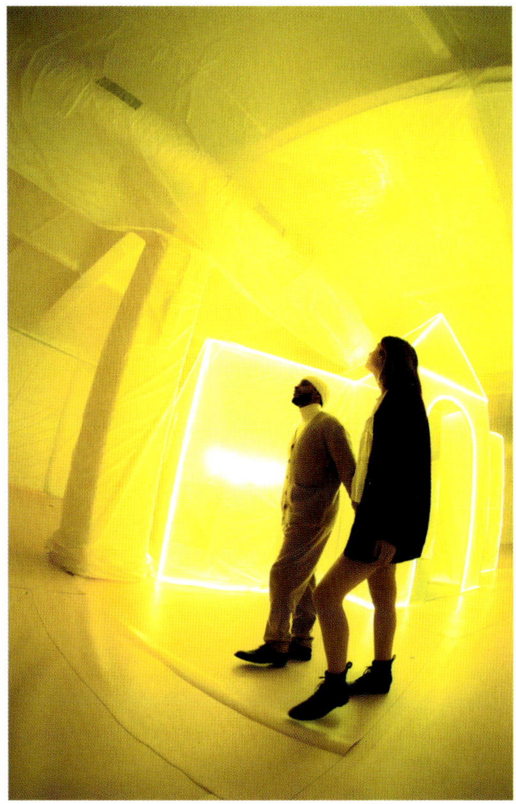

Giallo 368
With *Giallo 368*, the artists want to pay homage to the history of design in the city of Milan by inducing the viewer to reflect on the contemporary development of this artistic practice. Constructed from yellow plastic and uniquely designed for the Superstudio Più loft space, this installation guides viewers by a structure made of the same material. Adorning the structure, a LED-lit quote poses the question, “Who are we designing for?”. The experience is designed to prompt reflection on the motivations and goals of design.

Penique Productions
Giallo 368
Balloon Museum
Pop Air
Milan, 2022

Giallo 368 2022

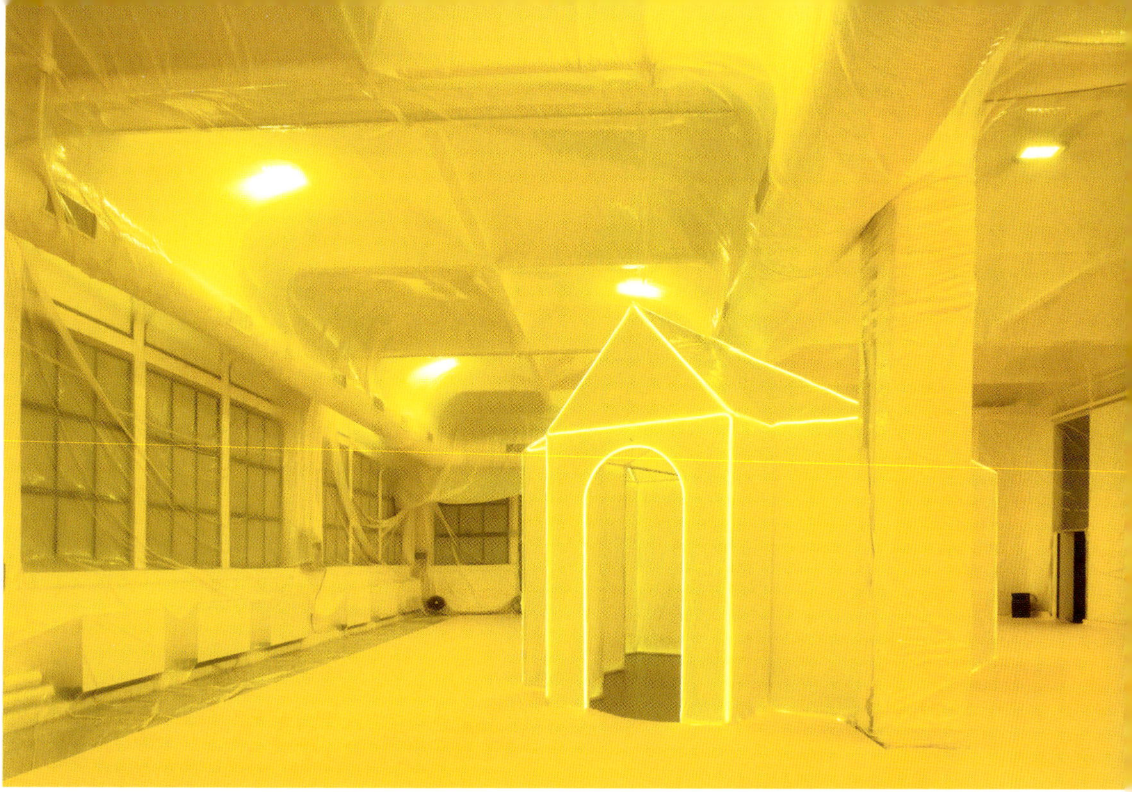

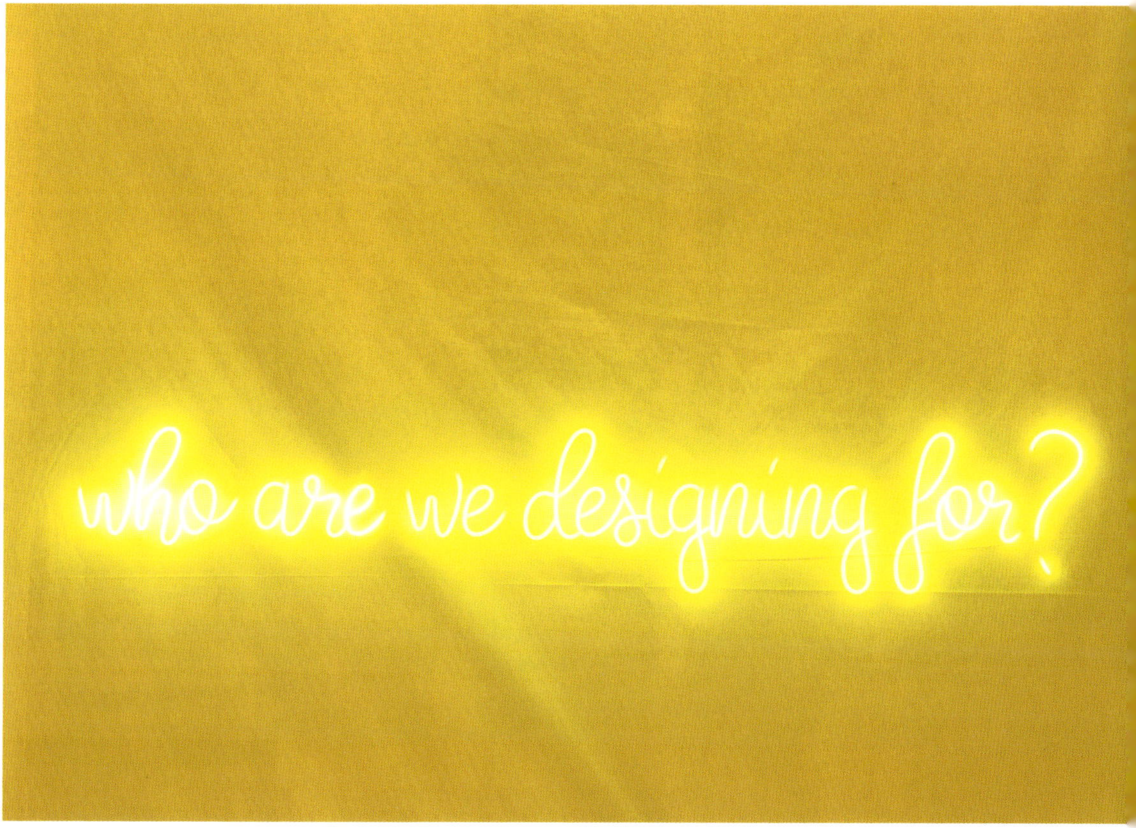
who are we designing for?

Rosâtre

This artwork was created for the *Pop Air* exhibition presented in Paris at La Villette in 2022. The architecture of the Grande Halle disappears to better reveal itself, covered by a layer of pink monochromatic plastic and by long LED wires. The work *Rosâtre*, with its evocative title drawing attention to the color used, is an installation that invites visitors to stop for a moment during their visit, with seats placed in the center of the space. Here, the balcony of the Grande Halle is totally transformed, allowing new shapes and details to appear in a fluffy and colorful atmosphere.

Penique Productions
Rosâtre
Balloon Museum
Pop Air
Paris, 2022

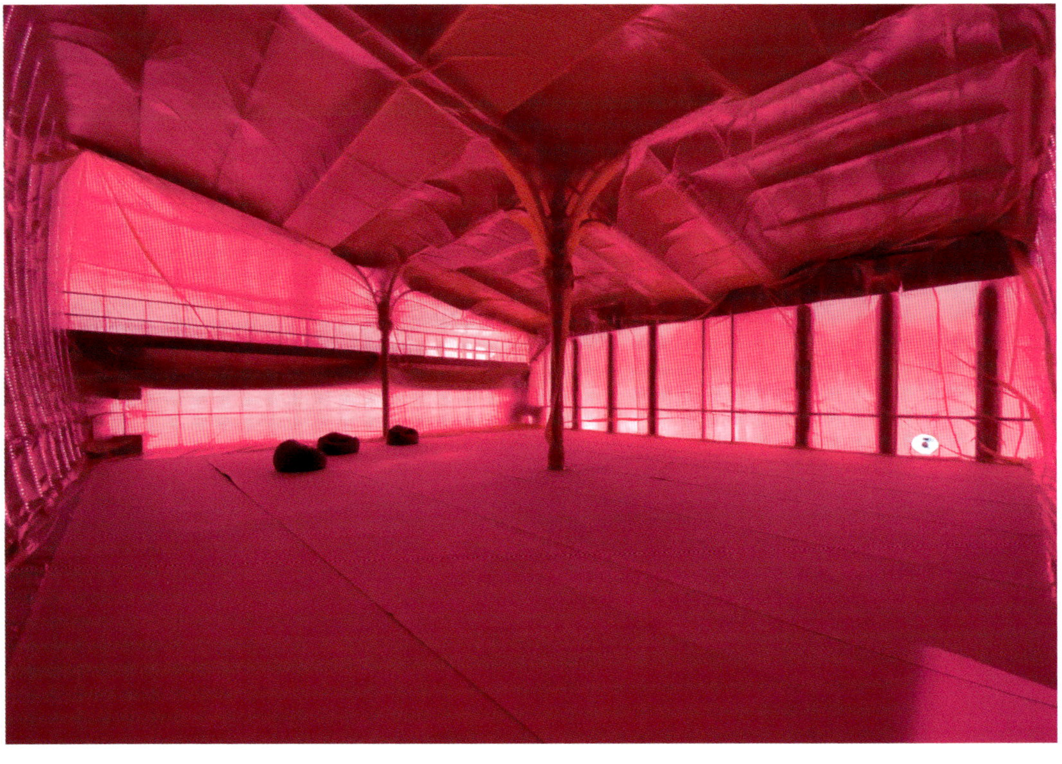

Rosâtre 2022

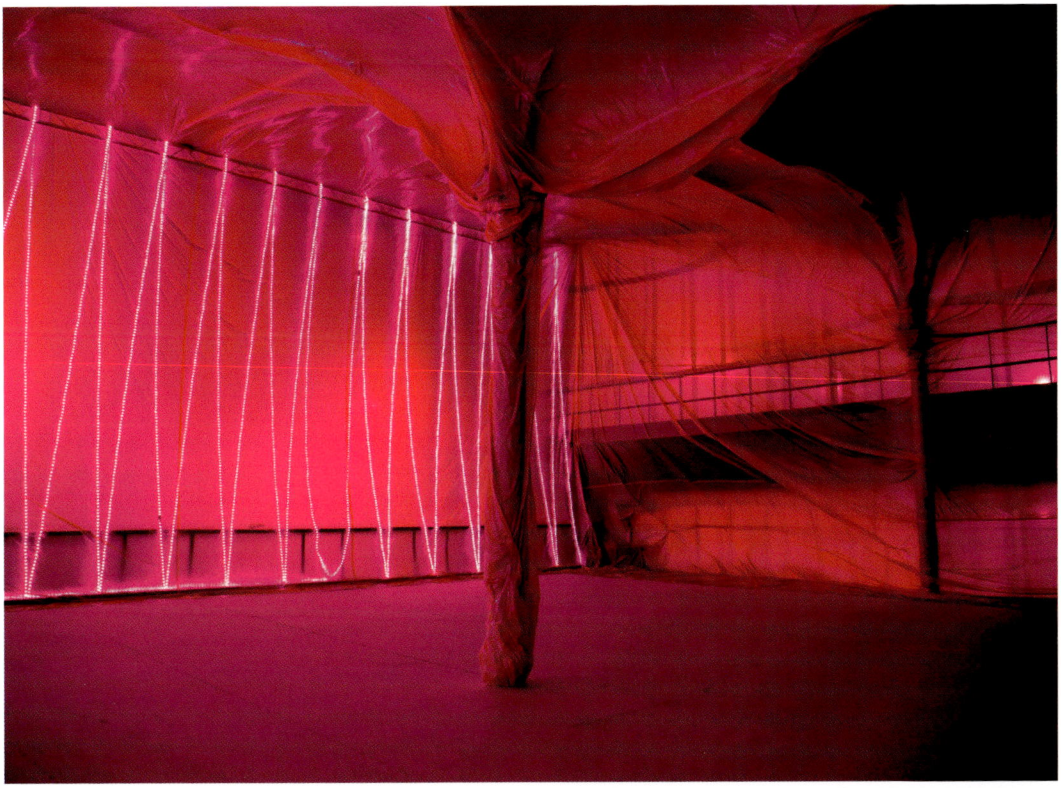

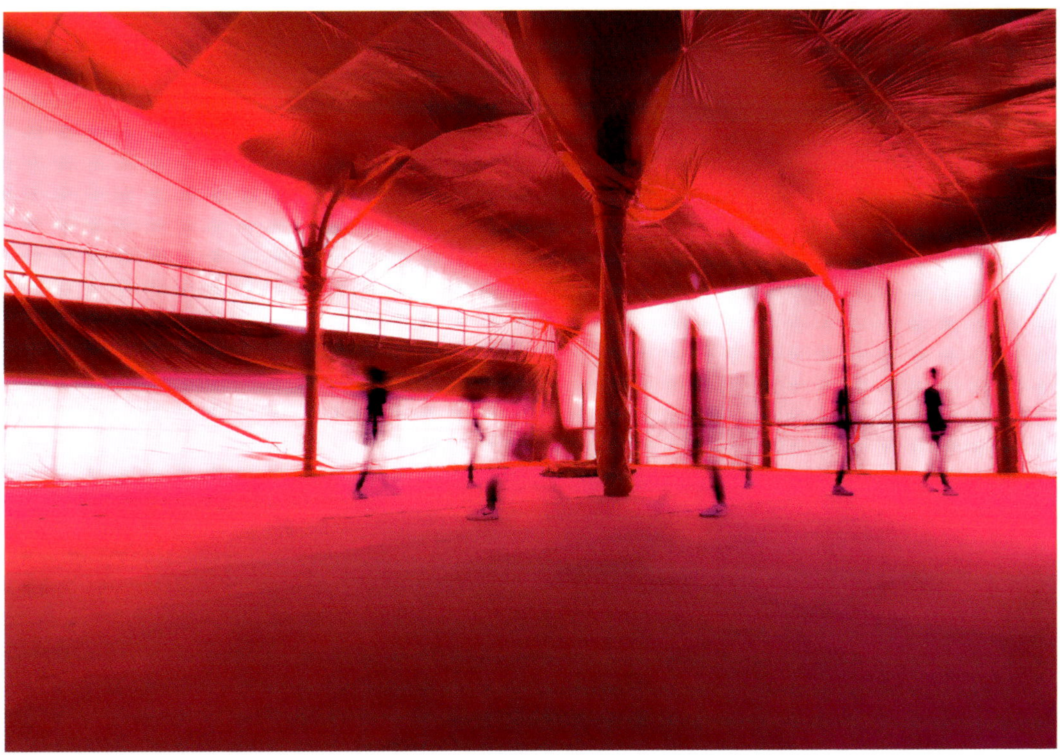

PEPPER'S GHOST

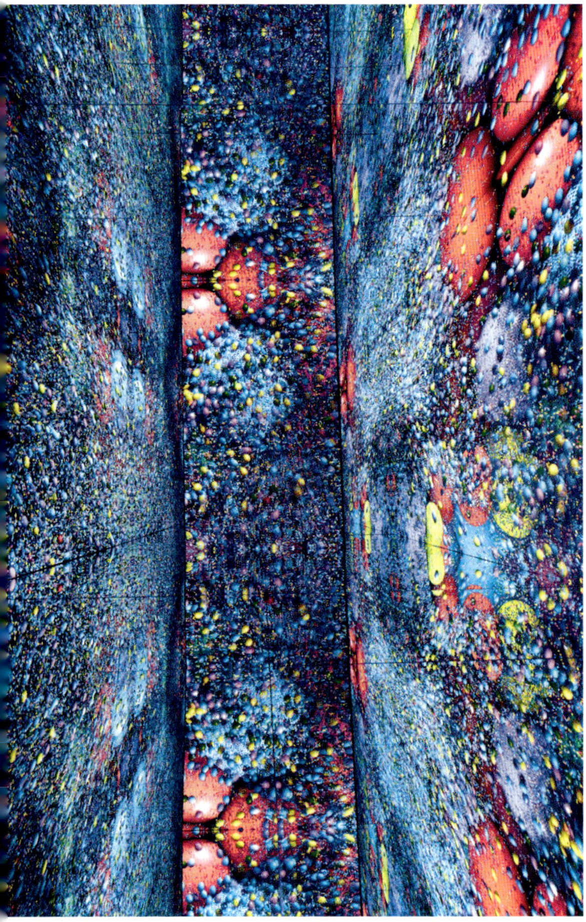

This name, recalling the first hologram effect ever created, refers to a collective comprised of digital artists, graphic designers, engineers, visual artists and video makers, lighting and sound designers, founded and guided by artist Anderson Tegon. They design and produce digital exhibitions and immersive experiences, 3D mapping, light shows, holographic performances; fostering creativity through the use of advanced hardware systems, by creating contents and delivering the proper support to produce and set up original digital artworks. Anderson is a digital art and digital Street Art pioneer able to transform a wall, a floor, a ceiling, every type of space or surface into a true, futuristic artwork. He has a "creativity first" approach where technologies are used as means of expression, as brushes for a painter. Thanks to his artistic vision, Pepper's Ghost created *Aura – The Immersive Light Experience* in Milan while, in March 2022, it launched *Ghost Over Banksy*, based on a Banksy's stencil, and it has proved to be the first Digital Street Artwork ever made. Pepper's Ghost motto is "CANVAS IS EVERYWHERE."

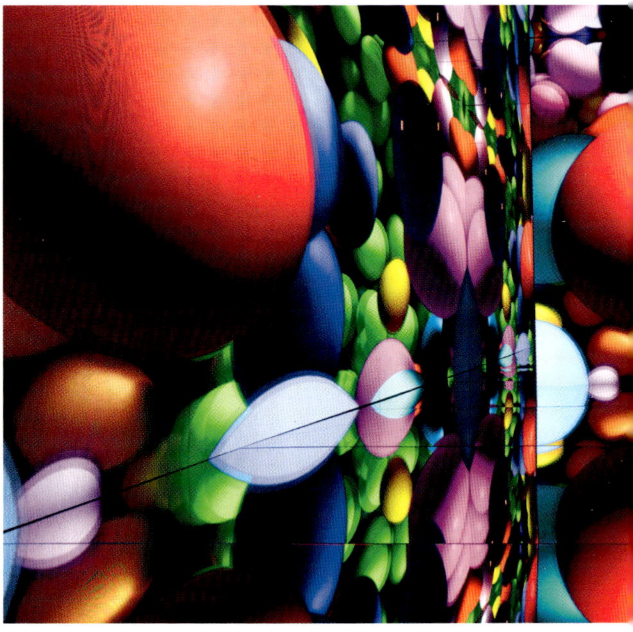

Pepper's Ghost
ARIA – The Breath
Immersive Experience
Balloon Museum
Pop Air
Madrid, 2023
Naples, 2023

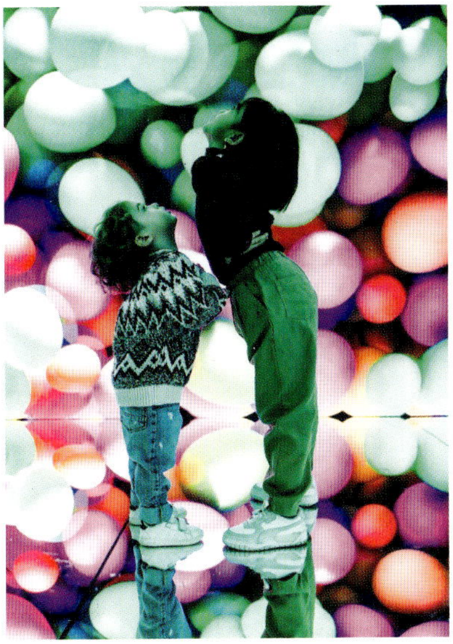

ARIA – The Breath Immersive Experience
It is an immersive experience, a digital interpretation of Inflatable Art in which the visitor finds themselves enveloped in a tight space, surrounded by a multitude of balloons lost in the sky. The visitor is taken on this flight of brightly colored elements, following their evolution through the metaphysical experience of suspension. The infinite concept of air is narrated through the apparition of Aria, which reveals itself through the form of a female face made up of thousands of tiny inflated spheres. Aria shifts and morphs in the storm of brightly colored spheres and then is absorbed into its surroundings. The immersive sound design is intended to bring back in sound the sensations created around the visitor with the same intensity and depth of a breath taken miles high with the unique intention of experiencing a space without limits.

"[Air] surrounds and encircles us, a bit like a companion, which certainly helps us of course to live and exist but it also gives life."

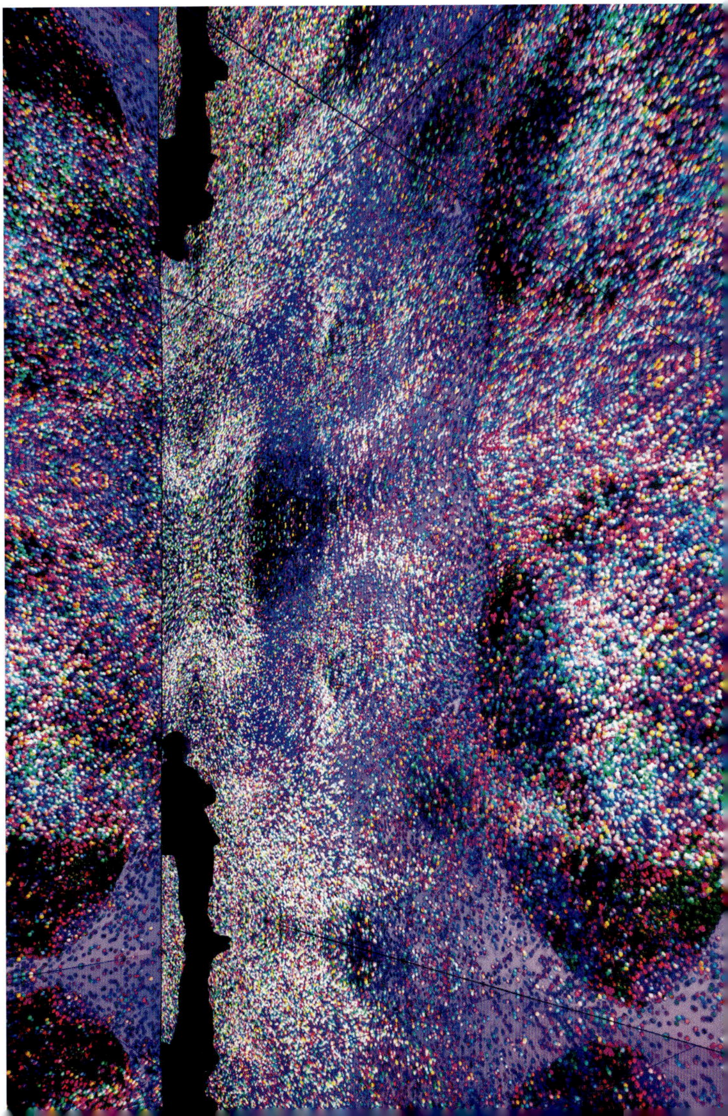

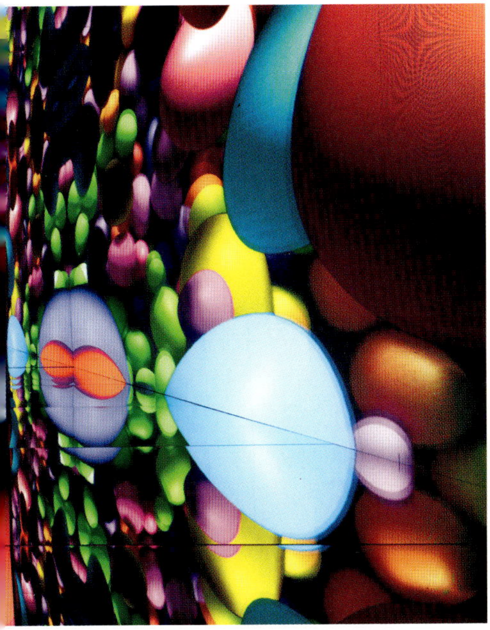

MICHELA PICCHI

Michela Picchi is a multi-disciplinary artist from Rome, currently based in Berlin. After graduating in Law and Economics and later in Graphic Design, she moved to Hong Kong, where she was able to explore, experiment, and develop her own distinctive style. Her work draws inspiration from collage and visual illustration, and her unique use of color is a key element in her output, diving into Pop and surrealist worlds. Constant motifs in her work are the "psychedelic" tigers that appear in her murals, prints and collaborations.

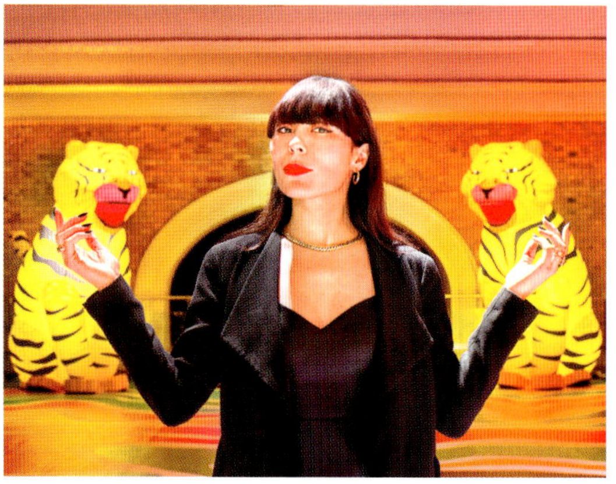

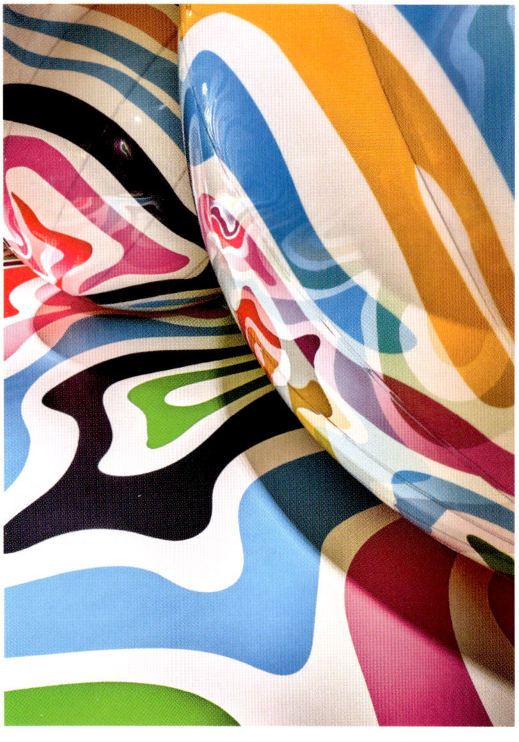

Picchi focuses on how perceptual experiences are linked to visions and how this relation can be transferred into artworks. She has had numerous solo exhibitions in Italy and has been featured in a variety of international group exhibitions, including at the Saatchi Gallery in London, Affordable Art Fair in Milan, Gerichtshof Gallery in Berlin, an artist residency at SPAZI in Venice, Italy, and at Creative Fusion Art Residency in Cleveland, Ohio. Notably, Michela Picchi delivered a TEDx Talk in Taipei, Taiwan.

Top
Michela Picchi
with her artwork
Playground Love
Balloon Museum
EmotionAir
London, 2023

Michela Picchi
Playground Love
Balloon Museum
EmotionAir
London, 2023

Playground Love 2023

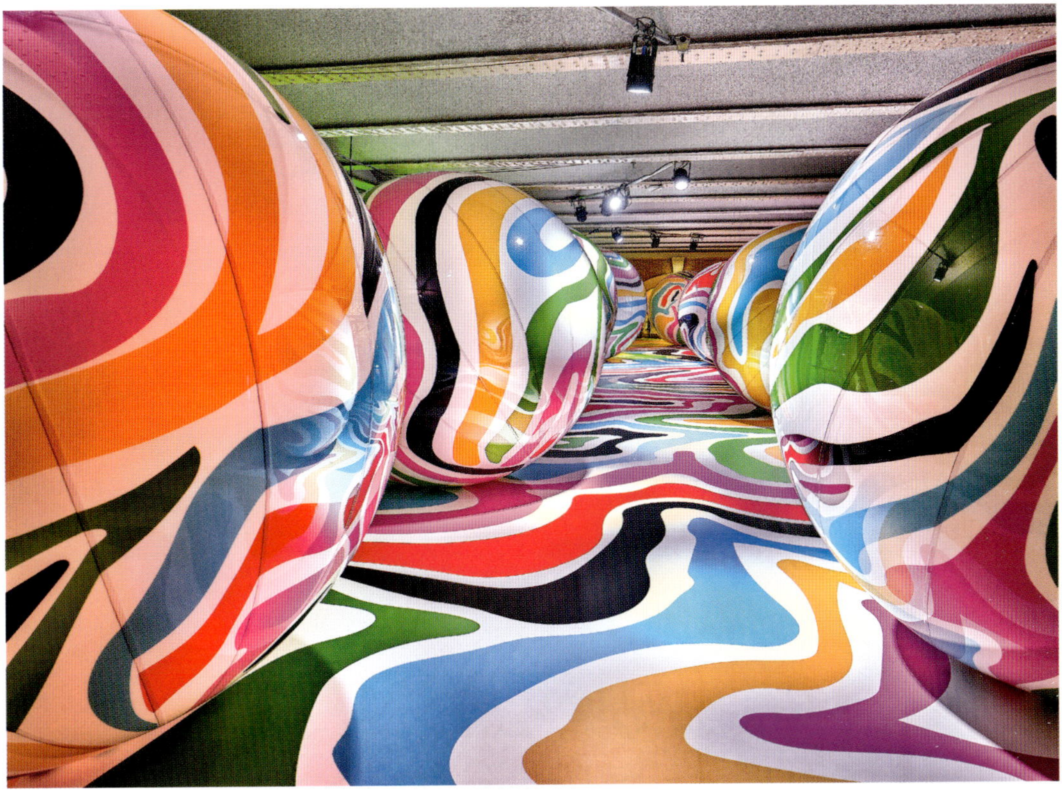

Playground Love

The title of the song by the famous French music group Air is just the beginning for Michela Picchi in the creation of her artwork. *Playground Love* becomes just that—a space of play and love, where all the creativity and esthetics of the artist are expressed. Large resonating spheres occupy the space, immersed in the colors and distinctive graphic research characteristic of Michela Picchi's production. At the room's edges, four giant tigers act as benevolent guardians of the space and the spectators' interaction. The artist intends to bring back the lightness typical of childhood, often associated with the act of play. There is a surprising rediscovery of childlike innocence and awe in the giant dimensions of each of the elements present. Undoubtedly, the theme of enjoyment fulfills a fundamental role in the interpretative and cognitive process of the artwork, offering a playful perspective inherently linked to the audience's experience.

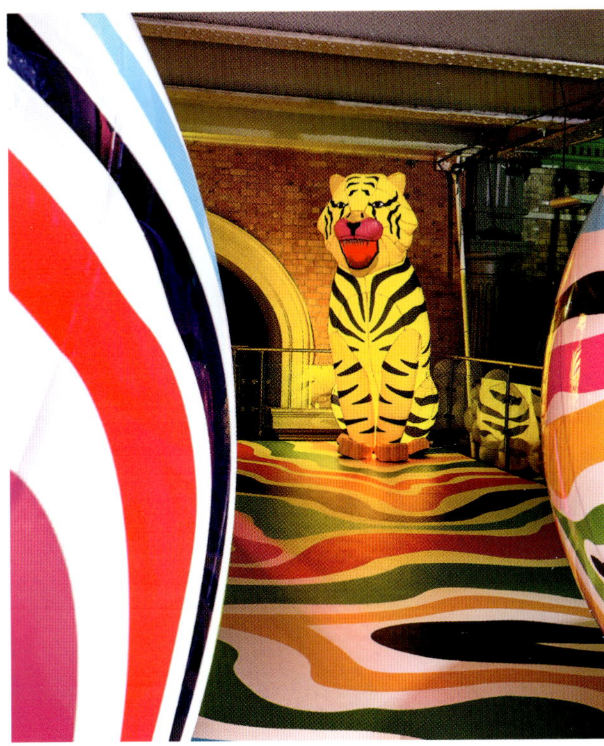

PLASTIQUE FANTASTIQUE

Plastique Fantastique is an art duo and collective founded in Berlin in 1999 and is now directed by Yena Young and Marco Canevacci. The multidisciplinary artists create immersive spatial installations, challenging the notion of reality and the limits of our senses. Each project invites the public to explore an imaginary landscape within the existing world, questioning the paradoxical nature of perception and the complex layers of our surroundings. These (in)visible installations merge art, performance, individual stories, people, and architecture to provide a multi-sensorial experience that blurs conventional boundaries and transcends the imagination. Most recently, the collective debuted RINGdeLUXE, a site-specific installation that surrounded the Passerelle Léopold-Sédar-Senghor footbridge in Paris on the occasion of Nuit Blanche 2023. They have also published their book, *PLASTIQUE FANTASTIQUE – A journey through an ephemeral realm*, an extensive monograph showcasing a selection of projects from the past two decades.

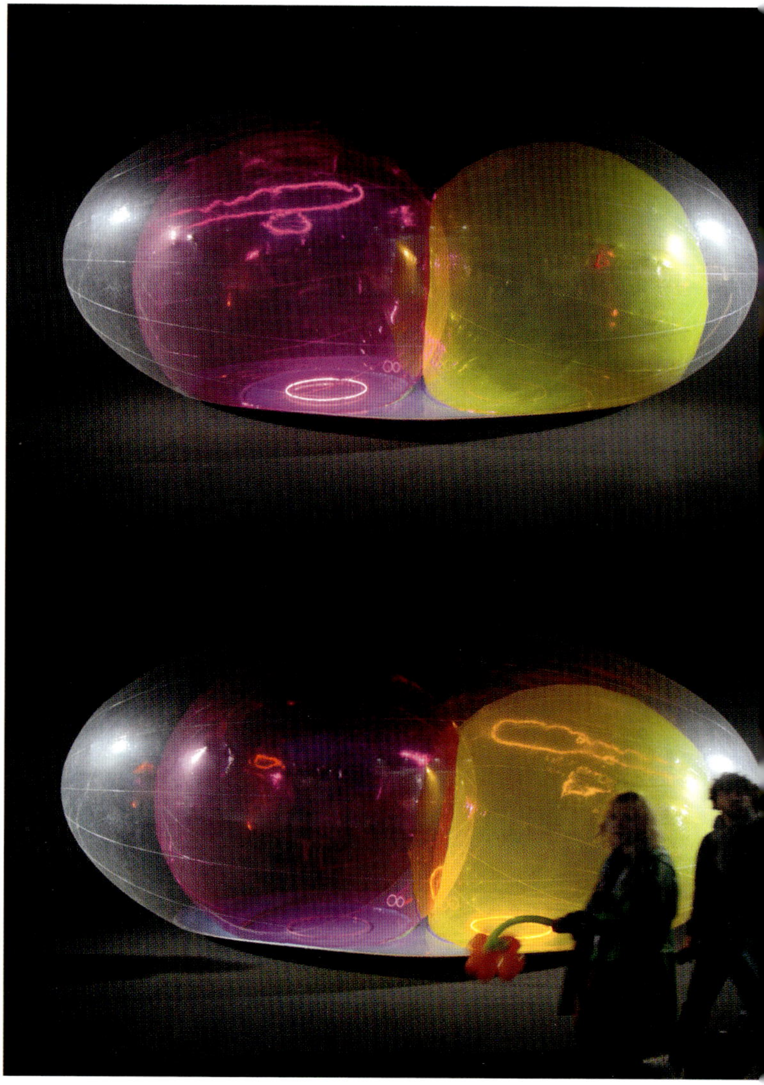

reSET THEORY

reSET THEORY is inspired by a mathematical concept known as set theory, established by the German mathematician Georg Cantor at the end of the 19th century. Dealing with the notions of element and belonging, the artists transpose this idea in the form of an oval and transparent inflatable sculpture inside which two colored spheres touch and continually inflate and deflate, stimulating each other and transforming the space into a breathing organism. Beyond the sensual and esthetic aspect, the artists deploy the process of subtractive synthesis. Using magenta and yellow for the spheres and cyan for the base, the artists arrive to the black. Always in movement, this work invites the visitor to rethink the possibilities of interactions and connections with the elements that surround us.

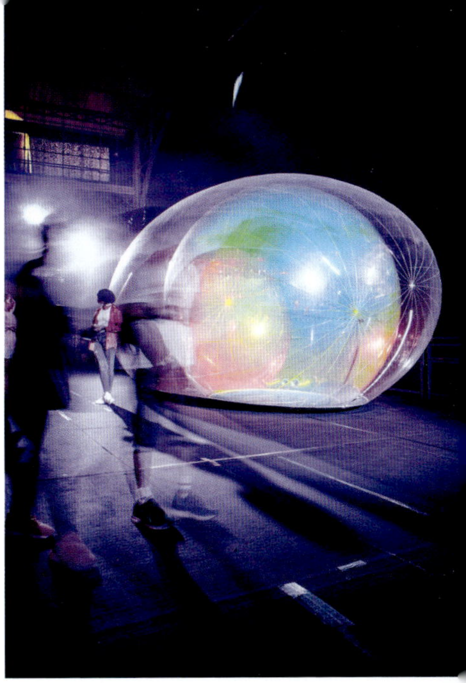

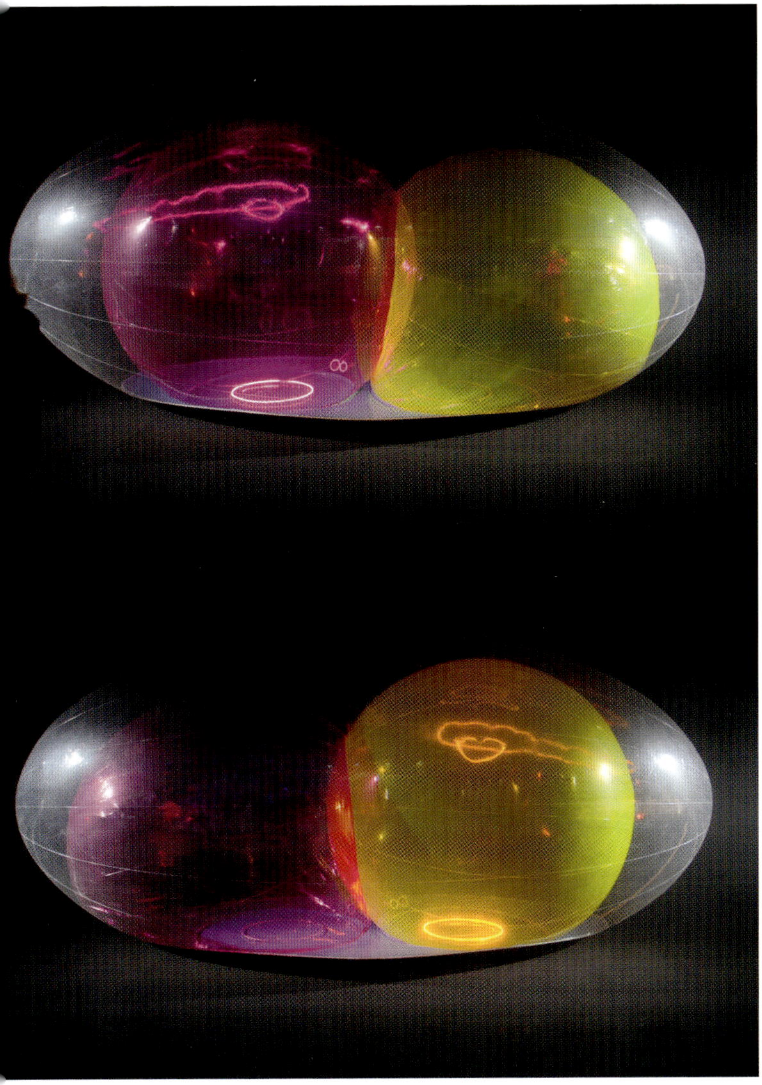

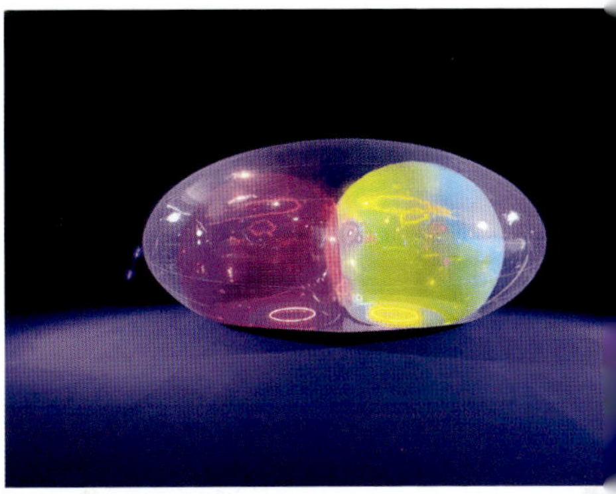

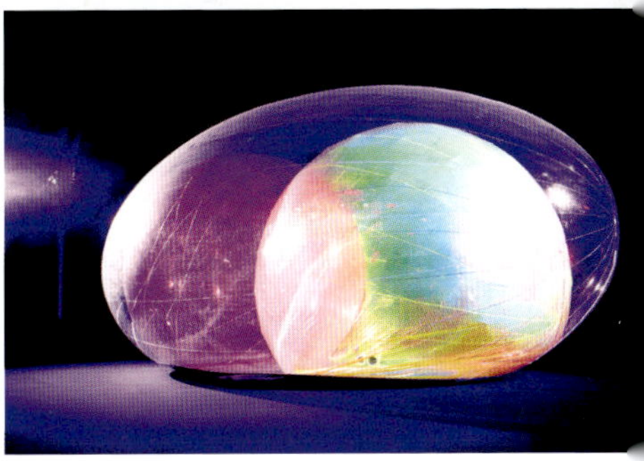

Plastique Fantastique
reSET THEORY
Balloon Museum
Pop Air
Paris, 2022

THOLOS

This work was first presented in the Balloon Museum *Pop Air* exhibition in Milan in 2022. The name recalls architecture of the past; in fact, in archaeology, the word Tholos refers to buildings with circular plans, composed of stone rings that create a pseudo-dome. An ode to geometry, this monument elevates the discipline to the stature of an ancient deity, housed within a seemingly immense structure that, with the aid of air, can be positioned anywhere, as required. Visitors will find themselves immersed in an architectural wonder, distinct from the outside world, as they journey into an infinite and replicated dimension, all courtesy of strategically placed mirrors.
The outcome is a mystic and humorous experience, which challenges visitors' conception of spatial geometry and gravity.

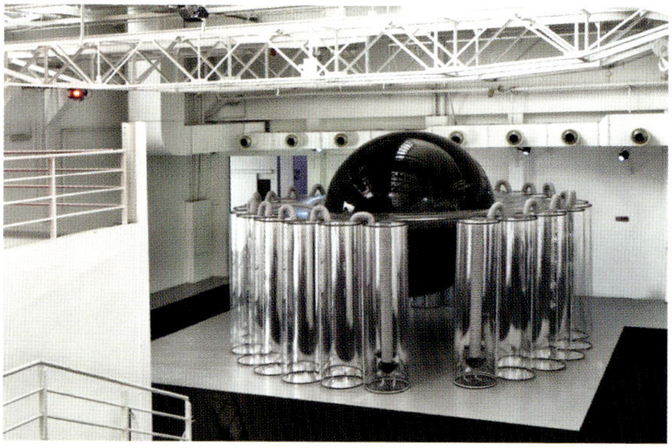

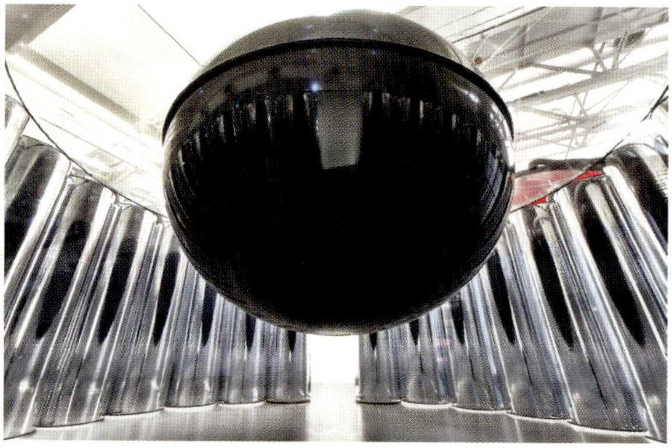

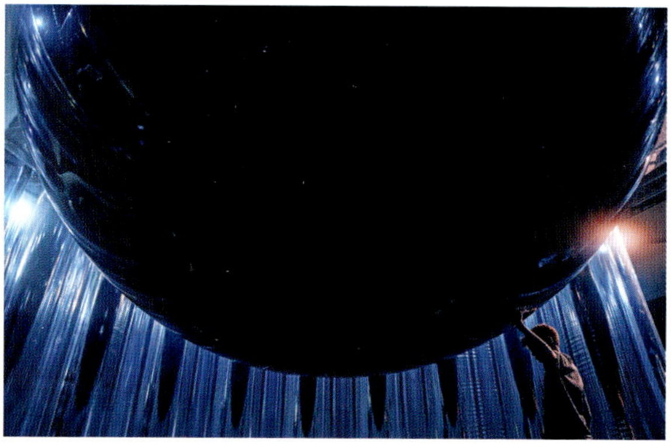

THOLOS 2022

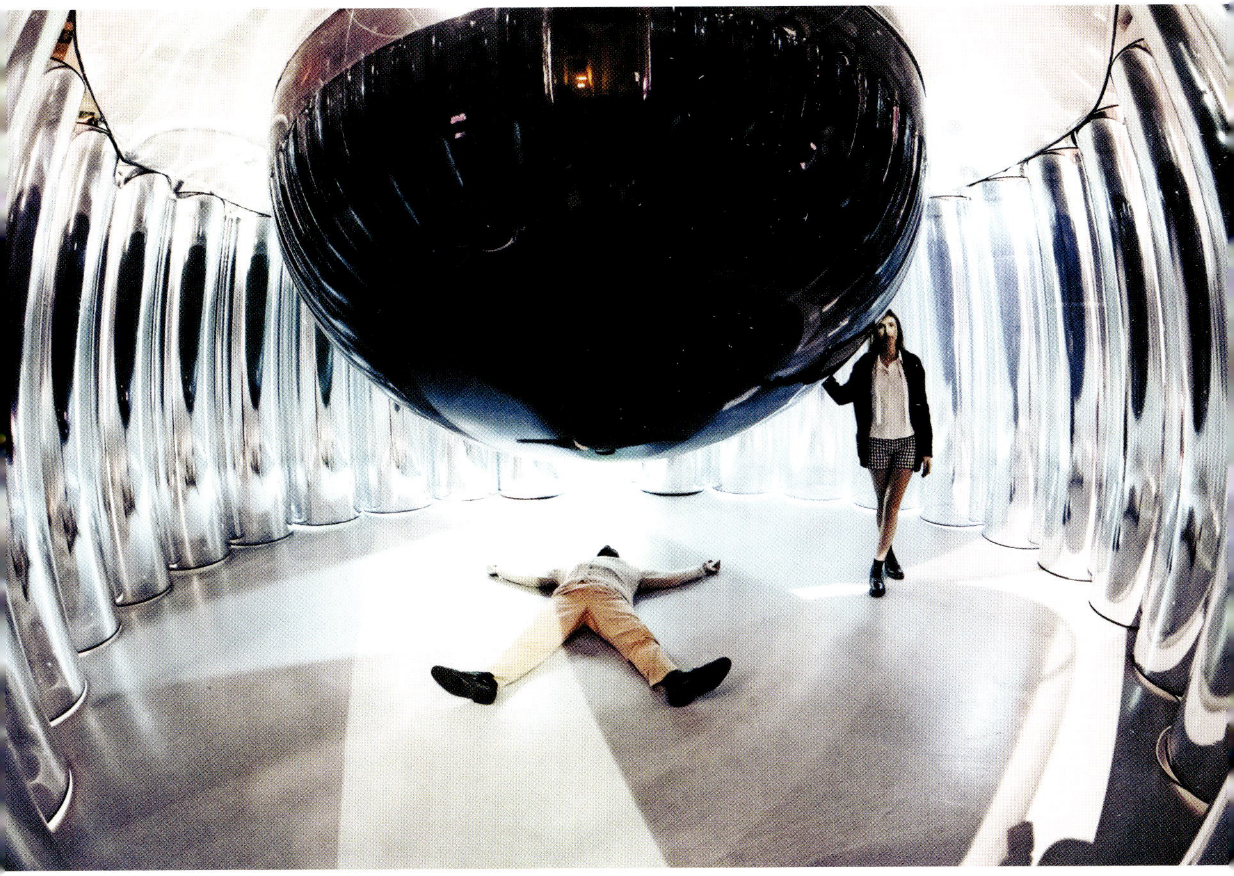

Plastique Fantastique
THOLOS
Balloon Museum
Pop Air
Milan, 2022

PNEUHAUS AND BIKE POWERED EVENTS

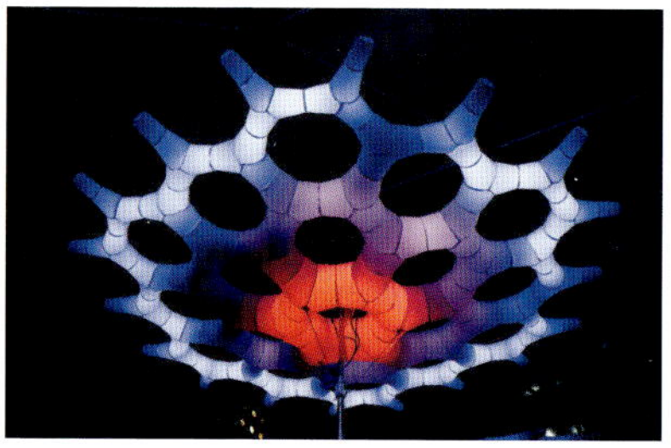

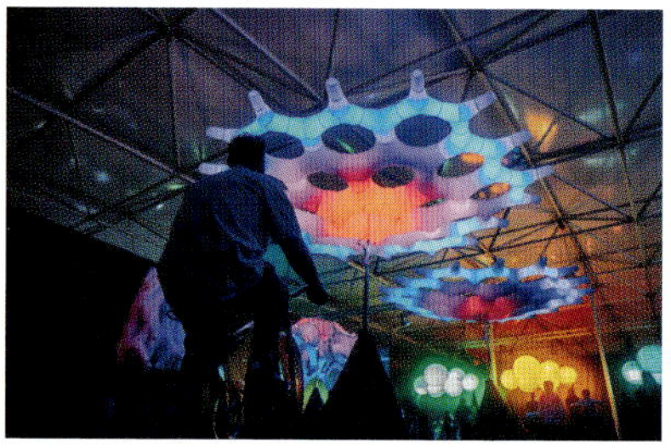

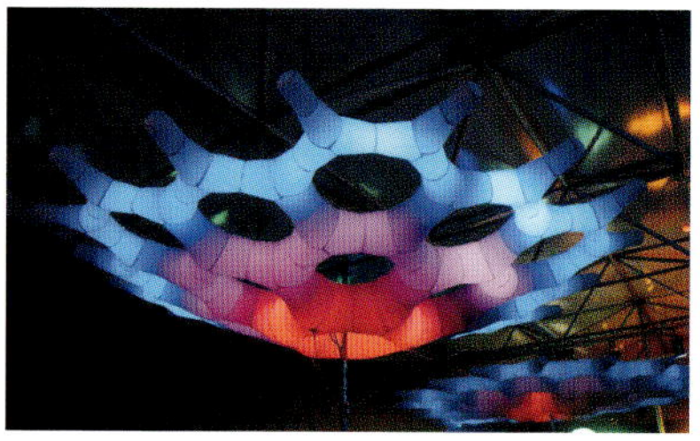

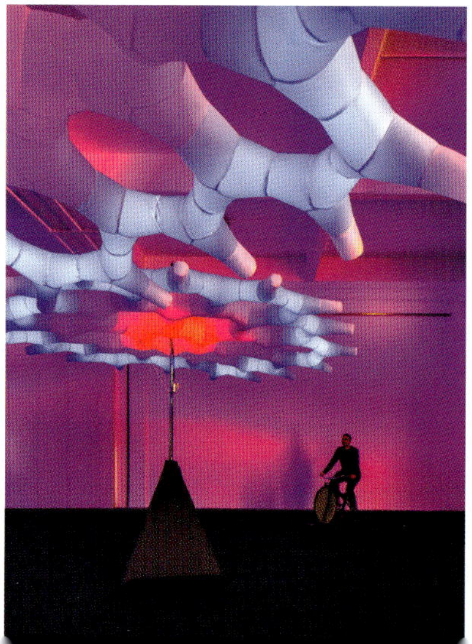

Pneuhaus is an American art and design studio that focuses on dynamic transformations of public space. Founded in 2014 as an interdisciplinary team with backgrounds in architecture, textiles, and furniture design, their practice is centered around developing the craft of inflatables. Through physically making and experimenting with the various properties of air and textiles, they seek to explore the ways in which we engage with the space around us and challenge our predominantly rigid built environment. Pneuhaus's sculptures and the immersive spaces lead visitors in the discovery of their senses, and in the joys of shared experience. From large to small, static to dynamic, analog to digital, the studio is constantly evolving and exploring new opportunities to create phenomenal experiences that stimulate their audience sense of play, curiosity, and wonder. The team's work extends across a variety of sectors including museum spaces, public arts festivals, and municipalities, as well as corporate collaborations including with NASA, Nike, and Spotify, to name but a few. Since its founding, Pneuhaus has completed over forty built projects and the team is engaged in actively installing their work both locally and internationally.

Bike Powered Events, an interactive design company led by artists in America since 2009, is renowned for a body of work that centers on sustainability, wellbeing, and the influence individuals have on shaping their environment. Utilizing stationary bicycles, the company designs and produces exhibitions and events that activate and illuminate spaces, generating all of the electricity from human power. Nationally and internationally recognized, Bike Powered Events excels in engaging diverse audiences, fostering meaningful connections through shared creative experiences, and spearheading the application of sustainable power sources into high-quality art. The intention is to deepen participants' connections to themselves and their bodies through simple movement that produces captivating and wondrous feedback.

Canopy 2019

"Canopy is about the exchange. Of being able to ride a bicycle, to put your energy into it, and it illuminates and brings to life a creature in front of you."

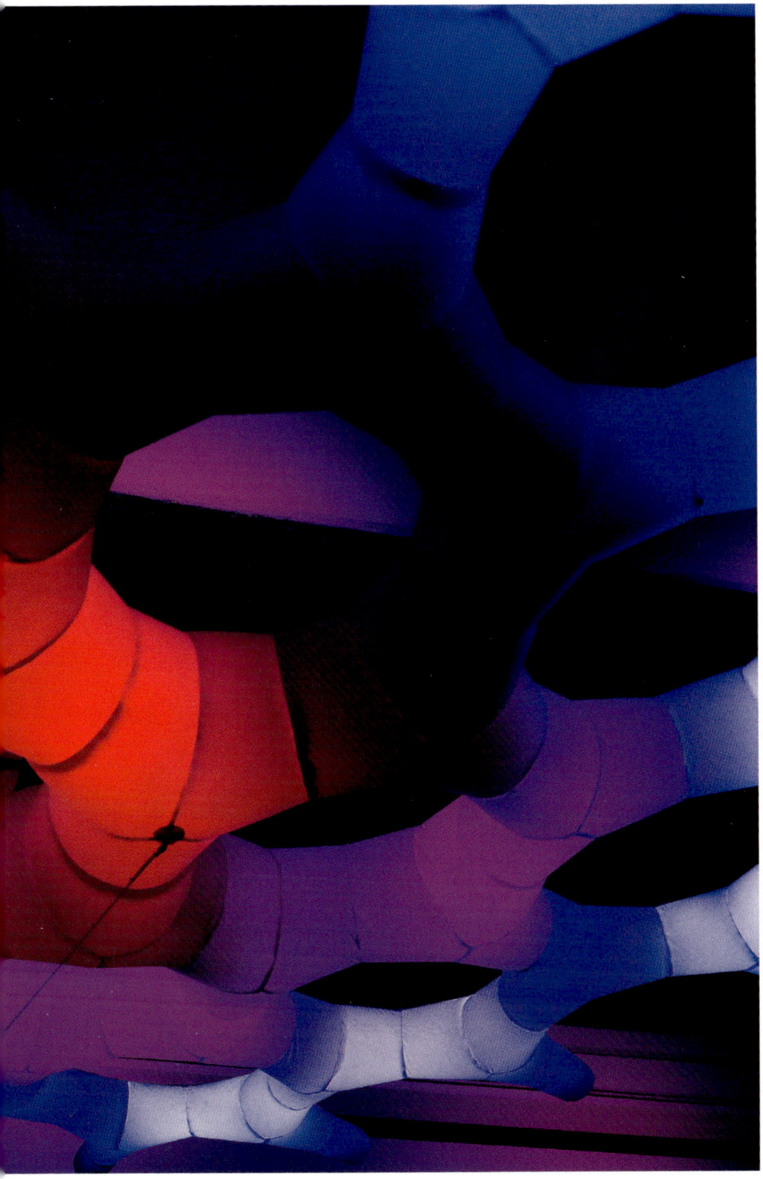

Canopy
This interactive installation invites viewers to amplify their experience by becoming part of it. Thanks to generators driven by participant's pedaling, the installation comes to life. The tree-like light sculptures transform, illuminate, and continuously expand from the energy of each bicycle. *Canopy* encourages its visitors by offering them an interactive experience that emphasizes the generation of green electricity. These sculptures are never still: they constantly change their movements through interaction. *Canopy* is the first collaboration between inflatable art and architecture studio Pneuhaus and Bike Powered Events. The work is inspired by the phenomenon of "crown shyness," where the foliage of several nearby trees grows and shapes itself so it does not touch, resulting in incredible patterns. When fully inflated, *Canopy*'s individual units come together to create a luminous web of color that extends to active users and viewers while activating a collaborative process whereby everyone shares and circulates energy.

Pneuhaus
and Bike Powered Events
Canopy
Balloon Museum
Pop Air
Milan, 2022
Madrid, 2023

KALMAN POOL

Kalman Pool completed his BFA at the School of the Art Institute of Chicago, followed by his MA in Painting at the Royal College of Art in London. Concurrently, he attended the Swatch Art Peace Hotel as an artist-in-residence, where he was invited to create a Swatch X You artist special WATCH. In 2023, he created a large-scale installation, *WEAVVY* 海宇, for Lincoln China, showcased at the biennial Auto Shanghai Show. Inspired by BioArt and natural history, Pool's interdisciplinary works examine the dialectical relationship between virtual and physical, seemingly reconciling both by means of fantastically inventing VR-made bio-mutated phantasms, inflatable simulacra, and invented pictographic language installations. Kalman was inspired by the inflatable dummies used by the U.S. top-secret "Ghost Army" in World War II, combining VR techniques and inflatables to create installations and digital pieces. Kalman Pool has exhibited internationally at the Jupiter Museum of Art Shenzhen and Saatchi Gallery London among other venues.

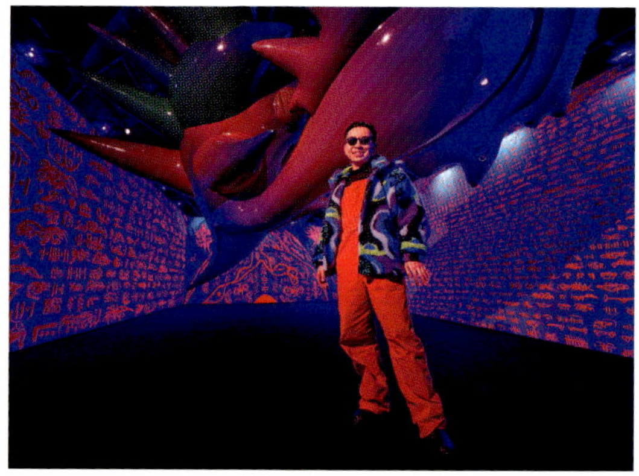

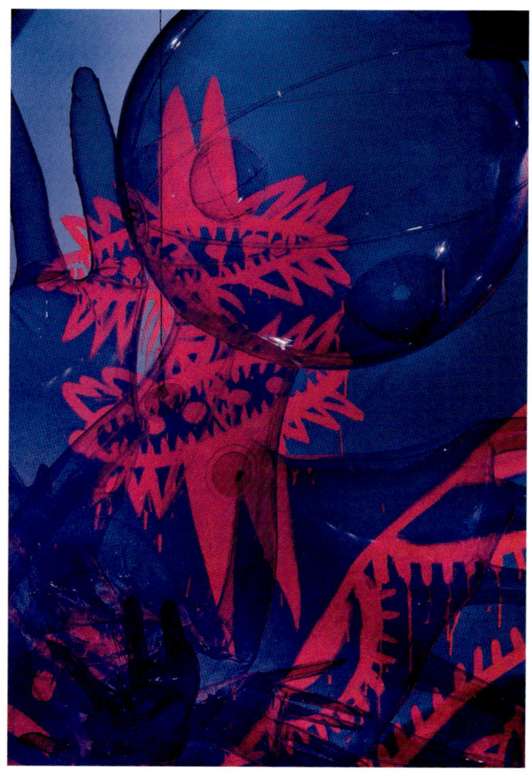

Top
Kalman Pool with his artwork *Voyage*
Balloon Museum
EmotionAir
London, 2023

Kalman Pool
Voyage
Balloon Museum
EmotionAir
London, 2023

Voyage 2023

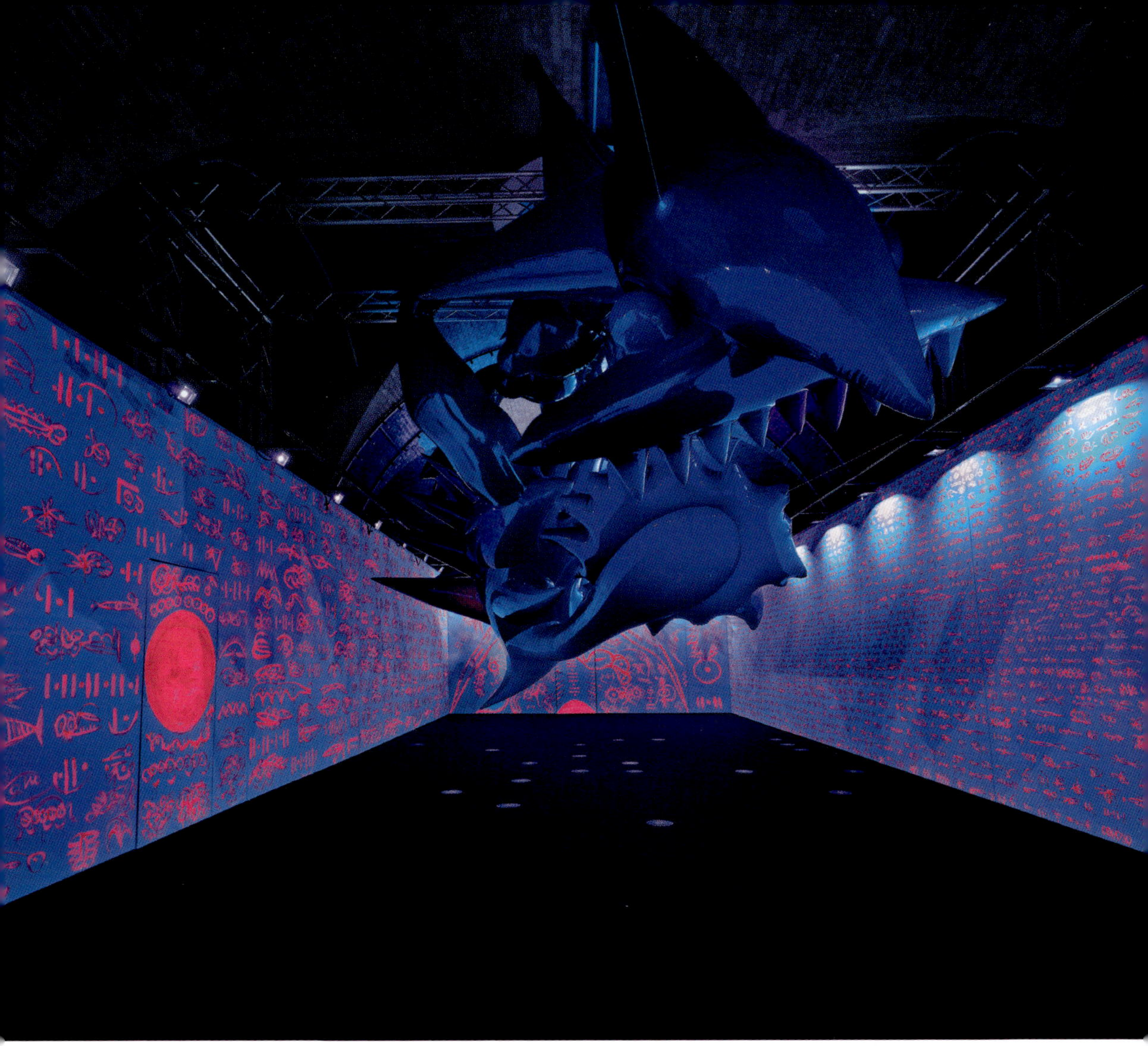

Voyage

This imaginary journey unfolds in a mysterious, historical, and futuristic realm; one might find oneself in the depths of the ocean as well as in space, encountering a new alien civilization, and remaining surprised by the new and unexplored. At the center of the installation, a colossal and divine creature, the Cosmic Dragon, towers above the heads of visitors, suspended as if in a museum of natural history. Continuing through the room, the spectator will also encounter ethereal inflatable phantasms seamlessly transitioning from invisible to visible.

On the walls appear fluorescent words in *Luminous Opera*, a new language created by the artist and inspired by East Asian languages, which he has been exploring and developing, here presented for the first time in Europe. The inspiration for these artworks stems from the artist's journey to the Mogao Caves, a divine Buddhist site with over a thousand years of history in northwestern China. Inside the cave, murals and statues depict celestial creatures and hieroglyphics.

QUIET ENSEMBLE

This creative studio is concerned with audiovisual unexpected experiences, producing immersive installations and light/sound-based works, researching and focusing on the balance between nature and technology as main tools for the creation. Founded in 2009 by Fabio di Salvo and Bernardo Vercelli, Quiet Ensemble generates audiovisual performances and installations by capturing the essence of various objects and creatures ranging from goldfish to pineapples to clouds. The research of Quiet Ensemble goes through the observation of balance between chaos and control, nature and technology, creating subjects that merge those elements, elements that take form from the relation between organic and artificial subjects, focusing on insignificant and wonderful events, such as the movement of a fly or the sound of trees. Celebrating the “invisible concerts” that take place every day, Quiet Ensemble strives to reveal hidden and often overlooked aspects of the environment around us. The duo has presented at many international festivals, including Sonar Festival in Barcelona, Noor Riyad in Saudi Arabia, and Signal Festival, Prague, and has also collaborated with international brands like ADIDAS, Mercedes, and Balik, among others.

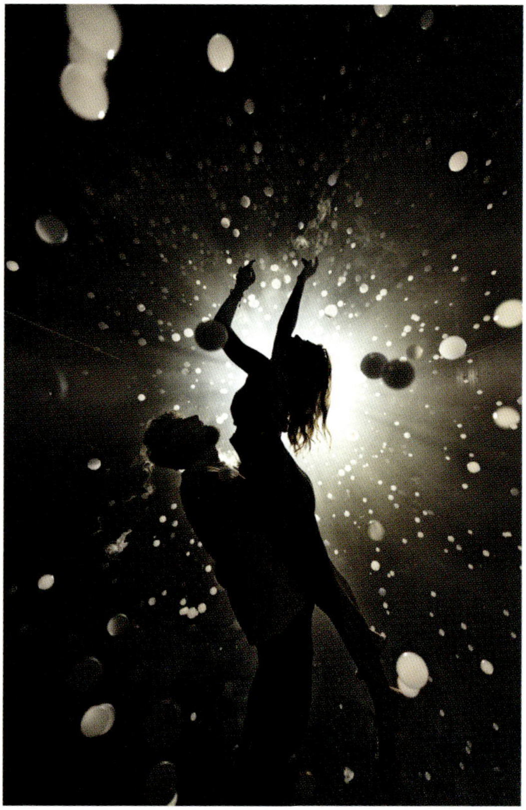

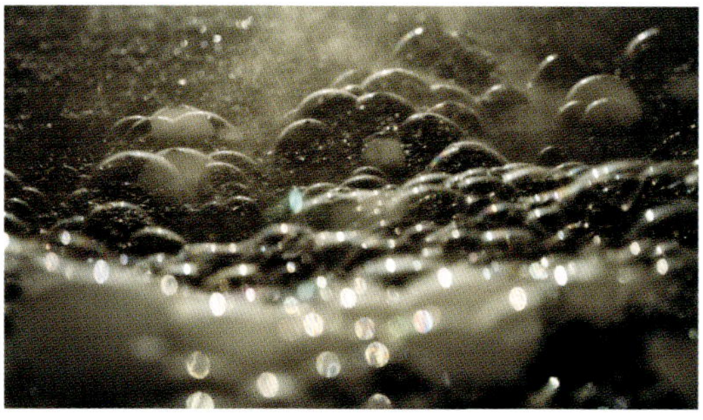

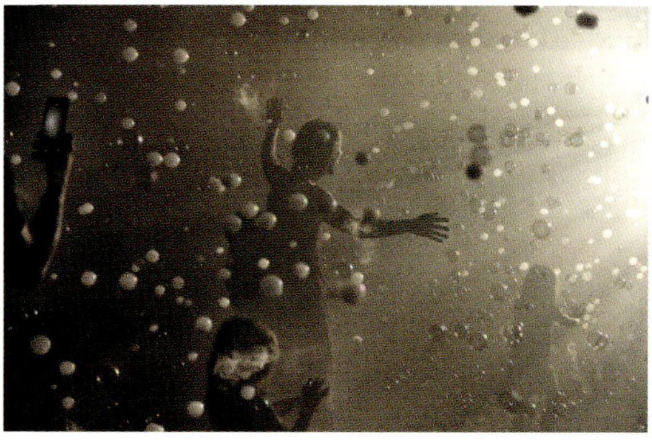

Quiet Ensemble
A Quiet Storm
Balloon Museum
Pop Air
Milan, 2022
Madrid, 2023
Naples, 2023

A Quiet Storm 2022

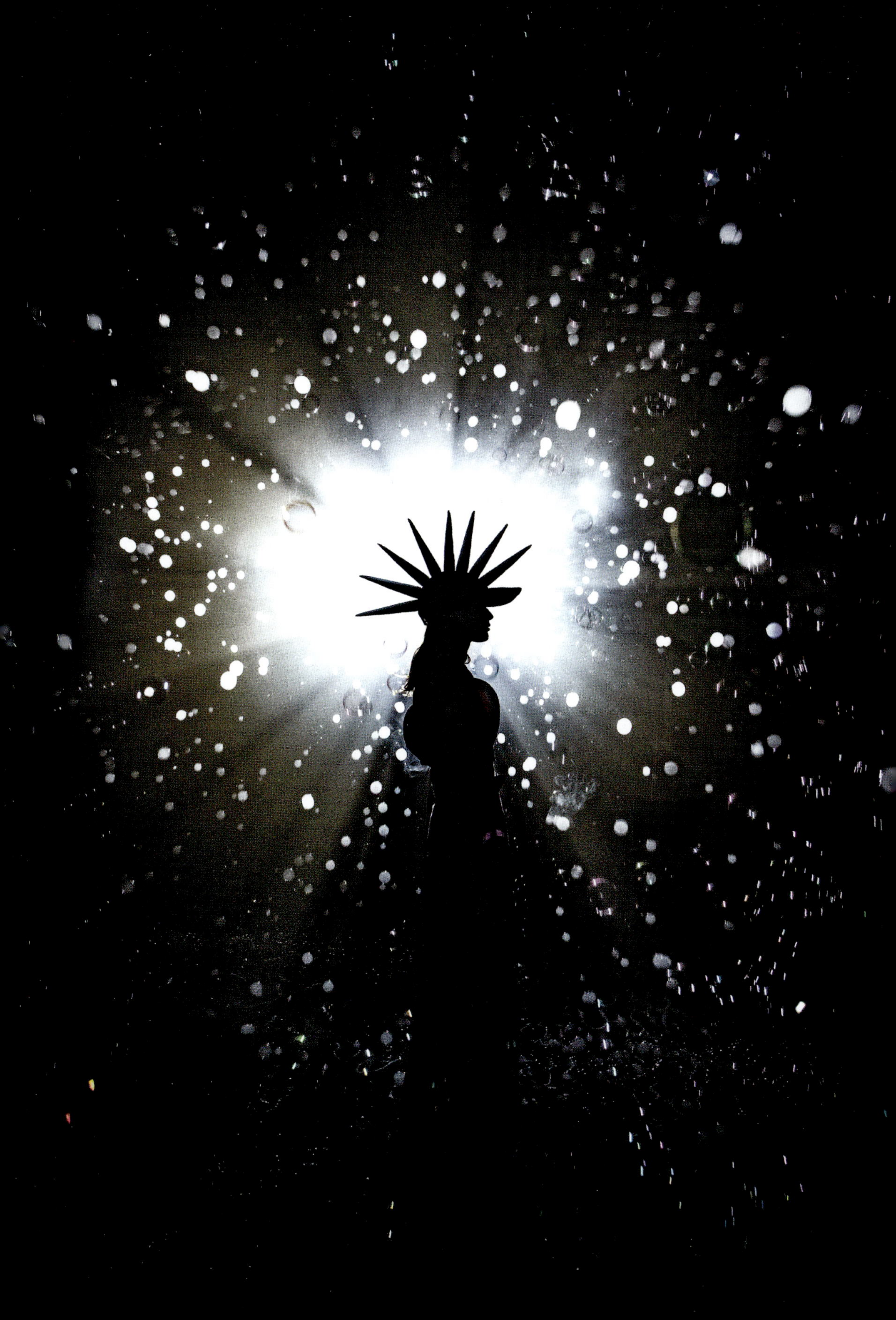

QUIET ENSEMBLE

A Quiet Storm

Once plunged into darkness, visitors are surprised to discover dozens of soap bubbles floating in space. All are filled with thick white smoke, making them opaque objects. At the first impact, the light, fragile soap bubbles explode, releasing their thick cloud. There's something magical about the installations by Italian duo Quiet Ensemble. Time seems suspended. A graceful moment in a world where everything is usually a rush. Generated by smoke machines, the bubbles move to the rhythm of a sound composition created by the duo.
This simple, but clever device allows the artists to blur our bearings and activate our perceptions, engaging our senses to evoke a feeling of wonder.

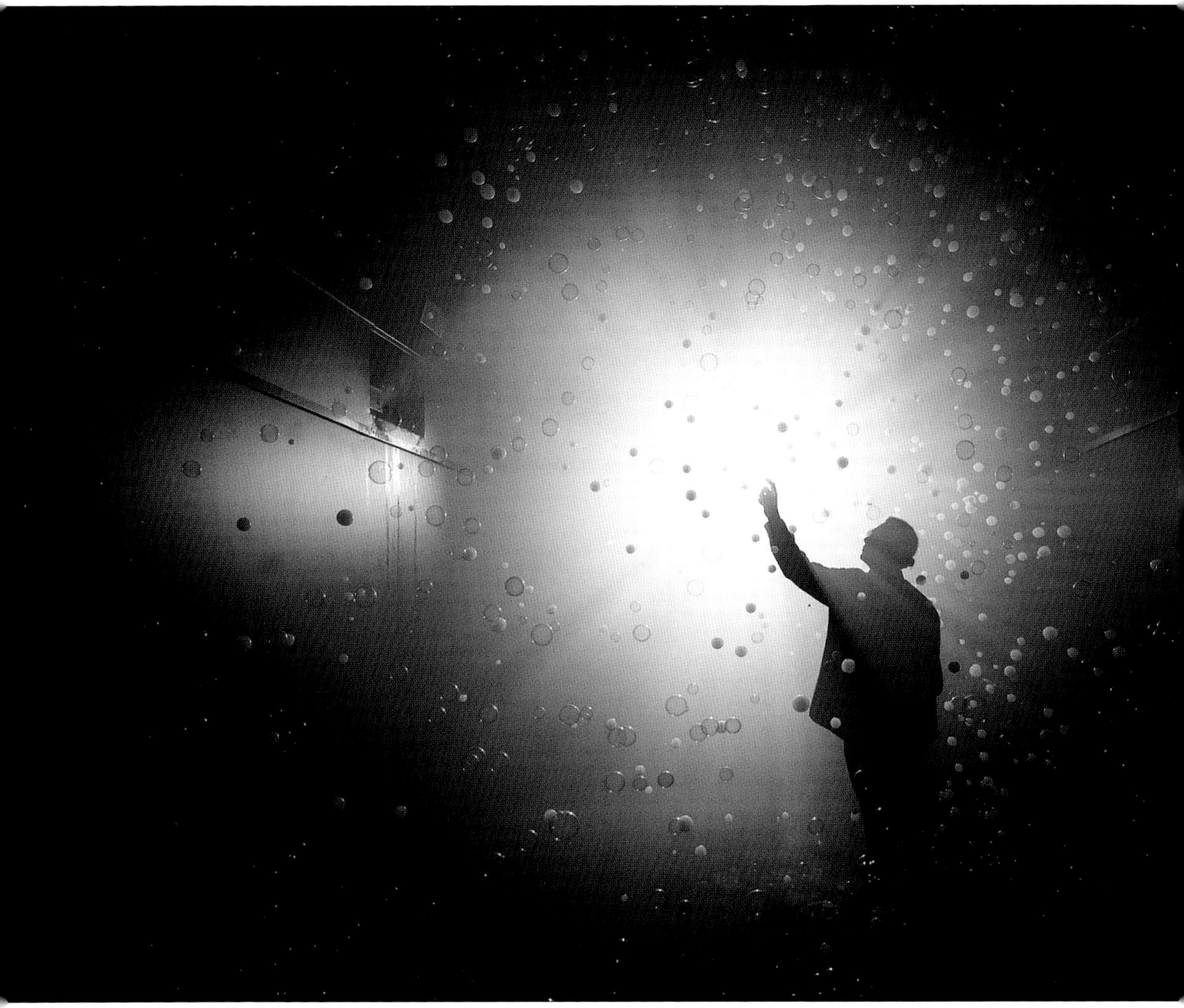

Quiet Ensemble
A Quiet Storm
Balloon Museum
Let's Fly
New York, 2023

A Quiet Storm 2022

"In all of our works, we have always tried to analyze small things, small elements that are around us and that we do not pay enough attention to.

Through the use of technology we try to magnify the things that might otherwise go unnoticed by the viewer."

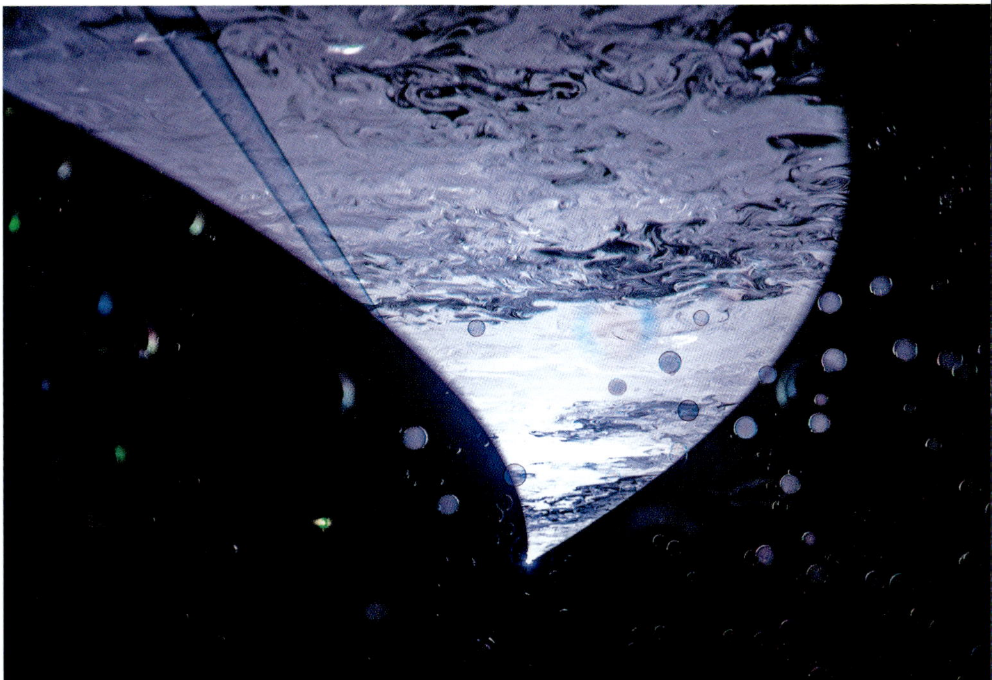

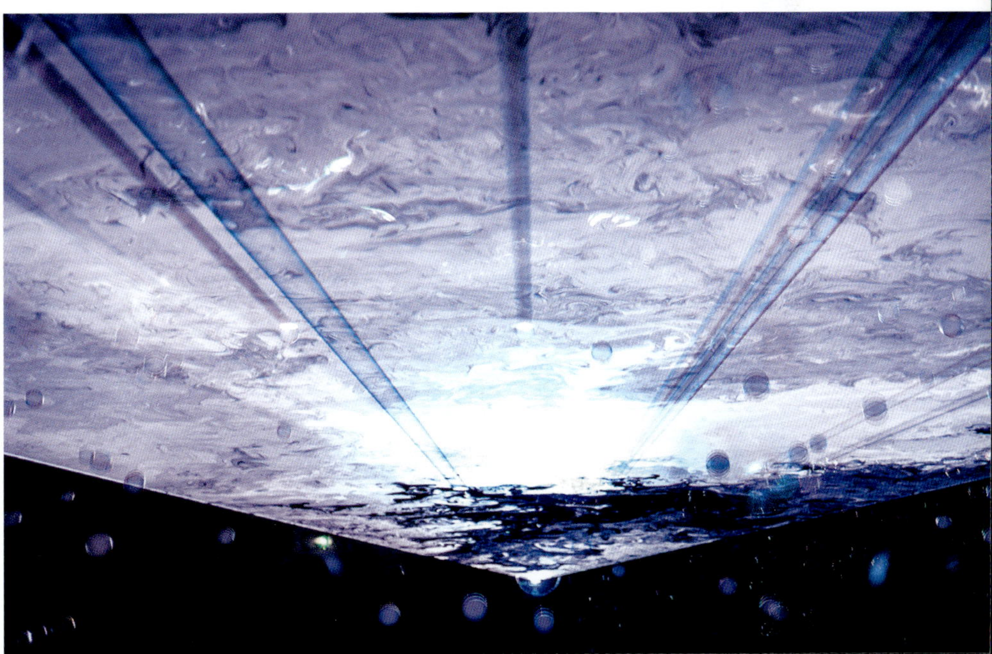

STEFANO ROSSETTI

A polyhedral artist based in Milan, Stefano Rossetti moves from graphics to immersive installations. Rossetti organizes events with Inflatable Art pieces that are part of the Rossetti Design Park world. His theme parks *Parcobaleno* and *Rainbow Park* have been welcomed by museums and city centers around the world. His work conveys values and positive emotions through vivid shapes and colors and addresses issues of common interest by touching consciences with a smile. Rossetti's output featured in the display at MUDEC Museum in Milan as well as making its international debut with an exhibition in Helsinki, Finland and another in Guadeloupe, French Antilles.

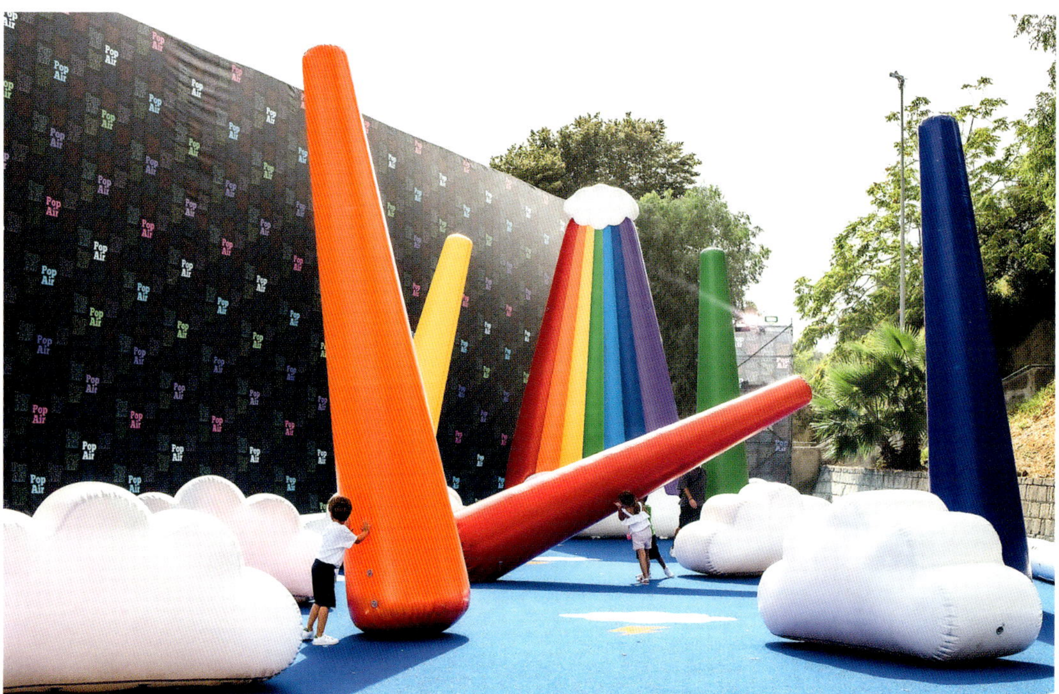

Parcobaleno 2020

Parcobaleno

This installation transforms the rainbow, a symbol of peace, into a place to live, play, smile, and feel free. *Parcobaleno* is based on the desire to build peace through play, because, to live in peace, you have to live by playing! In this installation, the rainbow becomes a real space with large oscillating colored rays to touch, clouds to walk on and Colorama, a large inflatable sculpture 10-meter high that celebrates the rainbow and its colors. *Parcobaleno* is an explosion of hope, *joie de vivre*, and an invitation to freedom, but the most beautiful aspect of this work is created by the visitor, who smiles and plays.

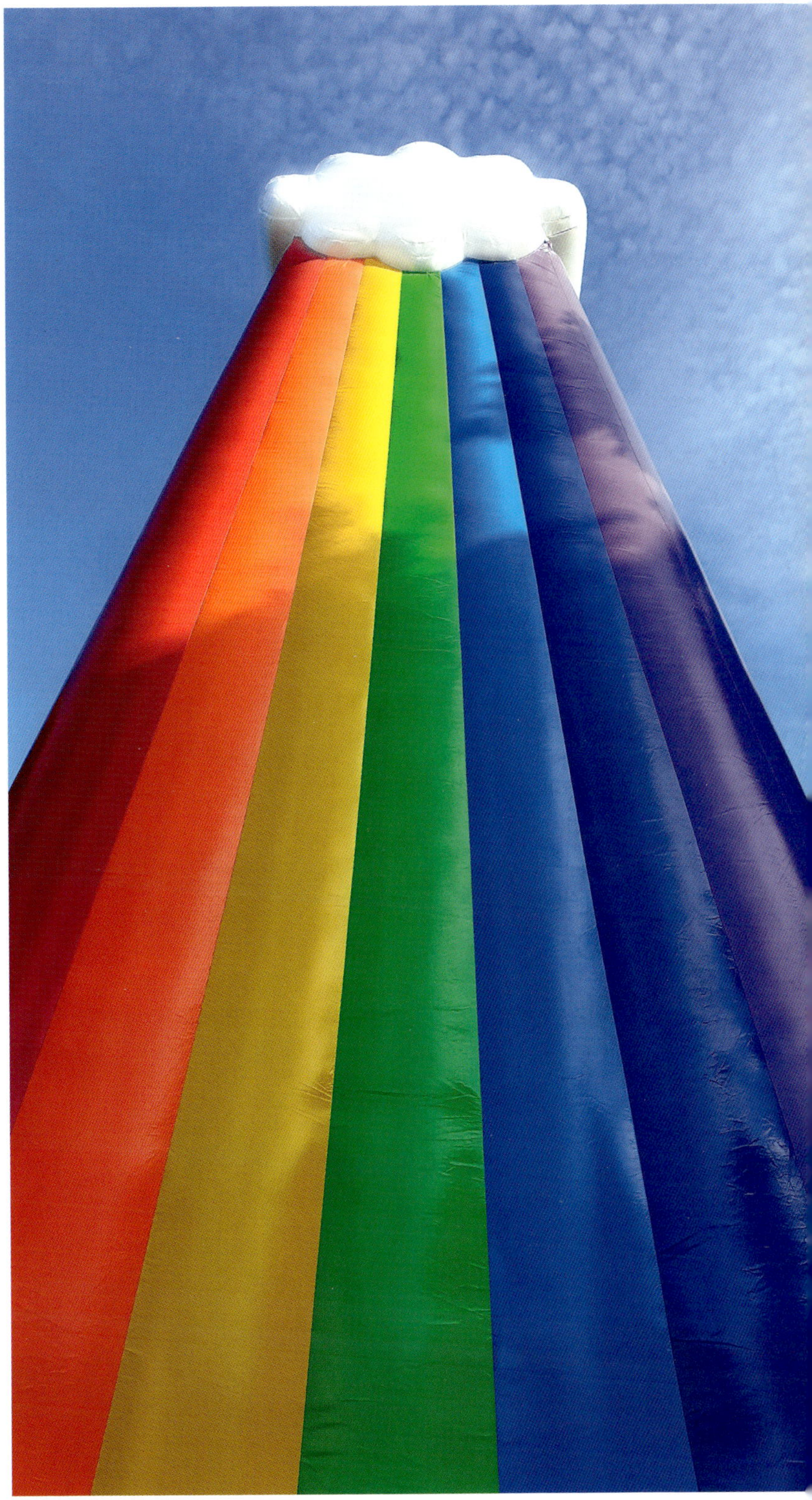

Stefano Rossetti
Parcobaleno
Balloon Museum
Pop Air
Naples, 2023

RUB KANDY

Rub Kandy aka Mimmo Rubino, born in 1979, is an artist who for 20 years has been moving between graffiti, contemporary art, urban art, and applied art. He has collected multiform interventions, different for media, style, technique, context. His research is free from the dictates of recognizability. The language is crossover and mixes fine art, vandalism, and conceptual art. The works alternate strict formalism, minimalism, the optical, social anger, childish emotionality, megalomania, and defeatism. He does not disdain Pop culture, design thinking, applied art. He has participated in several international events, including exhibitions, festivals, public art interventions, and urban regeneration projects. Among them: Panama Biennial, 2013; Outdoor Festival – Ex Caserma Guido Reni, Rome, 2015; SANBA Festival, San Basilio district, Rome, 2015; Manifesta 11 – The European biennial of contemporary art, Zurich, 2016; Artmossphere – Moscow Biennial of Urban Art, 2016; Paphos 2017 European Capital of Culture (Cyprus). His work has featured in international newspapers and publications, particularly in the field of urban art and post-graffiti.

Below
Rub Kandy
The GINJOS
Balloon Museum
Let's Fly
New York, 2023

Opposite
Rub Kandy
The GINJOS
Balloon Museum
Pop Air
Paris, 2022

Logo
***TheGINJOS* for**
Balloon Museum

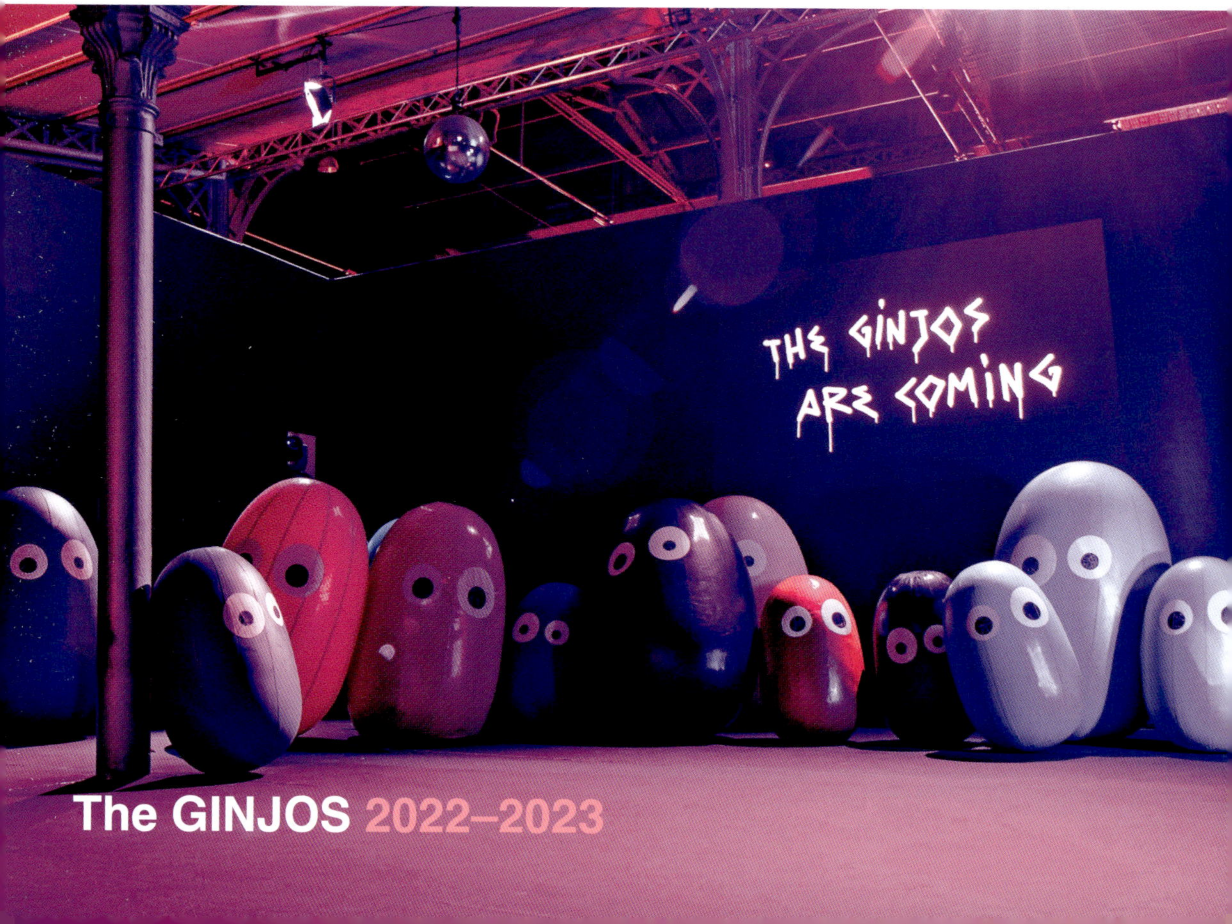

The GINJOS 2022–2023

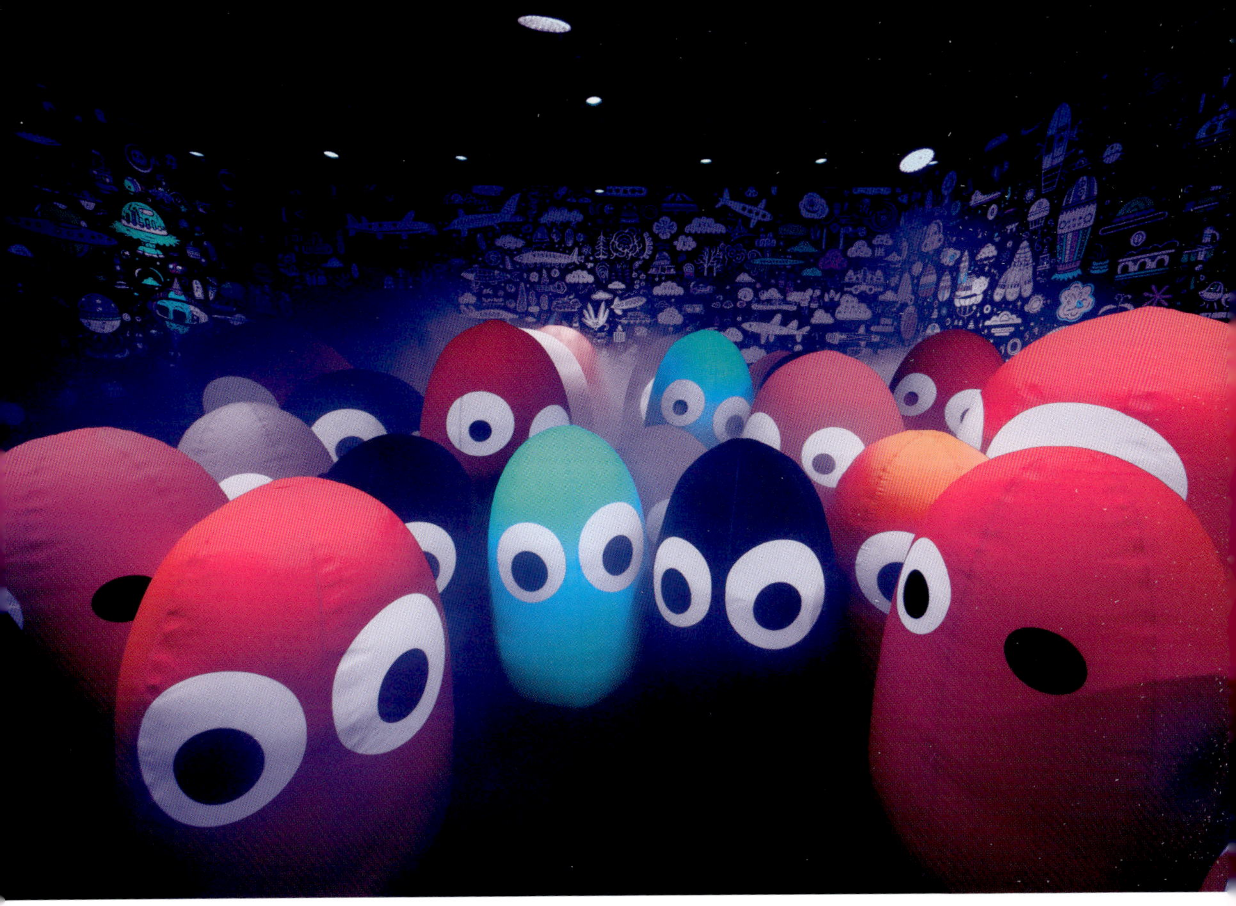

The GINJOS

These strange inflatable creatures have huge eyes that see everything. Following their debut at the *Pop Air* exhibition, they made another appearance at the exhibitions *Let's Fly* and *EmotionAir* at the Balloon Museum. Originating from the jungle on the Panama–Colombia border in Latin America, some of them glow in the dark. Irreverent, affectionate, and filled with contradictions, *The GINJOS* are predominantly silent: lacking mouths, they nevertheless manage to convey a smile through their form and colors. Their large eyes carefully scrutinize the visitors' every movement, creating the impression that they are waiting for them in their realm and are ready to accept interaction with the audience. From tender embraces to playful tugs, *The GINJOS* will be a constant presence, magically coming to life to enrich the exhibition experience.

THE GINJOS ARE COMING

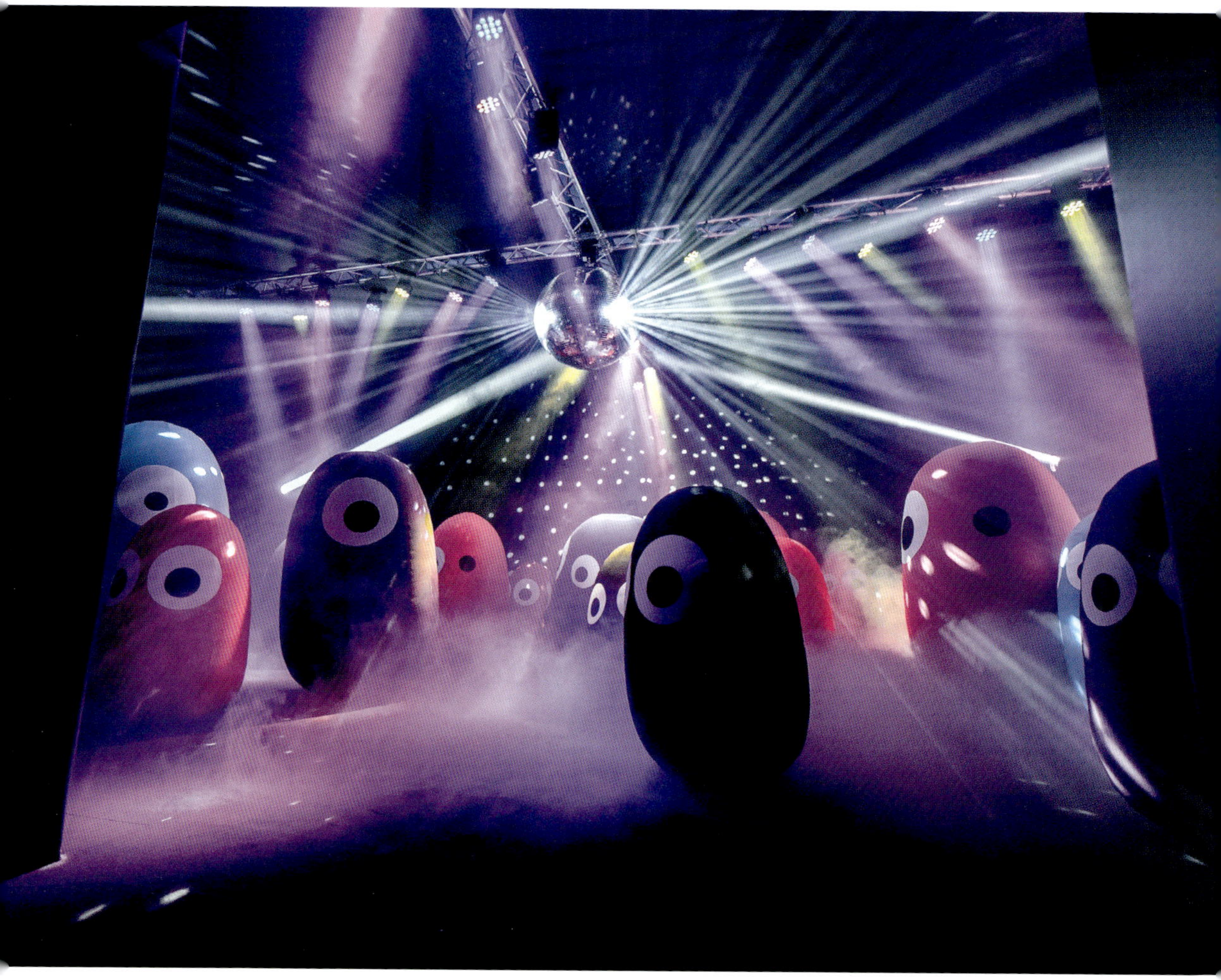

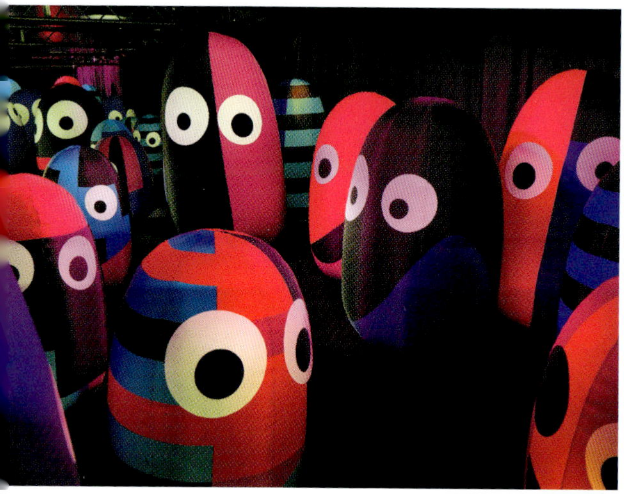

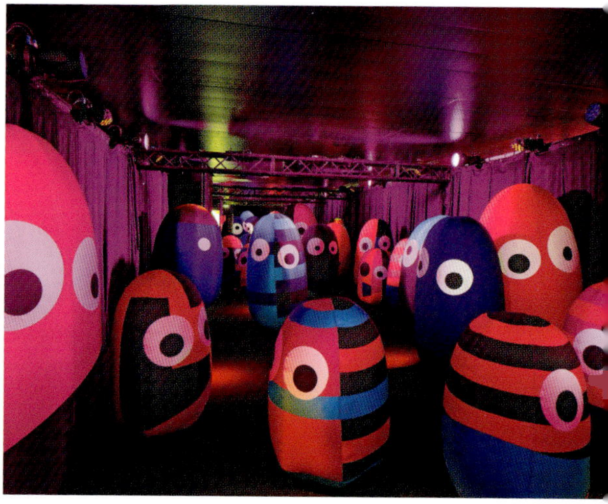

The GINJOS 2022–2023

"One day you wake up and find a GINJO in your house.
Ok, ok, you don't know it's called GINJO, but soon you will and you will also know that it is spelled in CAPSLOCK.
It is not clear where they are from or how long they have been here.
I think they are Portuguese, no, maybe Latino, I don't know, maybe Oriental.
I don't know. I saw the first one in Lisbon, but maybe it was there by accident.
They don't have mouths or they just keep their mouths shut. And I think I know why.
I find it hard to understand what they are thinking or how they communicate with each other.
I get the impression that they are careful not to be discovered by me, to show their feelings.
Or maybe they just ignore me.
They're reserved.
They're quiet, but I think it's actually me who doesn't hear them.
I was immediately intrigued by them, so I tried to learn all about them.
So: they come in Strawberry Red, Purple, Magenta Pink, Babyblue, Black.
I think they hate yellow.
They come in various sizes; I've identified roughly four.
For convenience, I call them the Baby, the Student, the Big, the Superbig.
I'm not sure that different sizes correspond to different ages.
I don't think there are boys and girls.
They also love to party.
Sometimes they are in groups but other times they are alone.
They have feelings.
Is hard to tell but I'm sure they do.
I swear I've seen some of them blush.
I couldn't find anything on Google about them.
I don't know if they are good or bad.
Maybe some are good and some are bad?
Who knows how many there are.
It is impossible to count them, they always change in number.
I don't know how that's possible.
Sometimes I thought they were a figment of my imagination.
I thought I was the only one who saw them.
Yet someone besides me has seen them.
Do you see them?
I swear I saw them."

Opposite top
Rub Kandy
The GINJOS
Balloon Museum
Pop Air
Madrid, 2023

Opposite bottom
Rub Kandy
The GINJOS
Balloon Museum
EmotionAir
London, 2023

Rub Kandy
The GINJOS
Balloon Museum
Pop Air
Naples, 2023

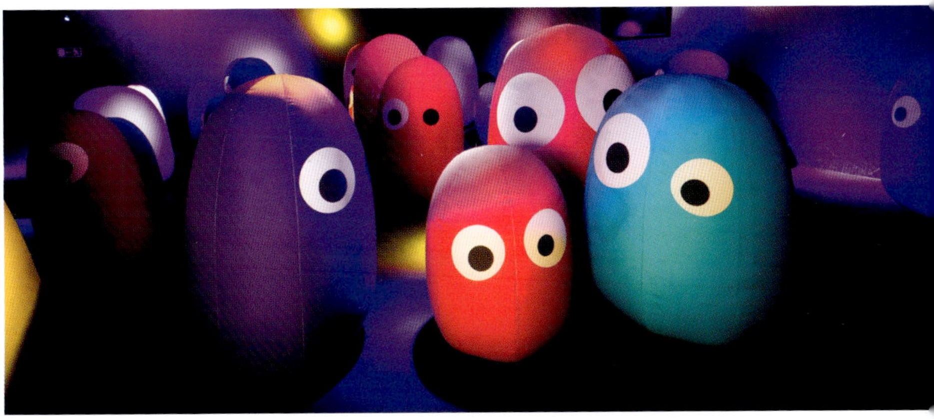

ALEX SCHWEDER

Alex Schweder describes his work as "Performance Architecture" due to the ways his environments develop through performance thinking. His projects include inflatables at a range of scales, extreme buildings that he occupies for periods of time, projections onto mist, and performed renovations of domestic space. By making architecture through performance, Schweder works with space toward questions rather than solutions. His work has been exhibited and collected internationally including by MoMA, Tate Britain, Performa 17, the Tel Aviv Museum of Art, the SFMoMA – San Francisco Museum of Modern Art, and the 2014 Venice Architecture Biennale. He is a fellow of the American Academy in Rome and currently lives and works in New York City.

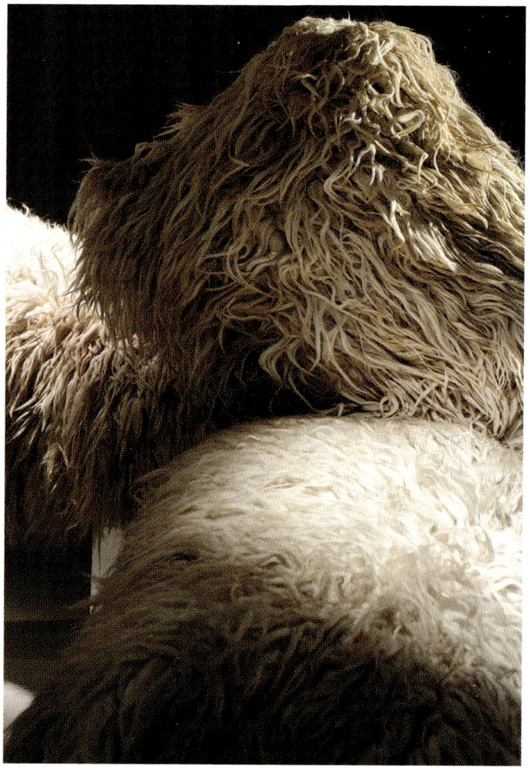

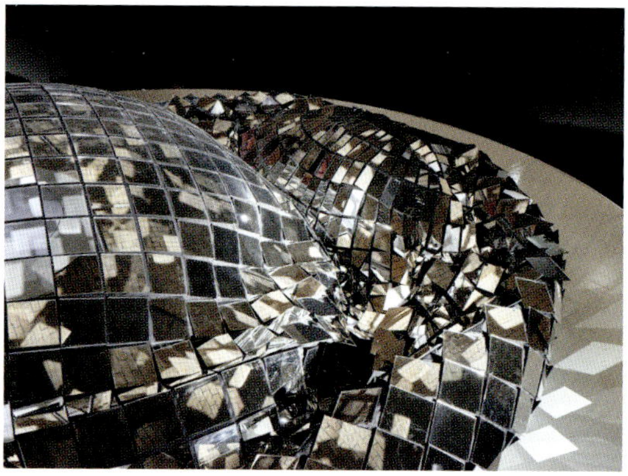

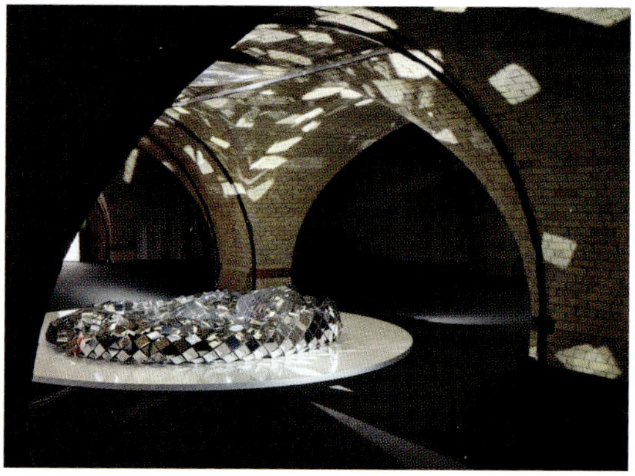

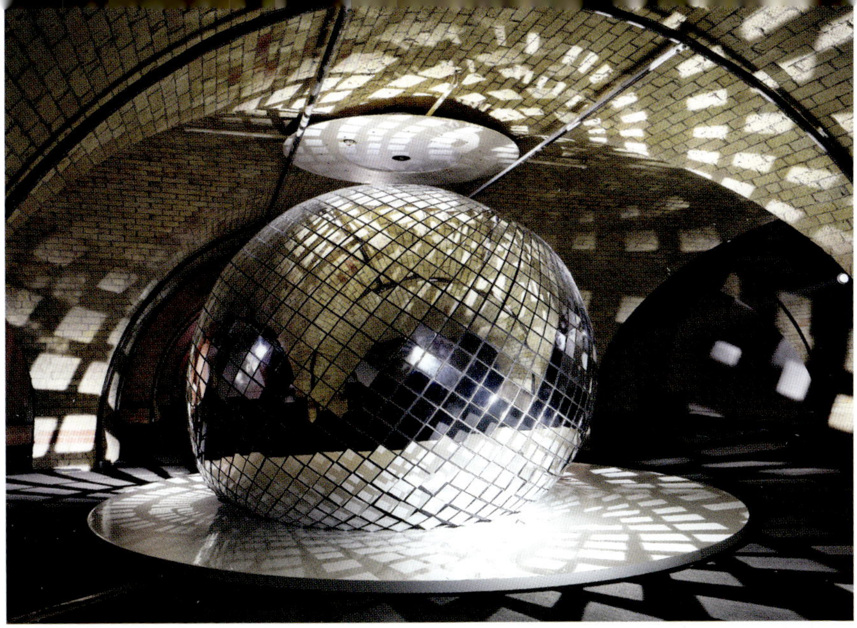

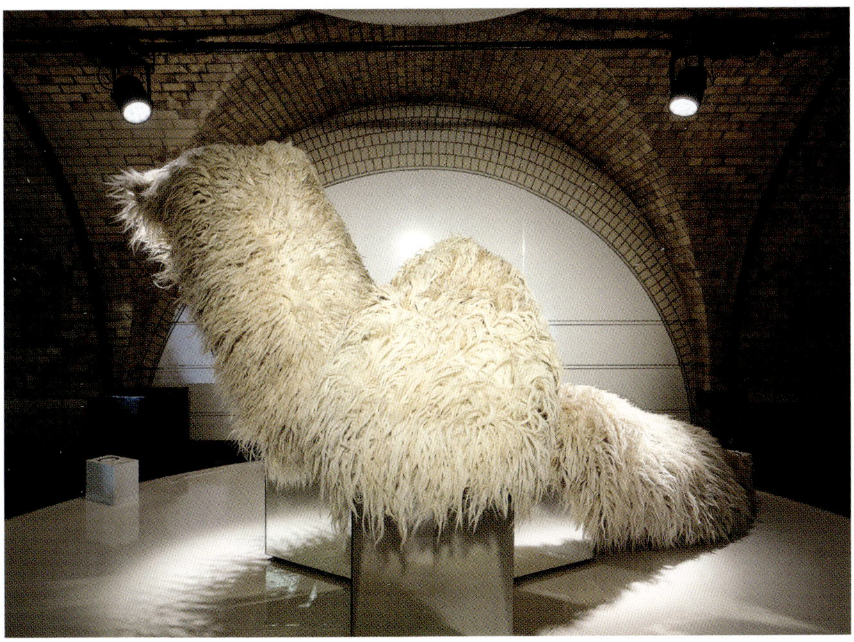

Alex Schweder
The Third Thing
Balloon Museum
EmotionAir
London, 2023

The Third Thing

Described as a cocktail of fur, mirrors, air, and sound, *The Third Thing* was born when the artist began exploring the possibility that the inflatable spaces he had been making for over a decade could also be sonic instruments. Conceived as a duo, the two works that comprise this experience are the mirrored vocalist, *Her Joy,* and the furry string player, *His Dilution*, who merge as they compose sound and space in an intertwined way. Rising and falling as she breathes, *Her Joy* is thought of by the artist as vocalist in the inflatable band *The Third Thing*. Her lyrics become either more or less muffled as the air of her breath is inhaled and exhaled, a rising and collapsing mirror ball at a size that dinosaurs might dance to. During this slow process the reflections of her mirrored dress let the sparks fly. Just as the party ends, it begins once more. The movement of this light that bounces on architectural surfaces and the audience of this band are like kinetic light paintings that fill the space of music.

MICHAEL SHAW

Born in 1973 in Cambridgeshire, United Kingdom, Michael Shaw is a curator, teacher and sculptor. He has been the curator of Burghley Sculpture Garden since 2005, is a lecturer in Fine Art at Loughborough University, UK, whilst also creating giant site-specific inflatables and sculptures at the request of museum collections. In 2005, he earned a doctorate based on Donald Judd's sculptural concept "Specific Objects." He has had many solo exhibitions in the United Kingdom as well as taken part in group exhibitions in Europe and abroad. Shaw has garnered many awards including from the Arts Council of England, artist in residency at *OPEMS,* the Collection, Lincoln, and at the Wirksworth Festival. He has exhibited internationally, most recently an inflatable artwork at the CICA Museum in Gimpo, Korea and Hi-Viz, a 46 x 20 x 5 meter sculpture for the 2024 Sydney Festival.

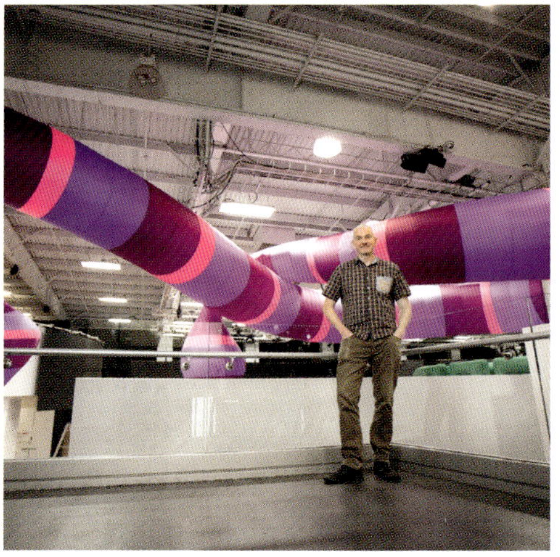

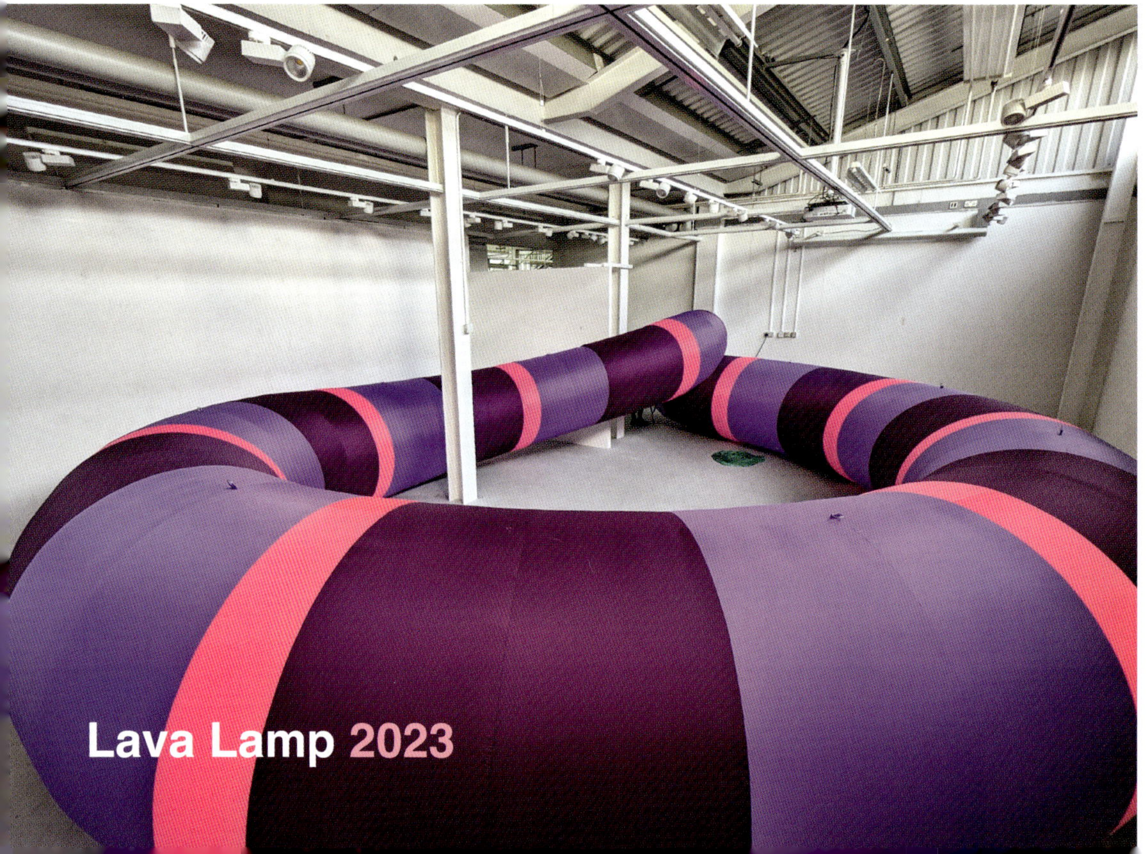

Lava Lamp 2023

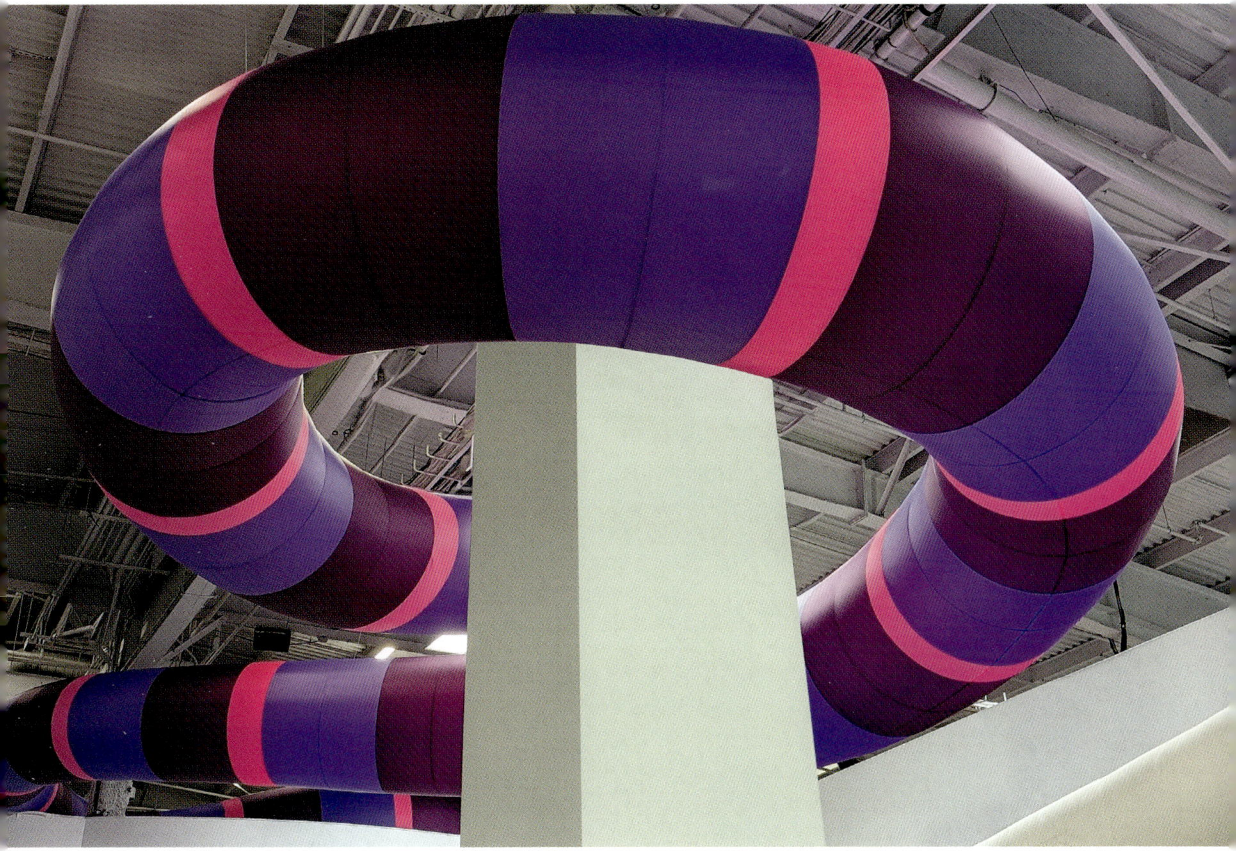

Lava Lamp

For the *Let's Fly* exhibition, Michael Shaw created an architecturally bespoke response: *Lava Lamp*, a monumental, inflatable and colorful sculpture. With this title, the artist refers to the lamp invented in 1963, a vertical glass globe containing a transparent liquid in which colored balls of melted wax circulate. Michael Shaw's sculpture is inspired by the colors, shapes, and movement of the lamp, which became a Pop reference in the 1990s. Like a sleeping creature, the inflatable gives the strange impression of breathing in and out. Indeed, its fans are constantly activated, blowing air cyclically into the structure. Measuring more than 44 meters in length, the artwork wraps itself around the space, overflowing at both ends. This psychedelic snake is composed of repeating violet, lilac, and pink stripes. A pattern of colors that accentuates its curvilinear course around the building. Thanks to its immensity and extravagance, Michael Shaw's sculpture is a striking installation to behold, and due to its partial suspension, is visible from many angles of the building.

Micheal Shaw
Lava Lamp
Balloon Museum
Let's Fly
New York, 2023

Opposite

Michael Shaw
with his artwork
Lava Lamp
Balloon Museum
Let's Fly
New York, 2023

Michael Shaw
Lava Lamp
The artist's studio
United Kingdom, 2023

SILA SVETA

Sila Sveta, founded in 2008 by Alexander Us and Alexey Rozov, is a multidisciplinary international media, production and conceptual design studio that combines innovative technology and creative expression to develop immersive digital art installations and experiences worldwide.
Sila Sveta is a pioneer and innovator in the field of big multimedia productions. The studio's DNA is of strongly musical and performative arts nature, boasting an exceptional portfolio, including names and brands like The Weeknd, Drake, Billie Eilish, FIFA, NBA, Mercedes, Audi, Porsche and AT&T. From the music world it has been almost natural for Sila Sveta to expand their interests to other scenes and innovative combinations of art and technologies, that they cover from concept to release. 90+ awards won, 700+ projects completed.
The essential idea: creating miracles.

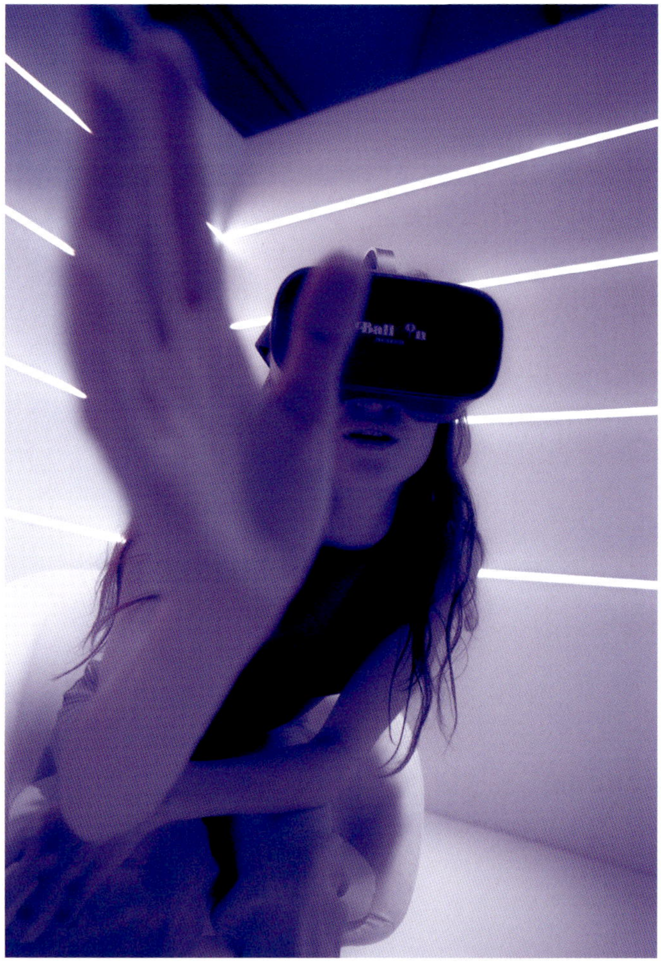

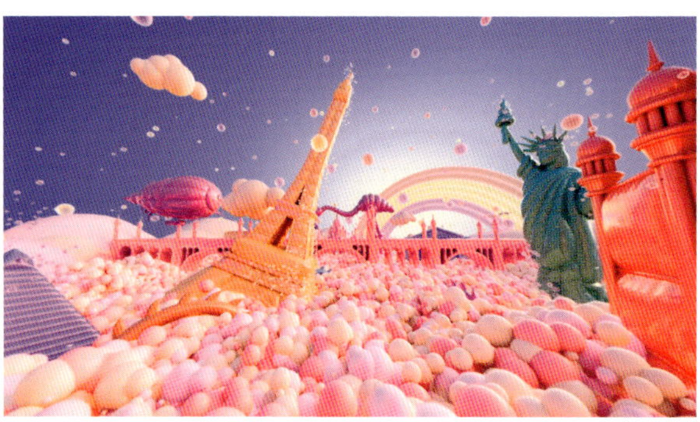

Top
Sila Sveta
Airscape
Balloon Museum
Let's Fly
New York, 2023

Still frames
from *Airscape*
by SIla Sveta
Balloon Museum
Let's Fly
New York, 2023

Airscape 2023

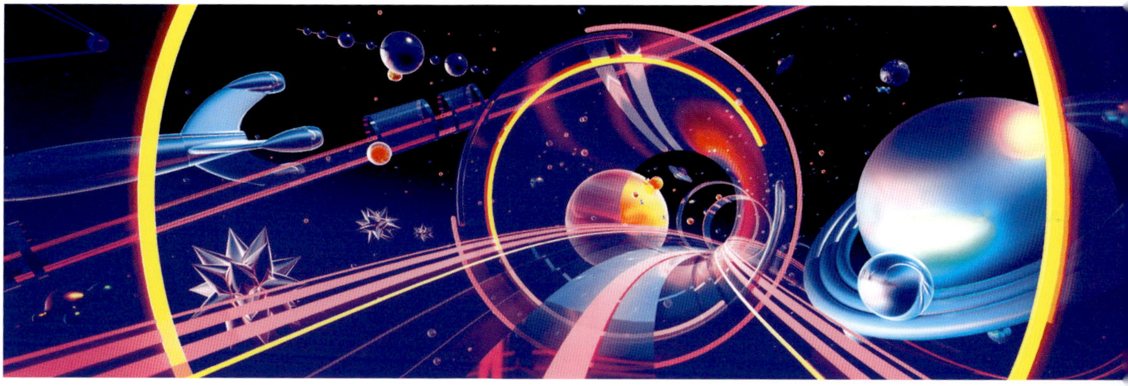

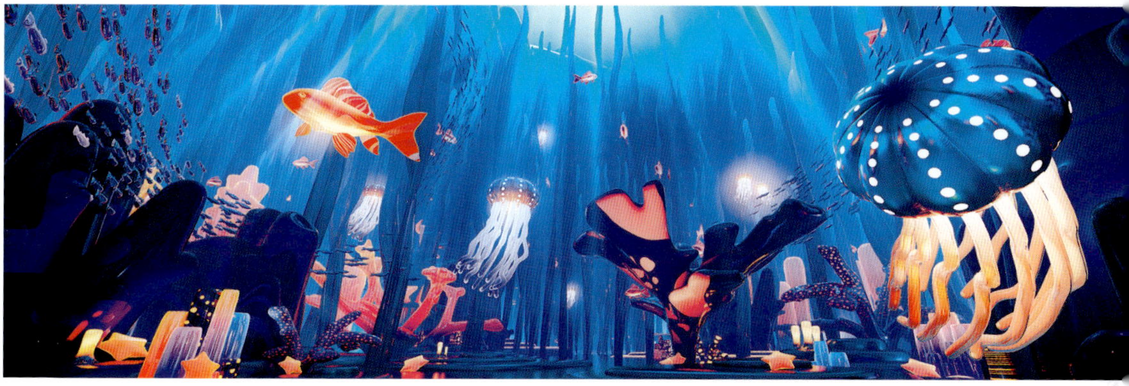

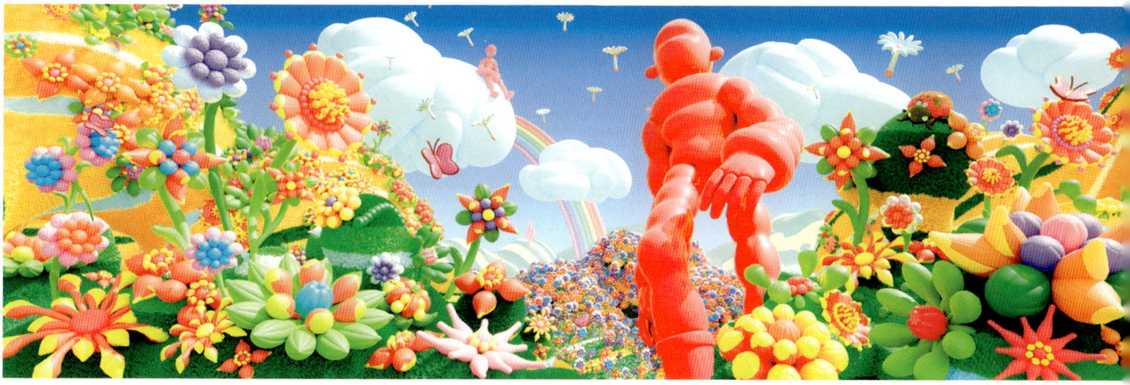

Airscape - *VR Immersive Experience*
The Sila Sveta collective immerses us in captivating inflatable worlds. Wearing a virtual reality (VR) headset, we are projected into a long tracking shot, as if through a video game. The artists transport us from world to world to discover bubbles, balloons, castles, grandiose palaces, rollercoasters, and unexpected underwater creatures. By alternating scales, from the infinitely large to the infinitely small, the artists produce the sensation of an unlimited universe, where anything seems possible. This video evokes anecdotes and references, notably, to what appears to be the Colosseum, an immense amphitheater in the heart of Rome. A fitting reference, given that the Balloon Museum's creators are based in Rome, Italy. With this dynamic sequence shot, viewers are plunged into a breathtaking visual journey, a unique immersive experience designed especially for the Balloon Museum.

KARINA SMIGLA-BOBINSKI

Karina Smigla-Bobinski
ADA
Balloon Museum
Let's Fly
New York, 2023

Opposite, top
Karina Smigla-Bobinski
with her artwork *ADA*
Balloon Museum
Let's Fly
New York, 2023

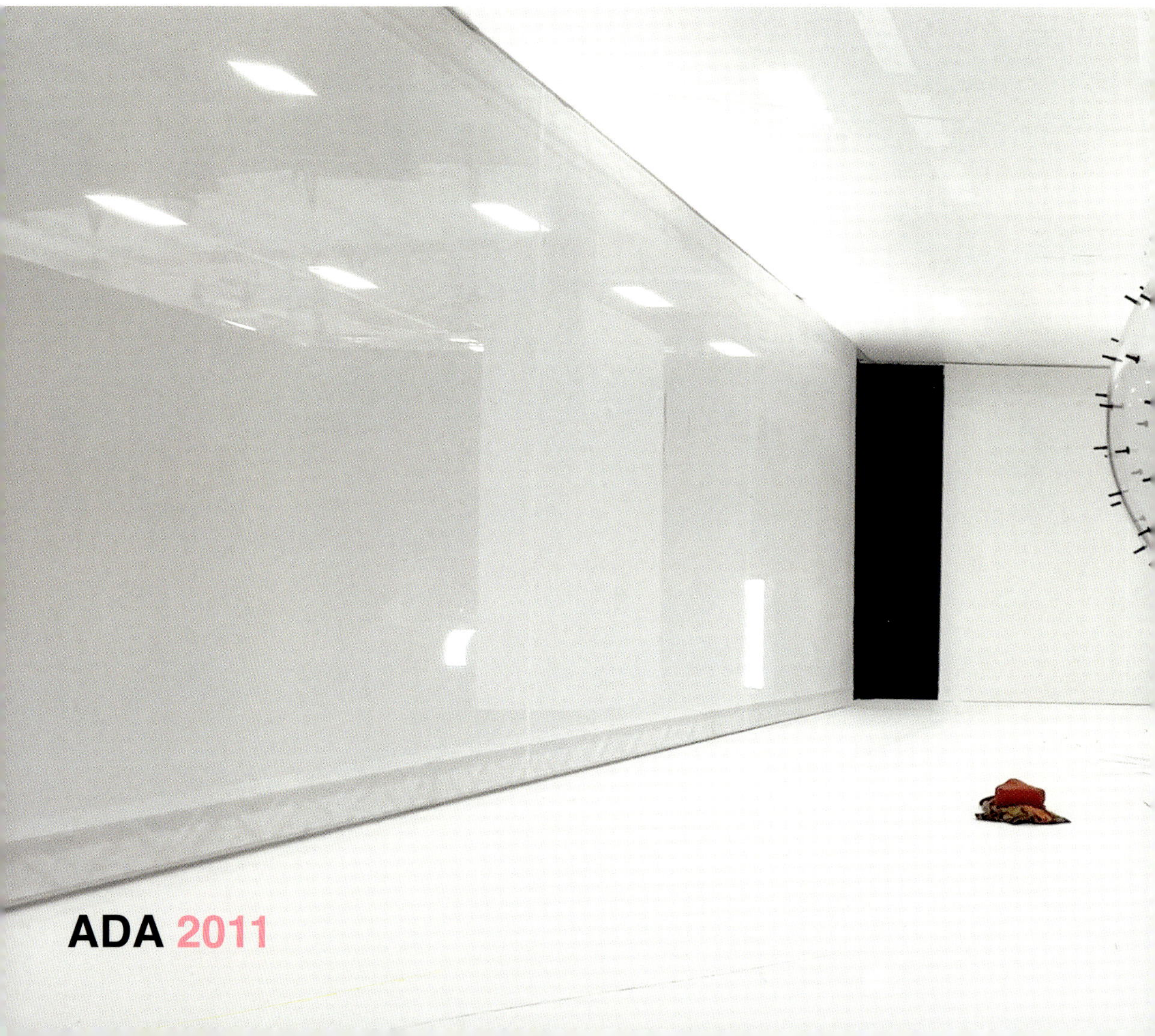

ADA 2011

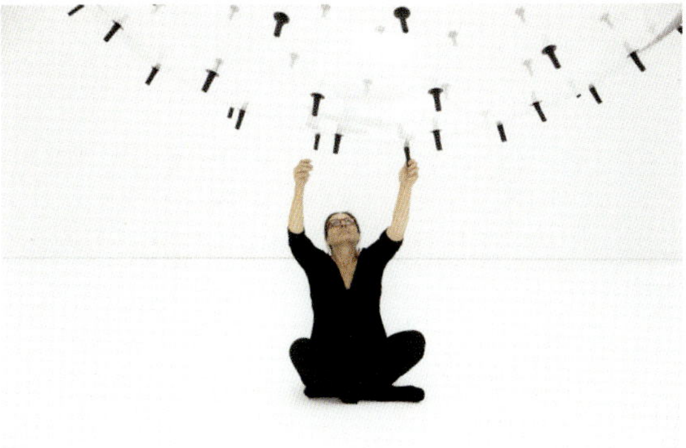

"My work is all about playing together between consciousness and body, between science and art, and between the artist and the audience."

Karina Smigla-Bobinski is an open-media artist who works with analog and digital media in the field of proprioceptive art. Her themes move between science, intuition, expression, and cognition. She creates and collaborates on projects ranging from painting, kinetic sculptures, interactive installations, art interventions, mixed reality objects, multimedia physical theater performances, and online projects. Her works have been shown in 53 countries on 6 continents at festivals, and in galleries and museums including the New Taipei City Art Museum in Taiwan, Chroniques Biennale in Aix-en-Provence, France, Ming Contemporary Art Museum in Shanghai, China, Mattress Factory – Museum of Contemporary Art / Pittsburgh as well as collaborative performances worldwide including at the Festival Montpellier, France, Grand Théâtre, Luxembourg, GoDown Art Center Nairobi, Kenya, and Biennale di Venezia – Arsenale, to name but a few.

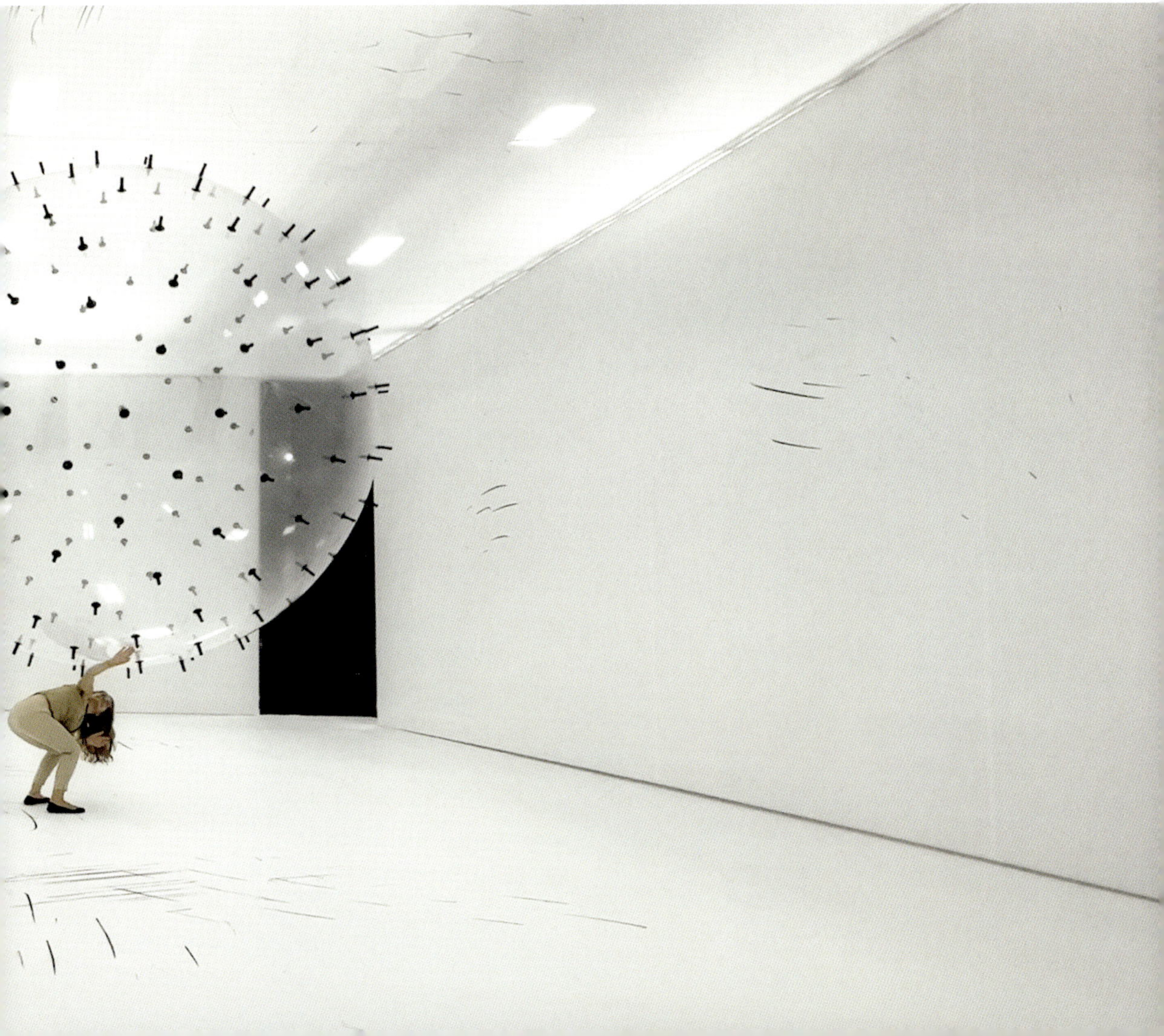

ADA

Named in honor of the eponymous 19th-century English mathematician Ada Lovelace, famous for having created the first true computer program and envisioning a machine capable of generating works of art, *ADA* is a self-generating work of art. Inflated with helium, it bristles with charcoal sticks. This PVC sphere floats freely in space and it is in this weightlessness that *ADA* leaves its mark. Activated by the gestures of

visitors, the sphere moves, rolls on itself, ending up on the floors and white walls of the rectangular room. Like a sheet of paper, the walls are completely scribbled over. No matter how hard visitors try to control it, they soon realize that *ADA* is an independent artist. Her movement expresses itself visually and, like a computer, produces unpredictable results. A unique, evolving interactive installation that grows with its audience.

Karina Smigla-Bobinski
ADA
Balloon Museum
Let's Fly
New York, 2023

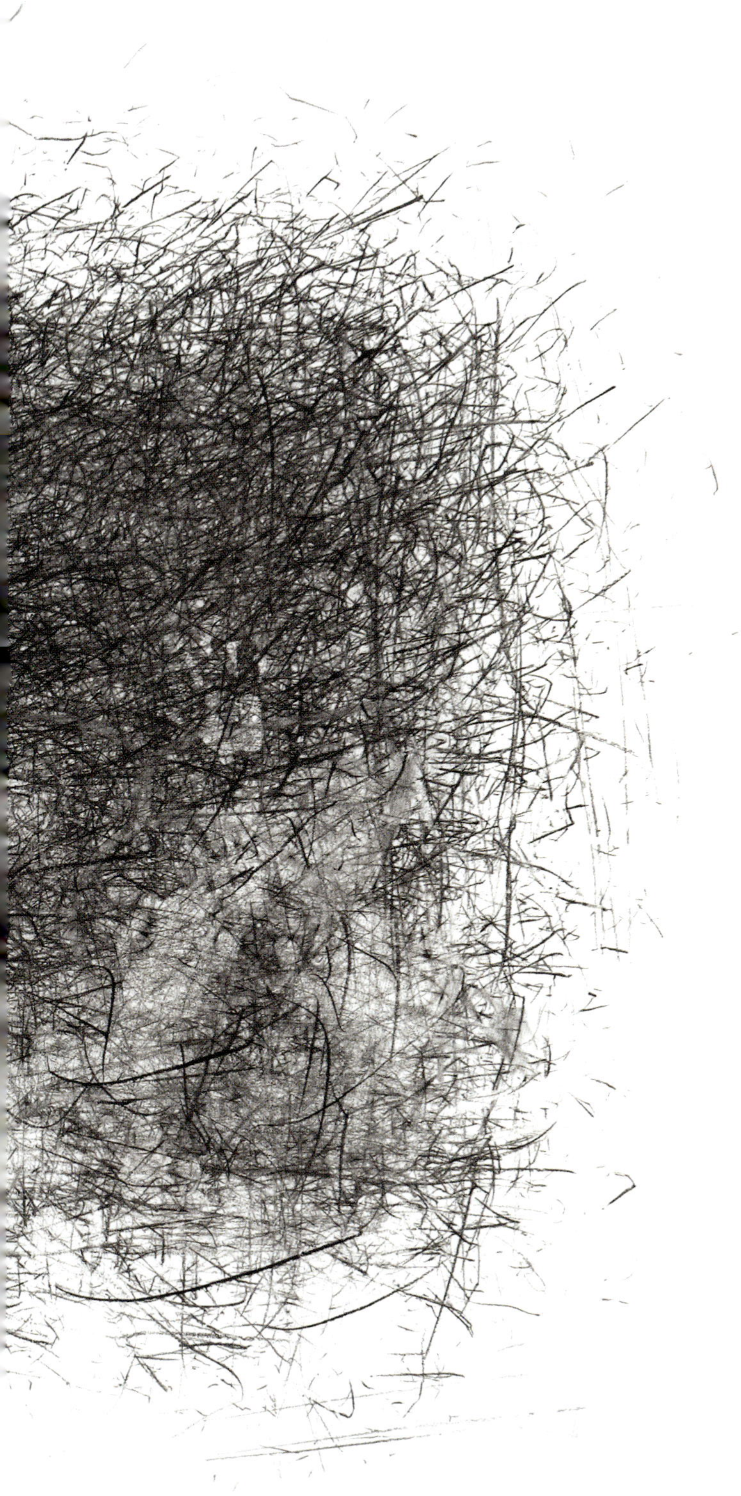

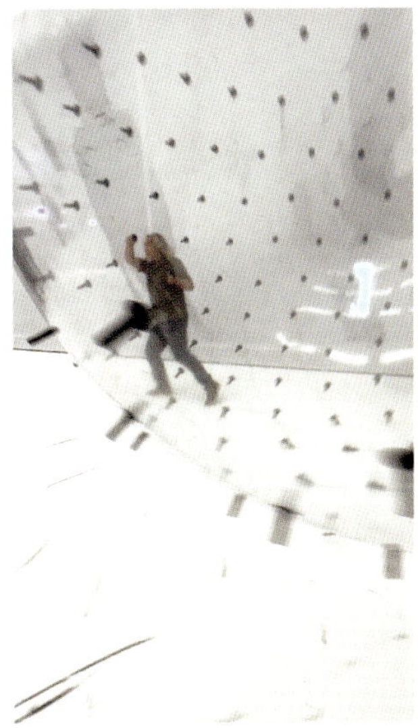

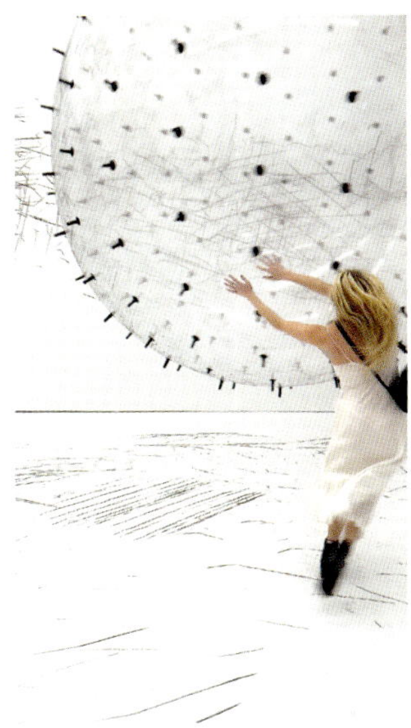

KARINA SMIGLA-BOBINSKI

POLYHEADRA

The interactive installation by Karina Smigla-Bobinski presented for the first time at the *Pop Air* exhibition in Milan in 2022 is called *POLYHEADRA*. The title is a play on words that combines the word POLYHEDRA, referred to three-dimensional geometric shapes ('poly' meaning many and 'hedron' base), and the word HEAD (head) resulting in the idea that there are many minds contributing to this work. All the opinions and ideas that come out of the many minds of the participants continually reformulate the composition of this collective work or, in other words, an open-source work of art. The idea is based on the self-configuration processes in nature, such as the selfs-configuration of the brain. In this installation, in fact, visitors can configure the artwork themselves. *POLYHEADRA* is intended for precisely that, a room filled with tubes of varying sizes and lengths with magnets placed strategically along the body and at its ends, asking the participants to create continuous and collaborative formations by connecting the tubes to each other, attaching them to the walls, and hanging them from the ceiling. The work is therefore also collaborative, with participants working together to create their own installations within the room. The artist encourages increasingly audacious arrangements that ultimately lead to the contents of the entire room collapsing to the ground, symbolizing life where pieces may tumble, leaving it to us to gather and reassemble them.

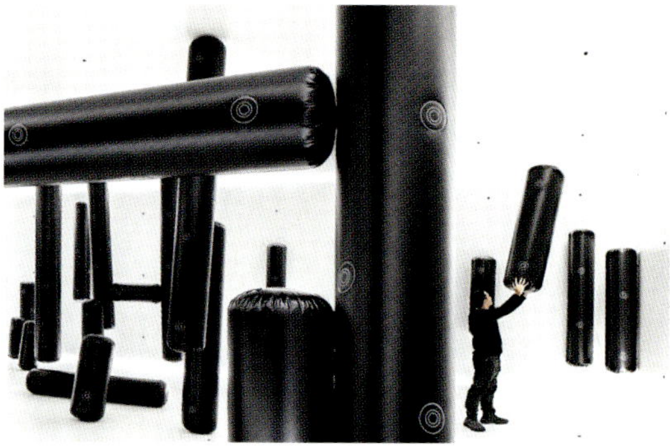

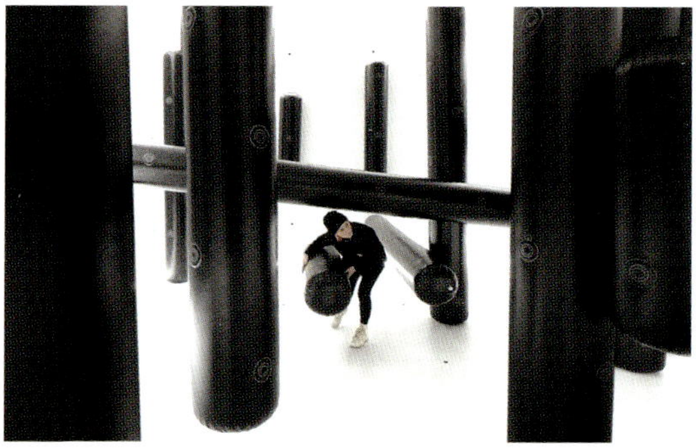

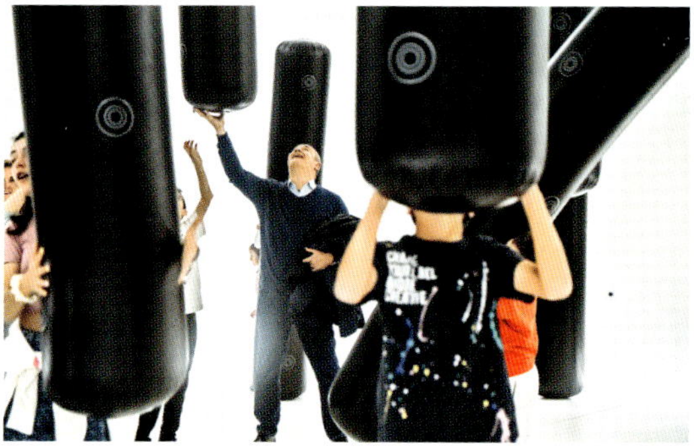

Here and overleaf
Karina Smigla-Bobinski
POLYHEADRA
Balloon Museum
Pop Air
Madrid, 2023

POLYHEADRA 2022

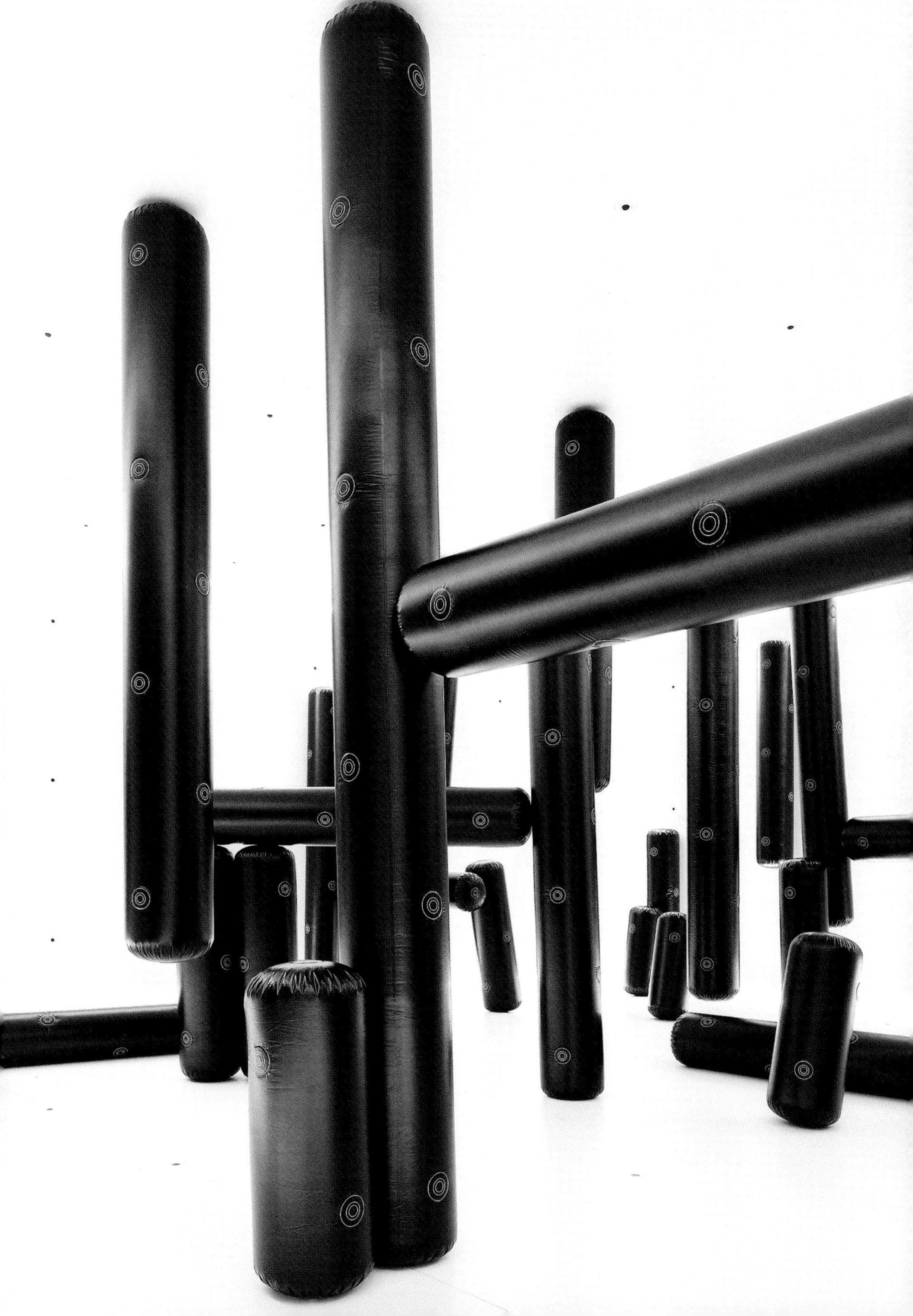

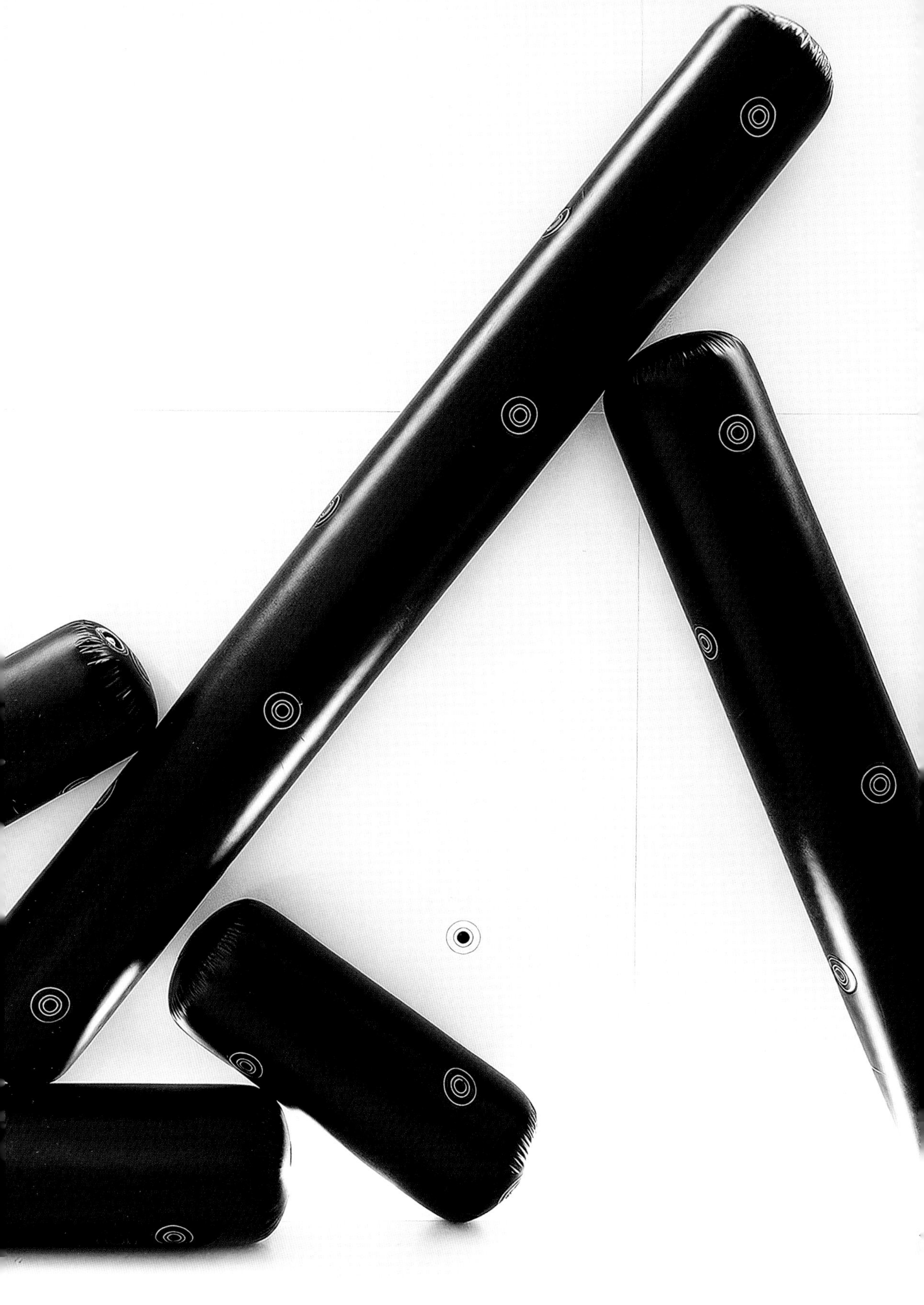

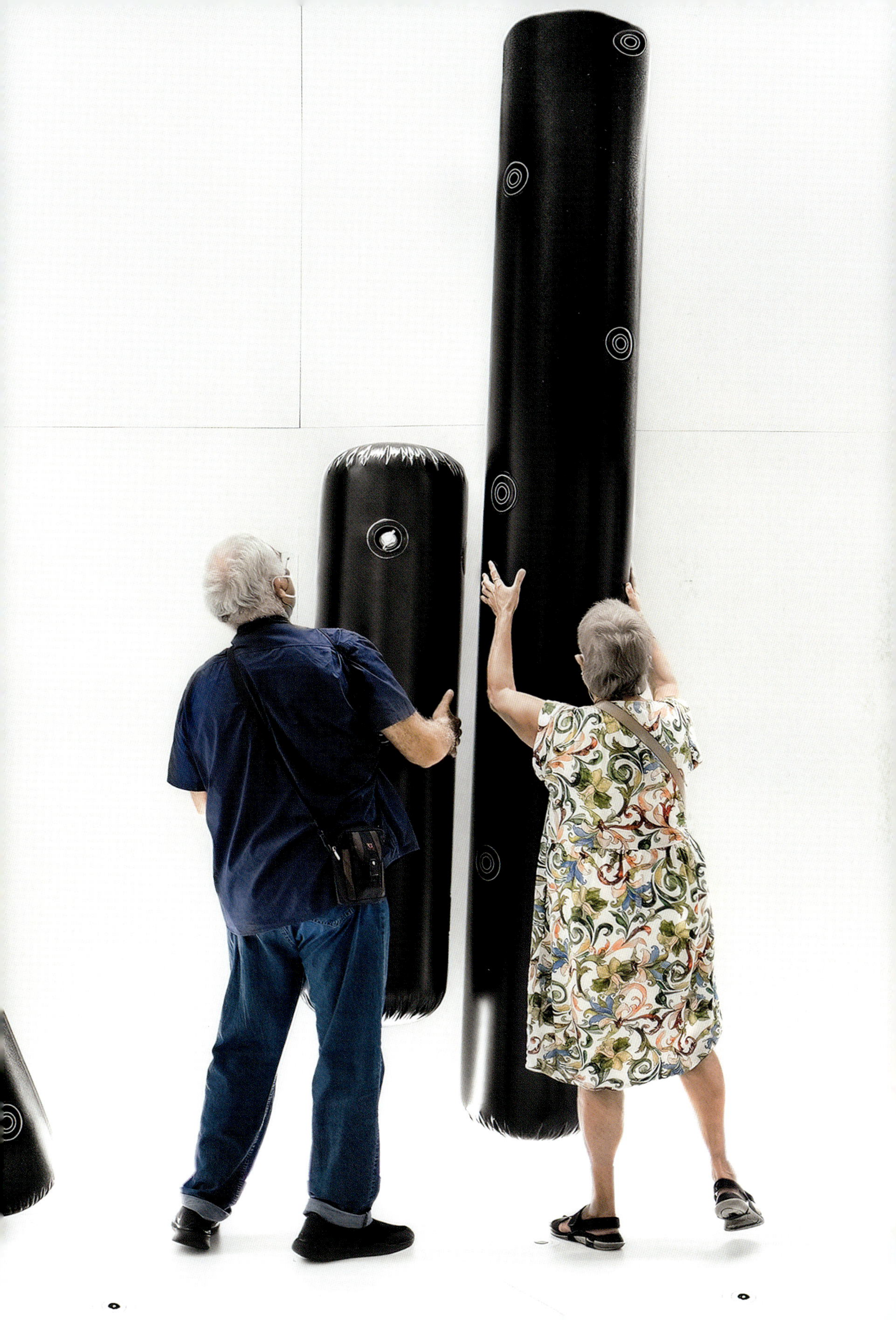

KARINA SMIGLA-BOBINSKI

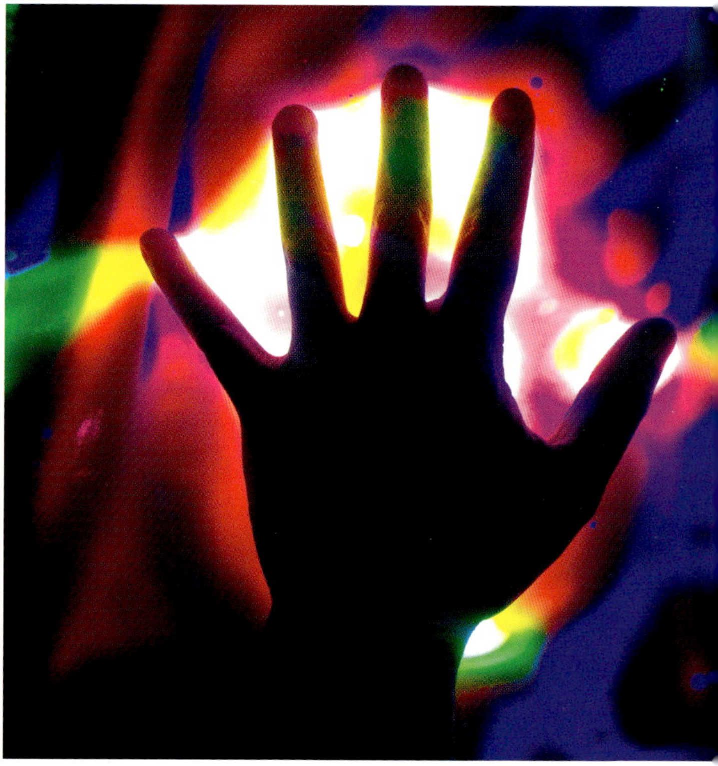

Kaleidoscope
This interactive artwork is composed of large luminous tables where cyan, magenta, and yellow inks float on the surface on separate levels. The word "Kaleidoscope" originates from the Greek, meaning "to see beautiful forms," inviting reflection on perception and beauty in their sensory dimensions. The piece explores how color can be a way to discover the world and our connection to it. Each touch from the audience shifts

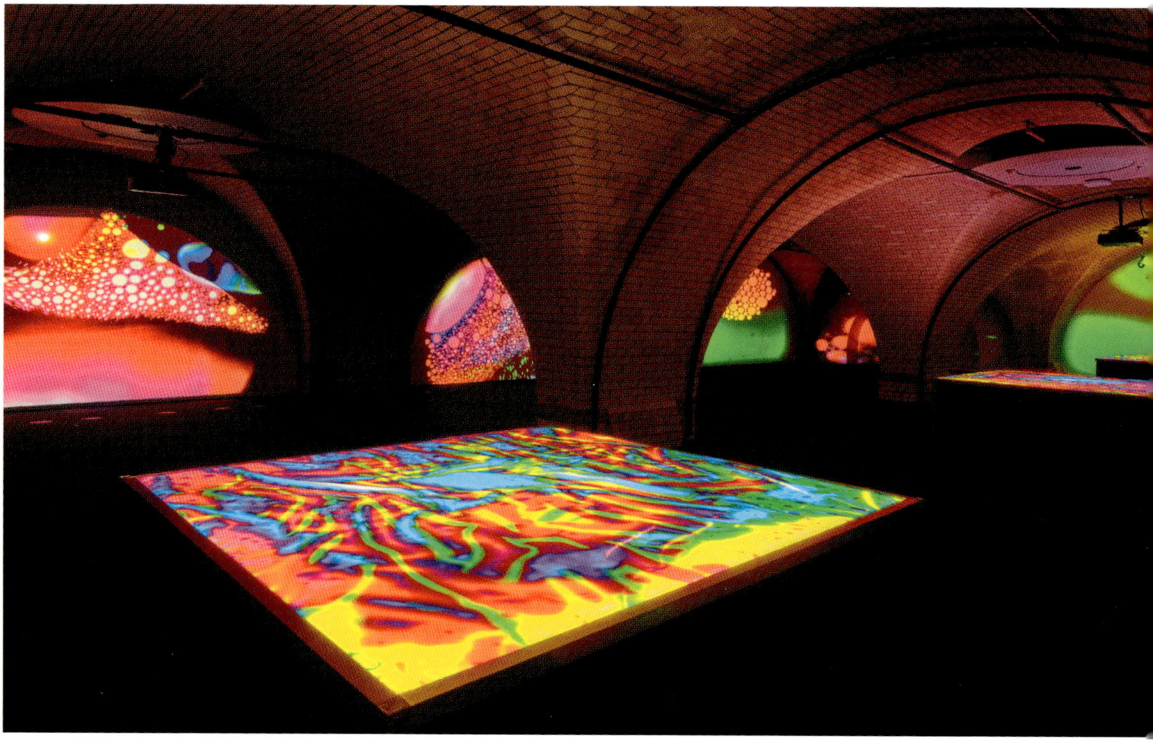

Kaleidoscope 2016

Karina Smigla-Bobinski
Kaleidoscope
Balloon Museum
EmotionAir
London 2023

and alters the inks, creating infinite combinations on the table's surface.
From the overlap of the CMY virtual colors (cyan, magenta, yellow) new true hues like RGB (red, green, blue) emerge that can be perceived by the human retina. This experience is enriched and amplified by projections all around the room, capturing every movement and combination created. Here the magic happens in exactly the opposite way, with the RGB light from the projectors creating the new virtual hues of CMY colors on the walls. The associated emotions multiply across various layers of the artwork: from the joy and fun of initial interaction to curiosity in understanding and creating multiple combinations, to the discomfort of leaving old thinking patterns. Subsequently, wonder and confusion arise, leading to the revelation of a new world.

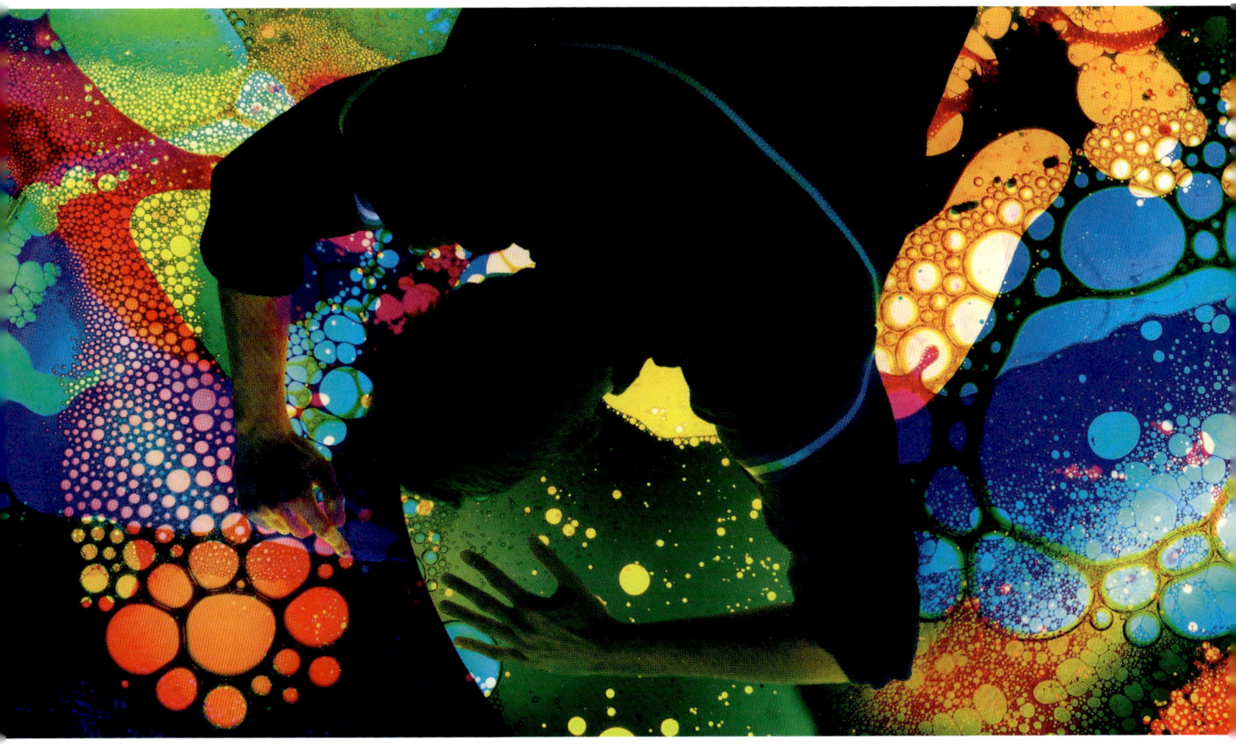

SpY

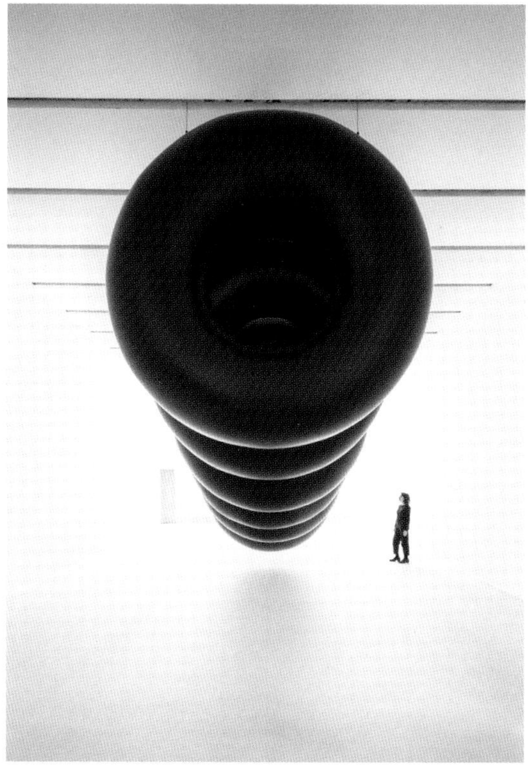

The contextual art projects of Spanish artist SpY are among the most original and talked-about contributions in the evolution from urban art to public art. Throughout his career, SpY's practice has developed into an increasingly spectacular body of large-scale installations and interventions, ever more ambitious and impactful, produced in cities across the world. SpY interpellates viewers while engaging them as active subjects in the artistic process. He works with incisive concepts and strong formal approaches, raising substantial questions about the reality of human relations. SpY designs and produces his artistic projects from his platform SpY Studio. The studio is both a laboratory space and an eclectic team of technical specialists and craftsmen, and is known for an unparalleled ability to bring to life unique, alluring, and formally solid artistic experiences.

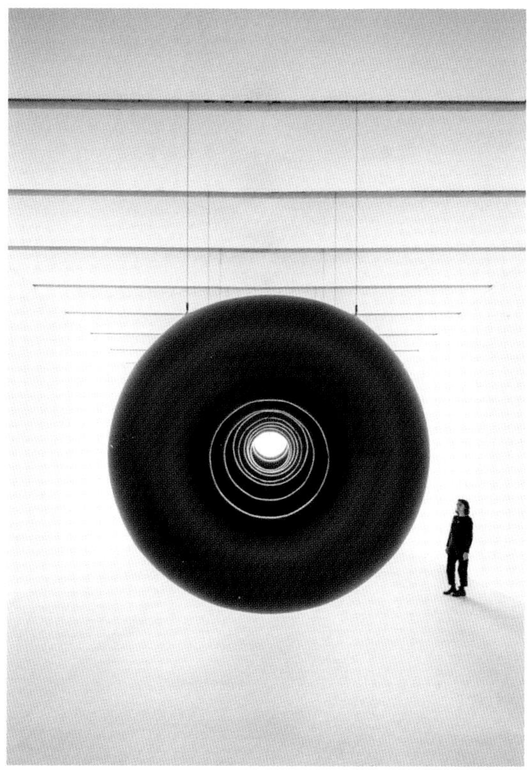

SpY
ZEROS
Balloon Museum
Let's Fly
New York, 2023

ZEROS 2023

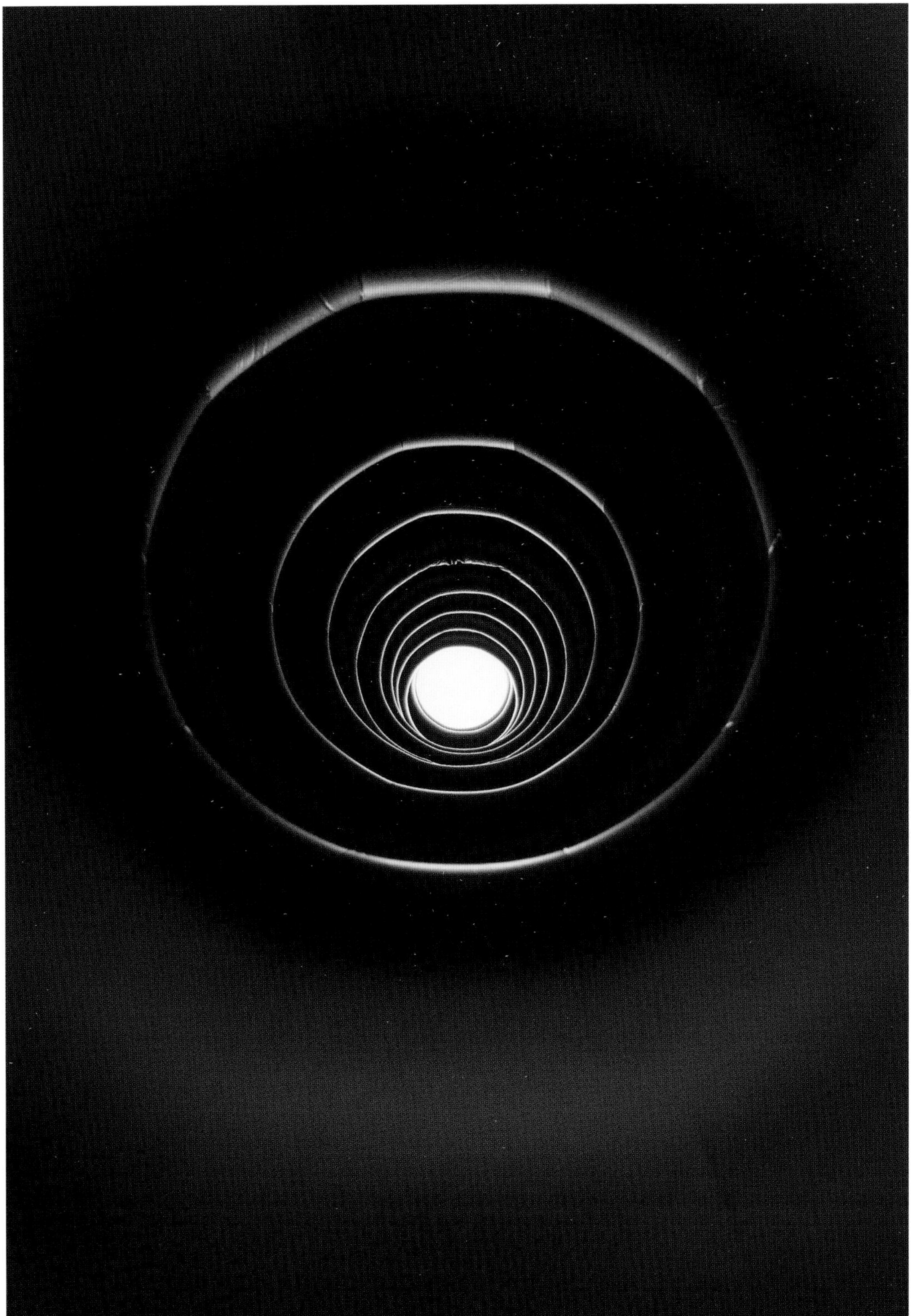

ZEROS

This is a kinetic inflatable sculpture, a work in motion. Made up of a dozen black inner tubes, each around three meters high, that move in a slow, undulating choreography. The contrast between the dazzling white light of the room and the intense, matte black of the inflatable rings draws the viewer's eye. In contact with this strange mechanical ballet, the heart slows down and breathing becomes hypnotized. The movements breathe life into this plastic animal, creating a unique visual and spatial experience. The installation recalls the creations of the ZERO group, pioneers of Inflatable Art, a collective that emerged in the 1950s and sought to turn inflatables into objects of communication, redefining the relationship between artwork and space. The group was founded by German artists Otto Piene and Heinz Mack.

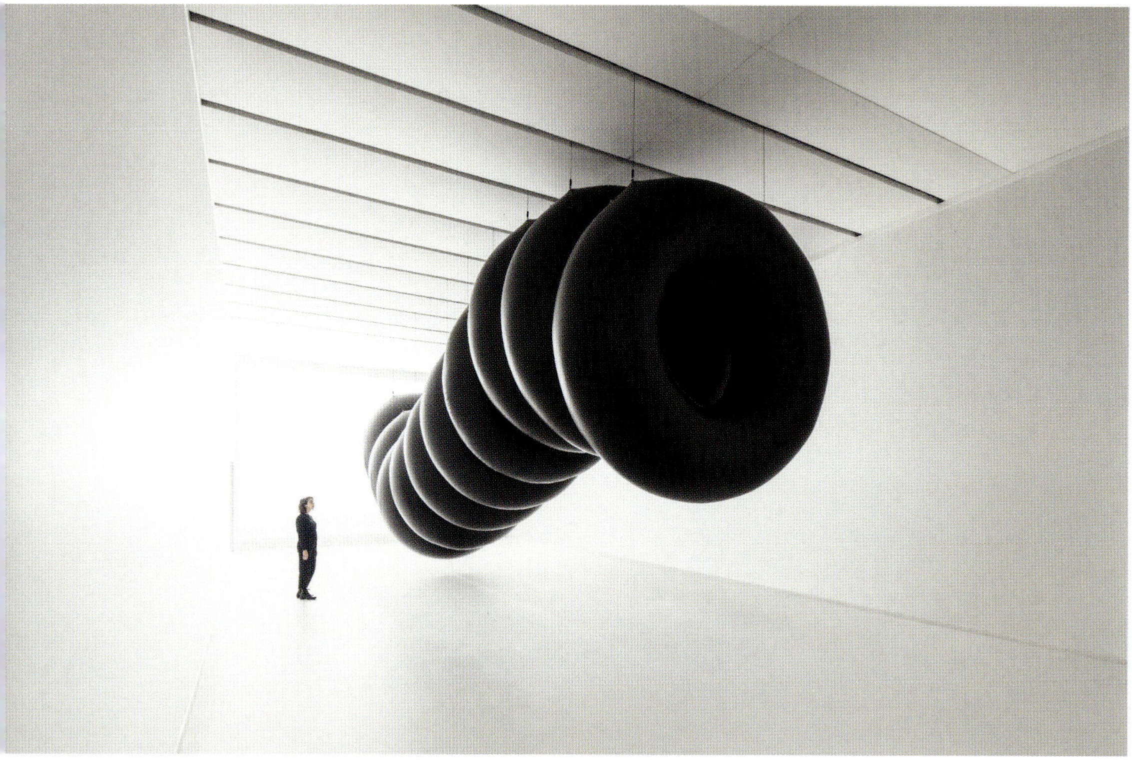

ZEROS 2023

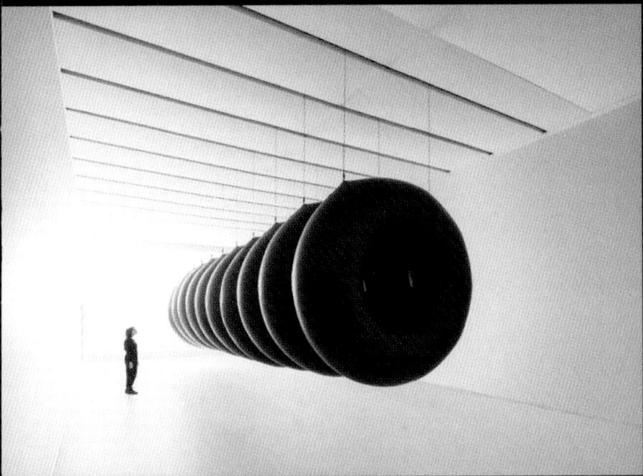
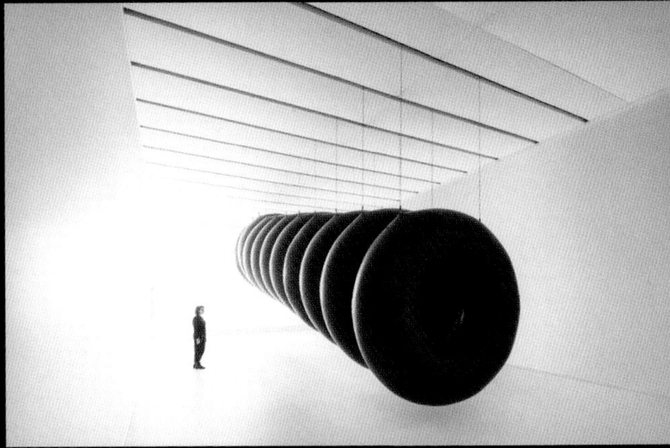
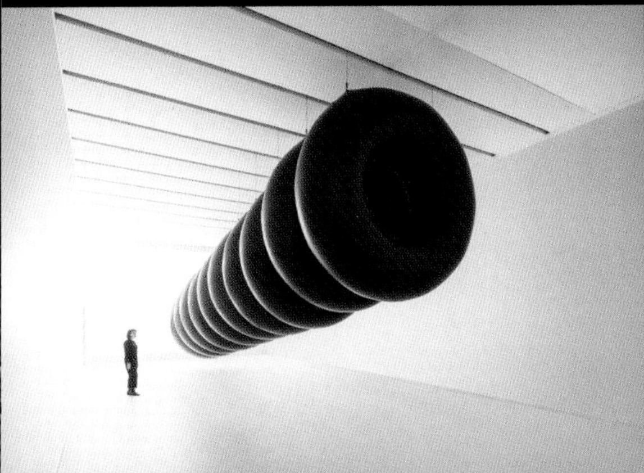
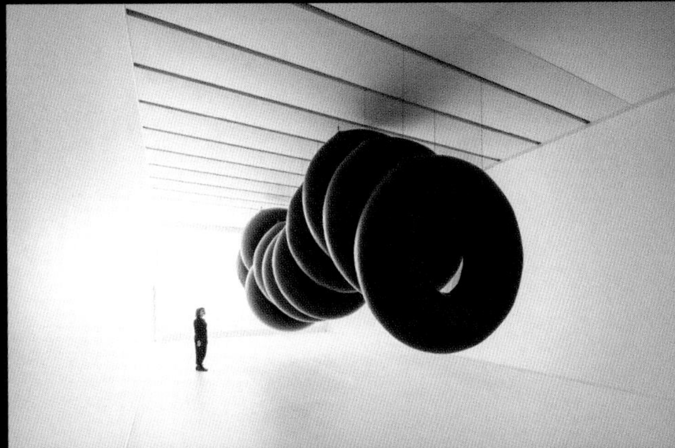
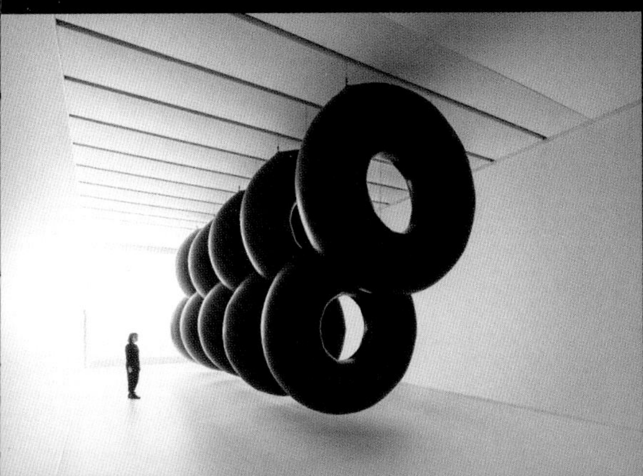
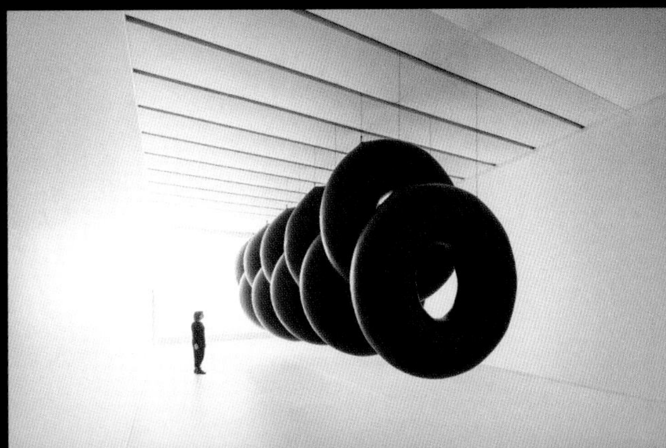

MAX STREICHER

Max Streicher is a sculptor and installation artist from Alberta, Canada, now residing in Toronto. Since 1989 he has worked extensively with inflatable technology in kinetic sculptures and installation works. In 2007 Streicher was a presenter at "Take a Deep Breath", a symposium hosted by Tate Modern, London, UK. He was a founding member of NetherMind, a Toronto-based collective of sculptors who, since 1991, have coordinated several exhibitions in alternative sites, such as abandoned factories. He has shown widely across Canada and internationally in museums, public galleries, and at cultural festivals. Streicher's inflatable works are in various collections, among them the Albertina Museum in Vienna, The Hara Museum of Contemporary Art in Tokyo, The Beaverbrook Art Gallery, Fredericton, New Brunswick, and The Art Gallery of Windsor, in Ontario.

Max Streicher
Battle of Cannae
Balloon Museum
Pop Air
Paris, 2022

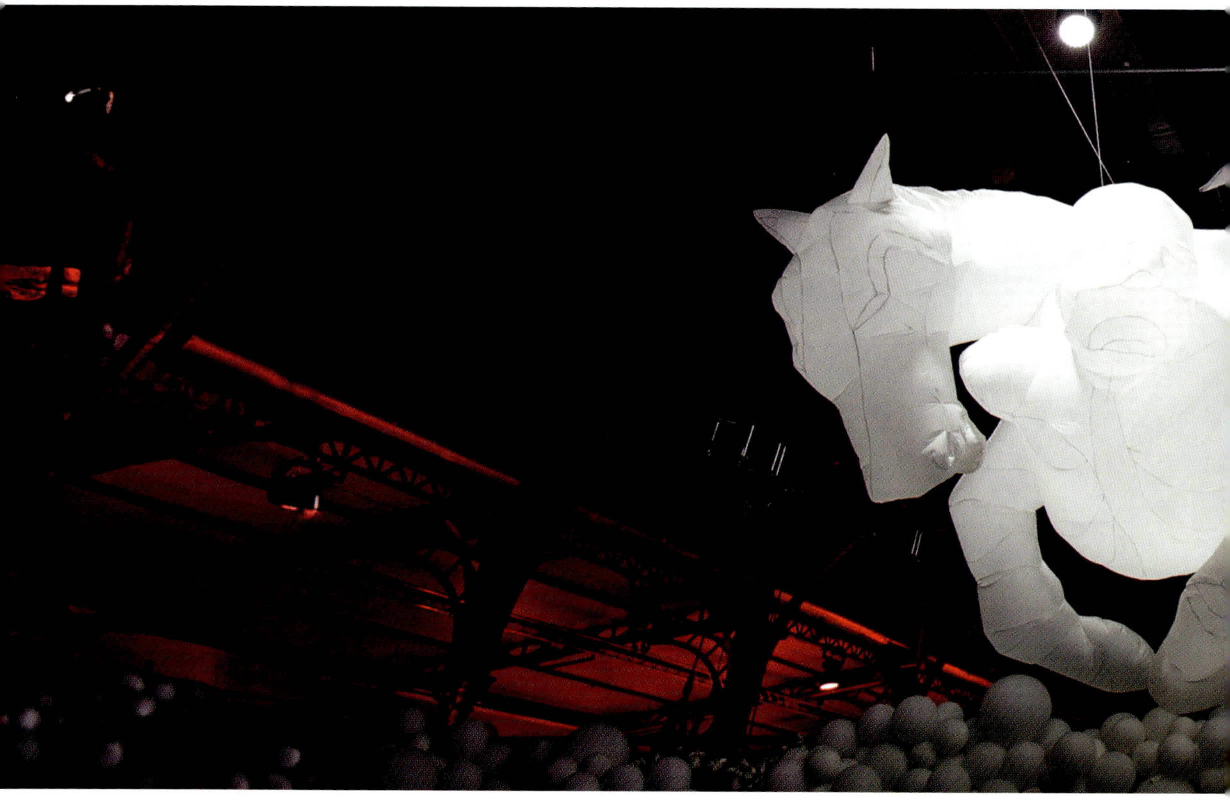

Battle of Cannae 2014

Battle of Cannae

Battle of Cannae could be an apparition in the clouds. Who has not looked for figures and creatures in passing clouds? Streicher renders this common creative impulse literal with his soldiers and beasts frozen in the melee of battle. He sees balloons as expressing a reach for the transcendent. They embody our desire to defy gravity, to fly, to be above it all. It was thus a natural progression for Streicher to begin working with the cloud form in installations that have a surreal, metaphysical quality.

In the real battle of Cannae, in 216 BC, Hannibal's forces routed the Roman army in a defeat that was so psychologically scarring to the Roman populace that people began to read various events as omens of a pending catastrophe. Notable is one peculiar event in the town of Cannae in which a bull jumped to its death from a third floor window.

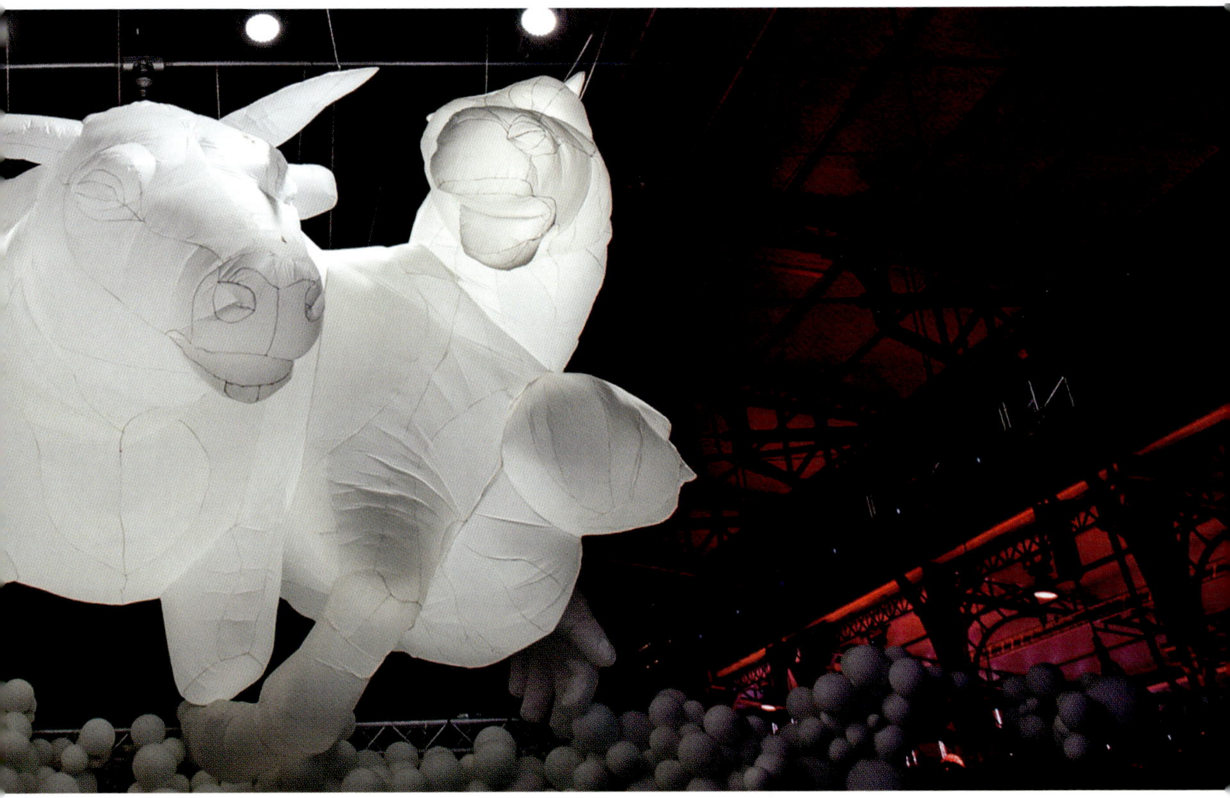

Max Streicher
Silenus
Balloon Museum
Pop Air
Milan, 2022

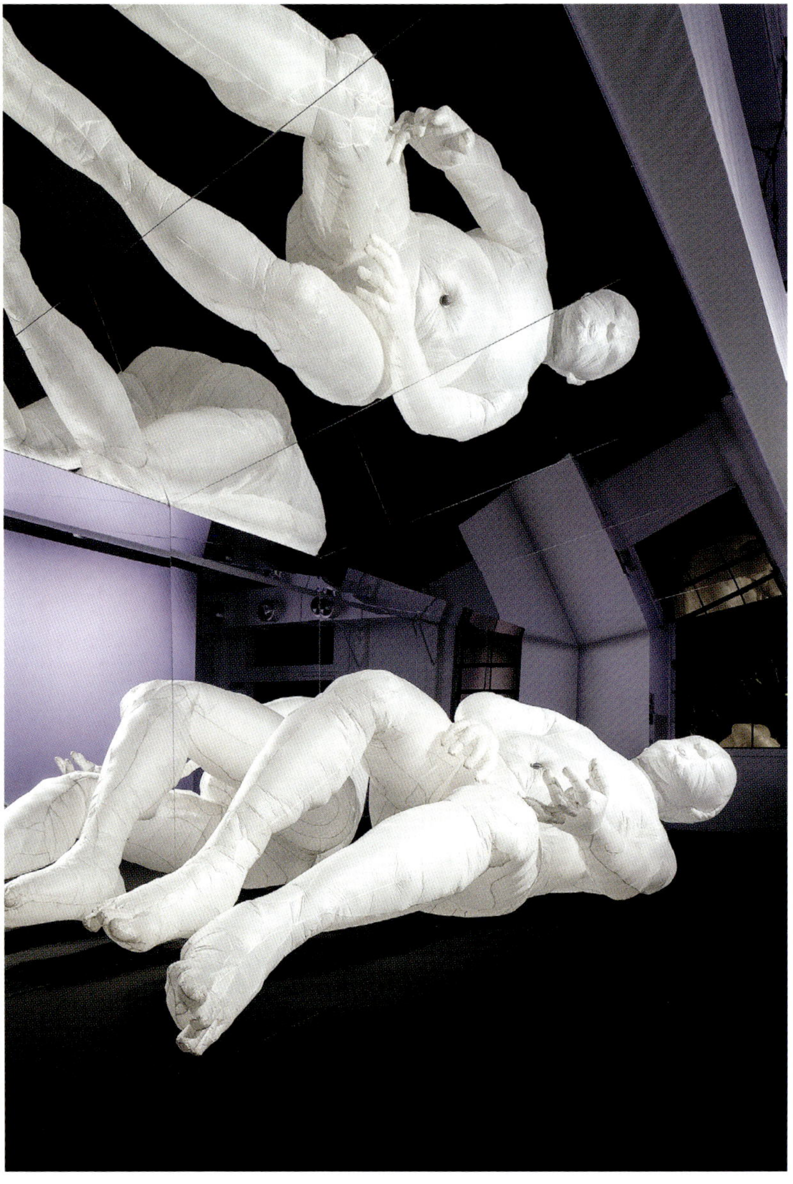

Silenus

Silenus is a transient presence, highlighted by the artist's use of an extremely light nylon spinnaker, a material that is fragile, translucent, ghostly, almost not there at all. Streicher is interested in the "kinesthetic" potential of the inflatable medium. More than kinetic, he is referring to the way that the movement of air within a sewn form can reflect our own body's experience of breathing and other life-like movements.

A life cast of a friend of the artist was used in creating the pattern for this work, resulting in its uncanny life-like detail. The stillness of this giant, who appears to be floating, like an astronaut in space, combined with the qualities of the nylon spinnaker, reinforces its sense of a transience—perhaps a spirit ready for ascent.

Opposite
Max Streicher
Waking Soldiers
Balloon Museum
Let's Fly
New York, 2023

Silenus 2002

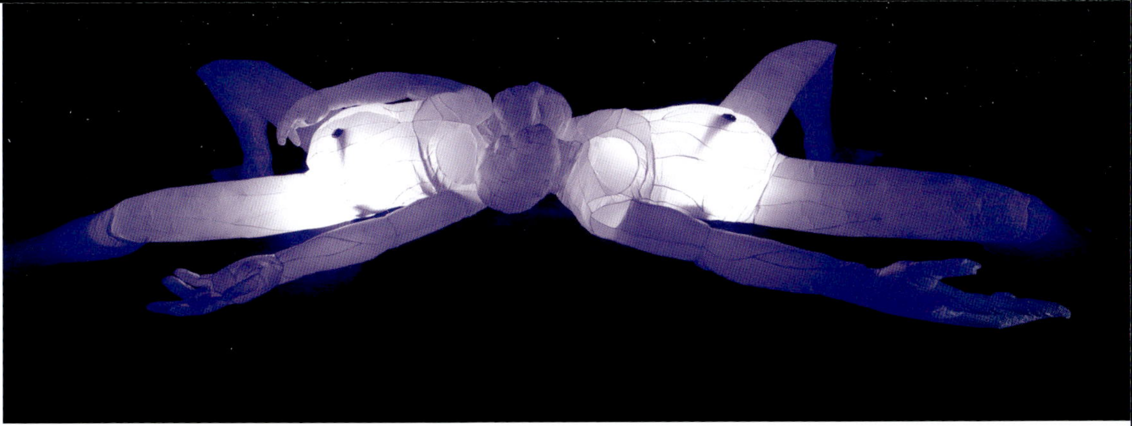

Waking Soldiers

The breathing figures of *Waking Soldiers* pay homage to the terracotta army of China's Shaanxi province of 200 BC, that was to resurrect with the emperor in his next life. The desire to see inert matter animated is an impulse that Streicher shares with his ancient artisan counterparts. In both cases life casts have been used. The Chinese cast the faces of real soldiers. Streicher used a cast of a model in the design of the patterns for his giant figures.

As with all of Streicher's inflatable works, these figures were fabricated by the artist himself, from beginning to end. The fact that the artist's hand is evident in the rendering of each line contributes to the distinctive way that *Waking Soldiers* comes to life as air moves through them.

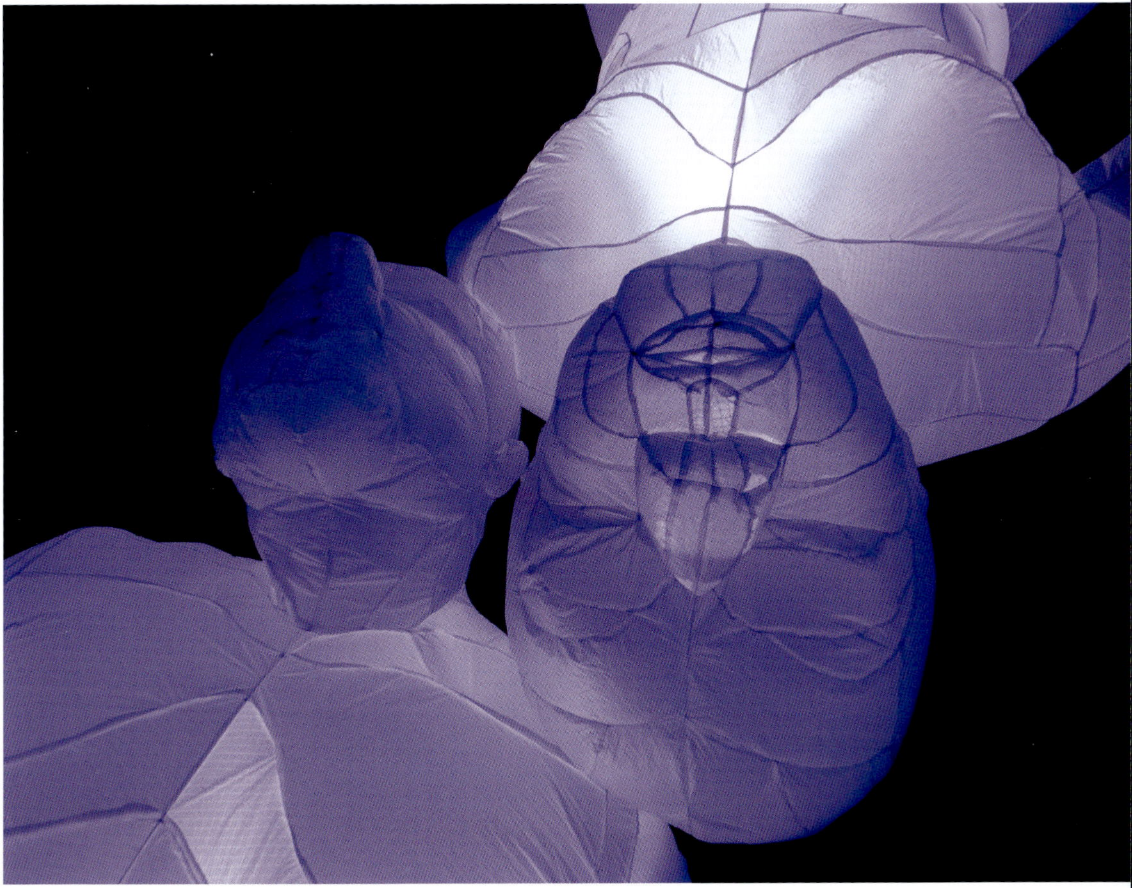

Waking Soldiers 2006

MOMOYO TORIMITSU

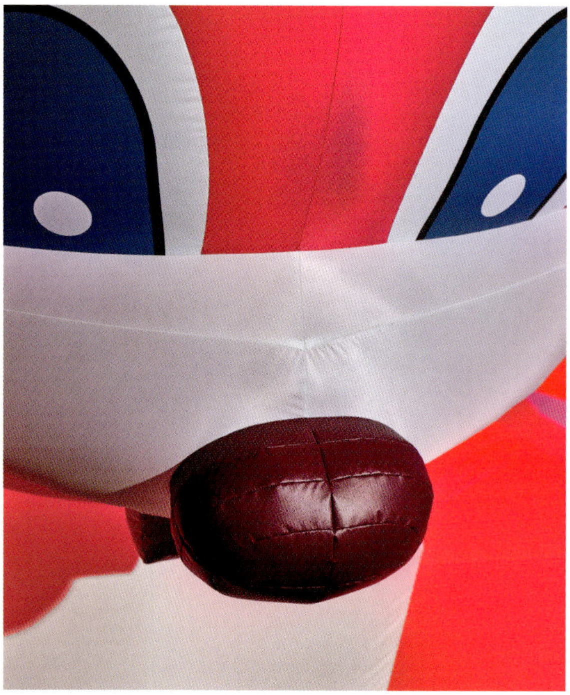

Born in Japan, Momoyo Torimitsu has lived and worked in New York since 1996, when she joined the P.S. 1 International Studio Program. She works in a variety of forms, including kinetic sculpture, installation, video, photographs, performance, and site-specific projects. Her work is inspired by the hypocritical imagery of corporate culture and media stereotypes of cuteness and happiness, reexamined through the lenses of irony and humor. Her best-known projects are a series of realistic crawling businessman robots that symbolize "corporate soldiers." Torimitsu's work often places the viewer in the tension between the realization of an underlying cultural truth, and the funny or lighthearted exterior, ultimately creating a feeling of disquiet, forcing participants to evaluate their own roles in the acceptance of certain social norms. Torimitsu has exhibited her works at Hawai'i Triennial *Pacific Century – E Ho'omau no Moananuiākea, Honolulu*, Frei_raum Q21 exhibition space/MQ, Vienna, Austria, ArtScience Museum, Singapore, Manifesta11, Zurich, Switzerland.

Somehow, I Don't Feel Comfortable
At the core of this creation is the artist's ambivalent feeling toward cuteness, particularly in its Japanese definition. The bunny represents a stereotypical image of cuteness: something innocent, pure, and small that should be protected. The artist portrays this endearing image in a distorted manner to express her own feelings about Japan's male-dominated society. Its uncomfortable position encapsulates the artist's sentiments about Japanese "kawaii" (cuteness) culture, associated not only with cute characters like Hello Kitty but, more broadly, with societal expectations regarding women's behavior in Japan. Women should be cute, have a submissive smile, and speak in a high-pitched voice.
Her frustration swells like a balloon. The intentionally oversized rabbit, exhibited cramped between the ceiling and the floor, looking down from above, evokes a critical sense of unease about the demands and expectations of cuteness culture.

Momoyo Torimitsu
Somehow, I Don't Feel Comfortable
Balloon Museum
EmotionAir
London, 2023

Somehow, I Don't Feel Comfortable 2023

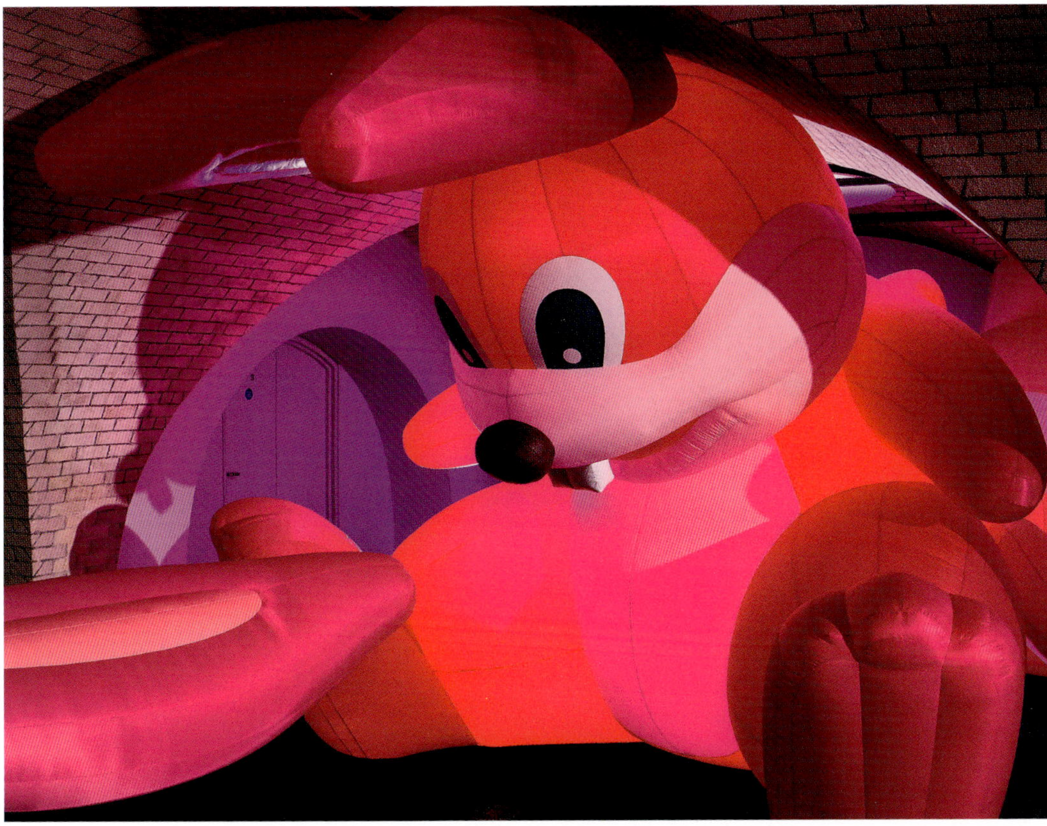

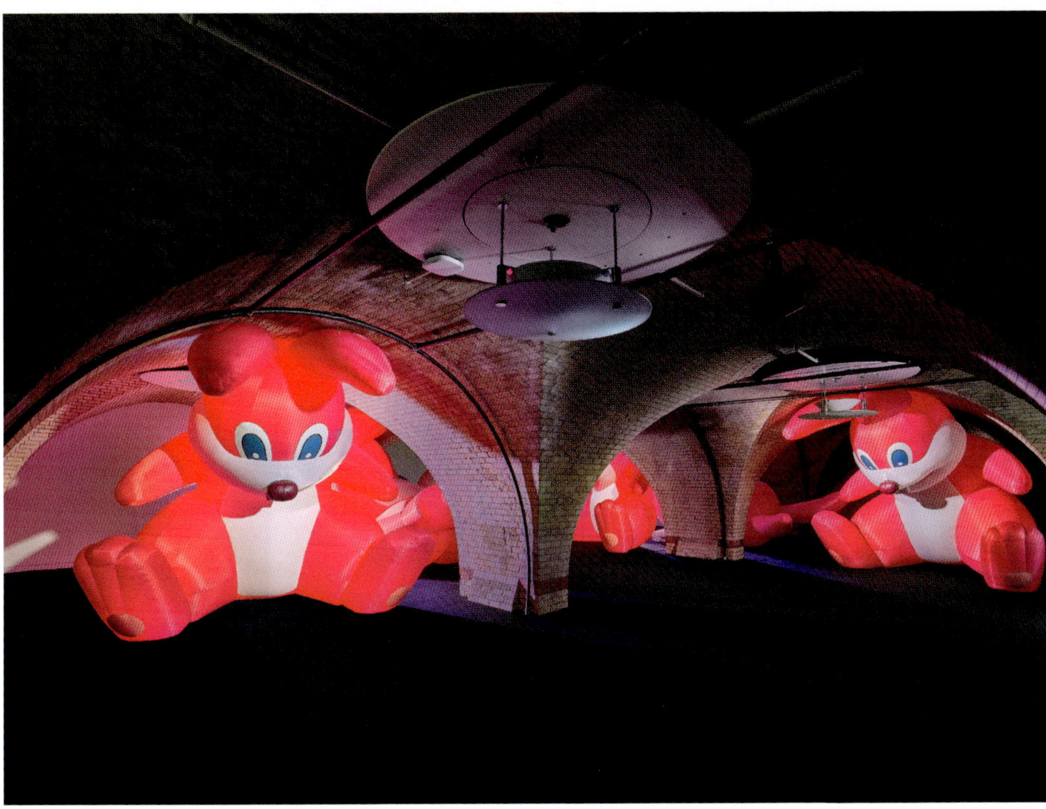

ULTRAVIOLETTO

Ultravioletto is an interactive design studio working in a multidisciplinary field that merges architecture and design, storytelling and installation, contaminating them with new technologies. Ultravioletto shows a marked sensitivity in experimenting with a path of expressive research that gives value to both communication projects and pure works of art. Engaging in a dynamic interplay between arts and new media, Ultravioletto specializes in creating interactive installations, performances, and immersive environments. The collective collaborates on projects that seamlessly integrate analog and digital dimensions, forming a language that enhances the overall experience while consistently exploring the relationship between humans and technology. Noteworthy collaborations and exhibitions by Ultravioletto include Bulgari – Magnifica Roma, Milan Fashion Week, Explora Museum, TAC Museum, among many others.

Ultravioletto
Into the Rainbow
Balloon Museum
Pop Air
Madrid, 2023

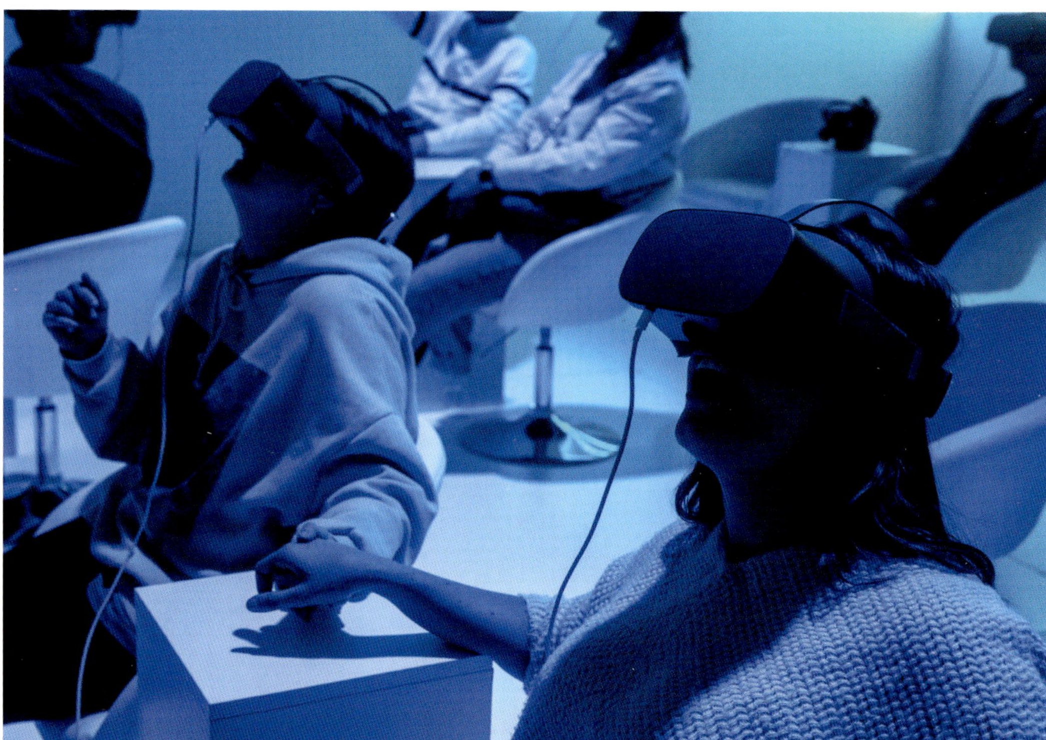

Into the Rainbow 2023

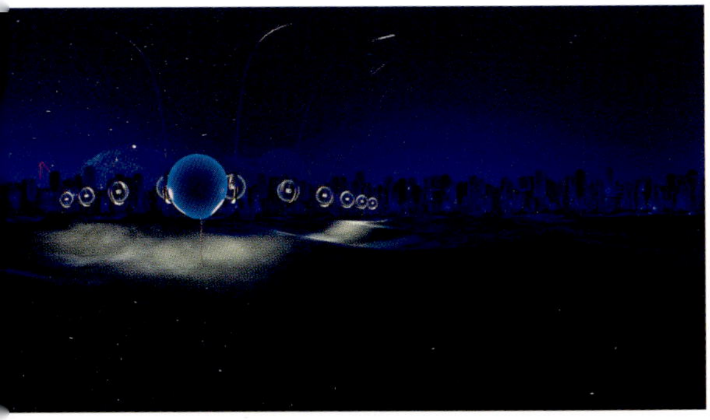
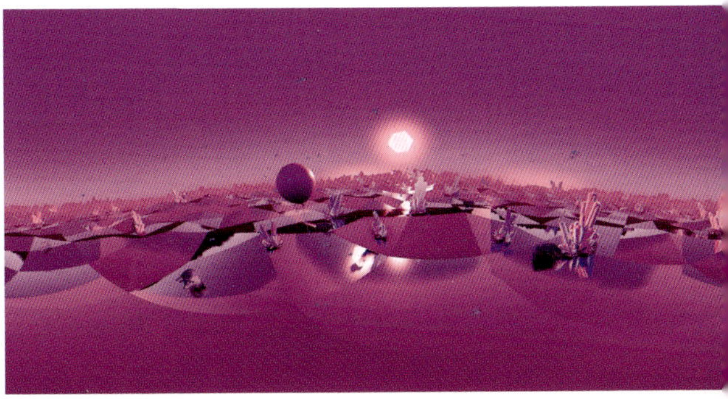
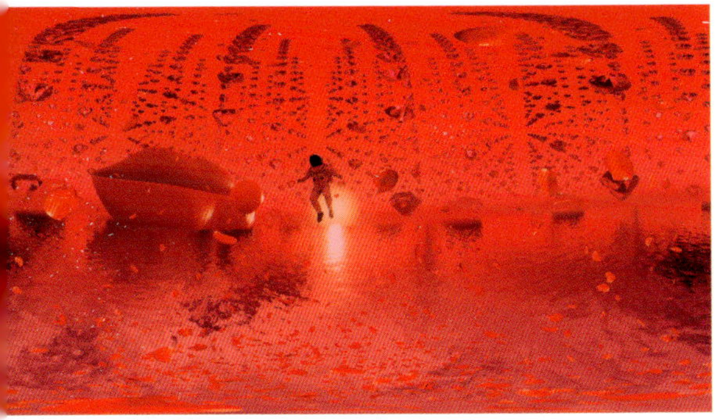
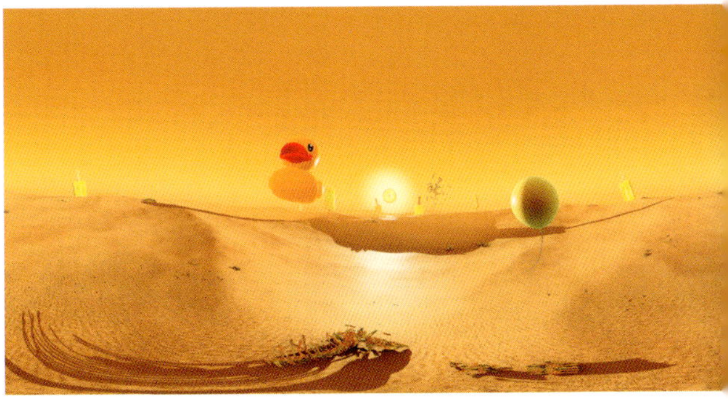

Still frames from
Ultravioletto
Into the Rainbow
Balloon Museum
Pop Air
Madrid, 2023

Into the Rainbow – *VR immersive experience*

This work offers a captivating first-person journey through the immersive realm of virtual reality. This adventure is centered around a vertical motion experience, guiding the viewer through a vibrant spectrum of colors mirroring the diverse hues of a rainbow. Within each distinct color realm, the viewer embarks on a whimsical exploration of surreal landscapes inhabited by equally enigmatic characters and objects, from a blue underwater realm to a flying rubber duck. The journey is punctuated by a series of eccentric and colorful travel sequences—an astronaut hovers above a bright red seascape, an orange egg yolk lays sunny side up on a bed of basketballs—where each space is facilitated by a magical elevator that seamlessly transports us between these enchanting worlds. Interwoven with these dynamic moments are interludes of tranquility, providing users with the opportunity to freely turn their heads and delve deeper into the captivating world that surrounds them.

JASON WILSHER-MILLS

Initially rooted in traditional painting within the realm of Fine Art, Jason's journey recently took a digital twist, courtesy of modern tools like the iPad and Wacom tablets. These devices, marked by convenience and accessibility, empowered him to create intricate, large-scale works despite the physical challenges presented by his disability. The transition from traditional to digital initially stirred Jason's artistic conscience, challenging his classical training. However, in recent years, he has wholeheartedly "embraced the pixel," expanding his portfolio to encompass interactive sculptures, 3D prints, lightboxes, and augmented reality experiences. Beyond his personal artistry, Jason actively engages in community projects, collaborating with diverse individuals. In 2020, he earned the prestigious Adam Reynolds Award from SHAPE Arts, leading to a commission for an interactive sculpture at the Folkestone Triennial, which was unveiled in September 2021, marking a pivotal moment in his career.

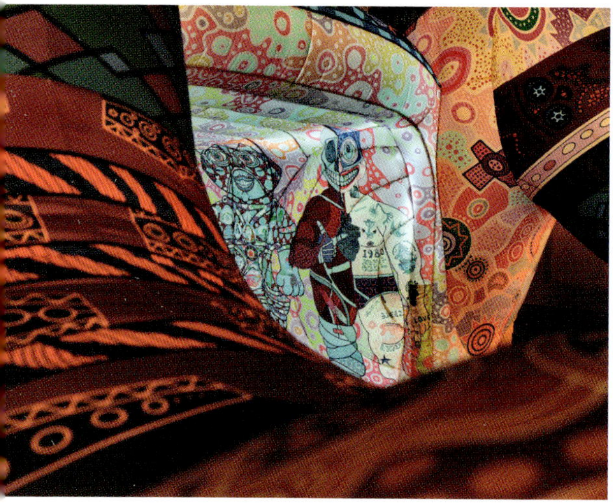

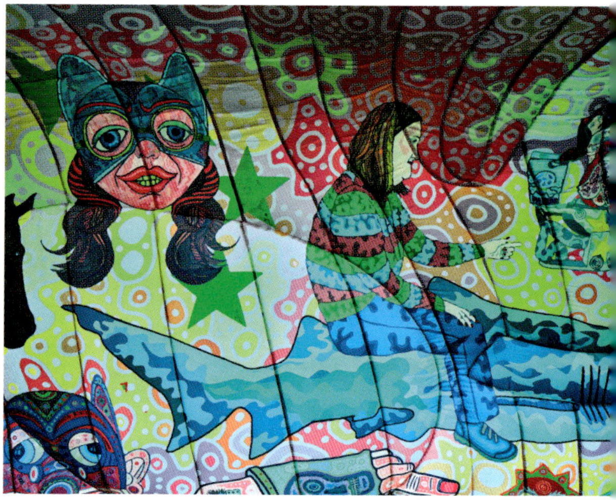

Jason Wilsher-Mills
The Argonaut
Balloon Museum
EmotionAir
London, 2023

The Argonaut

A grand installation, *The Argonaut* depicts a person with disabilities lying down like a vibrant Gulliver that viewers can traverse. Spectators have the opportunity to enter a lively world richly adorned with faces and other representations of the disabled communities with whom the artist has collaborated over the years. The title is inspired by its ancient Greek namesake, the vessel for which Jason sought the bravest Greek heroes to join him on his epic journey. Similarly, Wilsher-Mills has discovered new heroes within the disabled communities he worked with throughout his journey in Britain. The creation of this imposing work draws inspiration from the artist's experiences growing up in northern England, his love for British children's comics, 1970s' television programs, and the psychedelic décor that adorned his first home. The result is a rich tapestry of childhood memories, a love for popular culture, disability activism, and humor. Joy and rebellion are the two emotions the artist has chosen to associate with this work: spectators are captivated by the colors and images covering the character, almost provocatively carrying messages of activism. According to the artist, the world can be changed, one mad artwork at a time.

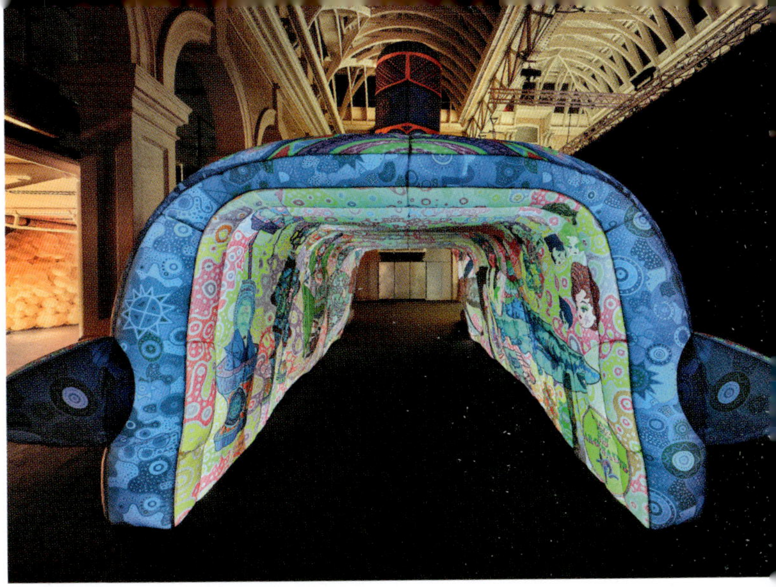

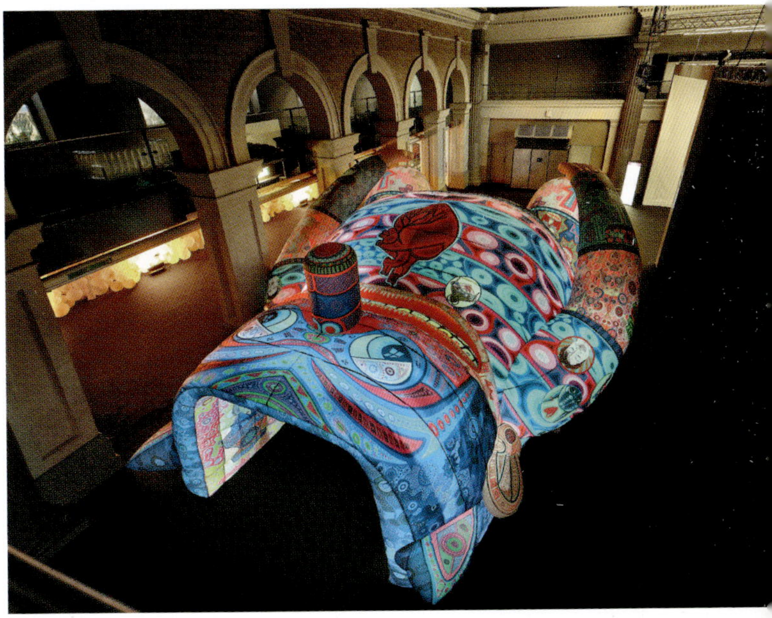

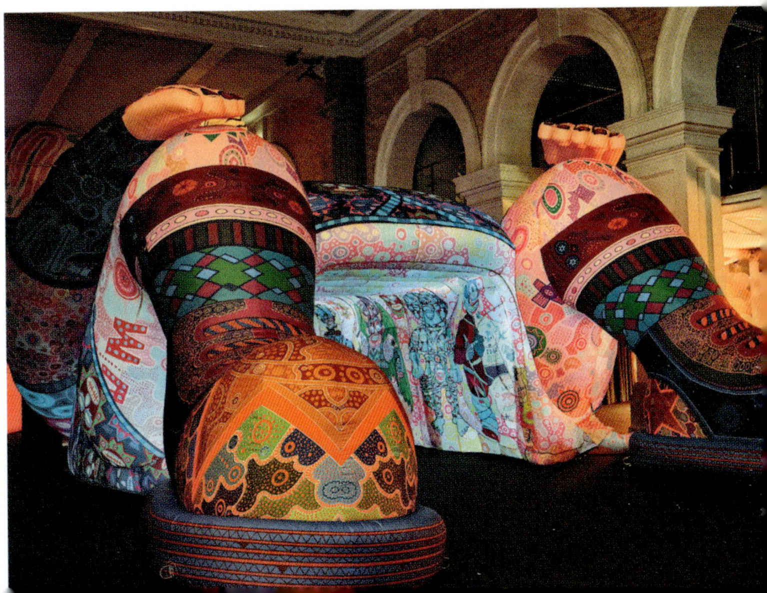

GERALDO ZAMPRONI

Architect, urbanist, and self-taught artist, Geraldo Zamproni has fully embraced art since 1998. In that year, he debuted in Brazilian exhibitions (3rd Brazilian Contemporary Art Fair in São Paulo); by 2005, he had showcased internationally (International Painting Competition in Kobe, Japan). Initially, he explored craft techniques and crafted unique pieces from industrial materials, simulating their existence in unconventional contexts through sculptures and installations. Notable works include *Silver Line* (2007), metal-folded "pillows," and *Untitled* (2006), nails on light poles. As his career progressed, he expanded scales and approaches, creating site-specific installations and interventions that interact with their surroundings. These projects aim to alter spaces through the relationship between object, environment, and observer, employing familiar images in unfamiliar contexts, fostering estrangement and instability. His art reinterprets the ordinary, offering new reflections, possibilities, and imaginative spaces. His unique architecture invites the viewer to discover a completely new place for themselves.

Geraldo Zamproni
Volatile Structure
Balloon Museum
Pop Air
Milan, 2022

Opposite
Geraldo Zamproni
Volatile Structure
Balloon Museum
EmotionAir
London, 2023

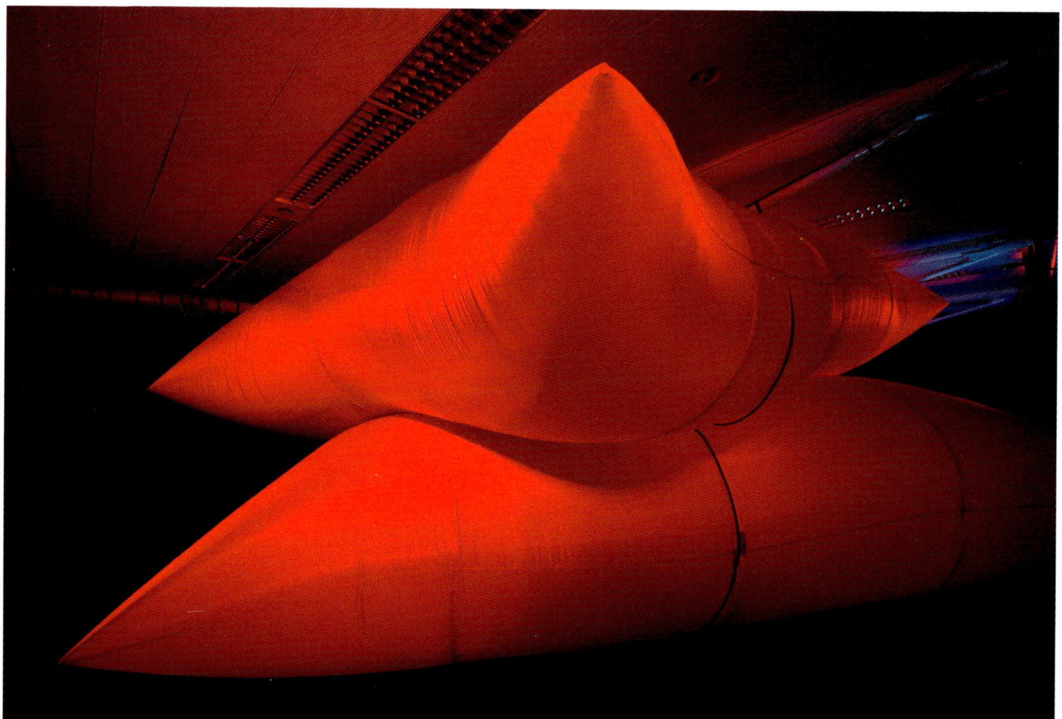

Volatile Structure 2011

Volatile Structure

With his work *Volatile Structure*, Brazilian artist Geraldo Zamproni places gigantic everyday items in architectural contexts, creating a constant tension between the object and the surrounding environment. The monumental red cushions, seemingly supporting the structure, aim to suggest the physical possibility of such an unpredictable juxtaposition but prove incompatible with reality. The cushion evokes the idea of affection, the desire to touch and caress. The artist uses this element as an ironic and contradictory intervention, as the massive structure and its weight are in stark contrast to the object presented. Zamproni's interventions question architecture and landscape, providing a new perspective on spaces that exhibit tension and discomfort, and inviting the audience to reflect on the dynamics between common objects and the built environment that surrounds them.

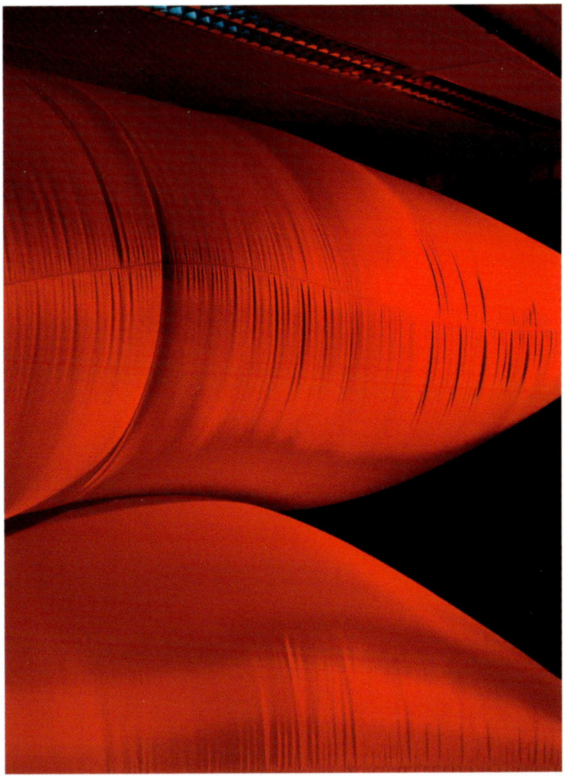

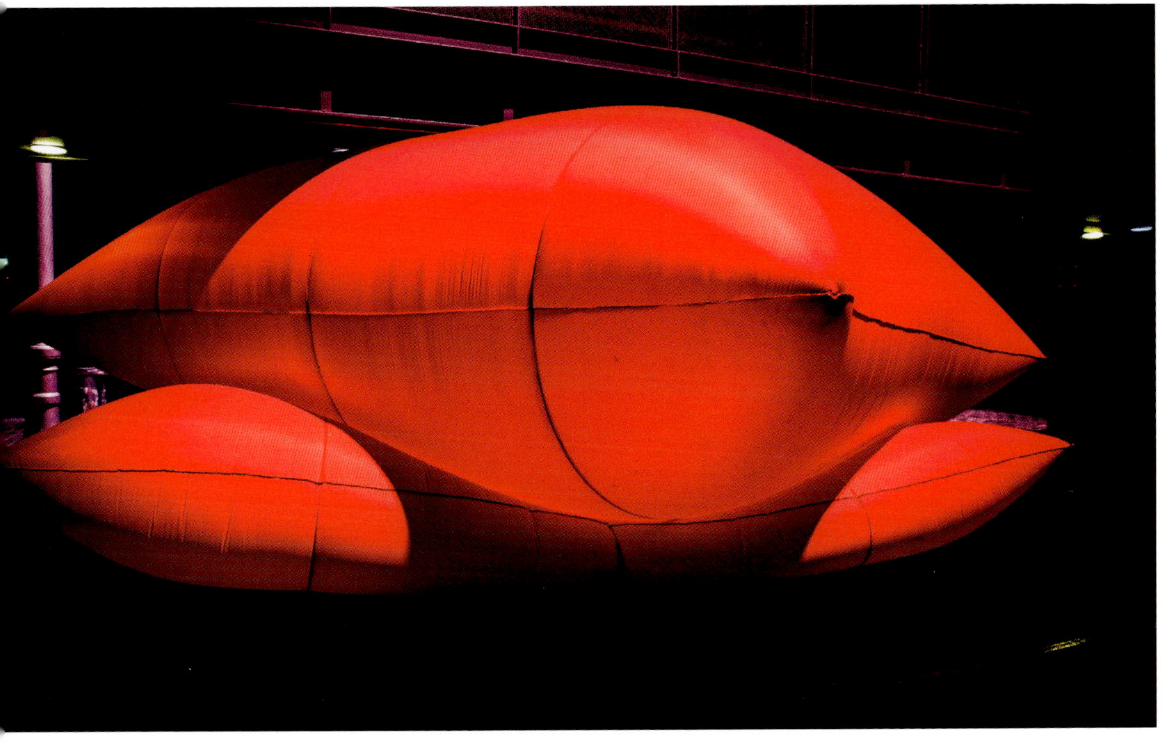

LUCAS ZANOTTO

Born in the Alps of Northern Italy, after years working in Milan, Barcelona, and Berlin, Lucas Zanotto is currently based in Helsinki. Zanotto began his career as a product designer, moving into character design and development with focused skills in 3D modeling and sound design. The founder of the company YATATOY, which focuses on children's content, is working with Inflatable Art and characters that emit, through a variety of media, charm and joy. First garnering huge recognition for his animated art videos online, he quickly moved to creating real-life kinetic videos, like EYES, a series of 6 installations, and PLANK a client-based project involving the use of ping pong balls, chairs, and coffee mugs, that have delighted viewers worldwide. Zanotto has won the Apple Design Award, the Golden Lion in Cannes, Gold at BDA Promax International, the Main Prize at ITFS, and Best Promotional Animation at Ottawa Animation Festival, among many others awards.

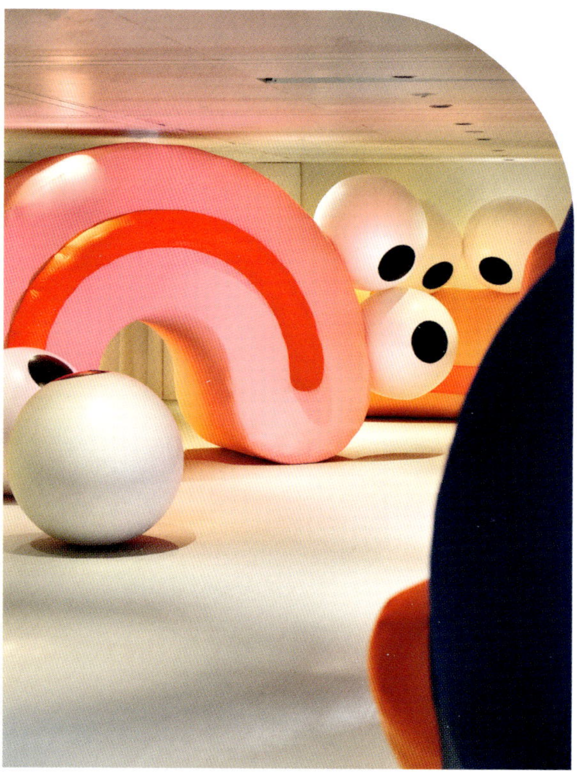

Lucas Zanotto
SQUEEZED IN
Balloon Museum
EmotionAir
London, 2023

SQUEEZED IN 2023

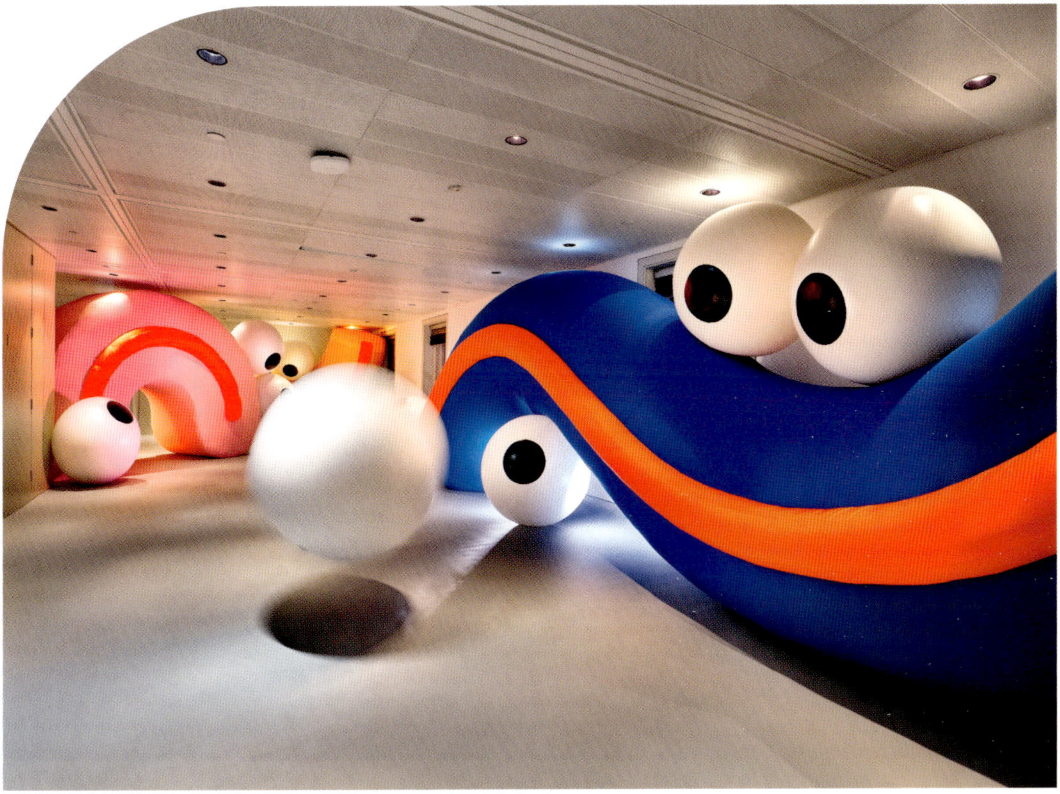

SQUEEZED IN
This interactive installation by Zanotto was specifically designed for the Balloon Museum. The title encapsulates the entire concept behind this work: considering the constraints of space, the idea was to emphasize this aspect and create characters that appear too large, giving the sensation of being squeezed. Far from a negative experience, this effect makes one feel small amidst these charming creatures. The artist's intention is to craft a colorful, light-hearted world populated by endearing oversized characters. The initial impact on the audience is sure to evoke surprise and joy, fostering a lively connection as they empathize with these characters, engaging in play and rolling their inflatable eyes throughout the room. For the artist, understanding the space was a crucial first step in creating *SQUEEZED IN*. By experimenting with simple and fundamental forms, he brought to life a space that is both compact and remarkably friendly, inhabited by these delightful characters.

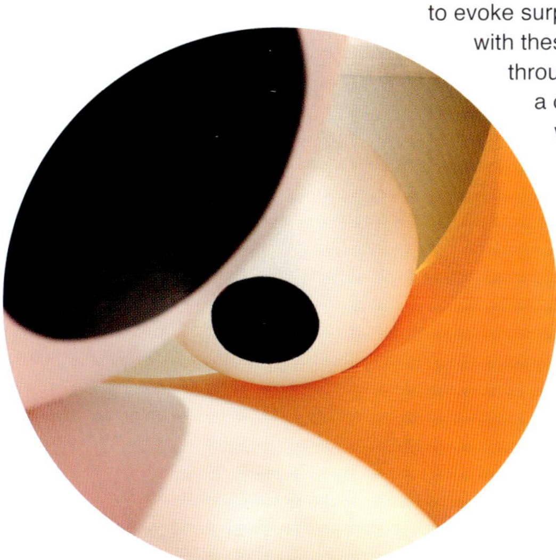

Ephemeral monuments. The new era of Inflatable Art

Valentino Catricalà

Inflatable Art, Inflatable Design, Inflatable Architecture... There are so many inflatable items today as interest grows in all things inflatable. A new era of the inflatable, we might say, of structures based on the ability to sculpt air by making air the primary material, the source of creation. But what do we mean by Inflatable Art? Here, we mean operations that use inflatable materials, usually PVC, to create large or small installations, performances, happenings, or sculptures. What distinguishes it from other art is that once the form is decided, it is the air that brings the work to life by creating soft, fragile, often flying structures.

We have become used to seeing inflatable structures in today's art, but if one thinks about it, it is clearly a new phenomenon, by virtue of the primary material used to make these works: air. This is an unconventional material for contemporary art. Air lacks the heaviness of marble, the malleability of wood, or the density of stone; it can be light and heavy, immaterial and material, virtual and real, invisible and visible. It is what gives us life and what takes life from us. Artists have long used many different materials, from the classical such as marble, wood, iron, and so on, to the 20th-century innovation of "almost anything"; they "willingly move from one discipline to another, from one medium to another, without introducing the slightest hierarchy between ephemeral action and a sculpture, video, installation, or gestural intervention."[1] Art "is made with everything," to use Angela Vettese's formula, and today it is increasingly made with air as well. Previously relegated to the spheres of play and entertainment, the use of air as a sculptural material has only sprung up forcefully in recent years with the emergence of a new society, with the advent of digital capitalism.

A bit of history

But let's take this step by step: if we really want to understand the preponderant role of air today, we need to look briefly at some historical moments. In fact, the history of the inflatable goes hand in hand with the emergence of the modern era of industrial capitalism on the one side, and technological and scientific development on the other. It is no accident—the idea of making flying air structures casually arose from the scientific experiments of English physicist Michael Faraday between the first and second industrial revolutions. Between 1820 and 1826, in fact,

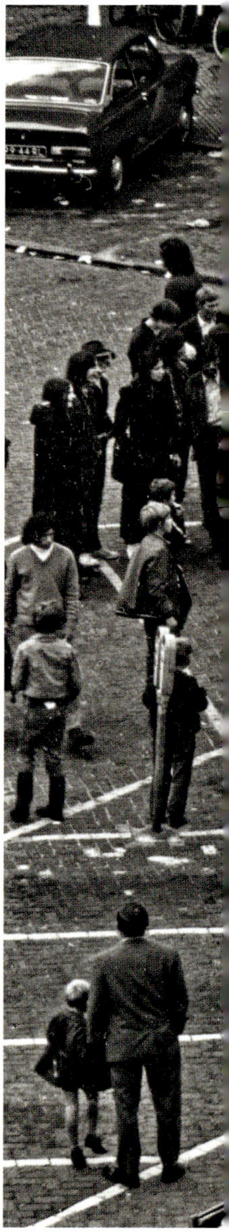

Jeffrey Shaw, Theo Botschuijver and Sean Wellesley-Miller (Eventstructure Research Group), *Cushion*, Nieuwmarkt Feesten, Amsterdam, 1971

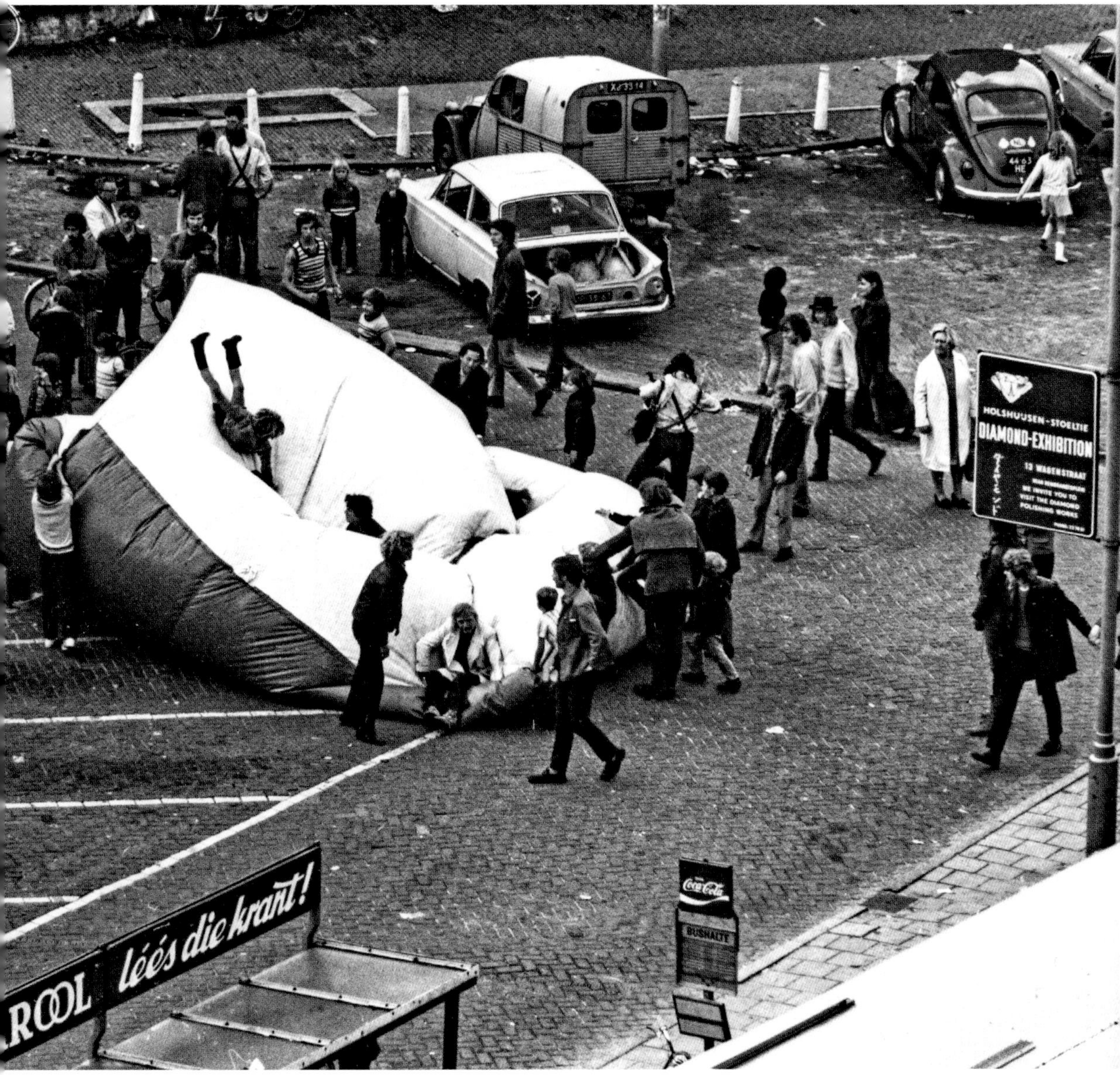
HOLSHUIJSEN-STOELTIE
DIAMOND-EXHIBITION
13 WAGENSTRAAT
WE INVITE YOU TO
VISIT THE DIAMOND
POLISHING WORKS
Coca-Cola
BUSHALTE
ROOL
lées die krant!

Faraday discovered vulcanized rubber, which became a key component for creating elastic balloons. Rubber was only commercialized in 1847 by Britain's Thomas Hancock, who patented the process of vulcanizing it, making it more durable and suitable for use in inflatable objects. During the same period, in the United States Charles Goodyear also reached the same conclusion. Rubber, then, is an industrial product, a technology, born of and made possible by scientific and technological development. As we will see, the success and typical use of the inflatable today has been made possible by the advent of a digital society.

If the scientific discovery can be contextualized within that flourishing period of scientific revolutions between the first and second industrial revolutions, commercialization of the inflatable coincides with the advent of capitalism when Neil Tillotson began the mass production of balloons in the early 20th century. The use of inflatables in art also began during this period, above all, with a reflection on air as a sculptural material, as the raw material of the creation process. Among the first to see its potential we must certainly mention Marcel Duchamp, who, while not exactly using balloons, sensed the leading role of air in the 20th century with the work *Air de Paris* (1919). Duchamp takes a glass ampoule for medical use (marked *Serum physiologique*) and, enlisting the help of a Parisian pharmacist, empties it of its contents and fills it with 50 cc of Paris air. The air becomes a souvenir to send, the theme of the artistic act.

Although he did not make inflatables we can identify Lucio Fontana, and his concept of spatialism as inaugurating a new relationship with the atmosphere, with infinite space to explore. Air, vacuum, ether, atmosphere, becomes the primary material to be investigated. It is as though, by violating the painting with a slash, as it were, the whole world is sucked into a new dimension. Fontana's approach influenced all the art to come, including artistic operations like those of Yves Klein and Piero Manzoni. Indeed, we recall Manzoni's *45 Corpi d'aria* of 1959 and *Fiato d'artista*, balloons containing the artist's own breath that would inevitably deflate, dispersing the breath of life. From then on, the way was paved for art practitioners who looked to air as a sculptural material including such world-renowned artists as Andy Warhol, Christo and

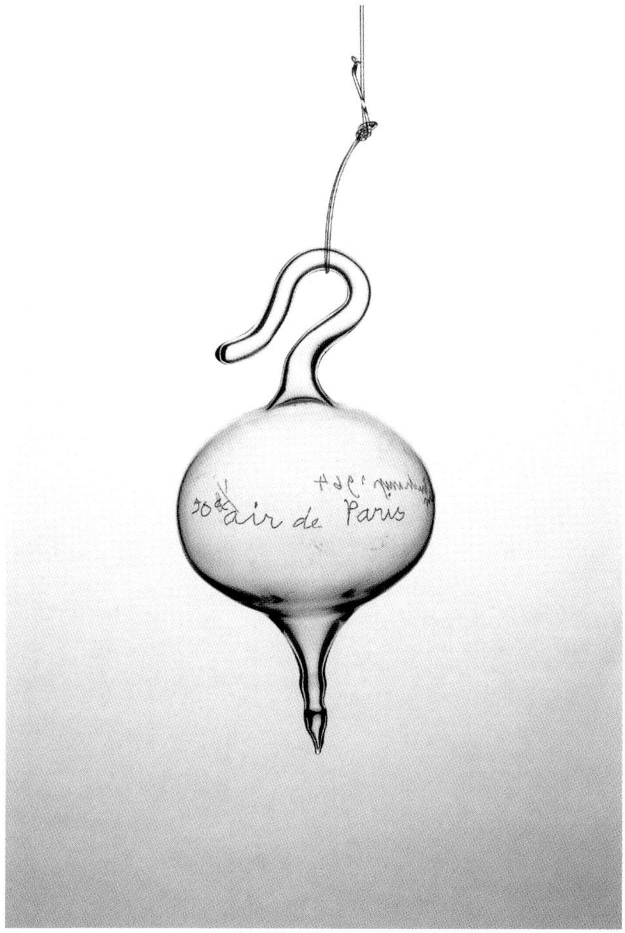

Marcel Duchamp
Air de Paris,
1919/1964
Ready-made
Staatliches Museum
Schwerin, Schwerin,
Germany

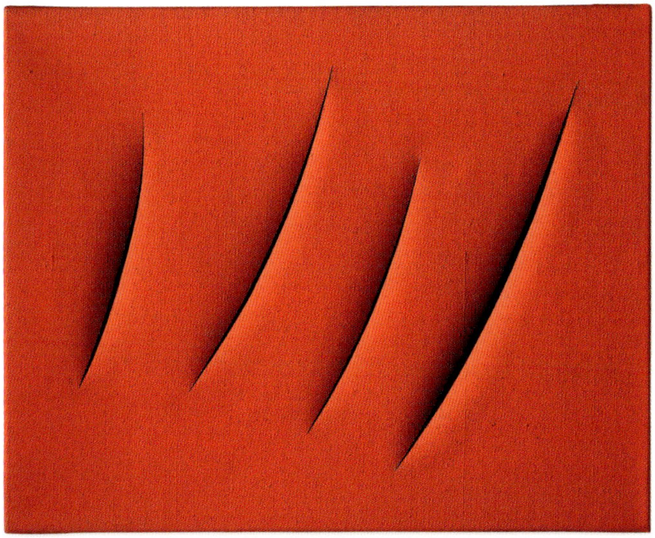

Lucio Fontana, *Concetto spaziale, Attese*, 1962, hydropaint and cuts on canvas, 47 x 56 cm. Private collection

Jeanne-Claude, Franco Mazzucchelli, and Jeffrey Shaw, among many others. Andy Warhol's *Silver Clouds* (1966) is an important example of this early use of the inflatable, a work created in collaboration with engineer Billy Klüver in 1966 and presented at the Leo Castelli Gallery in New York. An example that shows the way to an interactive and immersive use of the experience.

Less well known is the work *Cushion* (1969) by Eventstructure Research Group with Jeffrey Shaw. Shaw is an important artist for our discourse as epitomizes the link between early artistic experimentation with inflatables and the advent of technological capitalism. Shaw's reflection begins with a consideration of the new potential of images at a time when the inflatable was becoming a mass-market, entertainment object. We see this already with the work *Glove Screen* (1967) in which Shaw's film *Continuous Sound and Image Moments* (1966) was projected onto a shallow rectangular box with a series of translucent white surgical gloves inserted into a wooden panel on one side and a transparent acrylic panel on the opposite side. Interactivity already enters Shaw's work in that the viewer could push a pedal that activated the projector and the air that inflated the gloves. From here Shaw begins a reflection on the role of the inflatable through monumental public sculptures. *Corpocinema* (1967) is a 700-cm diameter, 400-cm high inflatable dome inside which film images are projected, a way of rethinking cinema in the wake of the expanded cinema of the time. Many experiments with inflatables would follow, including *MovieMovie* (1967), *Supertube* (1968), *Pneutube* (1968), *Octopus* (1968), *Aplavent* (1968), *Airground* (1968), *Black Airground* (1968), and throughout the 1970s with *Airground Mattress* (1970), *Auditorium* (1971), *Aqua Airground* (1972), *Teardrop/ Tearfall* (1977), to name but a few. Particularly noteworthy is the performance *Cushion* (1969), in which the audience was invited to carry a huge inflatable cushion around the city of Amsterdam.

In the 1980s, a new vision of the use of inflatables emerged linked primarily to the logic of consumer society, as evidenced by the work of Jeff Koons.

The era of digital capitalism

The era of the inflatable as we know it today is inseparable, as mentioned earlier, from the appearance of digital capitalism. Starting with the 2000s we have entered what Ruggero Eugeni calls "algorithmic capital", computational (or algorithmic) images, born from the connection between resources belonging to the political economy of light and vision and those pertaining to the economy of information and data. They are algorithms that are both objects and tools of the production, extraction, and distribution of common resources, to the point that "algorithmic capital" is the most appropriate name for defining the constitutive features of post-media society.

The digital environment we are experiencing is therefore no longer what we were familiar with even a few years ago. The reason for that, first, is purely quantitative, determined by what is called the big data phenomenon. The level of data quantity has reached an inconceivable degree, and the quantity of data affects the quality of its organization and management. And here we turn to a second level of interpretation. This quantity of data impacts us, society, and more generally the cultural perspective we use to look at the future of our ecosystems. This universe has generated new technological "actors" that are the driving force of new economies and social models. Think of the development of Artificial Intelligence (AI), made possible by the vast amount of data that feeds it. At the same time, AI is today a necessary resource for us to find our way in that world. In addition, there is the emergence of new economic systems, such as blockchain, that dispose of many of the typical actors of the "old" economic system, as well as the development of new modes of visualization. "Today, virtual, augmented, and mixed reality, 3D movies, immersive videogames, flight or driving simulators, navigation systems like GPS, artificial interactive environments, and so on, bear witness to the advent of new practices of imaging and consequently to new forms of visuality, which do not necessarily rely

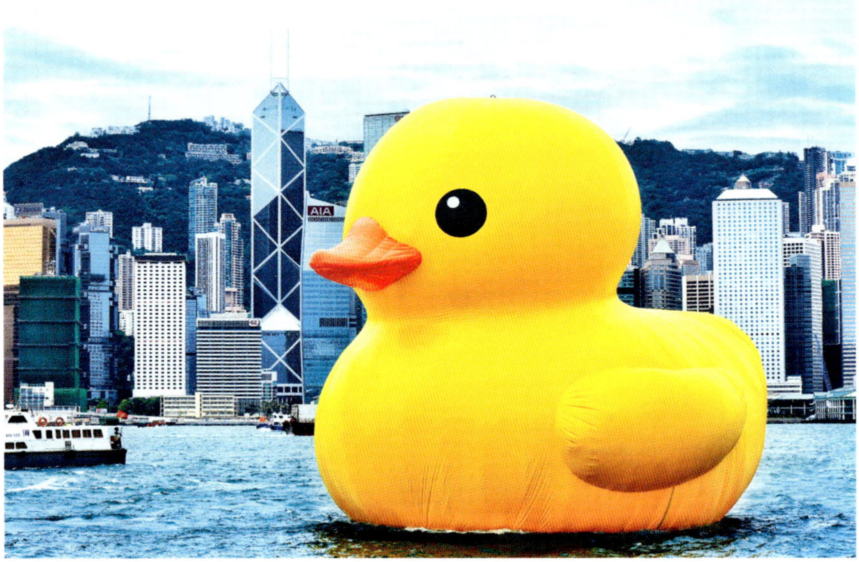

Florentijn Hofman, *Rubber Duck*, Hong Kong, 2013

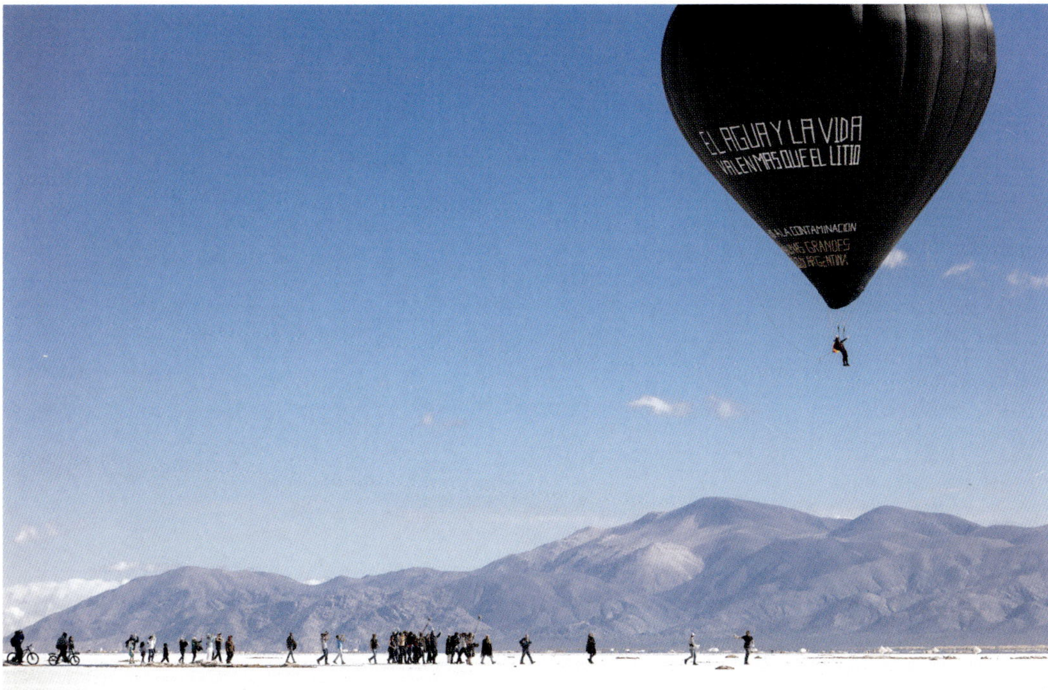

Film still from *Fly with Pacha, into the Aerocene*, 2017-2023, showing *Aerocene Pacha*, a free flight conducted by the Aerocene Foundation in Salinas Grandes and Laguna de Guayatayoc, Jujuy, Argentina, 2020. Piloted by Letícia Noemi Marqués, this solar flight, lifted only by the heat of the sun, broke 32 world records as recognised by the Fédération Aéronautique Internationale (FAI), becoming the most sustainable flight in human history, raising the message "Water and Life are Worth more than Lithium".

on an eye that tries to fill the gap between reality and its representation."[2]
All this has had an impact on art made evident by the generations born between the 1980s and 1990s, who, with their studies, are at the same time imagining and producing new futures, new possibilities for life within "technological ecosystems."
What does this have to do with inflatables, one might ask, with an art designed and built on an element as old as the world, namely air. The point, as explained earlier, is not the use of the material itself, but how to orient it, how to work with it, and how to understand its metamorphoses within rapidly changing societies. The new era of the inflatable responds to this need for large size, for a "wow!" effect, for immediate and direct consumption of the work, for monumentality existing somewhere between entertainment and artistic practice. We have entered a new phase of art, and the inflatable represents the pinnacle, the symbol around which we structure reasoning.
It is no coincidence that the inflatable in art has increasingly taken the form of monumental installations, the art form par excellence from the 2000s to the present. Massimiliano Gioni wrote some time ago, "More recently, the practice of installations in art has created immersive environments that pulverize any sense of unity. Still in its interconnected openness in the multiplicity of references and chaotic embrace of materials and objects of desire, installation creates experiences with the same grandeur associated with monumental sculpture. It is no coincidence that the triumph of the installation developed in parallel with that of a spectacle economy and a limited attention span. The installation reflects the bombardment of data that forms the mature phase of the information so-

ciety. It describes the ecstasy of communication, the sublime awareness of being just a node in an expanding stream of instantaneous connections spread across the globe."[3]

The use of the inflatable in art reflects this need to respond to the prevailing information society, to the bombardment of data, to the desire for magnificence of a society that conceives of the monument only in the negative: that is to say, as the annulment[4] of its solid function and perpetuation of memory to acquire one as ephemeral, fragile and delicate as our digital society: hence, the air sculpting inflatable sculptures.

A few examples...

Technological progress has certainly influenced the development of this new era of the inflatable. As technology has advanced, so artists have had access to more sophisticated materials and innovative production techniques. This has enabled the creation of more complex and detailed inflatable works, expanding artistic possibilities and pushing the boundaries of creativity.

The great recent interest in the inflatable by Yayoi Kusama, a celebrated Japanese contemporary artist, born on March 22, 1929, in Matsumoto, Japan, is but one example. Kusama was among the first to work with immersive environments, with the idea of the "infinity net," and is known for her extraordinary artistic output that spans installation, performance, painting, sculpture, poetry, and more. Her artistic career has gone through several phases, and her work is marked by distinctive elements such as the repetitive use of patterns, particularly "dots." In recent years Kusama has begun working with large-scale installations including inflatables, renewing the use of air sculptures, such as the 2019 giant yellow and black inflatable pumpkin that filled Place Vendôme in Paris for days.

In 2023 Kusama opened the new Factory International space in Manchester, the new home of the MIF-Manchester International Festival, with a major exhibition entitled *You, Me and the Balloons*. In this exhibition Kusama shows her recent work with inflatables, with installations over 10 meters tall, with the intention of creating a magical world. "It would be interesting if people experienced the exhibition as a wonderland," says the artist.

The peculiarity of art in recent times is its spectacular quality, and, not surprisingly, the inflatable is one of the most frequently used mediums, as with the installations of Florentijn Hofman, known for his large-scale public artworks, often made using unusual and surprising materials. *Rubber Duck* is a series of installations represented by a giant floating duck. The *Rubber Duck* is unusual for its extraordinary size. The sculpture can vary in size depending on its installation, but it is often several dozen meters tall. This imposing presence has a significant visual impact and exudes a joyful and playful vision of art, as it is an oversized, floating yellow duck with a cute, almost cartoonish shape. The work debuted in Saint-Nazaire, France, and was subsequently exhibited in many different places, including Beijing, Amsterdam, Baku, Lommel, Osaka, São Paulo, and Hong Kong.

A completely original way of working with air is found in *Aerocene* by Tomás Saraceno. *Aerocene* is an artistic and scientific project developed by the artist, and focuses on making inflatable aerostatic sculptures that float in

Yayoi Kusama, *You, Me and the Balloons*, Manchester, 2023

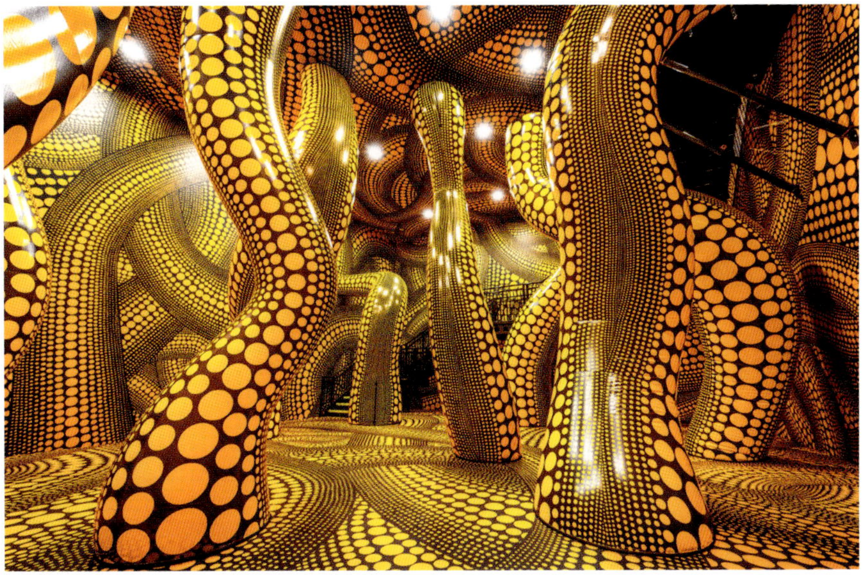

Cyril Lancelin, *Cube Abyss*, London, 2023

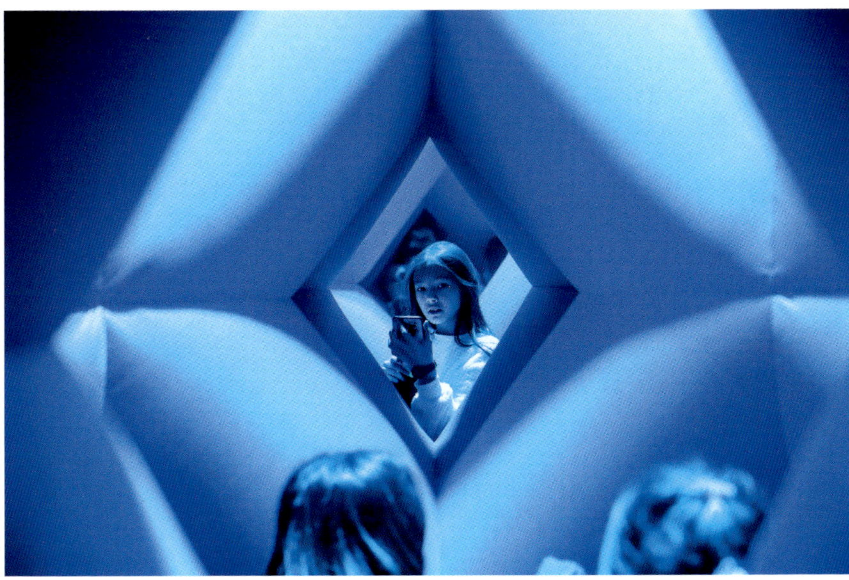

the air without the need for any kind of external energy, such as motors or propellers. *Aerocene* sculptures use solar energy to heat the air inside their structures. The warm air becomes lighter and then the sculpture begins to rise. Without the use of propellers or motors, the *Aerocene* can glide freely, driven by winds and atmospheric currents. The *Aerocene* project reflects Saraceno's vision of the need to transform our approach to the environment and human mobility. Through the levity of the *Aerocene* sculptures, the artist invites reflection on the connections between humans, air, climate and the Earth itself. Saraceno has organized events and performances around the world to present *Aerocene*. These events often involve audience participation, encouraging people to interact with the inflatable sculptures and explore concepts of sustainability and relationship to the environment. This helps to spread awareness about sustainability and the relationship between humanity and the environment.

Among the Italian artists who have pursued research on inflatables is Franco Mazzuchelli, who has been making works with inflatables from the 1960s until today. In 2023 the sculpture exhibition entitled, *Air, Earth, Water,* in the garden of Triennale Milano, celebrated Mazzucchelli with his inflatables from the 1960s to the present. Similarly, Loris Cecchini, invited by Galleria Continua to exhibit at the St. Regis Rome hotel, decided to display on the external facade *Blaublobbing,* "transparent extrusions," huge soap bubbles connected to each other, which protrude from the walls of the building, almost undermining the linearity of the architectural structures and giving them a surreal, dreamlike appearance.

Filippo Panseca, who had already designed a huge inflatable sphere for the Vesuvius archeological park in the 1970s, made the *Artificial Bionic Moon* during the 2019 Venice Biennale. It is a sphere measuring 12 meters in diameter sphere inflated with inert helium that activates photocatalysis through nano-technological elements (natural air purifiers) by means of the sun's UV rays, thus reducing pollutants in the air. The sphere takes on the appearance of a large artificial moon and was visible from all over Venice.

Many artists have contributed to this new era of the inflatable as a key to interpreting the present, including Filthy Luker and Pedro Estrellas, Dirk Schellekens and Bart Peleman, Carsten Holler, Ai Weiwei, and Steve Messam.

The New Era of the Inflatable

In March 1968, the exhibition *Structures gonflables* was presented at the Musée d'Art Moderne in Paris. It was organized by members of Utopie, founded in 1967 by a group of architects, urban planners, and sociologists. This was the first time the inflatable became the subject of an exhibition, to the extent that the museum's curator, Pierre Gaudibert, wrote in the introduction that the "aesthetics of everyday life penetrates the universe of museums that have hitherto constituted its negation through the conservation of unique, rare, used objects, torn from the fabric of everyday life." From the factory to everyday life, this was still the point of the critical interpretation of society, as in the 1960s, that saw the inflatable as something new, to be explored as a critical and social function.

As mentioned earlier, today we have moved beyond the social dimension and into one of the spectacle. This new era is admirably represented by the travelling exhibition *Pop Air*, curated by the Balloon Museum, and organized by the Lux Holding group, which has a curatorial committee. The project was initially presented in the city of Rome, and then traveled to Milan, Paris, Madrid, London, New York, Naples, and will, in the future, reach many other cities. The contemporary character of the exhibition is derived from the multifaceted nature of the invited artists in an interweaving of the art world, represented by Sila Sveta, Karina Smigla-Bobinski, MyeongBeom Kim, Max Streicher; the world of architecture, with Architects of Air, Penique Productions, ENESS, Hyperstudio; high-impact audiovisual experiences, namely Quiet Ensemble, Pepper's Ghost, Ouchhh, Tadao Cern; and the world of architecture and design with Ultravioletto, Cyril Lancelin, Camil-

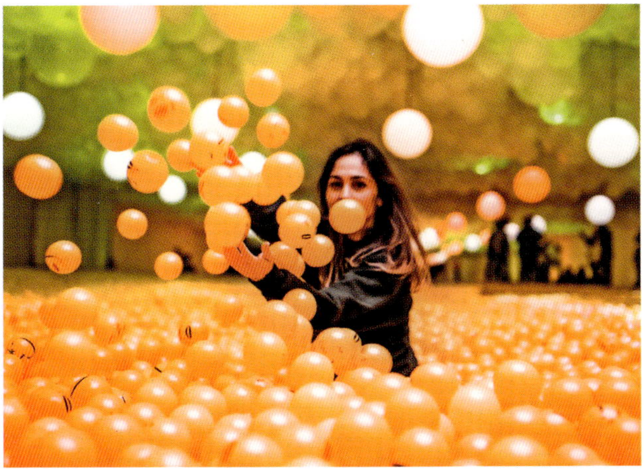

Hyperstudio, *Hyperfeeling*, London, 2023

la Falsini. This interweaving represents the complexity of a vastly changing art world that, at its zenith of maximum experimentation, touches disciplines that until recently were thought of as disparate.

Balloon Museum shifts the axis of interpretation to a society, where in the words of David Joselit, "what used to be called 'fine arts' are increasingly being distributed and consumed like any other mass media product".[5] The playful, interactive aspect, accessible to the public, is a pretext for bringing the viewer closer and to open a reflection on the role of art in an age when the great media bombardment leads the user to develop an interest in the immediate and the shocking. This attitude leads art to go as far as approaching forms seemingly outside of these parameters such as design, architecture, and quality forms of entertainment.

Interactivity creates active involvement by overturning the traditional passive role of the viewer, allowing them actively to participate in the artistic experience. This builds a more intimate bond between the work and the viewer, stimulating deeper emotional and mental involvement. The Balloon works go beyond mere viewing to foster a multisensory perspective. We see the *Cube Abyss* installation by Cyril Lancelin, whose inflatable architectures make us confront landscapes that arouse some of our deepest emotions, such as fear; or the Pop style of Momoyo Torimitsu, or the impossible architectures of MOTOREFISICO, as well as the architectural performances of Alex Schweder. From this point of view, the Balloon Museum represents the high point of art development that, as we have seen, has favored increasingly monumental, visually striking forms, while initiating a direct reflection on the information society.

1 Nicolas Bourriaud, *Estetica relazionale*, Postmedia, Milan, 2010, p. 56.
2 Francesco Casetti and Andrea Pinotti, "Post-Cinema Ecology", in Dominique Chateau, José Moure, *Cinema in the Post-art Era*, Amsterdam University Press, Amsterdam, 2020.
3 Massimiliano Gioni, 'Ask the Dust', in *Unmonumental. The Object in the 21st Century*, exhibition catalog, Phaidon, New York, 2012, p. 65.
4 I refer to Andrea Pinotti's book *Nonumento*, Johan & Levi, Monza, 2023.
5 David Joselit, 'Art in the Age of Media', in Francesco Casetti (ed.), *Art in the Age of Media*, Postmedia, Milan, 2012, p. 185

From breath to innovation. Inflatables through history and their impact on creation

Léa Hodencq

In 2022, the Balloon Museum team launched the *Pop Air* exhibition in Paris. This was the second chapter in a series of monumental art projects that began in Rome and continued in Milan, Madrid, New York and London. With the participation of some 15 international artists, the exhibition offers an immersive experience quite unprecedented in the panorama of Inflatable Art, managing to attract, in the age of social networks and digitization, a seemingly endless stream of visitors and followers from around the world. After years of severe, Covid-19 pandemic restrictions, public enthusiasm for tactile and immersive interaction was unanimous: within a few months, the Balloon Museum's colorful inflatable creations attracted more than 720,000 visitors.

To understand the reasons for this success we need to examine the history of inflatable objects. Where did they come from? What are they associated with? Why is their use nowadays synonymous with fun?

Inflatable objects are often linked to feelings of entertainment and spontaneity. With their ephemeral, volatile, and fragile character, they also evoke the imagery of travel and adventure. The idea comes directly from antiquity and finds its earliest example in the sails of boats inflated by the wind. These forms also find numerous expressions in nature: one has only to think of air-filled bubbles, with their instantly recognizable spherical shape; or the hooded seal, whose snout enlarges like a balloon in mating season; or even the fascinating puffer fish, capable of inflating in an instant to appear more imposing in the eyes of predators.

Many are the human inventions also dedicated to experimenting with the potential of the inflatable. The most famous example is certainly that of the Montgolfier brothers: since the time of Leonardo da Vinci, man had longed to soar through the air, and, finally, in the Age of Enlightenment, those dreams became a reality. Joseph-Michel and Jacques-Étienne, French industrialists and inventors of the aerostat, presented the hot air balloon to the public for the first time: a giant balloon weighing several hundred pounds took flight to the amazement and applause of the crowd. The story goes that it was Joseph Montgolfier, while warming his shirt in front of the fireplace, who noticed that the fabric inflated mightily thanks to the hot air. Convinced that he had discovered a new principle, but without analyzing how it worked, he then involved his brother in his intrepid research.

In the late 19th century, a German count named Ferdinand von Zeppelin began building airships, the famous

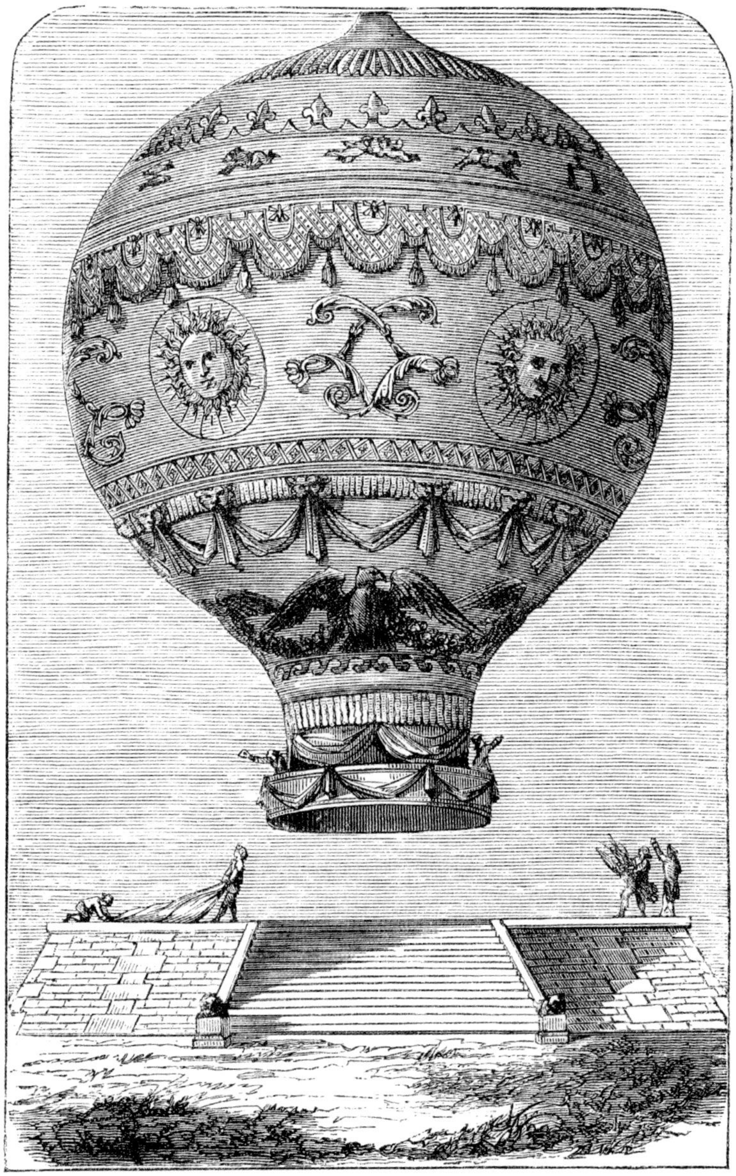

Balloon of Marquis d'Arlandes (1742-1809), a French ballooning pioneer. *Scribners Magazine*, 1870

Zeppelins. Used as bombers during World War I, in the 1930s they became the most luxurious craft for transatlantic flights. Their reputation, however, was soon tarnished. Inflated with hydrogen, which was highly flammable, they caused numerous accidents that received considerable publicity at the time and led to the end of their use.

As in the case of the Zeppelin, inflatable objects were first developed by the military, proving to be valuable tools because of their ease of transport and installation. In 1944, during World War II, a diversionary action was organized: Operation Fortitude. To simulate a nonexistent military force, Allied troops lined up dozens of inflatable tanks on the beach to deceive German aerial reconnaissance. Thus, these devices allowed the Allies to divert attention from the main front, contributing to the success of the landing.

Because of their great power of attraction, inflatable objects have made their way into various fields, including the art world: e.g. design, film, and architecture. The mid-1950s saw the birth in England of the new artistic movement called Pop Art,1 which then developed in the United States in the 1960s. This cultural phenomenon melds science fiction and technology but also advertising, design and everyday objects. In 1966 Andy Warhol, the movement's superstar, created the *Silver Clouds*. First exhibited at the Leo Castelli Gallery in New York, the *Silver Clouds* were cushion-like silver balloons filled with helium. Even then Warhol believed that art should not simply be enjoyed from a distance, but should rather become a physical, immersive experience. Indeed, his pioneering installation allowed visitors to interact with the balloons, walk around them and even touch them. In 1960 there was a strong desire to go beyond the traditional conception of sculpture and to push back the boundaries of the conventional materials associated with it, such as stone, wood or bronze. This was the era when industrial materials—polymers, viscose, and other elements—appeared, allowing for new forms and new interactions.

Special mention must go to the bouncy castles, spaces expressly dedicated to collective play and fun that first appeared in the late 1950s. At that time an American engineer named John Tom Scurlock was employed by

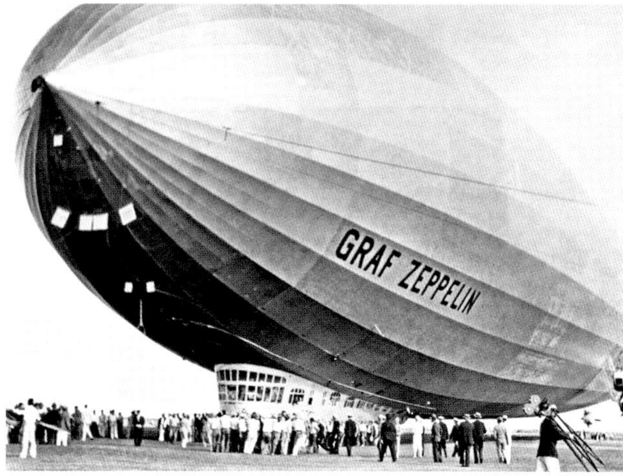

The LZ 129 Graf Zeppelin, making a stopover in Miami, on its way to the Century of Progress exposition in Chicago, circa October 23, 1933

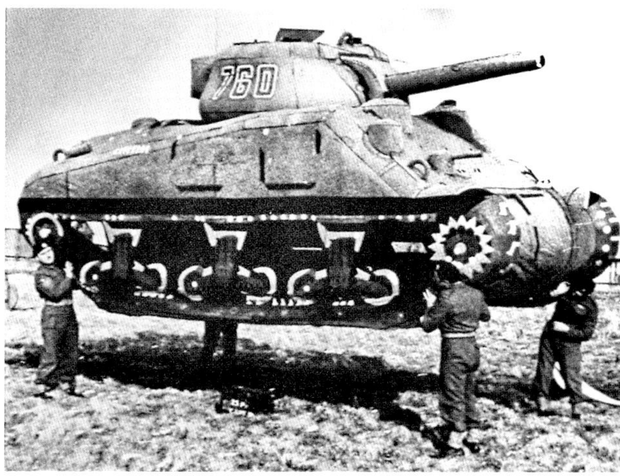

Inflatable Light Tank used in England during preparation of Operation Fortitude, 1944

an oil and gas company. While on site he noticed that workers used to put up tents to protect themselves from the weather and that this operation required a lot of time and energy. So, he decided to create an inflatable tent that was lighter and much easier and quicker to set up. From then on, every morning Scurlock was confronted by employees who, just for fun, jumped on the structure during installation, and the idea of inflatable games was born! A few years later, the engineer's wife, Frances, founded the first company dedicated to renting these kinds of objects. Today, bouncy castles are part of our collective imagination and several artists have used them in their work. One notable example is the *White Bouncy* Castle, a large inflatable castle created by Dana Caspersen, William Forsythe, and Joel Ryan and exhibited in 2022 at the Villette in Paris as part of the *Pop Air* exhibition. Also in the 1960s, the film industry relaunched by creating an inflatable character that has become iconic: the Rover. As mentioned earlier, inflatable objects usually hark back to a joyful and cheerful imagery, in fact they are often found at birthday parties or places where something is being celebrated, as well as at the beach or pool during the summer. However, they can also have a dark side. Such is the case with The *Prisoner*, the British television series in the fantasy-political genre that tells the story of a former secret agent trapped in a village on an inaccessible island. In his countless escape attempts, the agent is repeatedly captured by the Rover, a strange inflatable object that intervenes when prisoners try to escape. This character is shaped like a large, soft white ball that produces a dull rumble when it attacks and is capable of bouncing and gliding at high speeds and for long distances over both land and sea. Initially "the guardian" was to be a small remote-controlled vehicle topped with a flashing beacon. Difficult to maneuver, very noisy, and unremarkable, it ended up sinking into the sea. The series team then came up with the original idea of a conceptual vigilante: a large and very simple white balloon devoid of any mechanism. The Rover quickly became the emblem of surveillance, so much so that it appeared in *The Simpsons* in 1998.

The field of design was also strongly influenced by inflatable fashion, which in the 1960s emerged as a true cultural pattern and almost a way of life. Indeed, innovations in the field of synthetic materials offered new artistic possibilities, paving the way for previously unseen shapes and colors. In 1966 three Italian architects—Paolo Lomazzi, Donato D'Urbino, and Jonathan De Pas—met in Milan, where they founded Studio DDL and designed the inflatable *Blow* armchair. Conceived in 1967 and first presented in 1968, this creation became the icon of Pop furniture and a symbol of the revolutionary spirit of the times. Made of translucent PVC in acid colors, the *Blow* chair was much more affordable than other high-end design pieces, and as a result was to be found in many homes. Today it has earned a place in prestigious collections, such as that of MoMA in New York and the Centre Pompidou in Paris.

In the Europe and United States of the 1960s and 1970s, a socio-political context was being created that contrasted with the hyper-functionalist approach predominant in the postwar period. In the field of architecture, a new generation of profes-

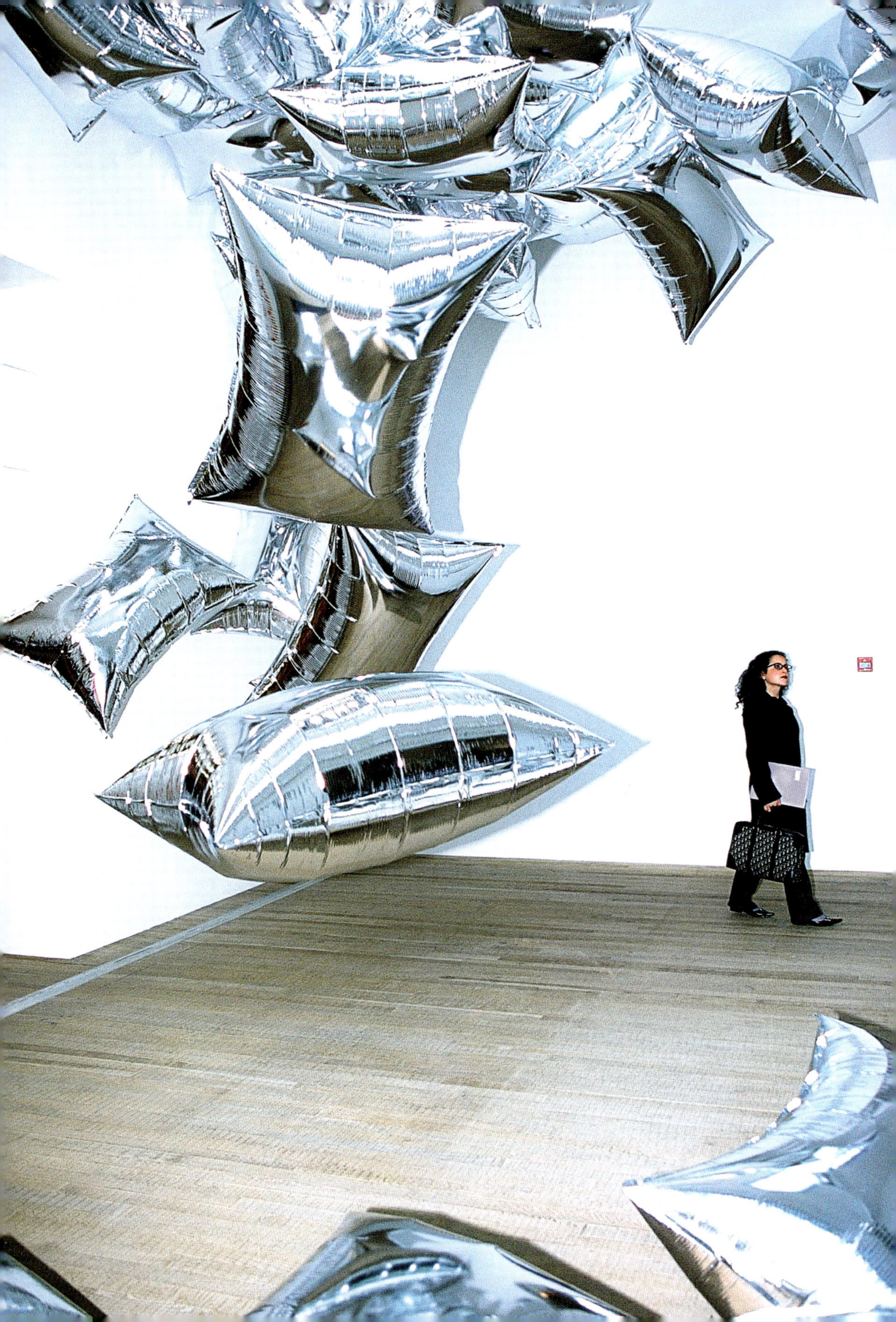

Andy Warhol Art Exhibition at the Tate Modern Gallery in London, 2002

Patrick McGoohan in the TV series *The Prisoner*, 1967

sionals began to propose alternative and sometimes utopian ideas in an attempt to humanize this discipline. Indeed, the theme of the 1970 Osaka World Expo was "Progress and Harmony for Humanity." For the first time this event was held in Japan, boasting the participation of more than seventy countries. It was the apotheosis of inflatable architecture. Among the most notable structures was Taneo Oki and Sihigeru Aoki's *Mushballoon*, a true architectural feat, consisting of huge air cushions held in suspension by some forty metal cables: an entirely revolutionary configuration at the time. The use of inflatable structures in architecture offered numerous advantages. Indeed, because of their immediate nature, they allowed a considerable saving of time, as well as being inexpensive to transport and install. The industrial materials of which they were made were significantly cheaper than traditional materials: PVC, neoprene, and polyurethane were unrivaled in the marketplace. Plastics were widespread, and designers continually experimented with their use. However, after the huge Expo 70, as it was known, inflatable structures went out of fashion. The first oil crisis in 1973 marked the end of the plastic ideology. The euphoria of inflatables ended with the realization of the harmful consequences of overconsumption as well as the environmental problems associated with pollution and non-recyclable materials.

Inflatable Art projects only made a comeback in the 2000s. And they re-

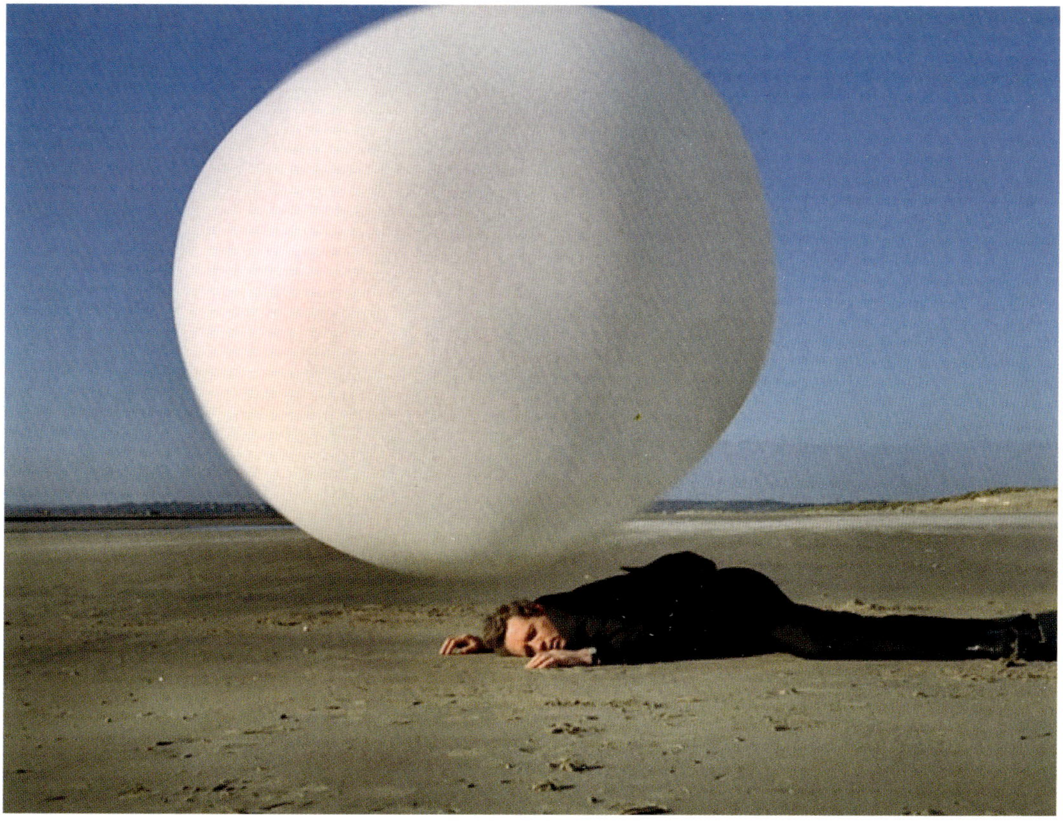

appeared with even more playful and interactive, sometimes more comical, characters. The materials used were more durable and environmentally friendly. Some notable exhibitions of Inflatable Art garnered international cultural and political recognition: among them, the exhibition *Air-Air: Celebrating Inflatables*, which opened on July 20, 2000, at the Grimaldi Forum in the Principality of Monaco, and showcased some 20 works by a variety of international artists and mixed all disciplines, providing an overview of Inflatable Art from the 1960s onward.[2]

Another from the same group was *Mobile M+: Inflation! a (Con)temporary Sculpture Park*, the outdoor exhibition set up at Hong Kong's West Kowloon Cultural District in 2013. Here several monumental inflatable sculptures by international artists including Choi Jeong Hwa, Jeremy Deller, Paul McCarthy, Cao Fei and Tomás Saraceno were on display.[3]

Even more recent was the exhibition *Aerodream: Architecture, Design and Inflatables 1950-2020*, which opened at the Centre Pompidou in Metz, France, on January 30, 2021. The exhibition offered visitors a journey through more than 250 works and audiovisual documents, reconstructing the history of inflatable structures from their earliest days to the present.[4]

In addition to exhibitions, individual artists and events were also becoming symbols of Inflatable Art: such was the case with Jeff Koons, undisputed master of kitsch, and his iconic *Balloon Dog* series. Created between 1994 and 2000, it consisted of dog-shaped balloons made of stainless steel. In this way, the American artist made a simple and ephemeral balloon durable and grand, immortalizing and amplifying a small object that was originally festive and popular.

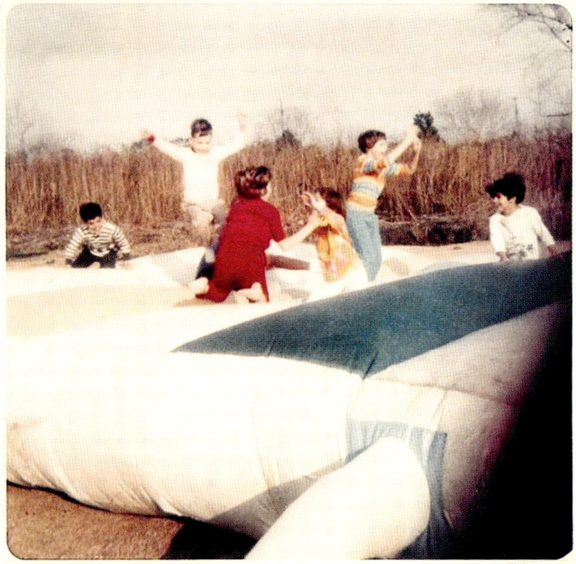

Children play on an early version of the bouncy house. Date unknown

Japanese artist Takashi Murakami was also among the followers of the inflatable, particularly for his famous *Mr. Dob.* Introduced in 1993 with the painting *Dob Genesis*, this character then went from two-dimensional to three-dimensional, becoming an inflatable figure in 1994. His appearance brought to mind a revisited Mickey Mouse: his round head and unmistakable ears, on which were imprinted the letters D and B, respectively, which with his O-shaped face formed the word "dob." This name encapsulated the phrase "dobojite, dobojite, oshamanbe," a parodic utterance partly inspired by a manga character from the 1970s. This figure, believed to be the artist's alter ego, quickly became the *kawaii* icon[5] we know today. Oher artists whose research explored the history of their country, showed an interest in the inflatables. Such is the case of Jeremy Deller, who in 2012 created a monumental inflatable sculpture entitled *Sacrilege*. With it, the British artist recreated the celebrated site of Stonehenge, one of the most impressive and mysterious prehistoric monuments in the world. Located in the United Kingdom, the imposing ruins take the form of a series of menhirs[6] arranged in a circle and included on the UNESCO World Heritage list, attracting about a million visitors annually. Deller transformed the Stonehenge monument into a vast inflatable playground using plastic materials to create a scale replica. The installation encourages interaction from the public, inviting visitors to climb, jump, and play. But what does the title refer to? The name "Sacrilege" literally means "desecration of sacred objects and places." In this way the artist tried to anticipate and defuse any potential criticism. The work, with its decidedly playful character, encapsulated an invitation to reevaluate British history and national identity.

Contemporary inflatable structures deliberately reinforce the link between art and entertainment. These new works are testament to the deep connection between art, mass culture, and the culture industry. Reference to the famous Macy's Parade is almost inevitable. The brainchild of the American department store chain of the same name, the Macy's Thanksgiving Day Parade is a procession that takes place in New York City on Thanksgiving Day in November. A parade of floats travels through the city streets, displaying large inflatable creations with the likenesses of various characters and celebrities. Helium balloons were introduced in 1927, and Felix the Cat had the honor of being the first to wave over the crowd. At the time, there was no way to deflate these floating figures, so they were dispersed in the air and burst as they soared into the sky. The following year, valves were

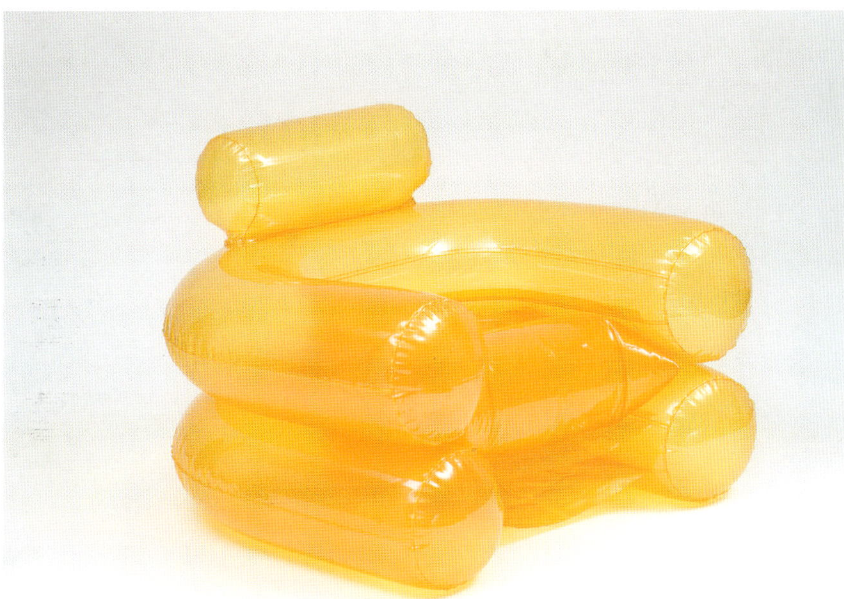

The inflatable armchair *Blow* by Paolo Lomazzi, Jonathan De Pas, Donato D'Urbino Design date: 1967. Manufacture date: c. 1967-1972. Manufacturer: Zanotta S.p.A., Italy PVC plastic 83.8 x 119.7 x 102.9 cm (inflated) Museum of Modern Art (MoMA), New York

applied that allowed the helium to escape as the balloons hovered in the air at the end of the parade. A return address was given and a reward established in the hope that the inflatable creations would be returned. Not all were returned, in part because, among other reasons, one landed in the East River and another fell into the ocean. It is said that in 1932 one of them wrapped itself around the wing of an airplane causing it to crash: from then on, the balloons were no longer dispersed in the air. Today the parade attracts 3.5 million people to New York City, and a similar number of spectators follow the festivities on television. Each year this parade of floats and giant inflatable puppets depicting SpongeBob, Spiderman, or Pikachu winds its way along a four-mile route.

In recent times, the inflatable object has become a real star of the runway. For the presentation of the Italian fashion label Diesel's spring-summer collection at Milan Fashion Week 2023, Dutch designer Dennis Vanderbroeck's design studio created a monumental installation: a giant inflatable sculpture composed of several disjointed human figures. In addition to causing a stir, the work—50 meters long, 38 meters wide and 14 meters high—broke the Guinness Book of World Records. A complementary un-

Balloon Dog by Jeff Koons at The Broad Contemporary Art Museum, Los Angeles April 9, 2016

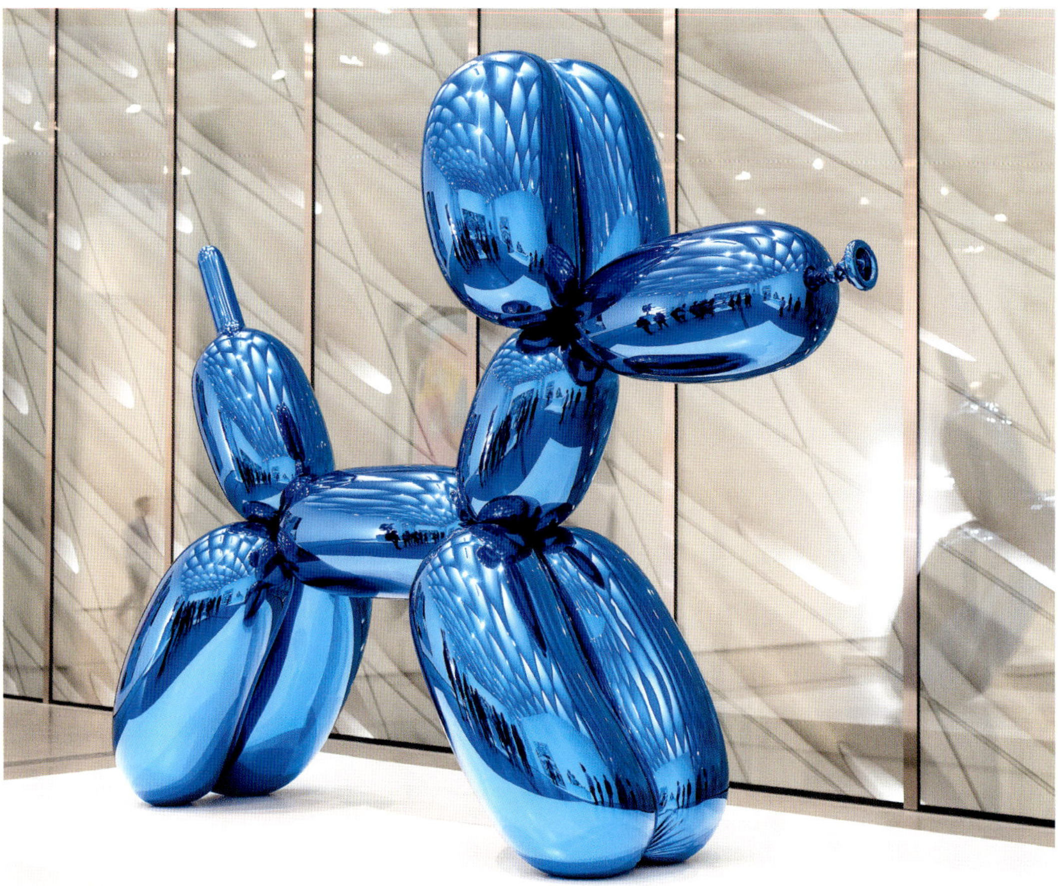

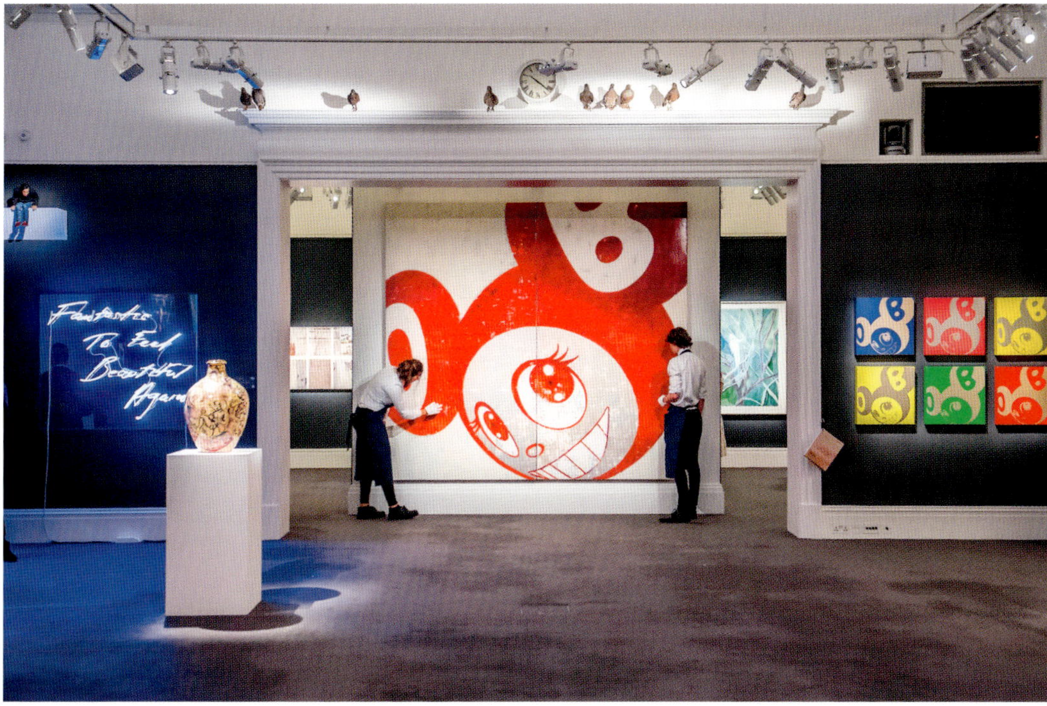

And then and then and then... by Takashi Murakami for Frieze week, Sothebys, London, 2018

derstanding has existed between art and fashion for decades, but in recent years sensational scenic creations have taken center stage. In addition to presenting clothes, today's fashion show gives designers the opportunity to offer to immerse audiences in their own artistic universe, thus trespassing into the realm of live performance. These new forms of presentation were adopted throughout the 20th century. In the 1960s and 1970s, catwalks became evermore surprising, with futuristic collections that definitively broke with the past.

In conclusion, inflatables are everywhere and manage to fit into every creative circuit. Whether they are filled with air, gas, hydrogen, helium or nitrogen, these objects can be found not only in the tires and airbags of our cars, but also in the world of fashion—thanks to designers like Harri[7] and their surrealist-flavored clothes—and even in space. Indeed, the recent LOFTID mission[8] involves the use of inflatable shields to improve rocket landings on Mars. Beyond everyday uses and the latest technical innovations, inflatables are today very much in vogue. In a context of economic, environmental, health and geopolitical crisis, the need for lightness is everywhere. The return of these volatile objects connected to the need for lightheartedness and the yearning to take off fits this mood. Such works offer a sense of peace away from heavy, anxiety-provoking themes, creating festive and comforting environments. Crossing the boundaries of formats and interactions with a light and playful step, the inflatable is open to all experimentation, definitively establishing itself as an art practice in its own right.

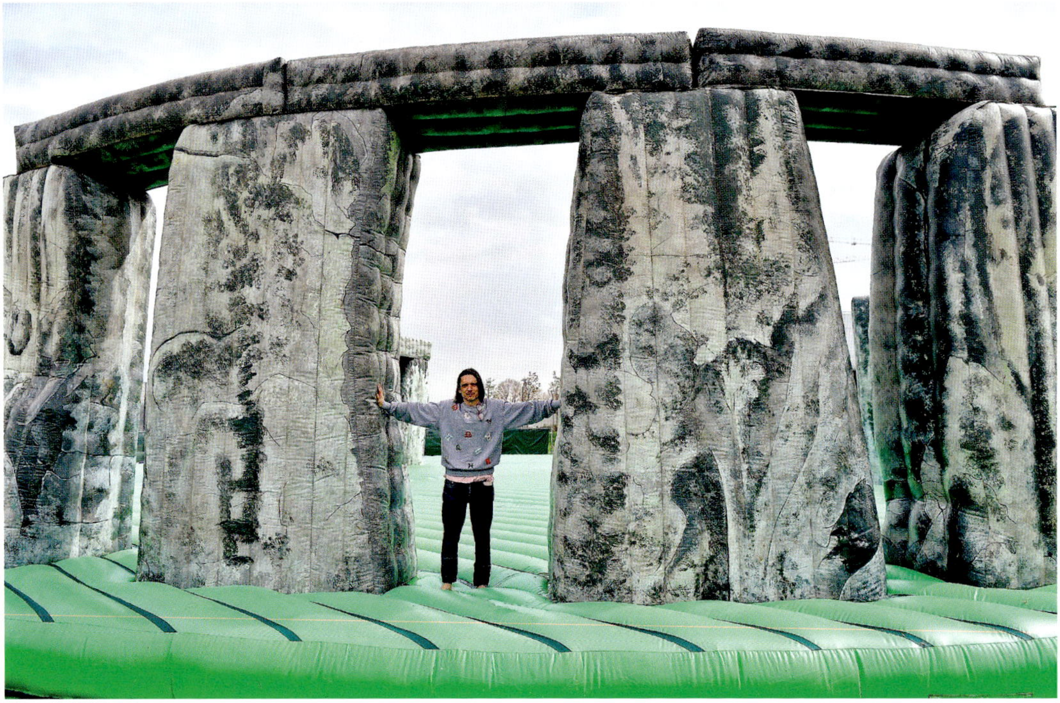

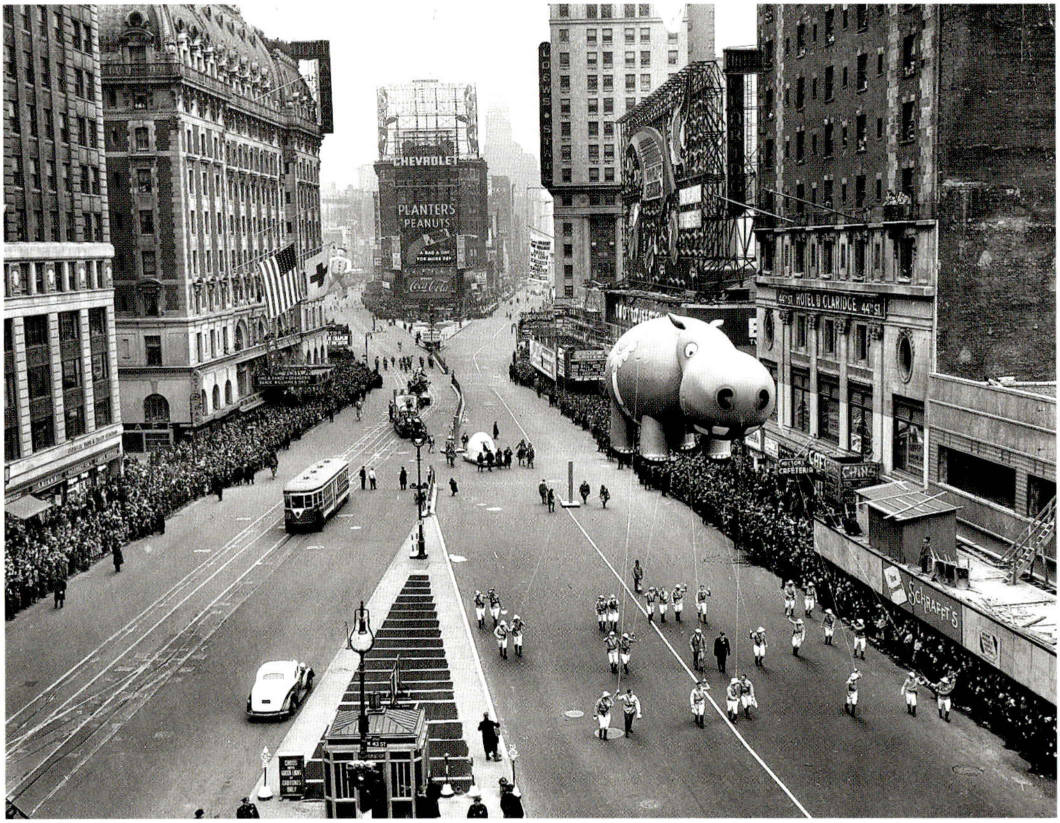
CHEVROLET
PLANTERS
PEANUTS
HOTEL CLARIDGE
SCHRAFFT'S

Opposite, top
Artist Jeremy Deller poses in front his installation *Sacrilege* at City Life Park, Milan, 2018

Opposite, bottom
A hippo balloon floats over Times Square during the Macy's Thanksgiving Day Parade, New York, 1940

Right
Singer Sam Smith in a design by HARRI at the 43rd BRIT Awards, Arrivals, The O2 Arena, London, 2023

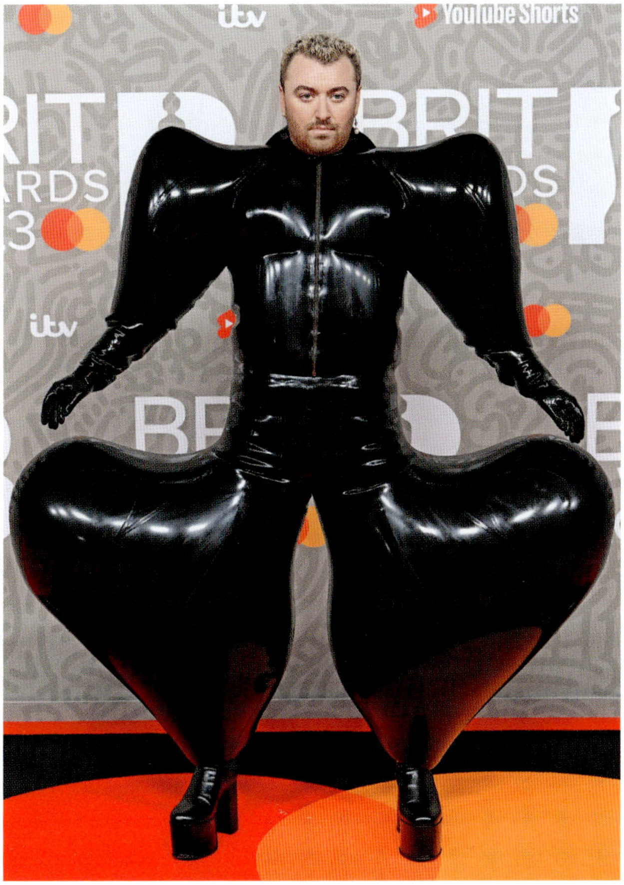

1 Short for Popular Art.
2 Held from July 21 to August 27, 2000 at the Grimaldi Forum in the Principality of Monaco.
3 Held from April 25 to June 9, 2013 in Kowloon, Hong Kong, at the West Kowloon Cultural District Promenade.
4 Held at the Centre Pompidou-Metz from January 30 to August 23, 2021 and then in Paris at the Cité de l'architecture et du patrimoine from October 6, 2021 to February 14, 2022.
5 Kawaii is a Japanese adjective that mainly means "cute."
6 Megalithic monument, stone rising vertically.
7 Fashion designer Harikrishnan Keezhathil Surendran Pillai.
8 The acronym stands for "Low-Earth Orbit Flight Test of an Inflatable Decelerator.

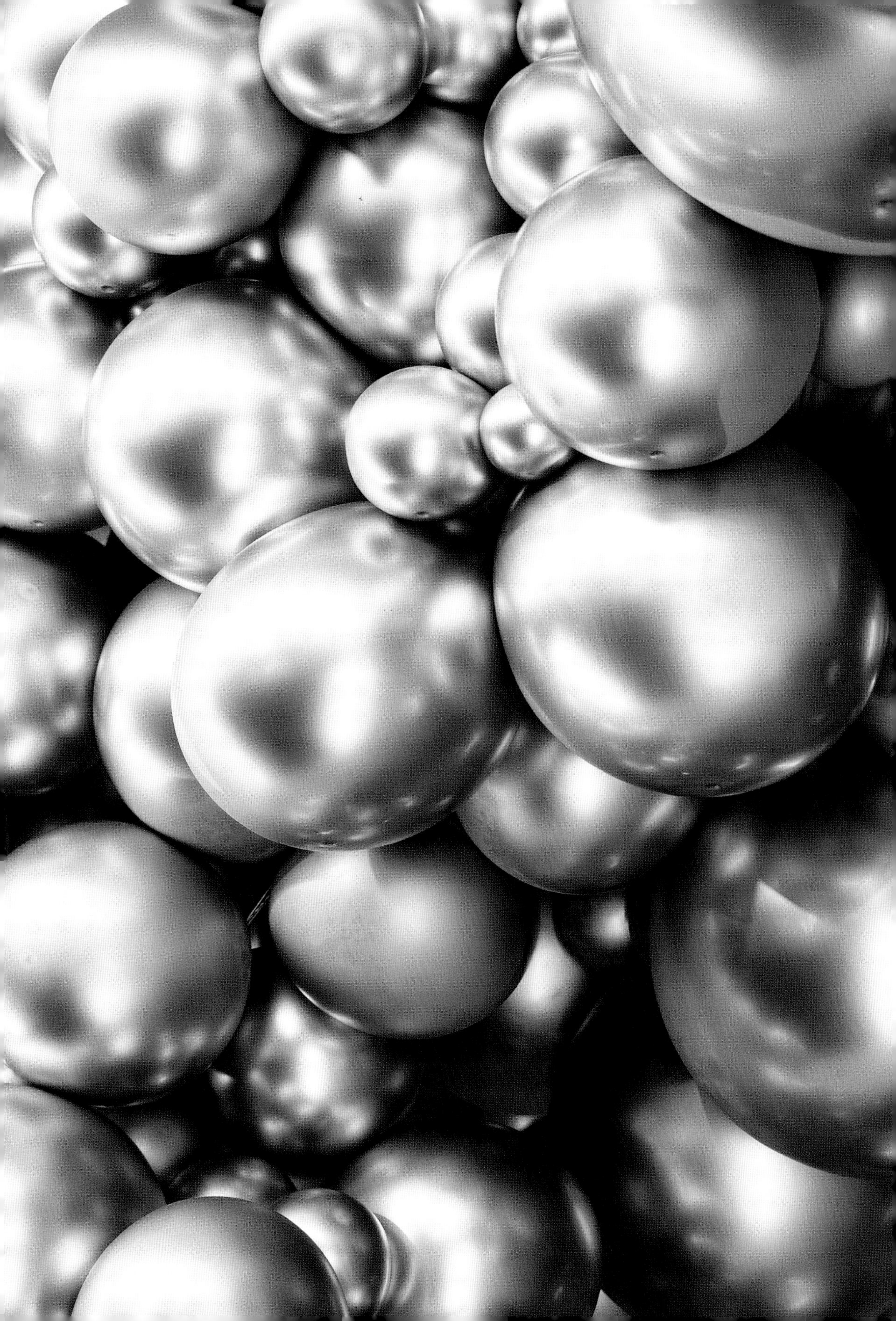

Appendix

A

Anotherview
Skyscape #1, 2023
Video, TV screen, and window
17 x 3 m
Balloon Museum - *EmotionAir*
pp 26-27

Architects of Air
Dodecalis Luminarium, 1992
Opaque grey unreinforced PVC,
translucent colour unreinforced PVC and
reinforced PVC
980 m^2
Balloon Museum - *Pop Air*, Madrid, 2023
pp 28-31

Ashley, Claire
Clown (Star Patrick), 2019
Ripstop nylon, spray paint, and fan
5.5 m
Balloon Museum - *Pop Air*, Paris and Milan, 2022
pp 32-33

Atelier Sisu
Evanescent, 2020
Dichroic PVC
8 x 8 x 7 m
Balloon Museum - *Let's Fly*
pp 34-35

B

Bauder, Christopher
ELECTRIC MOONS, 2018
36 ground-based KINETIC LIGHTS Winch XS, 36
90cm white helium balloons
8 x 8 x 6 m
Balloon Museum - *EmotionAir*
pp 36-39

Blahutová, Kateřina
Living Forest, 2021
Nylon fabric
3 - 6 m height, 30 - 60 cm diameter
Balloon Museum - *Pop Air*, Rome, 2021
Partner and co-author: PrusaLab
Production and co-author: Signal productions
pp 40-41

C

Cern, Tadao
BB, 2023
Mylar BoPET air inflated balloons
8 x 8 m
Balloon Museum - *Let's Fly*
pp 42-43

E

ENESS
Spiritus Sonata, 2023
PVC, polyester, and blower
16.6 x 16.6 x 4 m
Balloon Museum - *Let's Fly*
pp 52-53

Cupid's Koi Garden, 2022
Polyurethane coated polyester woven fabric, LED
eyes, speaker, and blower
Various dimensions
Balloon Museum - *Pop Air*, Paris
pp 44-47

Together Forever, 2023
Printed Woven polyester fabric, LED eyes, speakers,
and blower
15 x 5 m
Balloon Museum - *Pop Air*, Naples
pp 48-49

Kubli, Thom
Black Hole Horizon, 2012-2015
Polyurethane, soap bubble liquid, acrylic glass, and electronics
10 x 10 m
Balloon Museum - *EmotionAir*
pp 84-87

Kuehlne, Jimmy
Bau(ncy) Haus, 2018
Polyester and LED pixels
Variable 20 x 10 x 4.7 m
Balloon Museum - *Pop Air*
pp 88-89

L

Lancelin, Cyril
Flying Maze, 2023
Polyurethane coated polyester woven fabric
10 x 10 x 5 m
Balloon Museum - *Let's Fly*
pp 90-93

Cube Abyss, 2023
Polyurethane coated polyester woven fabric
10 x 10 x 5.45 m
Balloon Museum - *EmotionAir*
p 96

Knot, 2021
Polyurethane coated polyester woven fabric
8 x 8 x 5 m
Balloon Museum - *Pop Air*
pp 95

Duck One Arch, 2021
Polyurethane coated polyester woven fabric
2.50 x 1.80 x 2.20 m
Balloon Museum - *Pop Air*, Rome, Paris, and Milan
p 97

M

Makaroff, Miranda
Synchronized Chaos, 2023
Polyester, lights, and mirror
12 x 2 m approx.
Balloon Museum - *EmotionAir*
pp 98-101

Messam, Steve
Façade, 2023
Polyester, fans, and LED lights
39 x 4 x 2.7 m
Balloon Museum - *EmotionAir*
pp 102-105

MOTOREFISICO
Never Ending Story, 2021
Plastic balls and nylon
Various dimensions
SOUND DESIGN
Plume (Netlabel) Gentle music
Balloon Museum - *Pop Air*
pp 106-107

Swing, 2023
PVC, elastane, and polyester
1 m (each sphere)
Balloon Museum - *EmotionAir*
pp 108-1097

N

Nakamura, Motomichi
Cannonballs, 2021
PVC Balloons and projection
3.3 x 3.3 x 1.4 m (inflatable sculpture)
Balloon Museum - *EmotionAir*
pp 110-111

O

Ouchhh
AI DATA PORTAL, 2023
Flexible Curve LED tunnel, and mirrors
11 x 4.5 m
Balloon Museum - *Let's Fly*
pp 112-113

P

Penique Productions
Deposito Vittoria, 2021
Polyethylene film sheet, and car
10 x 25 x 7 m
Balloon Museum - *Pop Air*, Rome
pp 114-115

Rosâtre, 2022
Polyethylene film sheet, line lights, and pillow
15 x 15 x 9 m
Balloon Museum - *Pop Air*, Paris
pp 118-119

Giallo 368, 2022
Polyethylene film sheet, house structure, and neon lights
24 x 16 x 6 m
Balloon Museum - *Pop Air*,
Milan
pp 116-117

Pepper's Ghost
ARIA - The Breath Immersive Experience, 2022
LED screen tiles and mirrors
Balloon Museum - *Pop Air*
pp 120-121

Picchi, Michela
Playground Love, 2023
Kristal PVC and polyester
2.6 m, 3 m (spheres); 3 x 1.2 x 1.5 m (tigers)
Balloon Museum - *EmotionAir*
pp 122-123

Plastique Fantastique
reSET THEORY, 2022
TPU and blowers
8 x 4 m
Balloon Museum - *Pop Air*, Paris
pp 124-125

THOLOS, 2022
Black, transparent and mirrored TPU; aluminum, iron rings, blower, audio player, and dimmers
4.75 x 8 m
Balloon Museum - *Pop Air*
pp 126-127

Pneuhaus and Bike Powered Events
Canopy, 2019
Bicycle, LEDs, polyester, fan, and tripod
13 x 11.6 x 3.6 m
Balloon Museum - *Pop Air*
pp 128-129

Pool, Kalman
Voyage, 2023
Fluorescent acrylic, fabric, LED UV light, programmed spotlight, aluminum frame, wireless speaker and TPU inflatable
19 x 7 x 4 m
Balloon Museum - *EmotionAir*
pp 130-131

Q

Quiet Ensemble
A Quiet Storm, 2022
Smoke bubble machine, lights, and laser
Various dimensions
Balloon Museum - *Pop Air* and *EmotionAir*
pp 132-135

See *Hypercosmo*
Video projection, light, and sound performance
pp 68-69

See *Hyperstellar*
Video, light, and sound performance
pp 70-75

R

Rossetti, Stefano
Parcobaleno, 2020
Mar-Pol 1000
14 x 29 x 7 m
Balloon Museum - *Pop Air*
pp 136-137

Rub Kandy
The GINJOS, 2022 - 2023
Polyester, PVC, and air
Various dimensions
Balloon Museum - *Pop Air*, *Let's Fly* and *EmotionAir*
pp 138-141

S

Schweder, Alex
The Third Thing, 2022
Fur, mirror, music, air and electronics
5 x 3 m (fur installations); 3 m diameter (sphere)
collaborated with composer Geneva Skeen on the sound for *His Dilution*
Balloon Museum - *EmotionAir*
pp 142-143

Shaw, Michael
Lava Lamp, 2023
Ripstop Nylon fabric
17 x 11 x 2.4 m
Balloon Museum - *Let's Fly*
pp 144-145

Sila Sveta
Airscape, 2023
VR Video
Balloon Museum - *Let's Fly*
pp 146-147

See *Hyperfeeling*
Video, light, and sound performance
pp 76-79

Smigla-Bobinski, Karina
ADA, 2011
PVC balloon, charcoals, helium, and air
3 / 3.5 m (sphere)
Balloon Museum - *Pop Air*, Paris, and *Let's Fly*
pp 148-151

POLYHEADRA, 2022
PVC foil and magnetic rings
Various dimensions
Balloon Museum - *Pop Air*
pp 152-155

Kaleidoscope, 2016
Lightbox, cyan/magenta/yellow inks and projection
3 light boxes of 2 x 2 m
Balloon Museum - *EmotionAir*
pp 156-157

SpY
ZEROS, 2023
10-12 units of black inflatable toroid donuts,
PVC light and strong tarpaulin
5.5 x 11.25 x 8.20 m
Balloon Museum - *Let's Fly*
pp 158-161

Streicher, Max
Battle of Cannae, 2014
Polyester fabric, blower and cables
9 x 4.5 x 5.5 m
Balloon Museum - *Pop Air*, Paris
pp 162-163

Silenus, 2002
Nylon spinnaker and blowers
8 x 3.5 m
Balloon Museum - *Pop Air*
pp 164

Waking Soldiers, 2006
Nylon spinnaker, rotating louver mechanism,
and blowers
5 m
Balloon Museum - *Let's Fly*, New York
pp 165

T

Torimitsu, Momoyo
Somehow, I Don't Feel Comfortable, 2023
Flexible nylon fabric, blower, duct tube, silencer,
and speed controller
3 x 3.6 x 5 m
Balloon Museum - *EmotionAir*
pp 166-167

U

Ultravioletto
Into the Rainbow, 2023
VR Video
Balloon Museum - *Pop Air*
pp 168-169

W

Wilsher-Mills, Jason
The Argonaut, 2023
Nylon acrylic
10 x 7 x 4.2 m
Balloon Museum - *EmotionAir*
pp 170-171

Z

Zamproni, Geraldo
Volatile Structure, 2011
Polyester and motors
6 x 6 m (each)
Balloon Museum - *Pop Air*, Paris and Milan
and *EmotionAir*
pp 172-173

Zanotto, Lucas
SQUEEZED IN, 2023
Lycra and polyester
Various dimensions
Balloon Museum - *EmotionAir*
pp 174-175

AIR WE ARE

BALLOON MUSEUM

FROM A TO Z

Catalog

Edited by
Francesco Dobrovich

Content Supervision
Antonella Di Lullo

Coordination
Emma Hamilton

Contributing Texts
Roberto Fantauzzi
Valentino Catricalà
Léa Hodencq

Contributing Editors
Maria Serena Salvatore
Riccardo Lionello

Book Cover Design and Art Direction
Flavio Raimondi

Artistic Management
Maria Chiara Laurenti

Photographers
Alberto Alaggio
Kimberly Butler
Matt Chung
Will Ellis
Daniel Greer
Daniel Herendi
Ivan Lucas
Daniele Muzzi
John Owens
Tomaso Pignocchi
Alessandro Raboni
Vasilis Rallis
Zeno Ruzza
Tomáš Slavík
Alessandra Trucillo
Federico Villa

Acknowledgements
The Balloon Museum is hugely grateful for all of the support we have received in organizing *Air We Are, from A to Z,* and wish to thank all the artsts who have partecipated, our visitors for supporting us, and our partners for their invaluable assistance.

Photo Credits
Thank you to everyone who gave their generous permission to reproduce the material listed here. Every effort has been made to secure all reproduction permissions prior to publication. Lux Holding apologizes for any inadvertent error or omission. If notified, we will endeavor to correct these at the earliest opportunity.

28, 29 bottom e 31 bottom (sketch) Alan Parkinson; 29 top Ivan Lucas; 30 and 31 top John Owens; 34 Curiocity_Markus Ravik; 35 centre and bottom Andre Pattenden; 41 Tomáš Slavík; 52, 53 Daniel Greer; 56, 57, 60 © Terry Rook - Glance Image; 66, 67 Juan Zapata: 82-83 MyeongBeom Kim; 84-85 Florian Voggeneder; 88, 89 Jimmy Kuehnle; 100-101, 122 top, 130 top Daniel Herendi; 176-177 Pieter Boersma; 178 © 2024 Photo Scala, Florence/bpk, Bildagentur fuer Kunst, Kultur und Geschichte, Berlin; 180 Courtesy ARR; 181 © Tomás Saraceno, The Aerocene Foundation & the Indigenous Communities of Salinas Grandes and Laguna de Guayatayoc. Photography by Studio Tomás Saraceno, 2020; 183 top Paul Cooper/Shutterstock; 187 J Sandvik/imageBROKER/ Shutterstock; 188 top Everett/ Shutterstock; 188 bottom © Bridgeman Images; 190 Nils Jorgensen/Shutterstock; 191 ITV/ Shutterstock; 192 Courtesy of Space Walk; 193 © 2024. Digital image, The Museum of Modern Art, New York/Scala, Florence; 194 Hayk_Shalunts/Shutterstock, 195 Guy Bell/Shutterstock, 196 top Mario Romano/Agf/Shutterstock; 196 bottom Scott Cornell/ Shutterstock; 197 David Fisher/ Shutterstock.

LUX Holding

Founder and CEO
Roberto Fantauzzi

Legal Representative
Vanessa Arcangeli

President
José Linguella

Managing Director
Andrea Lucentini

Creative Director
Riccardo Lionello

Head of Scenography
Alessia Petrangeli

Head of Communication
Fabio Fantauzzi

Head of Marketing
Simone Mariani

Art Director
Flavio Raimondi

Int. Business Development & Strategy
Andrea Giombini
Caterina Calò

Balloon Museum

International Manager
Federica Di Paola

Executive Project Manager
Stefano Achilli

Exhibition Project Manager
Lydia Daini
Giada de Luca
Federica Muscolo

Project Controller
Alina Sirbu
Sofia Saleri

Production Manager
Simone Rubei

Light and Set Designer
Daniele Davino

Exhibition Designer
Elena Raimondi
Alice Di Cicco
Giuditta Marucci
Mattia Alongi

Balloon Artist
Francesca Sacchetti

HR Specialist
Vittoria Ascione
Giulia Asper

Exhibition Production
Andrea Zecca
Giacomo Pasciuto
Giorgio Verderame

Customer Relations
Marta Pavone
Giulia Francescangeli

Head of Art & Curation
Francesco Dobrovich

Curator
Antonella Di Lullo

Artistic Management
Maria Chiara Laurenti

Artistic Production Coordinator
Chiara Caimmi

Exhibition Manager
Jesus Gonzalez

Special Projects Coordinator
Emma Hamilton

Press Officer & PR
Maristella Burchietti

Marketing & Communication Coordinator
Rosapia De Vinco
Elisa Bono
Maria Serena Salvatore

Video Content
Alessio Marini

Graphic Designer
Marino Spitoni

Web Designer
Giordano Chiappelli

Merchandising
Luca Trombini
Eleonora Musa
Arianna Ciccarelli
Nadia Zdanovich

Scientific Committee
Paula Perissinotto
Damiana Leoni
Léa Hodencq
Valentino Catricalà

Silvana Editoriale

Chief Executive
Michele Pizzi

Editorial Director
Sergio Di Stefano

Art Director
Giacomo Merli

Editorial Coordinator
Maria Chiara Tulli

Graphic Design and Layout
Annamaria Ardizzi

Copy-editing
Mariangela Palazzi-Williams

English translation from French
Lenore Rosenberg for Scriptum, Rome

Production Coordinator
Antonio Micelli

Editorial Assistant
Giulia Mercanti

Photo Editor
Silvia Sala

Press Office
Alessandra Olivari, press@silvanaeditoriale.it

ISBN 9788836657773

Available through ARTBOOK | D.A.P.
155 Sixth Avenue, 2nd Floor,
New York, N.Y. 10013
Tel: (212) 627-1999
Fax: (212) 627-9484

Silvana Editoriale S.p.A.
via dei Lavoratori, 78
20092 Cinisello Balsamo, Milano
tel. 02 453 951 01
www.silvanaeditoriale.it

Reproductions, printing and binding
in Italy
Printed by Tipo Stampa s.r.l., Moncalieri (TO)
in June 2024

Cover
Graphic rendering by
Flavio Raimondi

Pages 8-9
Hyperstudio
Hypercosmo
Balloon Museum
Pop Air
Paris, 2022

Pages 12-13
Cupid's Koi Garden
ENESS
Balloon Museum
Pop Air
Paris, 2022

Pages 16-17
ADA
Karina Smigla-Bobinski
Balloon Museum
Let's Fly
Atlanta, 2024

Pages 20-21
Emogram Balloons
kissmiklos
Photo courtesy of the artist

Page 198
Balloon Street
Balloon Museum
Pop Air

FSC
www.fsc.org
MIX
Paper
FSC® C150257